PERSPECTIVES ON THE NEW AGE

SUNY Series in Religious Studies
Harold Coward, Editor

PERSPECTIVES ON THE NEW AGE

Edited by
James R. Lewis and J. Gordon Melton

State University of New York Press

Published by
State University of New York Press, Albany

For information, address the State University of New York Press,
State University Plaza, Albany, NY 12246

Library of Congress Cataloging-in-Publication Data

Perspectives on the new age / edited by James R. Lewis and J. Gordon
     Melton.
          p.   cm. — (SUNY series in religious studies)
     Includes bibliographical references and index.
     ISBN 0-7914-1213-X (acid-free). — ISBN 0-7914-1214-8 (pbk. : acid
     -free)
          1. New Age movement. 2. United States—Religion—1965-
     I. Lewis, James R. II. Melton, J. Gordon. III. Series.
     BP605.N48P46   1992
     299'.93—dc20   91-39093
                                                                                    CIP

10 9 8 7 6 5 4 3 2

CONTENTS

INTRODUCTION

For the better part of this century, nonmainstream religions did not attract much in the way of sustained public attention. This situation changed with the "cult" controversies of the 1970s. As important as those controversies were, however, the public's focus on highly structured groups like the Unification Church and the Hare Krishna Movement during that decade tended to obscure a far more significant development, namely the emergence—in the wake of the sixties counterculture—of a large-scale, decentralized religious subculture that drew its principal inspiration from sources outside of the Judeo-Christian tradition. While this subculture was in many respects a continuation of a preexisting occult-metaphysical tradition, the addition to its ranks of a sizable number of former counterculturists in the postsixties period meant that metaphysical religion was no longer a marginal phenomenon: by the eighties, it had become an integral part of a new, truly pluralistic "mainstream."

In North America, the single most important event prompting general awareness of this subculture was the airing of the televised version of Shirley MacLaine's *Out on a Limb* in January of 1987. The success of this TV miniseries stimulated the mass media to begin investigating and, in time, to begin generating articles and programs about what came to be called the "New Age" movement. The media's interest was still high at the time of the Harmonic Convergence gatherings in 1987, causing the Convergence to attract more public attention than any New Age event before or since.

The widespread interest in the New Age, which was intensified by curiosity about the Harmonic Convergence, led, in turn, to the *Time* feature, "New Age Harmonies," in December of 1987. This piece was the most significant general article on the movement to appear in a major news magazine. Like many previous treatments in the mainstream media, "New Age Harmonies" focused on the flashier, less substantive aspects of the movement. However, perhaps because of the greater weight of *Time* magazine, this article, unlike earlier, similar pieces, influenced many of the more serious individuals within the New

Age subculture to back away from the label *New Age*.

Partially because the mass media portrayed the movement as trivial, and partially because of previously established habits of scholarship, academics were slow to pay attention to the New Age. Even scholars interested in alternative spirituality had tended, like the general public, to focus on high-profile groups like the Moonies and consequently missed the more subtle, but in the long range more important, shift that had occurred in the general culture. Based on superficial impressions, new age spirituality appeared shallow and faddish—a phenomenon that would disappear like Hula-Hoops and bell-bottoms. As a result, little or no attempt was made to study the movement. However, as should now be evident even to casual observers, there are many elements of the New Age that will survive its current wave of faddishness; like it or not, the New Age will persist in some form (though perhaps under a different name) into the foreseeable future.[1] In response to this revised perception of the New Age movement, the present volume has been undertaken in an attempt to fill the gap that exists in the scholarly literature.

Delimiting the New Age

One of the difficulties encountered while compiling this anthology was deciding where to draw the line between what was and what was not "New Age." Part of the problem is a direct result of the media attention that this phenomenon has attracted over the past four or five years. As has already been indicated, many movement participants have distanced themselves from this label because of the mass media's focus on the more superficial and outlandish aspects of the New Age. This distancing has served to complicate further an already fuzzy boundary problem.

To avoid some of the confusion which has thus come to be associated with the term, it is useful to distinguish at least two meanings of "New Age." The first meaning is what we might think of as New Age in the *narrow* sense, which we can take to refer to the phenomena, personalities, and events given prominence by the media (e.g., channeling, Shirley MacLaine, and the Harmonic Convergence). Prior to the current cycle of media-created faddishness, however, the expression *New Age* was claimed by a broader spiritual subculture—a subculture in which the prominence of things like channeling, crystal healing, and so forth is a relatively recent development. With a certain amount of justification one can, therefore, also talk about New Age in the *broad* sense and include within its scope people and groups who would, at present, explicitly *reject* this particular label. Without ignoring the faddish aspects of the movement, the papers in the present compilation incorporate much material that lies outside the narrower meaning, but within the broader meaning, of the New Age.

Background of the New Age Movement

While the New Age is a synthesis of many different preexisting movements and strands of thought, its most influential predecessor was the occult-metaphysical community, represented organizationally by such groups as the Theosophical Society. The New Age can be distinguished from this older metaphysical community by the New Age movement's emphasis on transformation.[2] For example, while traditional astrologers (such as the Reagans' astrologer) focus on such matters as the timing of actions and the prediction of events, New Age astrologers focus on how individuals can use the self-understanding derived from the study of their astrological charts to guide their transformation into better people.

In addition to individual transformation, the very label *New Age* implies a millenarian vision of world transformation that distinguishes the New Age from the majority of its predecessor movements. The most important—though certainly not the only—source of this transformative metaphor, as well as the term "New Age," was Theosophy, particularly as the Theosophical perspective was mediated to the movement by the works of Alice Bailey. Other preexisting movements, religions, and strands of thought brought together in the new age synthesis were Spiritualism, New Thought, the Human Potentials Movement, the Holistic Health Movement, some of the religions imported directly from Asia, and the religions of such traditional peoples as Native Americans.

When we change our focus from the movement's intellectual heritage to the background of the majority of its participants, we get a very different perspective on the origins of the New Age. As many observers have pointed out, a significant proportion of New Agers are baby boomers, people who two decades earlier were probably participating, at some level, in the phenomenon known as the counterculture. As the counterculture faded away in the early seventies, many former "hippies" found themselves embarking on a spiritual quest—one that, in many cases, departed from the Judeo-Christian mainstream. Thus one of the possible ways to date the beginnings of the New Age movement is from the period of the rather sudden appearance of large numbers of unconventional spiritual seekers in the decade following the sixties.[3] In the early seventies, the movement's focus was somewhat different from what it had become by the mid-eighties when the media began to pay attention. Those early years were characterized by the prominence of newly imported Asian groups, although many of the older occult-metaphysical organizations were also experiencing a growth spurt. These various groups, in combination with a significant number of less formally affiliated individuals, constituted a fairly substantial spiritual subculture that became the successor movement to the counterculture. This initial phase of the New Age movement looked forward to the transformation of society but did not place an emphasis on many of the things that outside observers now regard as quintessentially New Age (phenomena such as channeling and crystals).

One of the traits of the New Age is that major subjects of interest vary from time to time, so that, particularly to the outside observer, this subculture appears to go through transformation after transformation. The movement away from the prominence of Eastern spiritual teachers (particularly characteristic of the seventies) to an emphasis on channeled entities (in the eighties) is an example of one such transformation. In a similar manner, the interest in channeling seems to be waning as we move into the nineties, and the new emphasis appears to be shamanism and Native American spirituality.

Outline of Volume

Without claiming to offer final answers, the introductory essay outlines the definitional/evolutionary problem of distinguishing New Age from non-New Age, both methodologically and conceptually. The balance of the book is divided into four sections: The five chapters in Section One examine the historical roots of the New Age phenomenon. Section Two contains six chapters that look at some of the range of the movement, as well as certain reactions to the New Age. The three chapters in Section Three compare the New Age with certain other movements. The anthology concludes with four chapters surveying the New Age's international impact.

Chapter 1

Approaches to the Study of the New Age Movement

―――――――――― *James R. Lewis*

When studying an amorphous movement like the New Age, one almost always has difficulties deciding where the phenomenon begins and ends, and one usually encounters certain pitfalls into which it is all too easy to stumble. Because this volume is the first of its kind on the new age movement and hence likely to stimulate further work in this area, the present essay has been included for the purposes of steering the researcher away from a few dead ends, outlining some of the issues with which each researcher must grapple, and suggesting a few directions for future research.

Boundary Issues

In a recent edition of *Body Mind Spirit*, one of the more widely distributed New Age magazines, the editor, Paul Zuromski, raises the question, "Is 'New Age' Dead?" This question is asked in the context of a short piece on the editor's page which explains why the magazine has dropped its banner "Your New Age Information Resource" in favor of "Tools for Creating a Richer, More Fulfilling Life." After asserting that he never cared much for the *New Age* label anyway, the editor proceeds to cite Gallup Poll findings, as well as certain other evidence, which indicate that the label has acquired negative connotations in the mind of the general public. Partially because of this negative press, even book publishers are abandoning the new age category for a series of "more accurate labels like self-help, new science, metaphysics, Eastern religions, philosophy, natural living," and so forth (meaning that the term has been dropped without abandoning any of the topics that were formerly marketed under the new age label). Zuromski further observes that, "The change in consciousness that the New Age Movement sought to explain and encourage will happen whether we give it a name or not," and advises his readers that it is "Time to let go [of the label *New Age*] and move on." He is also of the opinion that the answer is *not* to find a new term to replace *New Age*, but rather "to recognize that there is no need for a general label."[1]

For anyone researching the new age movement, the reflections found in "Is 'New Age' Dead?" raise several important issues. In the first place, because individuals, institutions, and periodicals who formerly referred to themselves as "New Age" no longer identify themselves as such, studies built around a distinction between New Age and non-New Age (e.g., the Feher survey reported elsewhere in the present volume[2]) become more complex. In particular, one can no longer simply ask respondents in a straightforward manner whether they consider themselves part of the New Age. One must instead rely on more indirect kinds of questions—such as assent to beliefs in reincarnation, planetary consciousness, holistic healing methods, et cetera—to determine whether respondents belong to the movement.

In the second place, we should ask whether "New Age" is a meaningful category of study at all. Following Zuromski's advice, perhaps we should entirely abandon the label as well as the temptation to coin other, less loaded, terms. The problem with dropping this comprehensive category, however, is that there quite obviously exists a subculture of significant size which considers itself to be more or less unitary, at least when contrasting itself with "mainstream" culture. The existence of such a coherent subculture is clearly implicit in Zuromski's remarks (i.e., the implied audience to which he is addressing his observations).

The problem with abandoning the particular expression *New Age* is that, at the present time, there exists no comparable term which covers all aspects of the movement. If we were, for example, to substitute *metaphysical community* for *New Age*, then we would be excluding certain important phases of the holistic health movement—phases which do *not* consider themselves "metaphysical," but which *do* consider themselves part of the New Age (or which, to take into account the emergence of widespread aversion to the term, formerly considered themselves "New Age"). "Metaphysical" also tends to encompass certain religious communities, such as Christian Science, which do not fit into the New Age category. And there are similar problems with other terms. For these reasons, I tend to favor retaining "New Age" as an etic category, at least until a more adequate replacement is coined.

The admission of "New Age" into scholarly discourse does not, however, entirely solve our boundary problems. The movement emerged out of a preexisting occult-metaphysical subculture that—especially in such institutional embodiments as the Theosophical Society, New Thought churches, traditional Spiritualist denominations, and so forth—was affected by, but was never completely absorbed into, the New Age.[3] It thus makes sense to distinguish the New Age from its predecessor movements. There is, however, no easy, unproblematic criterion for making such distinctions. Gordon Melton has proposed an emphasis on social and individual transformation as the distinguishing characteristic of the New Age,[4] and for certain studies, such as the Feher study to which we have already referred, this is useful as a heuristic distinction. However, because certain strands of the older occult-metaphysical tradition also emphasize transformation, it would be possible to imagine other kinds of studies for which this distinguishing attribute would be much less useful. Researchers whose studies require them to make a distinction between New Age and Non-New Age would thus be well-advised to utilize whatever criterion is best suited to their particular project.

In my own research, I encountered complexities in the New Age subculture that required me to modify certain preliminary criteria I had adopted. For example, a common observation one finds in the literature on the movement is that New Age channels, unlike their most obvious predecessors, Spiritualist mediums, focus on conveying metaphysical truths rather than on messages from the dead. On closer observation, however, one finds that the characterization of Spiritualists as primarily message bearers from the other side of life is an oversimplification derived from undue focus on the traditional mediums of the nineteenth century. Twentieth-century Spiritualists, while continuing this aspect of their tradition, also regularly convey metaphysical discourses from spirits, although the specific *content* of their metaphysics differs somewhat from that of most New Age channels.[5]

I also found that the characterization of New Age psychism as being "woo-woo" and "airy-fairy" was true of only some of the more public New Age channels. When I began to explore the New Age subculture in northern California, I came across a number of *psychics* (a term often avoided for the same kinds of reasons people shy away from *New Age*) who had turned their talents to therapeutic and business counseling. One such person is Evelyn Oliver, D.D., a Neuro-Linguistic Programming (NLP) practitioner who advertises herself as the "ultimate business strategist." In addition to bringing her intuitive ability into her very effective (from what I have been able to observe) NLP work, she also runs a successful business consulting practice. Her clients run the gamut from lawyers to investment brokers, and she has ongoing retainers with a variety of mainline businesses.[6] To provide the reader with a sense of what Berman's business clients feel they receive from her consulting, it might be useful to cite from one of the testimonials found in her promotional literature:

> I believe that Eve's work with me was a major factor in whatever success I have achieved in the business world. She involves her clients in a total process, and she helped me get in touch with the intuitive part of myself, from personnel decisions to individual stocks I may have purchased as an investment advisor. Eve's work with me has been instrumental in my development on an emotional, spiritual and business level.[7]

In this testimonial, we see a blending of different areas of life—business, personal, and spiritual—which would have been more compartmentalized in traditional religions (even in more traditional occult-metaphysical organizations). This tendency to blur the barriers between different areas of life (a tendency New Agers would view positively as "holistic") is characteristic of New Age spirituality, although, for the reasons I have already discussed, Oliver and people like her would never label themselves "New Age."

Larger Issues

The question of distinguishing the New Age from the spiritual subculture out of which the movement emerged should cause us to ask certain other kinds of questions, such as, Just how extensive is this larger subculture? My impressionistic sense of the New Age is that it is merely the most visible part of a more significant cultural shift. While the popularity of phenomena like channeling and crystals may well be on the decline, the larger spiritual subculture which gave birth to these more particular phenomena is growing steadily. These impressions are reinforced by Gallup Poll statistics which indicate that one out of every four Americans believes in astrology, and that one out of five Americans believes in reincarnation. Similar surveys taken in the United Kingdom turn up the interesting statistic that 30-35 percent of the British population hold a belief in reincarnation.

Statistics of this magnitude indicate that we are no longer talking about a marginal phenomenon. Rather, we appear to be witnessing the birth of a new, truly pluralistic mainstream.[8] This especially seems to be the case in northern California where a recent newspaper survey found that roughly 25 percent of San Francisco Bay area residents agree with certain key New Age ideas, such as the notion that "nature, or Mother Earth, has its own kind of wisdom, a planetary consciousness of its own."[9] While it might be inaccurate to conclude from this survey that 25 percent of all Bay area residents should be regarded as New Agers, it would not be inaccurate to assert that approximately 25 percent of Bay area Californians adhere to certain holistic, ecological, and metaphysical points of view that depart significantly from traditional perspectives.

At this point we might well ask how this important spiritual subculture has escaped the attention of scholars. Beyond the points already made in the introduction to the present volume, one of the answers to this question is that large, amorphous movements are difficult to study. By way of contrast, a researcher investigating a group with explicit boundaries such as the Hare Krishna Movement can, with the cooperation of the local temple president, simply pass out questionnaires to temple residents and anticipate a 90-100 percent return rate. Clear membership boundaries in combination with cooperative subjects allow one to construct highly accurate profiles of Hare Krishna devotees with minimal expenditures of time and energy. Considering the complexities that would be involved with conducting similar surveys of an amorphous subculture, need we wonder that social scientists have focused on more structured religious movements?

The vagueness of this subculture is further complicated by the manner in which it tends, particularly at its more diffused extremities, to cross certain taken-for-granted boundaries and "infiltrate" subcommunities that one might anticipate would be hostile to nontraditional spirituality. There are, for example, many members of mainstream religious denominations who practice yoga and meditation, explore alternative healing practices, follow astrological advice, and even believe in reincarnation.[10] Such people often continue to consider themselves good Methodists, Presbyterians, Catholics, or whatever and thus are easy to miss in surveys that classify populations into mutually exclusive categories.

One also needs to take account of the many people who consciously avoid being associated with the New Age. In contrast to the media stereotype of the colorful New Ager who walks around in conspicuous crystal jewelry while spouting incoherent New Age philosophy, most movement participants tend to keep a low profile with respect to their religious beliefs and practices. In northern California, for example, one can find a significant number of professional people who keep their unorthodox spiritual orientations "in the closet" (Wiccans sometimes say that nonpublic members of the Craft are "in the broom closet") to avoid possible negative ramifications for their professional practices. The presence of large numbers of movement participants at elite levels of society is thus not immediately evident to the casual observer.

While the preceding discussion may have had the negative effect of convincing researchers that they should avoid studying the New Age at any cost, I hope that it has had the more positive effect of convincing readers of the importance of this movement. Particularly if we think in terms of the larger spiritual subculture in which the New Age is rooted, the cultural shift anticipated by New Agers (usually under the rubric of a "paradigm shift")[11] has already occurred—though most people have not as yet recognized it as a *fait accompli*.

Characterizing the New Age

Given the amorphous nature of the New Age, How can one recognize its manifestations? What are its identifying traits? The problem with characterizing this movement is that it is so diverse that it would be possible to find exceptions to almost anything we might say about it. As Eileen Barker has observed, "the 'movement' is not so much *a* movement as a number of groups and individuals that have a number of beliefs and orientations that have what the philosopher Ludwig Wittgenstein has called a 'family resemblance'—two members of the family may bear almost no resemblance to each other, although they both resemble a third member."[12]

The diverse, decentralized nature of the movement thus frustrates any attempt to characterize it in a final, decisive manner. It is, nevertheless, still possible to develop a list of "New Age" traits, as long as one bears in mind that any given manifestation of this subculture is unlikely to be characterized by all of them. In an effort to develop such a list, I have found it useful to begin with earlier scholarship that has been carried out in this area.

Because the expression *New Age* was not generally utilized outside of this subculture until 1987 (the year of the Harmonic Convergence and of Shirley MacLaine's televised miniseries, "Out on a Limb"), all but a few of the relatively small number of relevant papers that were composed prior to that year did not present themselves as studies of the New Age. These studies were carried out under the older rubric, *new religious movements*. For example, much of Robert Ellwood's work on new religious movements is clearly relevant to the study of the New Age. Approaching alternative religiosity from the discipline of religious studies, Ellwood is able to put forward many suggestive comparative observations, such as the one he makes in *Religious and Spiritual Groups in Modern America* between certain new religious movements and shamanism. Like shamanism, one of the characteristics of the New Age movement is a marked emphasis on healing, and, like shamans, many New Age teachers unite the roles of spiritual guide and healer. Also, some of the traits he lists as "General Characteristics"[13] of new religious groups are relevant to the New Age movement, for example:

- Emphasis on healing
- A desire to be "modern" and use scientific language
- Eclecticism and syncretism
- A monistic and impersonal ontology
- Optimism, success orientation, and a tendency to evolutionary views
- Emphasis on psychic powers

Out of the considerable sociological literature on new religious movements, one can also uncover much relevant material. One piece I found especially useful is an older paper by Roy Wallis, "Reflections on When Prophecy Fails." In this short article Wallis notes two important traits of the "cultic milieu" (a term coined by Colin Campbell to apply to the alternative spiritual subculture out of which the New Age emerged):

> First, there prevails in the milieu an attitude of "epistemological individualism," that is, a belief that the individual is the ultimate locus for the determination of truth. Secondly, there prevails an ideology of "revelational indeterminacy," that is, a belief that the truth may be revealed in diverse ways and through diverse agents. No individual or collectivity possesses a monopoly of the truth.[14]

When we shift over to the relatively scant scholarship which discusses this subculture under the rubric *New Age*, we come back to the trait Gordon Melton put forward as the defining characteristic of the New Age, transformation:

> The New Age Movement can be defined by its primal experience of transformation. New Agers have either experienced or are diligently seeking a profound personal transformation from an old, unacceptable life to a new, exciting future. . . . Having experienced a personal transformation, New Agers project the possibility of the transformation not of just a number of additional individuals, but of the culture and of humanity itself.[15]

Melton further observes that, for the New Age, the experience of transformation is identical to what is usually termed a "religious experience," and that one prominent model for this transformation is healing. Somewhat more generally, it can be said that in this subculture transformation and healing are more or less equivalent to what is usually referred to as spiritual growth.

Another term that is used interchangeably with spiritual growth is learning. In *New Religions and the Theological Imagination in America*, Mary Bednaroski calls attention to the New Age emphasis on "learning": life is learning, death can be a learning experience, spiritual growth is a learning process, and so forth. Although she keeps her discussion of this theme within the boundaries of her chapter topic (death), looking at the broader New Age phenomenon through the "lens" of the learning theme helps us to notice that, in contrast to many other religious movements, the dominant New Age "ceremonies" are workshops, lectures, and classes, rather than worship ceremonies.[16]

In viewing the New Age as an expression of American culture, Bednaroski is drawing on Catherine Albanese's work on the New Age. Albanese puts forward a broad interpretation of the significance of the New Age in "Religion and the American Experience."[17] In this article, she argues that the New Age movement and the fundamentalist movement are *both* expressions of what she characterizes as an emerging American "ethnicity." She makes this argument with respect to five points on which these two movements appear to converge—points that flow directly out of emphases characteristic of American culture:

1. To begin, for both, personal transformation and direct spiritual experience are at the heart of one's life project, and, for both, private transformation must find its twin in the transformation of society.
2. Both fundamentalists and New Agers hear voices more than see visions: their mysticism comes clad in a rhetoric of newness that is expressed as ongoing revelation.
3. Both fundamentalists and New Agers stress healing. . . . For both movements, physical health is a sign of blessing, part of the empowerment that comes through close contact with what is sacred. And for both, another sign of blessing is material prosperity.
4. In both fundamentalism and the New Age, a kind of ontological positivism predominates, linking both to the religious materialism they share. [e.g., adherence to biblical literalism and belief in literal reincarnation]
5. The "new voluntarism" of fundamentalism and the New Age is expressed in the popular, nonelite, "do-it-yourself" quality that characterizes both.

Albanese's analysis has the distinct virtue of seeing the New Age movement as a direct expression of Western culture rather than as an aberration or as an exotic transplant. Academics undertaking a study of the New Age would profit from this broader perspective on the movement.

One of the earliest articles to focus explicitly on the New Age was Hans Sebald's "New-Age Romanticism: The Quest for an Alternative Lifestyle as a Force of Social Change." Sebald's work contains some thoughtful generalizations, such as the traits he lists that allow one to characterize the New Age as a coherent movement:

1. A sense of belonging—"A large number of persons . . . unequivocally identify with the [New Age]."
2. Common values—values that Sebald sums up as living in attunement with the "life forces in and around us," and that lead to such concrete practices as vegetarianism.
3. Goal of the movement—by which he means that New Agers are attempting to create an alternative society that they believe will eventually supplant mainstream society.
4. Common Style—which Sebald describes as an antimaterialistic simplicity. (This particular characteristic applies to only part of the movement.)
5. Jargon—by which is meant that there exists a certain discourse within the movement which outsiders have difficulty understanding.
6. Mass communication—by which Sebald means that there are a large number of alternative sources of information, such as New Age magazines and the like, which circulate news within the movement and which rarely appeal to people outside of the movement.[18]

While other traits of this subculture could be mentioned, enough has already been said to provide students of the New Age with a starting point for their investigations. Researchers interested in compiling a truly exhaustive list of all characteristics of the movement can consult other articles in the present collection.

Pitfalls

Although Hans Sebald's "New-Age Romanticism: The Quest for an Alternative Lifestyle as a Force of Social Change" is in many ways a useful point of reference, it contains a number of important weaknesses that other explorers of the New Age landscape would do well to avoid. Using "New-Age Romanticism" as a starting point, I will indicate in the present section a few of the more prominent pitfalls one can encounter on this terrain.

In the first place, Sebald bases many of his generalizations on *one* field work experience—in this case exposure to a single New Age commune in Arizona. On several points I found the perspective of these communards to deviate from the perspective of the larger movement. For example, at one point Sebald talks about the "New-Age scorn" for science and technology that is held to be in opposition to the movement's appreciation for the "mystical" (p. 111). This aspect of his analysis misses the considerable New Age literature on what has come to be referred to as "New Science," a field represented preeminently in the writings of Fritjof Capra, whose work attempts to reconcile science and mysticism.[19]

In the second place, we might note that while "New-Age Romanticism" is only seven years old, parts of its analysis are already antiquated. For example, Sebald's characterization of the New Age as a movement with which large numbers of people unequivocally identify no longer applies (for reasons that were noted earlier in the present paper). Also, his discussion of the New Age "scorn" for science may have been more generally applicable to this subculture before the rise of "New Science" as a popular topic. These changes are indicative of the process of transformation which the New Age community is constantly experiencing. This steadily changing nature is a trait in the movement's deep structure that researchers should carefully note. Without adopting such a perspective, the waning popularity of channeling and crystals— to take current examples—could be misinterpreted as indicative of a general decline in the New Age movement. Instead what is happening is that the New Age subculture is merely shifting its focus to such new topics as (at the time of this writing) "inner child" work, shamanism, and American Indian spirituality.[20]

Finally, the article is unnecessarily burdened by tendentious rhetoric that causes the reader to question not only the objectivity, but also the accuracy, of Sebald's observations. For example, at one point he asserts that the New Age movement "substitutes fantasy and imagination for the facts of life and for an objective assessment of one's own personality. It thrives on the childlike, hedonistic, picturesque, bizarre, unknown, and mystical" (p. 108). Needless to say, such gratuitous value judgments add nothing to the substance of Sebald's analysis, although they do provide one with some insights into the biases of rationalist secularism.[21] Similar remarks apply with even more force to the many anti-New Age books produced by the conservative Christian community, although, unlike rationalist analyses of the same phenomenon, most Christian treatments make no pretense of being value-neutral.[22]

More generally, researchers should note that studies of the New Age which attempt to dismiss it as foolish or faddish usually fail to advance our understanding much beyond the negative—and often inaccurate—stereotypes proffered by the mass media.[23] To take one oft-repeated criticism as an example, a large number of observers have accused the New Age of being excessively narcissistic,[24] but one does not have to look far to see the fallacy in this simplistic generalization. With a change of focus, one can perceive significant numbers of "New Agers" trying to make the planet a better place on which to live by being active in Earth Day gatherings, Green politics, and the recycling movement—to name only a few of the movement's more prominent activities.[25] Even the Harmonic Convergence, which the mainstream media universally ridiculed, was motivated by a desire (however inadequately expressed) to heal the planet—not an enterprise one would expect to be undertaken by a subculture composed entirely of selfish narcissists. While it is not difficult to find aspects of the New Age that are less than inspiring, evaluating the movement solely on the merits of its least reputable manifestations is comparable to judging Christianity on the merits of televangelists like Jim and Tammy Bakker: Few people would be willing to condemn all of Christianity on the basis of its least exemplary side, and the New Age deserves to be approached with a similar kind of even-handedness.

Directions for Future Research

While much remains to be done in every area of research on the New Age, the present work, in combination with Gordon Melton *et al.*'s *New Age Encyclopedia*, provides enough descriptive and historical information to support other kinds of studies. One direction that should immediately be pursued is quantitative research. Although, for reasons that have already been mentioned, such research is less rewarding than studies of more highly structured religious movements, it would not be difficult to conceive and carry out survey research at New Age gatherings using Shoshana Feher's study reported in "Who Holds the Cards? Women and New Age Astrology" (elsewhere in this volume) as a model. While generalizations to the larger subculture from the sample surveyed at such gatherings might be problematic, it would be nice to have at least a little empirical data with which to shore up our speculations.

Part of what is striking about the current state of scholarship on the subject is that most of us are working from impressionistic data. It is possible to assert, for example, that most of the participants at such gatherings as Whole Life Expos are baby boomers—white, middle class people in their forties.[26] But, while few people would disagree with this observation, it would be good to be able to refer to a little hard data for support. I am reluctant to make certain generalizations when I call to mind generalizations in other areas of study that were based on impressionistic data which, after quantitative research had been carried out, were found to be inaccurate or incomplete.

Another kind of research that should be pursued is to take the categories and theoretical frameworks that we already have, apply them to the New Age, and see how they pan out. A study that can be taken as a paradigm for this kind of work is Phillip Lucas's "The New Age Movement and the Pentecostal/Charismatic Revival" (found elsewhere in the present volume) which sets the movement in the context of McLoughlin's work on cycles of revival and Wallace's work on revitalization movements. Such studies would be good starting points for the "frontier" stage we are at with respect to research on the New Age subculture.

There has, for example, been much good theorizing about millenarian movements beyond the classic Wallace study mentioned by Lucas that one could attempt to apply to the New Age.[27] While the New Age is not a millenarian movement in the same clear-cut sense as a Melanesian cargo cult, there are some rather obvious millenarian overtones in the term *New Age*, as well as in New Age discourse about apocalyptic "earth changes" and "pole shifts."[28] Gatherings like the Harmonic Convergence, to mention one final example, are the New Age equivalent of the Ghost Dances of the late nineteenth century, in the sense that they were ceremonies designed to bring in the new world.[29]

While none of these suggestions for future research are particularly subtle or remarkable, they are appropriate for the current undeveloped state of New Age scholarship. And, while the difficulties involved with careful examinations of the New Age are not inconsiderable, the present paper's discussion of the scope and significance of the movement should encourage potential researchers to undertake studies of the New Age subculture in spite of the obstacles.

PART I

Historical Roots

Part One of the present volume deals with the historical roots of the New Age. In the first chapter in this section, "New Thought and the New Age," J. Gordon Melton discusses the relationship of the New Age movement with New Thought and the New Thought churches. While he sees the roots of the movement as lying more in Theosophy and Spiritualism than in New Thought, New Thought denominations were important in the spread of the New Age because of the forum and ready clientele that their churches provided for New Age books, speakers, and classes. He also argues that the New Age is a revivalist movement held together by a vision of personal and social transformation—a movement that will eventually fade away as a mass phenomenon, passing on its momentum to more stable denominational bodies.

Kay Alexander's "Roots of the New Age," while noting the importance of New Thought and Theosophy as influences on the New Age, focuses on the contribution of the human potentials movement and its offspring, transpersonal psychology. Transpersonal psychology developed out of an expansion of humanistic psychology to include such human potentials as ESP and the states of awareness available through meditative disciplines. The exploration of these potentials at growth centers like Esalen eventually spilled out into the spiritual counterculture of the early seventies, and helped to shape the face of the New Age movement.

Andrew Grace Diem and James R. Lewis's "Imagining India" examines the impact of South Asian spirituality on the New Age. While many of the core ideas of the New Age world view, such as reincarnation and a monistic ontology, are part of the West's own metaphysical tradition, these notions were revitalized and modified in response to the influx of Asian religious texts in the nineteenth century and Asian religious teachers in the twentieth. Diem and Lewis analyze the complex interaction between the West's changing images of India and the forms of Indian spirituality that eventually took root in the West.

Robert Ellwood's "How New is the New Age?" argues that the New Age is a contemporary manifestation of the West's alternative spirituality tradition, a tradition which goes back at least as far as the mystical Neoplatonism of the Hellenistic world. In this particular essay, Ellwood focuses on the parallels between the present-day New Age movement and nineteenth-century spiritualism.

Catherine L. Albanese's "The Magical Staff" looks at the New Age in terms of its emphasis on healing. In the New Age movement "healing" has become a comprehensive metaphor for physical healing, spiritual growth, restoring ecological balance, and achieving world reconciliation. While this use of "healing" has its roots in the harmonial spirituality of the nineteenth century (a spirituality that viewed spirit and matter as parts of a single continuum), the New Age has recast this harmonial tradition in terms of twentieth-century physics (or, rather, in terms of modern physics as interpreted through a theosophical lens). In addition to "healing through harmony," New Age healing involves a kind of shamanic journey (a journey that was also characteristic of certain forms of nineteenth-century healing) into the realm of nonmatter where subtle forces can transmute material substance.

Chapter 2

New Thought and the New Age[1]

———————— *J. Gordon Melton*

New Thought and the New Age designate two segments of contemporary popular religion which have intermingled with each other in a rather complex fashion in the 1980s. In spite of their obvious impact upon the American religious community and American culture as a whole and the vast amount of source material readily available about each, both have been somewhat neglected by the scholarly community. It shall be the purpose of this paper to explore the nature of the relationship between New Thought and the New Age with the hope of revealing new information about each while gaining some insight into the ever-shifting scene of late twentieth-century religious pluralism in North America. Before pursuing the primary task, however, it is necessary to get a clear handle on each movement.

Much of the literature about the New Age Movement expresses some difficulty with defining it. A significant part of that difficulty derives from the general hostility to nonconventional religion in America. Overwhelmingly, the secondary sources on both New Thought and the New Age movement have been written from an anti-cult perspective.[2] Authors have assumed that all cults were pretty much alike and a threat to society and serious religion. While much of this material is simply the product of popular religious prejudice, a disturbing amount of it has been generated from or sanctioned by national offices of mainline Christian and Jewish bodies.[3] Even the academic community has not been entirely free of such nonsense.[4]

Moreover, lacking the kind of basic descriptive material on both New Thought and the New Age which is available in abundance about most of the older denominational traditions, analysts who have attempted to sort out the relationship between New Thought and the New Age have not surprisingly often misunderstood their very different natures. New Thought arose in the 1880s as a schism from Christian Science. From the beginning its leaders established it as a new and separate religious movement. It has subsequently grown into a distinct religious family tradition analogous to the Lutherans or the Baptists. The New Age movement, on the other hand, is a revivalist movement more analogous in form to the post-World War II healing movement in the Pentecostal churches, the Ecumenical movement among liberal Protestants in the 1960s, or the Jesus People Movement of the 1970s. Each assumed the existence of stable religious (denominational) structures from which they drew their basic ideas. Rather than attempting to begin a new "denomination," each has attempted to revitalize the older bodies and unite them in a common cause. As a denominational family, New Thought has become a permanent part of the religious landscape. As a revivalist movement, the New Age (like the healing revivals, the Ecumenical movement, and the Jesus People movement) will come and go. Its major impetus will be absorbed by the older bodies from which the movement derived its basic ideas. In its wake we will be able to catalog the hundreds of ephemeral organizations which it spawned and learn to live with a few new esoteric and metaphysical organizations which originally formed to embody New Age ideals.

New Thought

Of the two communities, New Thought is the easiest to isolate and define. It emerged as a new religious tradition in North America and England in the late 1800s, though it has its intellectual roots in some popular movements (such as Swedenborgianism and Transcendentalism) from earlier in the century. Its beginning can be traced to Emma Curtis Hopkins who, in 1885, separated herself from Mary Baker Eddy and moved to Chicago where, in 1886, she founded a school that eventually became known as the Christian Science Theological Seminary. Like its parent body it placed its major emphasis on spiritual healing, was organized around practitioners, and trained its students through the Christian Science "class" structure.[5]

During the decade from 1886 through 1895, Hopkins trained a number of students who went on to found those "denominations" which today constitute the core of the New Thought tradition. Among her students were Melinda Cramer (founder of Divine Science), Myrtle and Charles Fillmore (founders of the Unity School of Christianity), Annie Rix Militz (founder of the Homes of Truth), and Kate Bingham (who in turn trained Nona Brooks, who founded Divine Science in Denver, Colorado). In the years after leaving Chicago and settling in New York

City Hopkins taught Clara Stocker (who in turn would teach Albert Grier, the founder of the Church of Truth) and Ernest Holmes (who founded Religious Science).

As originally constituted, New Thought was a decidedly feminist movement. Approximately 90 percent of Hopkins's students were women who left her class to assume roles as professionals in the religious community. She actually ordained over 100 ministers who moved on to create centers and mobilize a mass following (and in the process became the first female in modern history to assume the office of bishop and ordain other females to the ministry). In the 1890s, Hopkins students, cut off organizationally from Christian Science and feeling the freedom to develop their own variations of Eddy's basic approach, began to drop the term *Christian Science* and designate their rather scattered and diverse work as *New Thought*.

By the turn of the century, New Thought had established itself in every corner of the United States (most frequently on the heels of Christian Science), though its strength was in the western half of the country. It had spread to England by 1887 through feminist editor Frances Lord, an early student of Hopkins, whose *Christian Science Healing*[6] became the first New Thought text published in Europe.

During the early twentieth century, New Thought was structured around the several major New Thought churches (Unity, Divine Science, Homes of Truth), but also included a few smaller denominations (most of which proved ephemeral), and a continuing host of independent churches. In 1916 an ecumenical organization, the New Thought Alliance (now the International New Thought Alliance) was formed and several years later adopted a creed-like "Declaration of Principles." In 1957 the Alliance revised the statement, at which time all specific references to Christianity were deleted. The new declaration affirmed the "inseparable oneness of God and Man," the possibility that humans can "reproduce the Divine perfection in [their] body, emotions, and all [their] external affairs," and that the "Universe is the body of God, spiritual in essence, governed by God through laws which are spiritual in reality even when material in appearance."[7]

Thus during the twentieth century, New Thought emerged as what has been elsewhere termed a "new family tradition." It is one of several distinct new denominational families (such as the Latter-day Saints, Spiritualism, and the Theosophical/Ancient Wisdom Tradition) which arose in nineteenth-century America and which has in recent decades had marked success in diffusing around the world. New Thought congregations can now be found across Europe, the West Indies, Australia, New Zealand, South Africa, Nigeria, India, the Philippines, and Latin

America. It has shown particular strength in England, Switzerland, and West Germany. By the time the New Age movement appeared, New Thought, through its several thousands of relatively stable congregations, could be found across North America in every state and province.

The presence of New Thought (not to mention the other alternative religious traditions) in strength in North America goes a long way toward explaining the quickness with which the New Age movement spread once it appeared in the early 1970s. Rather than build a new organization, New Age prophets simply mobilized the preexisting strength of the membership of the older esoteric, Eastern, and metaphysical groups, many of which were in the midst of a major growth phase. While the groups were gaining members, the movement was supplying a new esoteric model around which the groups could expand their program. Most "New Age" groups are simply old organizations which adopted the New Age perspective. Of course, as has been true throughout the entire twentieth century, new esoteric and metaphysical organizations have been formed during the 1970s and 1980s, and many of these (thought by no means all) adopted the New Age peculiarities at the time of their formation.

The New Age Movement[8]

In comparison to New Thought, the New Age movement is a relatively new phenomenon. It developed in the late 1960s and emerged as a self-conscious movement in the early 1970s. As a movement, it both absorbed New Thought themes and reached out to New Thought groups with its message, but drew most of its inspiration from Theosophy and Spiritualism, and, to a lesser extent, the Eastern religions. It arose, not so much as a new religion, but as a new revivalist religious impulse directed toward the esoteric/metaphysical/Eastern groups and to the mystical strain in all religions. It found its first support among the numerous splinters of the Theosophical Society (over 100 in the United States alone)[9] and the many groups which were centered upon the phenomenon which would come to be termed "channeling," in which the leader(s) is(are) believed to be in regular touch with a supernatural source of information from whom teachings are regularly received. Usually, the channel (medium) moved into an altered state of consciousness (trance) and the entity spoke through him or her. In channeling groups the words of the channeled entity are normally transcribed and circulated to interested parties as the basis of study and enlightenment. (Many of the theosophical splinters were engaged in channeling from the ascended masters while Spiritualist groups were typically channeling from the spirits of the dead. After 1952, UFO contactee groups began to channel from the inhabitants of spacecraft. It is among the contactees that the term channeling was developed.)

The message of the New Age movement is its hope in transformation. Exponents of the New Age have undergone a personal transformation which changed their lives. They have witnessed a similar change in others and believe it possible that every person can also be transformed. Very real spiritual energies are available to create change, and numerous techniques function to harness that energy to produce change. Most of the various New Age activities aim at facilitating that personal transformation through such diverse activities as body work, spiritual disciplines, natural diets, and renewed human relationships.

As with the older esoteric/metaphysical groups, the New Age metaphor of transformation has been imposed on many of the older occult practices such as astrology and tarot cards, thus altering their use in several subtle but important ways. The New Age perspective provided a thoroughgoing critique of astrology and tarot as fortune-telling devices, while providing a shield from the constant need for scientific verification of astrological pronouncements. The New Age sees both astrology and the tarot as symbol systems that provide a means of self-understanding. In the New Age, the planetary arrangements in the zodiac, for example, are not seen as determining forces so much as a report on an individual's particular set of cosmic resources which s/he can draw upon to transform a life.

But if personal transformation on a large scale is possible, argues the New Age, then social and cultural transformation is also possible. The world can be changed from the crisis-ridden, polluted, warlike, and resource-limited world in which we live into a New Age of love, joy, peace, abundance, and harmony. This generation is also especially lucky as special spiritual energies are now available to transform humankind into the Golden Age heretofore only dreamed about. It is, of course, this hope of the complete transformation of society that gives the movement its name. Various New Agers have proposed quite different mechanisms for accomplishing this worldwide transformation. Some, such as Ruth Montgomery, look to a world wide catastrophe while others see an almost magical change occurring as a critical mass of individuals accept the New Age perspective. This second group has been most active in sponsoring events such as the Harmonic Convergence. A third group sees the New Age becoming manifest through the efforts of individuals in this generation to further New Age values in every arena of life. This latter group has led in the alignment of New Agers with the larger environmental, peace, alternative technology, and feminist movements.

Historically, the New Age movement can be traced to England in the 1960s. There a small number of what were called "light" groups (i.e., theosophical and channeling groups) began to meet together and speak of the prophecies of a New Age which had been passed to them through the writings of the theosophical tradition, especially the predictions of the coming of a "World Savior" first espoused by theosophical founder Helena P. Blavatsky. Many had read the theosophist Alice A. Bailey's book, *The Reappearance of the Christ*,[10] which looked for the return of the Maitreya, the theosophical Master whom Bailey's Arcane School identified with Jesus of Nazareth. Among the several light groups, the Findhorn Community emerged as especially prominent.

The New Age movement arose in the United States with the convergence of two forces. First, the work of the light groups was brought to the United States through the Universal Foundation and its executive, Anthony Brooke. Among the purposes of the foundation was to "link" other similar groups in a world wide community as individual "points of light." Each group was dedicated to spreading the spiritual light (energy) of the universe through its particular esoteric work. The foundation established what seems to be the first international New Age network.

The establishment of the Universal Link network coincided with a major change in American society. In 1965 the United States rescinded the Asian Exclusion Act which for over forty years had kept Asians out of the country. Since 1966, the new quota for Asian immigration has been filled annually. Among the millions of new Asian immigrants to the United States were a representative number of religious leaders (evangelists or missionaries) of the traditional Asian faiths (which had split into the same diffuse array as denominational Christianity and orthodox Judaism). While treated in a somewhat tongue-in-cheek fashion by the media, the Indian gurus, the Zen masters, and the Sufi sheikhs were as a whole serious religious teachers on divine missions to spread their faiths among the Western materialists. (The distinctive interaction of these Asian leaders with the New Age is the subject for another paper.)

The New Age movement took the message of the Universal Link and the fresh vitality of the new Eastern missionaries and began to articulate the vision of a transformed people and world. There was no better symbol of the New Age than Richard Alpert. In the 1960s drugs had almost destroyed him. But he turned east, and in an Indian guru, Neem Karoli Baba, he found the agent who transformed his life. He returned from India as a new person, Baba Ram Dass, a most articulate exemplar of the transformation he advocated. In a similar manner, theosophist/channeler David Spangler traveled to England to visit the "light groups," only to remain for three years at Findhorn. He returned in 1973 to author the books that provided a theoretical base for the movement already quietly spreading through the esoteric/metaphysical world.[11]

In Berkeley, in the early 1970s, a small group of scholars, primarily sociologists, recognized the importance of the new spirituality and the new Asian groups which were forming, but had trouble placing it in context. To them it was new, different, exciting, and some were swept up in it. Maybe, some hypothesized, it had the possibility of transforming the West now mired in the swamp of a decadent, spiritually-dead Christianity. Himself caught up somewhat in the hopes and possibilities of the new impulse from the East, philosopher Jacob Needleman wrote an optimistic appraisal of the groups as the "new religions." The term was certainly a step above *cult*, and it became the focus of a wave of valuable sociological research. However, the term also fostered a certain myopia. By focusing upon the "newness" of religious ferment in Berkeley in the 1970s, Needleman turned attention away from the pluralistic religious ferment that had been building globally for the past century. Needleman would go on to write what have been considered among the best presentations of the New Age perspective in his books *Lost Christianity*[12] and *A Sense of the Cosmos*.[13]

Channeling and Crystals

Beyond its basic transformational metaphor, two aspects of the New Age movement are especially helpful in understanding it. First, if the sheer volume of New Age literature is any indication, channeling is possibly the single most important and definitive aspect of the New Age. It is certainly the activity which has had the greatest success in mobilizing support for the movement as a whole. It also provides an excellent illustration of the manner in which the movement has interacted with the older esoteric groups already established in the culture. Channeling is simply another name for spirit contact, no different in form than that practiced in Spiritualism for the last 150 years. However, channeling, a term derived from the extraterrestrial contact movement of the 1950s, distinguished itself from Spiritualist mediumship in its purpose and content. What is now termed "channeling" made a definitive appearance at the end of the nineteenth century.

Throughout Spiritualism's history, its mediums have specialized in contact with the "spirits of the dead" for the purpose of demonstrating the continuance of individual life after death. Its typical format was the séance or the public-platform work before an audience in which a number of supposed spirits would be contacted so that those in attendance could talk briefly with a loved one on the "other side."

However, once convinced of spirit survival, the believer was often led to the further conclusion that spirits should be able to tap extraordinary and authoritative sources of information about the great questions of human existence. Indeed, throughout the early decades various mediums published books which contained discourses spoken by various spirit entities through them. However, at the end of the century several books appeared which, quite apart from the work of the medium in general spirit contact, purported to be a new revelation or teaching around which a new religious group could be and was organized. The first of these "channeled" volumes was *Oahspe*,[14] published in 1882 by John Ballou Newbrough (1828-1891). In 1888 *The Secret Doctrine*, the major work of Theosophy, purporting to be derived from a spiritual hierarchy of masters in contact with Madame Blavatsky, appeared. *The Secret Doctrine* set the stage for other Theosophists to produce documents received from the masters. Then in the early twentieth century, Levi Dowling channeled one of the most important Spiritualist works, *The Aquarian Gospel of Jesus the Christ*.[15] Through the decades other channeled volumes appeared as the new sacred writings of yet another new group. Some Spiritualist mediums became channels, but subordinated their channeling to their platform and seance work and only channeled for, or circulated transcripts of the sessions to, the most dedicated inner group of their supporters. Some channeled works, however, such as *The Betty Book* series edited by Stewart Edward White, became perennial best sellers in Spiritualist circles. Edgar Cayce became possibly the best-known channel of the pre-New Age era.

In the 1970s, two selections of channeled material heralded a new wave of spirit contact. In 1970 the first volume of *The Seth Material*[16] appeared. Seth was an entity who spoke through Jane Roberts, a housewife who lived quietly in upstate New York. The unexpected response to her first volume led to a sequel, *Seth Speaks*[17] (1972), and more than ten others. In 1975 *A Course in Miracles*[18] appeared. Channeled by a New York psychologist Helen Schucman, the *Course* purported to be from Jesus Christ. Spread quietly by word of mouth and without advertising, the *Course's* popularity rivaled that of the Seth material. Though a few groups were established around Seth's communications, literally hundreds of study groups emerged to study *A Course of Miracles*, which was published complete with a student's study guide and teacher's manual.

Within the New Age movement, channeling has been accepted and redirected to the goal of facilitating the personal transformation of the channelers' clients. The Spiritualist concerns of proving life after death and the psychical research issues which arose out of testing mediums to see if any produced paranormal data have been swept aside. Channeled entities developed their variations of New Age philosophy, and the only criteria for their value have been their internal consistency and their ability to resonate with the audience of seekers after transformation. Private meetings with a New Age channel become more of a counseling session for the discussion of personal problems than the traditional séance, which offered the possibility of a continuing relationship with those now dead. Thus, while the form of the older mediumship is preserved, the New Age has altered its purpose and function completely.

The popular wave of channelling in the 1980s created a problem for certain New Agers. Some, like Spangler, saw the movement growing as they hoped it would (hence creating a larger audience for their books and lectures) but were repulsed by the movement's loss of innocence under mass marketing techniques and the obvious movement of large sums of money for New Age services. It was a particular problem for Spangler, who had started as a channel and whose early works were channeled transcripts. Spangler had the unenviable task of salvaging his own channeled works (which have recently been reprinted) while denouncing the more successful channels as merely the product of "psychic glamour" (in esoteric circles, a harsh derogatory term).

A second distinctive aspect of the New Age is its attention to crystals. Again, occult attention to gem stones and crystal substances goes back many centuries. They were valued as healing agents, and they appeared on magical tables of correspondences. However, through the medium of channeling crystals have been assigned an unprecedented central role in the transformational process. That central role began with Edgar Cayce. In the years after Cayce's death, people began to scrutinize the vast stenographic records of his many sessions for material on a variety of subjects. In 1960 a booklet attempted to correlate his teachings on crystals and gem stones.[19]

In the 1980s, a longtime Spiritualist medium who had become attuned to the New Age, Frank Alper, began to expand on Cayce in his channeling sessions at the Arizona Metaphysical Association. In three books ostensibly about the lost continent of Atlantis,[20] he developed a comprehensive myth of the use of crystals to power the civilization of Atlantis and gave detailed instructions on the personal use of crystals to tap into the cosmic powers that facilitate transformation.

Crystals are among the better illustrations of the New Age movement's attitude toward science. Far from being an escape into prescientific irrationalism (an image which its ideological antagonists have tried to pin on it), the movement has been most open to both science and technology. Science, rightly subjected to a proper ethical perspective, can be instrumental in the New Age, just as its capture by modern rationalist materialists has brought world culture to the brink of disaster (a replay of Atlantis). But science should not only turn its attention to the great social problems that are bringing about the crisis of this day, it should also expand to include the paranormal sciences. Such an expanded science would then encounter the more important subtle "spiritual" energies which are fueling the coming New Age. The spiritual energies are analogous to those physical energies already brought within the scientific paradigm and in the New Age will become accessible to all.

As we turn to a discussion of the relation between the New Age movement and New Thought, some further reflection on the future of the New Age seems necessary. Whatever else it is, the New Age movement is an apocalyptic movement. It has drawn its life from a hope in a radical change for the better in society. In this respect it is most similar to the Jesus People movement and its hope that Jesus would return before its adherents had to begin the hard work of being adults, holding jobs, raising families, and paying taxes. The loss of belief in the imminent Second Coming played a crucial role in the dissolution of the Jesus People movement and its absorption by Pentecostals and Baptists. In like measure, as the signs of the New Age fail to appear in the larger society, the movement will be unable to sustain its coherence and begin to disappear.

The New Age Approach to New Thought[21]

The New Age arose as a revivalist movement within the larger esoteric/metaphysical milieu of the 1970s. It had a distinctive message, yet like other revivalists from Charles Finney to Billy Graham, the New Age evangelists were not out to build another organization but to revive, transform, and coordinate those already existing. Thus, they turned to the older esoteric groups as an initial audience for their message. Already in place across North America and Europe, the numerous occult and metaphysical groups welcomed the heralds of the New Age (as they were welcoming each new teacher who arrived from Asia) to their programs and pulpits. In the United States such national organizations as Spiritual Frontiers Fellowship, the Association for Research and Enlightenment, the Theosophical Society in America, and the several Spiritualist church fellowships were more than happy to open their forums to the bearers of the New Age Message.

Within the occult/metaphysical milieu, the New Thought churches were especially valuable assets for the New Age movement. Most New Thought congregations owned or rented permanent facilities. Not only were there weekly worship services and Sunday school classes in which to make guest appearances, the New Thought church had facilities which could be borrowed or rented and in which weekly New Age classes could be held. They also had a potential audience of somewhat sympathetic church members. New Thought ministers saw the New Age leaders as resources for expanding their churches' weekly program of offerings, while the exponents of New Age disciplines saw the churches as offering a ready-made clientele.

And while the New Age movement tended to be more theosophical in its perspective, it resonated with New Thought in several important particulars. It affirmed an impersonal deity, the importance of spiritual law, and the need for personal change. New Thought had wrestled with belief in reincarnation and was open to those who professed their faith in it. At the same time, New Thought prided itself on freedom of belief and the privilege of exploring diverse ideas. Thus, during the 1970s a cordial relationship began to develop between New Thought and the New Age. This relationship is ably illustrated by the spread of *A Course of Miracles*.

The content of *A Course of Miracles* is quite compatible with the basic ideas of New Thought, especially those of the Unity School of Christianity. Thus it was not surprising that as the *Course* spread, study groups began to emerge in Unity and other New Thought churches. Many of the New Thought ministers became enthused with it. Prominent among Unity ministers, Sig Paulson taped a series of lectures on the course which were circulated by the Unity School of Christianity and sold in Unity church book displays. By the middle of the 1980s, the majority of New Thought congregations had *A Course in Miracles* study group meeting in their facilities.

The new channelers also found a place in New Thought churches. Penny Torres, the channel for an entity called Mafu, got her start in weekly sessions held at the Unity church in Santa Barbara, California. As Mafu became nationally known, Torres's audience outgrew the church and then even Santa Barbara, but they were soon replaced by Azena Ramanda (a public religious name) and her channeled entity, St. Germain.

Other aspects of the New Age also found a home in New Thought churches. The soothing sounds of New Age music were welcomed as an aid to meditation. Crystals also invaded the New Thought churches, many of which in the mid-1980s began to display and sell them to members. Healing, always a central emphasis of New Thought, was expanded to include various other nonmedical practices such as body-work (massage, shiatsu, yoga). Many New Age therapies from rebirthing to psychosynthesis added spice to the weekly calendar of events.

By the mid-1980s, New Thought leaders began to see in the New Age a movement with a distinct new clientele of its own. It was growing and attracting the rich and famous. They began to see that it had more to offer them than rental fees for the use of their facilities and an enriched program for church members. The many non-New Thought people attracted to the New Age could become an expanded audience for New Thought. New Thought distinctives could simply be repack-aged as New Age. During the 1980s, therefore, a number of New Thought spokespersons began to describe themselves as New Agers and began to appear at New Age events. Most notable among these was Terry Cole-Whitaker, a former Religious Science minister.

Cole-Whitaker is also a symbol of one of the more important con-tributions of New Thought to the ever-changing New Age Movement. She has been one of the main exponents of what is termed "prosperity consciousness." From the beginning within New Thought, the idea that God is the source of all good led to the understanding that just as attunement with God could overcome disease it could in like measure overcome poverty. God's abundant supply was for the claiming. It is not surprising that New Agers found prosperity consciousness appeal-ing. It is the one aspect of New Thought which has been able to pene-trate the mainstream of American religious life through the work of ministers such as Norman Vincent Peale and Robert Schuller and Pen-tecostal evangelists such as Kenneth Hagin, Kenneth Copeland, Fred-erick Price, and Rex Humbard. At the same time, the idea of prosperity consciousness stood in stark contrast with New Age concerns about the environment and the need to live more simply for Mother Earth's sake.

As the New Age movement grew in prominence, the boundaries between New Thought and New Age became increasingly blurred. At this point, a reaction began to take place as New Thought leaders took a critical look at the movement's agenda. Unity minister Dell deChant has noted a growing resistance in New Thought to what became increasingly seen as New Age encroachment. A general alarm was sounded as early as the 1986 meeting of the International New Thought Alliance. The 1988 meeting included a panel of speakers who challenged the compatibility of New Thought and New Age perspectives. Most cited problems with channeling and made note of the stricture against mediumship as a prominent theme in early New Thought writings.

Particular attention was also drawn to New Age apocalypticism. Speakers called attention to New Thought's central affirmation of the availability of the fullness of God to each person in the immediate present. It contradicted New Thought to think in terms of new, heretofore unavailable spiritual energies. It was also somewhat offensive to champion spiritual energies available today which had been unavailable to past religious greats, such as New Thought's founders.

While the freedom-loving ministers and members of the New Thought congregations were slow to respond to the concerted attack on the New Age, some national leaders moved against New Age encroachments. Teachings of the Inner Christ, Inc., a member of the International New Thought Alliance which had built a significant part of its program around the channeling activity of its leader, Ann Meyer McKeavor, was told to drop its channeling activity or leave the INTA. When TIC refused, it was dropped form membership.

The president of the International Association of Religious Science Churches sent a letter to all of the association's pastors requesting their cooperation in removing the influence of the New Age movement from member churches. Various leaders in the United Church of Religious Science have let their opposition to the New Age be known in less formal manners.

More quietly, the Unity School of Christianity, whose president, Connie Fillmore, had become concerned about New Age distortions of Unity teachings, removed New Age material from its center in Unity Village, Missouri. Though the leaders of the Association of Unity Churches share Fillmore's anti-New Age bias, they have had less luck in removing *A Course in Miracles* classes from the independent-minded local churches and New Age paraphernalia from the bookrooms.

The movement against the New Age has not received universal approval, but has also failed to produce a pro-New Age reaction. On the one hand, no groups rallied to the support of Teachings of the Inner Christ, Inc. when it was pushed out of INTA; on the other hand, one can still find the New Age very much represented in the materials circulating in New Thought congregations. But just as certainly as the New Age movement will fade in the 1990s, so the New Age will quietly disappear from the churches' weekly schedules. New Thought will continue, having absorbed any elements of New Age it finds useful while it discards the rest.

Conclusion

If the popularity of the New Age movement is anything of importance, it is a symbol of the growth and maturing of the esoteric and metaphysical religious traditions of the modern West. Like Mormonism, these traditions have spread to all parts of North America and Europe and have begun a marked diffusion around the world. Like Mormonism, they are still having to contend with important pockets of intense opposition but meanwhile have found space to operate openly and accommodated in some degree to the larger religious community. It is of no little interest that this maturing is occurring just at the time Christian churches are experiencing their first decade in which a majority of Americans have consented to become church members (with no slowing of growth trends in sight).

In its interaction with New Thought, the New Age movement also vividly illustrates the vitality and staying power of religious family traditions and the denominational structures they foster. Denominationalism is the pattern in which religious structures function in a free society. Denominations provide the stable week by week and year in and year out religious activities and services that are the heart and soul of popular religion. As new religious impulses, new religious causes, and new revivalistic thrusts come and go, the denominations agree, disagree, react, change, and occasionally splinter. But most importantly, denominations remain after the revival dies, after the cause is won or lost, and after the excitement has run its course. They print the weekly educational lessons, stock hymnals and prayerbooks, and do the hundred-and-one tasks which can ease the pain of congregational traumas and insure their survival through periods of transition. Amid the "glamour" of paradenominational movements, the vital roles of the denominations show no sign of decreasing.

While the esoteric and metaphysical movements were maturing, the West has become home to all of the world's religious traditions, which have also gone about the business of reorganizing themselves in denominational patterns (urged along by legal structures and the IRS). In the 1980s the majority of the Asian teachers touted a decade ago as leading the wave of New Age transformation have settled into the more mundane tasks of recruiting members, training leaders, and teaching their own variety of Buddhism, Hinduism, Sikhism, Sant Mat, etc. and have quietly withdrawn from any participation in New Age gatherings. Given the withdrawal of New Thought and the Eastern religions, the New Age movement has been left with its base in theosophical and channeling groups. The older theosophical groups are continuing with their set agenda. That leaves the channeling groups as the remnant of the movement most likely to survive. Already the major channelers have established organizations and begun the hard task of mobilizing followers into stable "religious" groups. These groups will in turn settle into the landscape of the larger esoteric world as variations of theosophical and Spiritualist religions, while the esoteric community prepares itself for the next "movement" which will offer to revitalize its life.

Chapter 3
Roots of the New Age

──────── *Kay Alexander*

It has been widely observed that the variety of practices and interests which have been gradually grouped together since the early seventies under the general rubric *New Age* have their genesis, in part, in interests in powers of the mind, in spiritualism, and in the occult that have been evident in America since its inception. It is less well known that two main roots of the New Age movement, one theosophical and the other New Thought,[1] are directly traceable to Franz Anton Mesmer and Emanuel Swedenborg. On the one hand, their practices were studied by New Thought groups interested in spiritual or psychic healing which first developed in the transcendentalist milieu of Boston in the nineteenth century. On the other hand, the theology of Swedenborg influenced a variety of Americans beginning with members of the New Church, or Church of the New Jerusalem, founded by his followers in the same milieu. Their interest in Swedenborg was transmitted to Theosophists, through whom it passed to the founders of transpersonal psychology which developed in the following century on the opposite coast. A tracing of these two roots illustrates the degree to which they remained intertwined—though sometimes in overt opposition—and reveals the contributions of a seminal group of thinkers and practitioners to the worldview which lies behind more recent New Age developments.

Origins of New Thought and Theosophy

New Thought groups had their genesis in the Congregational, Unitarian, and transcendentalist milieu of sophisticated, educated, urban Boston. A study of the metaphysics and healing practices of early New Thought leaders such as Emma Curtis Hopkins, Horatio Dresser, and

Charles Brodie Patterson reveals common themes drawn from even earlier thinkers, most importantly from four New Englanders: (1) the Maine clockmaker, inventor, and healer, Phineas Quimby, (2) the Methodist minister turned Swedenborgian, Warren Felt Evans, (3) the great transcendentalist, Ralph Waldo Emerson, and (4) the founder of Christian Science, Mary Baker Eddy, who synthesized the thought of the previous three as early as 1881 in her Boston Metaphysical College, which trained students to do mental healing.

Further back, the source of New Thought is evident in the works of the Austrian hypnotist Franz Anton Mesmer (1733-1815) and the great Swedish scientist, philosopher, and mystic, Emanuel Swedenborg (1688-1772). Mesmer, through his experiments in hypnotism, came to understand himself as having tapped an occult force through which he could influence others. J. Gordon Melton points out that

> Evans in *Esoteric Christianity and Mental Therapeutics* (1886) . . . seems to return to a "Mesmeric model" by positing the existence of a "mental energy" transmitted by the mind. He identified that energy with the Hindu *akasa*, the *astral light* of Western occultists, the Christian *Holy Spirit*, and the Platonic *world-soul*.[2]

Modern Theosophy, which developed contemporaneously with New Thought out of The Theosophical Society, founded in New York in 1875 by H. P. Blavatsky, also has roots traceable to Mesmer. The stated goals of the Theosophical Society—to form a nucleus devoted to the Universal Brotherhood of Humanity without distinction of race, creed, sex, caste, or color, to encourage the study of comparative religion, philosophy, and science, and to investigate unexplained laws of nature and the powers latent in man—were remarkably similar to those of the New Thought leaders. New Thought members and theosophists shared an interest in universal brotherhood and comparative religion, and like many New Age groups, both groups were early dominated by the concerns and interests of feminine leaders. The writings of early theosophists such as Blavatsky formed an important part of the intellectual environment of developing New Thought groups.

In *Isis Unveiled* (1877) and *The Secret Doctrine* (1888),[3] Blavatsky claimed she was conveying the essence of all religions which had been the universally diffused religion of the ancient and prehistoric world, and she predicted the imminent dawn of a new age in which man would be transformed. She understood herself to be conveying esoteric teachings which had been kept alive in occultism, mysticism, and free masonry. When she opened an Esoteric Section of the Theosophical Society in England, in 1889, early members included Annie Besant, the leader of Blavatsky's lodges following her death, George R. S. Mead, a leading early scholar of Gnosticism and editor of *The Quest*,[4] and the poet, William Butler Yeats.

The Theosophical Society in England dated from 1876, the year after the first society was organized in America by Blavatsky and Henry Steele Olcott. It developed somewhat independently of Blavatsky and attracted the attention of circles of scholars and intelligentsia already interested in eastern religions, occultism, and psychic phenomena. Its leadership, which tended to change often at the beginning, at one time or another overlapped with that of the Society for Psychical Research, which included William James as an important member. Members were in conversation with the National Secular Society (of atheists) and the Fabian Society of Socialists, as well as with branches of the Theosophical Society in Paris and Germany. And while some of these leaders were interested in Blavatsky, it was often in terms of trying to discover how she could manifest psychic phenomena. To many of them, she was a piece of the data.

When the American leadership of the Theosophical Society moved to India, finally establishing its headquarters at Adyar near Madras, it gradually became involved with the growing Indian Nationalist movement. If the Church of England could be brought down, British rule would be consequently weakened. So ran the logic. Dharmapala, who represented Buddhism at the World Parliament of Religions held in Chicago in 1893, had earlier been recruited to Theosophy by Blavatsky and Olcott. Vivekananda, who represented Hinduism at the Parliament and who subsequently founded Vedanta in America, was another important Indian political, as well as religious, leader.

An interest in Theosophy and politics also emerged among British Theosophists. Annie Besant, along with George Bernard Shaw, was one of the early organizers of the Fabian Society, a socialist society founded in London in the winter of 1883-1884 with the declared object of reconstructing society in accordance with the highest moral possibilities. The Fabian Society participated in the founding of the Labor Party in 1900. Nearly all the leading socialists in England were at one time members of the Fabian group, and for many of them religious and political rebellion went hand in hand with atheism or interest in the occult.[5]

The founders of New Thought in America and of Theosophy in England, America, and on the Continent were reforming contemporaries and were part of a larger thought world fascinated with the powers of the mind and its ability to influence others. Later, socialist or revolutionary politics coupled with an interest in powers of the mind as it developed on the Continent were to feed into humanistic psychology, discussed below, through members of the Frankfurt School in Germany who moved to America with the rise of Hitler. Frankfurt-am-Main, between the two world wars, was an important intellectual center for secular Judaism, which had resulted from the weakening of religious Judaism during the nineteenth century by historical-critical study of biblical texts.

This scholarship also had an impact in England, and Walter Truett Anderson, in discussing the background of the New Age precursor, Alan Watts, describes one of the results:

> London in the 1930s was teeming with Oriental scholars, eclectic students of world religions, charlatans, seekers, yogis, gurus. One major organizational focus of this spiritual energy was the Theosophical Society . . . responsible for introducing many people—including a sizable segment of the British aristocracy—to the great works of Buddhist and Hindu philosophy, and it was a major force behind the spiritual ferment that Watts discovered in London.[6]

Traditionally, the Anglican Church, with its support of the royal, aristocratic, and intellectual status quo, had a strong appeal to those who considered themselves a part of these groups. But the intellectuals and aristocrats who read the new scholarship had their faith challenged, and some turned for confirmation of old or discovery of new spiritual verities to Swedenborgianism, Spiritualism, Theosophy, and older heresies kept alive in Gnosticism.

Gnosticism was an important intellectual strand of theosophy from the beginning. At the evening party in 1875 when the American Theosophical Society was first proposed and formed, the main speaker on "Egyptian Cabbalism" was brought and introduced by Charles Southern. A high ranking Mason, Rosicrucian, and student of Gnosticism, Southern exercised an important influence on the New York society during its early years, though he later dropped out. He helped Blavatsky with the editing of *Isis Unveiled* and contributed to its Gnostic slant. Another student of Gnosticism, George R. S. Mead, published the first full bibliography on Gnosticism[7] as an appendix to this *Fragments of a Faith Forgotten.*[8] His bibliography makes it evident that access to Gnostic texts and commentaries in the eighteenth century was available to anyone as fluent in Latin as Swedenborg.

The method of scriptural interpretation of Swedenborg, which depended on his finding inner esoteric meanings in the Bible through correspondences given in revelations by angels, bears similarities to early Gnostic techniques. His followers denied that he was doing allegorical interpretation on the model of Philo and Origen. But the reliance of Swedenborg on finding an inner sense in the Bible and his claims that he received direct revelations from the angels and took out-of-body journeys to heaven and hell are consistent with the purposes and claims of many of the Gnostics.

The ideas of Swedenborg were conveyed to the New Thought movement through Warren Felt Evans. Evans went to Phineas Quimby in 1863 for healing. Horatio Dresser credits Evans with detecting the resemblance of the ideas of Quimby to those of Swedenborg and with finding Quimby's theories of spiritual healing in Swedenborg's writings. These writings were accessible to Quimby because, as Marguerite Beck Block observes, an interest in Swedenborgianism emanating from Boston had swept over America in the eighteen-forties and then died down.[9]

Block credits Robert Hindmarsh, a convert to the New Church Society formed in England around Swedenborg's ideas, with giving major impetus to the movement. Hindmarsh formed an organization in 1783 which he "called 'The Theosophical Society', instituted for the purpose of promoting the Heavenly Doctrines of the New Jerusalem."[10] The purpose of his organization was to translate and publish the writings of Swedenborg. The New Church was in New York as early as 1795[11] and in Boston, which was later to become its real center, by 1816.

A letter from an English New Churchman on a visit to America in 1843 notes the involvement of the American Church in the homeopathic system of medicine.[12] And, though the beginnings of Spiritualism in America were later to be identified with the Fox sisters in 1848, Block finds Spiritualism to be "mentioned in New Church writings much earlier."[13] Magnetism, or Mesmerism, was an interest of the New Church in America which preceded spiritualism. Block chronicles the difficulties caused for the early New Church in England and on the Continent by spiritualist experiments and the practice of magnetism.[14] She notes that, though practicing magnetism and participating in Spiritualism were officially condemned, a connection between "these practices and the doctrines and truths of the New Church" existed "in the minds of many New Church people."[15]

New Thought leaders were later to adopt Swedenborg's distrust of practicing spiritualism along with his basic theology of one God, who is Jesus Christ, in whom there is a Divine Trinity. The Divine Trinity was understood by Swedenborg on a Platonic model. God is infinite and uncreated love, wisdom, and use, or end, replicated in man as finite and created. The final ends of all things, he held, are in the Divine Mind. These ends are the causes of all things in the spiritual world, and their effects in the natural world. The Oneness of God as well as the themes of divine love, divine wisdom, and the necessity of opening oneself to the divine plan became recurrent motifs in New Thought.

Evans derived a theological interpretation for Quimby's healing from Swedenborg, and the combination was carried forward by the New Thought leader Julius Dresser in his writings on medicine, philosophy and theology. Dresser taught that healing is accomplished by "keeping the windows of the soul open to the higher light"[16] which makes it possible for man to use "unused sources of power and energy."[17] We can aid in the healing of each other, claimed Dresser, through soul cooperation because ". . . all souls are united in the mental world. We are not detached, separated individuals affecting one another only through physical interchange. We are bound together by ties of thought—by thought atmospheres and emotions."[18] New Thought leaders taught that the essence of New Thought is Truth. However, they believed, as was stated by Patterson, that all people have had prophets and "no religion is devoid of truth,"[19] therefore, doctrinaire positions are to be rejected. It was acknowledged that Buddha, Krishna, Mohammed, Zoroaster, and Confucius were prophets of God.

Summary of the Origins of New Thought

New Thought began as a late nineteenth-century New England healing movement within self-consciously Christian circles. It developed nation-wide against a background of a wider interest in comparative religions promoted from such intellectual centers as Harvard and through publications such as James Freeman Clarke's *Ten Great Religions* (1871), which went through twenty-one editions. The World's Parliament of Religions, organized in 1893 by a group of liberal Protestant ministers led by Presbyterians and Congregationalists, was the culmination of this interest.

While New Thought groups pursued their interest—shared with others—in powers of the mind and eastern religions, study of early Gnostic heresies was pursued more privately in theosophical circles. Melton notes that "during the early years of the New Thought movement, leaders interacted with both spiritualists and members of the Theosophical Society."[20]

Charles Braden titled his definitive history of New Thought *Spirits in Rebellion*,[21] but intellectual rebellion in the late nineteenth century was hardly a new phenomenon in New England. John Winthrop, Jr. arrived at Massachusetts's Bay Colony with a substantial library of alchemical books which may have contributed to his father's decision to send him to defend Ipswich on the most remote northern edge of the colony. Harvard, established in the Colony in 1636 to provide an educated clergy, was soon regarded as too free thinking by the Puritans who established Yale in 1701 to guarantee orthodoxy, a move which they made long before Harvard nurtured both Unitarianism and transcendentalism. Free masonry developed as a strong movement in the colonies, and the founding fathers made memorable its influence when they adopted its symbol of the all-seeing eye above the pyramid on the Great Seal of the United States. Nineteenth-century communal movements such as Brook Farm and the utopian Oneida Society, established by John Humphrey Noyes with its Fourieristic views on sex and marriage, grew lushly in the same fertile soil.

An interest in world religions was nurtured by New England Unitarians and transcendentalists; when representatives of religions from around the world arrived in Chicago for The World's Parliament of Religions in 1893, they were eagerly welcomed. One of them, Vivekananda, remained in America after the meeting to establish the Ramakrishna Society, or Vedanta Society. When his disciple, Prabhavananda, came to California, he became the guru of Aldous Huxley, Gerald Heard, and Christopher Isherwood in Hollywood.

Educated New Englanders could easily spend a day in the Windsor chairs of the Boston Library pursuing esoterica or visit local booksellers to collect primary sources for their private libraries. The latest information was readily available to them through lecturers reporting on the new German historical critical study of the Bible, the latest archeological finds, and on the esoteric and exotic in general. Charles Braden, writing in the early 1960s, identified New Thought as "perhaps the chief channel through which some flowing-together of oriental—chiefly Hindu, Buddhist, Taoist—and Christian thought and practice is taking place."[22] However, from the beginning the interest of New Thought leaders in Hinduism, Buddhism, Zoroastrianism, Islam, and Taoism was an interest they shared with many.

Origins of The Human Potential Movement

A much-reported event important to the genesis of both transpersonal psychology and the New Age movement which took place on the west coast at Big Sur, also in the early sixties, had a very different ambience. Picture Abraham Maslow, then a professor of psychology at Brandeis University, and his wife driving down narrow Highway 1 which winds along the cliffs high above the Pacific surf pounding the rocks between Monterey and Hearst's castle. The year is 1962, the night is dark, and the Maslows are looking for a place to stay in the rugged, sparsely populated area. They turn in where they see some lights and find a group of people meeting at Esalen, an old hot springs spa and cluster of cabins which Michael Murphy, a Stanford graduate interested in Eastern religions, had inherited some years earlier. At this moment the fundamental link between humanistic psychology and Esalen, the earliest and most important of the Personal Growth Centers, was forged.

Proper Bostonians would not have supported the life style which had developed within the bohemian colony led by Henry Miller in the wildly beautiful Big Sur country below Monterey—a life style with roots in Fourierism which, with its doctrine of free love, had swept the country in the early 1840s but had been rejected by both Swedenborgians and later New Thought leaders. However, Bostonians interested in Transcendentalism might have been sympathetic to aspects of the religion.

Walter Truett Anderson quotes Mildred Edie Brady's description of the Big Sur country as the mecca for postwar bohemians, including their "belief in something that went by such names as 'the life force' or 'the great oneness.'"[23] Members of the Big Sur bohemian colony were not the first or the last romantic mystics in the area. Anderson describes the diffuse spirit of the early sixties in California in terms of an inner life running near the surface.[24]

Big Sur was not the only Californian bohemian colony in the fifties. Kenneth Rexroth describes a second developing on Mountain Drive in Santa Barbara where "sex, food, clothing, and shelter and mild intoxicants are abundant."[25] However, if the diffuse mood of California in the sixties could have been focused through a crystal, the pinpoint of light would surely have been on Big Sur.

During this period, Aldous Huxley, as a Professor-at-large at the University of California in Santa Barbara in 1959, lived on the fringe of the Santa Barbara bohemian community while he rented a house on the beach in Isla Vista and toured universities and colleges in California, conveying his vision of unused human potentialities. Huxley focused on "a great many potentialities—for rationality, for affection and kindliness, for creativity—still lying latent in man,"[26] and suggested that "as no human being has ever made use of as much as ten percent of all the neurons in his brain . . . if we set about it in the right way, we might be able to produce extraordinary things out of this strange piece of work that a man is."[27] Huxley, a member of the famous Huxley family in England, was part of the London scene of the thirties previously described in connection with Alan Watts. Huxley continued to combine an interest shared with other family members in mysticism, religion, and philosophy after his move to California in 1937. He studied Vedanta along with his friend Gerald Heard under the guidance of Prabhavananda, befriended Krishnamurti in the theosophical community of Ojai, and published voluminously, including *The Perennial Philosophy* (1945), *Vedanta for Modern Man* (1951), *The Doors of Perception* (1954), and *Island* (1962). Michael Murphy consulted with Huxley and Heard when first organizing his Esalen project.

Abraham Maslow introduced humanistic psychology into this cosmopolitan and bohemian milieu. Humanistic psychology, known as Third Force psychology to differentiate it from the First and Second Force psychologies of behaviorism and Freudianism, was a post-World War II creation of psychologists interested in studying psychology scientifically from the perspectives of healthy individuals as well as in discarding behavioristic models based on observations of animal behavior. Abraham Maslow was a key figure in the movement from the beginning and, as early as 1954, kept the roster of approximately 200 individuals to whom relevant papers were privately circulated during the fifties.[28]

Carl Rogers, with his person-centered therapy focused on uncovering the meaning of events in the present, was also an early leader of the humanistic psychology movement. Rollo May was another who, through his study in Europe, helped to link the movement to Continental philosophies developed between the two World Wars and to postwar existentialism. He introduced psychologists to philosophers such as Wilhelm Dilthey, Edmund Husserl, Martin Heidegger, Martin Buber, Jean-Paul Sartre and Maurice Merleau-Ponty. Going back to an even earlier period would permit the inclusion of the psychologist/philosopher, William James—influential in both America and Europe—who, with his writings on Mind Cure and Mysticism, brings us back into the ambience of New Thought. Though these philosophers would be variously described as spiritual or nonspiritual, taken together, they kept alive an approach to understanding man which was contrary to the developing logical positivism which represented the other main philosophical movement of the period.

Maslow provided an important link between humanistic psychology and psychologies developed in Germany between the two world wars. He frequently acknowledged his intellectual debt to Kurt Goldstein, who first developed a theory of self-actualization in his work with brain damaged soldiers in Frankfurt-am-Main, Germany after World War I, though Goldstein was later to claim that Maslow's use of the term was different from his.

Fritz Perls, the principle founder of Gestalt therapy, who became associated with humanistic psychology through Esalen, provided another link to European psychology which James Simkin describes as follows:

> One of the centers of intellectual ferment in Europe in the mid-1920s following World War I was Frankfurt-am-Main where [Fritz] Perls was exposed to some of the leading Gestalt psychologists of that era as well as existential philosophers and psychoanalysts. After acquiring the M.D. degree, Perls had gone to Frankfurt-am-Main in 1926 as an assistant to Kurt Goldstein at Goldstein's Institute for Brain Damaged Soldiers.[29]

Perls met his future wife Laura Posner at the University of Frankfurt. By 1950, after a period in Holland and South Africa, Laura and Fritz Perls were living in an apartment in New York City where they organized and established the New York Institute for Gestalt therapy, offering therapy and workshops. There they were part of the intellectual circle connected to the New School for Social Research, a haven for philosophers and sociologists connected to the Frankfurt School.

> Simkin describes Gestalt therapy as an existentially based system of psychotherapy having a primary focus on the here and now. . . . The focus in Gestalt therapy is on immediate present awareness of one's experience. Cognitive explanations or interpretations of 'causes' or 'purposes' are rejected.[30]

This emphasis on the here and now grounds a state of mind and assumptions which Donald Stone finds common to all human potential groups and which leads to a *gestalt consciousness* which he describes as follows:

> It is both behavioral and ideological. It underlies transpersonal experience as well as body work and encounter. As a state of awareness it is similar to the results of Eastern meditation in the way perceptions are organized and in the techniques used to attain it. Gestalt awareness is an altered way of looking at experience with the aim of witnessing it in a more direct, nonevaluative, noncognitive way. The techniques are designed to focus attention on an immediate situation in order to stay in present time in the present continuum of awareness. This is frequently called staying in the "here and now" or "present centeredness" or "going with the flow." A cat watching a ladybug climb a twig shows gestalt awareness.[31]

Fritz Perls moved to California in 1960, and in 1964 the first Gestalt training workshop was held at Esalen by his students. The primary

Gestalt Therapy Institute continued to be located in the residence of Laura Perls in New York City, but other Gestalt Therapy Institutes were organized around the country.

While Fritz Perls was in Frankfurt, Wilhelm Reich, the developer of bioenergetics, was his analyst. Reich represents another important early influence on the development of humanistic psychology. From Reich is derived the emphasis on working directly with the body as it interacts with the psyche, an emphasis which became an important component of experiential psychotherapy and, in turn, part of humanistic psychology. Eugene Gendlin notes that experiential psychotherapy emphasizing the "felt sense of the complexity of situations and difficulties,"[32] is based on existential psychotherapy which "holds that one can change oneself in present living. One's past does not have to determine how one lives."[33]

Gendlin points out that "felt meaning is neither muscles nor emotions, nor both together. It is the bodily felt sense of one's living in one's situation."[34] Experiential psychotherapy derives a philosophical justification from Merleau-Ponty's insistence that existence is to be understood in terms of bodily concreteness, that is, "we are in the world through our body."[35] Therefore, therapeutic change can take place "on the bodily plane as one works with diet, breathing, muscles as in Yoga and Reich's system."[36] This emphasis on the necessary embodiment of existence appears contrary to New Thought's insistence that it is the impact of the spiritual on the material which is essential. As Charles Brodie Patterson had earlier stated it, ". . . the body of man, to some degree, represents man's spiritual and mental life; that by the influx of man's spiritual consciousness the mind is renewed, and the body is strengthened and made whole."[37] Unless Yoga and Reich's systems are seen as vehicles for the influx of spiritual consciousness, New Thought and humanistic psychology appear to be somewhat at odds. And it is exactly this claim to facilitate the influx of spiritual consciousness which transpersonal psychology was soon to make.

In addition to Kurt Goldstein, a second important precursor whom Abraham Maslow frequently acknowledged was Jacob Levy Moreno, a psychiatrist who came from Vienna to New York in 1925. Moreno, from his earliest period in Vienna, was interested in interpersonal themes, and Leon J. Fine notes that "terms such as 'here and now' and 'encounter' so popular in the human potential movement were to be found as key ideas in Moreno's writings of this period."[38] These ideas were developed in group dynamics at the National Training Labs at Bethel, Maine, another precursor of the human potential movement.

Key Concepts of the Human Potential Movement

The human potential movement grew out of the previously noted link between humanistic psychology and personal growth centers such as Esalen, from which it derived an early emphasis on self-actualization, the experiential, encounter, the importance of the here and now, the role of the body in psychic growth, and group dynamics. The Association for Humanistic Psychology, which grew out of the *Journal of Humanistic Psychology* founded by Abraham Maslow and Anthony Sutich in 1961, was organized in 1962 with its headquarters in San Francisco and had 5000 members by 1970. Sutich stated the goals of the *Journal* in its opening issue as follows;

> The *Journal of Humanistic Psychology* is being founded by a group of psychologists and professional men and women from other fields who are interested in those human capacities and potentialities that have no systematic place either in positivistic or behavioristic theory or in classical psychoanalytic theory, e.g., creativity, love, self, growth, organism, basic need-gratification, self-actualization, higher values, ego-transcendence, objectivity, autonomy, identity, responsibility, psychological health, etc.[39]

In the lead article of the inaugural issue, Maslow made extensive reference to "some data [he] presented in a 1951 paper called 'Resistance to Acculturation.'"[40] He was referring to studies he had made of what he came to call self-actualizing individuals. In his interest in studying healthy individuals, Maslow had originally identified what he called "higher values" and then interviewed individuals to see if any conclusions could be drawn by grouping and studying individuals who evinced these values. An early finding was that his group had significantly higher occurrences of what he came to call "peak experiences." Maslow's numerous and various subsequent descriptions of his "peakers" would function importantly in the development of the human potential movement. In his 1951 paper Maslow had described his "peakers" as resisting acculturation, that is, transcending their environment, as follows: "In practically all of them, I found a rather calm, good humored rejection of the stupidities and imperfections of the culture with greater or lesser effort at improving it. They definitely showed an ability to fight it vigorously when they thought it necessary."[41] Though Maslow later identified his "peakers" collectively, citing many individuals who were unavailable for interviews, they tended to appear anonymously grouped as in the above quotation; however, Maslow, on this occasion, provides a footnote giving Walt Whitman and William James as "examples of this kind of transcendence."[42]

The human potential movement mushroomed from these rather clear and simple beginnings into a many branched, diverse phenomenon. Within the parameters of the here and now and the experiential, anything that could conceivably contribute to human growth, whether scientifically verified or not, was admissible—and was admitted. Growth centers on the model of Esalen began to spring up elsewhere, either in remote and naturally beautiful areas or in urban centers of population. And as techniques for growth proliferated, ancient spiritual techniques such as yoga were included. It was a short step to understanding experiences happening in the groups as somehow transpersonal, spiritual, or even mystical. Transpersonal psychology, emphasizing, as the name implies, personal experiences transcending the usual range of humanistic investigations, was born out of a new interest in the spiritual dimensions of experience in what had, as humanistic psychology, been a secular movement.

John Mann observes that "so many different methods are used within a human-potential context that it is difficult to single out a few for special treatment."[43] However, he identifies certain concepts which cut across "most, but probably not all, HP methods."[44] First he lists the concept of the "*peak experience*," which Maslow defined as follows: "The word peak experience is a generalization for the best moments of life, for experiences of ecstasy, rapture, bliss or greatest joy."[45]

A second important concept is "life force." Mann notes that "the emphasis on the release and flow of vitality frequently occurs,"[46] an emphasis which had been central to the bio-energetic analysis of Wilhelm Reich. From the beginning New Thought leaders had also been interested in the flow of force. Whereas in New Thought the flow of power passes from one person to another, the orgone energy of Reich which pervades the natural world is made available to an individual by such techniques as sitting in a box. Mann discusses a similar concept found in yoga known as "prana" and notes, "The basic purpose of yoga is to contact and absorb prana in ever increasing quantities. Certain forms of yoga are specifically directed toward the channeling of energy in a very direct manner. Kundalini yoga, for example, is described in classical texts as 'the Yoga of Psychic Force.'"[47] Mann also identifies two basic assumptions of the human potential movement: first, that *people are more similar than different*, therefore anybody can play. "The main criterion for participation," he states, "is wanting to belong."[48] The second is that *different methods can be successfully combined out of context*. Accordingly, "An HP workshop is likely to be wildly eclectic, bringing together concepts and means developed by people who have never heard of each other, working in different fields, countries, and historical periods. It is precisely this quality which characterizes the experience."[49] It is out of this "wild eclecticism" that transpersonal psychology was born.

Development of Transpersonal Psychology

As the human potential movement grew, the transpersonal aspect of it received increasing emphasis. Mann describes its eclectic diversification:

> Approached from different directions by seekers, scientists, gurus, and clinicians, the varied areas of meditation, altered states of consciousness, and parapsychology all help the individual to relate to a more cosmic level of experience. In some respects, many of the methods employed are ancient, but the context is new and from a modern Western viewpoint, it is all new to us.[50]

Mann attributes the transpersonal direction taken by some in the human potential movement to theorists such as Maslow and the psychiatrist Roberto Assagioli, both of whom agreed "that in addition to ego and unconscious aspects of human behavior, there is a higher level of conscious experience that is possible."[51]

Donald Stone describes Assagioli's technique of psychosynthesis as explicitly training for the transpersonal experience of a euphoric state of spiritual awakening. Assagioli pictures this state as follows:

> A harmonious inner awakening is characterized by the sense of joy and mental illumination that brings with it insight into the meaning and purpose of life; it dispels many doubts, offers the solution to many problems, and gives one a sense of security. At the same time there wells up a realization that life is one, and an outpouring of love flows through the awakening individual towards his fellow beings and the whole of creation.[52]

With an emphasis on the ability of each individual to achieve a higher consciousness, the splinter group interested in transpersonal psychology within the human potential movement took a new turn.

Donald J. Mueller suggests that the emergence of transpersonal psychology had already been seeded in a variety of ways by professionals who were: (1) willing to define the human condition as something more than merely biopsychosocial; (2) interested in experiences of human consciousness previously avoided by Western psychologies, as well as in (3) "the evolution of new values that include the desire to

harmonize better with one's own mind, body, group, planet and especially the cosmos (including God or Soul) as and how this might be the
case."[53] The main emphasis of the new movement, according to Sutich,
was on the experiencing individual.[54]

Mueller characterizes the goal of transpersonal psychology as "soul
actualization"[55] rather than self-actualization. Referring to the peak
experiences studied by Maslow, he states "transpersonal psychology
seeks to trace and record these 'mystical' experiences,"[56] and notes that
it is concerned with the B-values (i.e. Being Values) of Maslow—values
such as truth, perfection, unity, and necessity.

The transpersonal psychology movement was formally launched by
an address given by Maslow and sponsored by the Esalen Institute in
September of 1967 at the First Unitarian Church of San Francisco. Looking forward instead of backward, one can glimpse the variety of interests which transpersonal psychology was to subsume under its aegis in
Mueller's footnotes, where he provides a "tentative list of descriptive
expressions"[57] which were early used pertaining to "the mystical, peak,
or transcendent experience."[58] Under "Expressions of Awareness, Consciousness, or State" Mueller includes,

> Awakened, Christ, Core-religious, Cosmic, Field, Illumination,
> Mystical, Omega, Point Omega, Peak, Plateau, Religious, Self,
> Soul, Spiritual, Super-, Transcendent, Transpersonal, Ultimate,
> Unitive, Visionary, and Also Expanded and Heightened.[59]

Under "States of" Mueller lists

> Adam-Kadmon, Al-insan al Kamil, Alpha, Ananda-maya-kosa,
> Atman, Atonement (At-one-ment), Awe, Bliss, Buddhi, Ecstasy,
> Essence, Higher Mind, Joy, Nirodh, Nirvana, Oneness, Over
> Mind, Peace, Pneuma, Purusa, Rapture, Ruarch Adonia,
> Samadhi, Satori, Supreme Identity, Tathagatagarbha, Unity,
> Wonder and also Buddhahood, Jhana, Liberation.[60]

The practice of combining techniques out of context and divorced
from theoretical structures had already been well established. As individual interests branched out, a diversity was born under the rubric
New Age which made the earlier "wild eclecticism" of the human potential movement look narrow and circumscribed.

A Comparison of the Roots of the New Age

New Thought and Theosophy both were born in a period when ortho-
doxies within Christianity and Judaism were being threatened by the

historical-critical study of their sacred texts. If the Bible could no longer guarantee the Truth, then what could? For some, New Thought in the late nineteenth century provided one way of answering this question. For others, particularly members of medical circles in Vienna and Frankfurt between the two world wars, psychiatry guaranteed answers to ancient questions. When these members brought their research to New York, particularly in the ambience of the New School for Social Research, their ranks broadened to include a diverse group of Americans. Together they developed an interest in "Third Force" or humanistic psychology. Out of humanistic psychology linked with certain growth centers developed the human potential movement and, finally, as experiences interpreted as sacred broke into the secular milieu, the new movement known as transpersonal psychology was born.

New Thought thinkers had earlier had a central interest in describing their techniques as a science, but they were hampered by nineteenth century limitations on what is actually known about the brain. Transpersonal psychology also understood itself as a science, and blended ancient spiritual and modern scientific techniques as it sought to understand how consciousness is expanded. The experiments of transpersonal psychologists developed in diverse directions, ranging from attaching electrodes to Zen masters and Hindu yogis to interest in new scientific theories based on left brain and right brain research. As they discussed their results at the annual Council Grove Conferences, in Kansas, and published their results in the *Journal of Transpersonal Psychology*,[61] terms such as *biofeedback* and *alpha* and *beta waves* became household words.

The choice of the Council Grove conference ground as a major point of sharing and dissemination of information may ironically suggest a difference between New Thought and transpersonal psychology. It will be recalled that New Thought was developed originally in Calvinist New England. Its followers remained firmly convinced that it is God who heals and that the healer is only the "conductor" of the power or energy that heals. Transpersonal psychology, rooted in the "peak experience" of Maslow, was much closer in ideology to the Methodism which established the Camp Grounds in which those interested in the development of transpersonal psychology met.

Having the "peak experience" came to function as a guarantor of growth toward perfection, much as the experience of the Second Grace preached by Phoebe Palmer and other Holiness preachers did in Methodism. If the Methodists and Holiness churches remained convinced that it is God that gives the Grace, as did the Calvinists involved in New Thought movements, transpersonal psychology, with its secular origins, had no such conviction. The "peak experience," though not intended to become an end in itself, became ultimately desirable whatever its source.

But if there is an important difference between New Thought and transpersonal psychology, there are also important similarities. Mueller notes that the roots of transpersonal psychology include hypnosis and clairvoyance, spiritualism and mediumship, psychical research and the survival issue, parapsychology and ESP, and such diverse "esoteric" schools as Anthroposophy, Rosicrucians, and an interest in past lives.[62] Early New Thought groups shared many of these interests even though some were to be specifically rejected. By adding a few more interests to the list—such as holistic medicine, astrology, crystals, ecology and vegetarian diets—it is easy to sketch in the general parameters of the New Age movement.

Retracing the Roots of the New Age

The New Age movement can be understood as developing broader, more applied versions of the interests of transpersonal psychologists who, even though they made a careful effort to remain academically respectable, attained only a modest acceptance in the academic and psychological circles which had previously rejected humanistic or "Third Force" psychology. A religious-mystical emphasis was further encouraged in the New Age movement through participation of members in such groups as the San Francisco Zen Center, Sufi groups, and Catholic monks in contemplative centers.

In the early seventies, transpersonal psychology maintained strong academic ties through psychologists teaching and working at recognized institutions such as the Menninger Foundation and the Center for the Study of the Person in La Jolla. The invitational Council Grove Conferences on Altered States of Consciousness were originally designed as academic and scientific meetings.

Activities at Esalen and its more than one hundred copies across the country reflected current scientific and academic interests. Academicians interested in transpersonal and humanistic psychology, Eastern religions, new developments in physics and philosophy, as well as a variety of other topics took part in the academic programs as leaders and participants. Residential programs provided a community in which this eclectic variety of interests was combined.

If the New Age movement can be seen as one of the results of the transpersonal movement, it, as has been shown, came directly out of the human potential movement nurtured in growth centers during the sixties. The human potential movement had two distinct and important sources. The first reached back through the organization of the Association for Humanistic Psychology to its founders such as Abraham Maslow, Carl Rogers, and Rollo May. These, in turn, had ties to the Frankfurt School and the existential Continental philosophy developed between the two World Wars.

The second important root transmitted to it by Esalen reached back through the Beat scene of the fifties in San Francisco and through individuals such as Aldous Huxley, Alan Watts, and academicians interested in Eastern religions to the London of the thirties. Esalen, when it was organized on its lonely stretch of Highway 1, would be approached by car from either of two directions. Either the pilgrim could come south from the University of California at Berkeley and the bohemian community of San Francisco which developed into the Haight-Ashbury district, or proceed north through Santa Barbara, with its branch of the University of California, its bohemian community on Mountain Drive and the Center for Democratic Institutions. All of these eventually became involved with Esalen in one way or another, and Santa Barbarans included theosophical Ojai and Krishnamurti in its ambience of intellectual forces.

Also important during this period was the intellectual coalition of liberal politics and the human potential movement represented by such participants as the then governor, Jerry Brown, and state senator John Vasconcellos, who carried on a combination of spiritual and political interests already noted in earlier political reformers. Since the early rapprochement in England between the Theosophists and Fabians and in America between exponents of modernist theology and the Social Gospel Movement, liberalism and an interest in Eastern religions have often gone hand in hand.

As the one hundredth anniversary of the World's Parliament of Religions is approached, it is interesting to consider the New Age ambience in which any anniversary celebration will take place. The Parliament can be seen in one sense as a result of forces set in motion by Calvinist Congregationalists, Presbyterians, Unitarians, and Transcendentalists with an interest in the ideas conveyed by the world's religions. The New Age movement is more interested in their practices, which it combines with an interest in practices derived from Spiritualism, Mesmerism, and Swedenborg. Little did John Winthrop, Jr., with his library on the occult, or the Founding Fathers, with their Masonic lodges, know that Theosophy, New Thought, and the New Age would be their spiritual heirs.

Chapter 4

Imagining India: The Influence of Hinduism on the New Age Movement

——— *Andrea Grace Diem and James R. Lewis*

The New Age movement represents a unique synthesis of many pre-existing movements and religious traditions. A significant component of this synthesis is the South Asian religious tradition, particularly certain strands of Hinduism. The Hindu influence is clearly evident in the Indian yoga and meditation techniques, as well as certain key notions such as chakras and karma, that are omnipresent within the New Age subculture. In addition, at an earlier stage of American interest in Oriental thought, Asian influences blended with and revitalized the West's own traditions of monistic and reincarnationist thinking, and these ideas eventually became important parts of New Age ideology.[1]

After briefly outlining the history of the importation of Hindu spirituality into the United States, the present paper undertakes the task of coming to grips with the issue of how and why Hinduism became such an important component of the New Age synthesis. The focus of the discussion will be on the interaction between specific historical factors and certain general social-psychological influences.

Historical Overview

South Asian religion entered the United States in at least three distinct waves. The first wave was almost purely literary: In the later half of the eighteenth century, a group of scholar-officials working for the British East India Company translated some of the more important Hindu religious scriptures into English. The ideas contained in these texts directly influenced the transcendentalist movement (evident in such compositions as Emerson's "Over-Soul" essay) and, both directly and indirectly, influenced New Thought.[2] Translated Hindu scriptures also contributed to Theosophy, and the literary presence of Hinduism was at least partially responsible for inspiring Madame Blavatsky and Colonel Olcott's visit to India—a visit that further reinforced the Theosophical tendency to draw inspiration from Mother India.[3]

The second wave was set in motion by a handful of Hindu religious teachers who visited the United States in the late nineteenth and early twentieth centuries. While Protap Chunder Mozoomdar was probably the first Hindu to lecture to American audiences,[4] the reformed Hinduism of the Brahmo Samaj which he represented did not make a lasting impression on the American religious imagination.[5] Far more significant in terms of long-term influence was Swami Vivekananda, who visited the United States in 1893 and who was the most popular speaker at the World's Parliament of Religions in Chicago. Vivekananda eventually gathered enough support to establish the Vedanta Society in New York, an organization which, because of its publishing activities, has had an influence out of proportion to its membership. Another important Indian religious teacher to enter the United States during this early period was Swami Paramahansa Yogananda. In addition to the ongoing influence of his organization, the Self-Realization Fellowship, his *Autobiography of a Yogi* has inspired thousands of Westerners to undertake Eastern spiritual disciplines.[6]

Following the raising of immigration barriers in 1917, Asians were unable to enter the United States in large numbers until after these barriers were lowered in 1965. In the late sixties and early seventies, a new wave of Indian gurus found a receptive audience among young Americans seeking religious inspiration from nontraditional sources. While the spiritual subculture of the seventies was comprised of Buddhists, Sufis, and other non-Hindu groups, Indian spiritual teachers were the most numerous (as well as, in the long run, the most influential). This spiritual subculture, which was in many ways the successor movement to the counterculture of the sixties, led directly to the New Age movement of the eighties.

The Idealized Image of the East

A number of years ago, a physicist named Fritjof Capra published a book on the "parallels" between modern physics and Asian religion. This work, *The Tao of Physics*, became a best-seller, highly acclaimed in New Age circles. One of the more interesting aspects of the book was the way in which it seemed to misinterpret Asian religions and cultures on almost every page. To cite one particularly glaring example:

> Contrary to most Western religions, sensuous pleasure has never
> been suppressed in Hinduism, because the body has always been
> considered to be an integral part of the human being and not
> separated from the spirit. The Hindu, therefore, does not try to
> control the desires of the body by the conscious will, but aims at
> realizing himself with his whole being, body and soul.[7]

Such statements cause one to wonder whether Capra's study of Asian
traditions ever progressed beyond a reading of Alan Watts. Although
certain phases of Tantrism might support his understanding of Hinduism, even a cursory reading of more mainstream Hindu religious literature refutes Capra's characterization.[8]

Yet one suspects that Capra *did* read more deeply into the tradition than his statements reflect. One further suspects that Capra's misinterpretations were engendered by his need to create an idealized Oriental spirituality—an idealized image against which to critique the
perceived deficiencies of the West. This motivation can be clearly perceived in such statements as the following:

> The organic, "ecological" world view of the Eastern philoso-
> phies is no doubt one of the main reasons for the immense pop-
> ularity they have recently gained in the West, especially among
> young people. In our Western culture, which is still dominated
> by the mechanistic, fragmented view of the world, an increas-
> ing number of people have seen this as the underlying reason
> for the widespread dissatisfaction in our society, and many
> have turned to Eastern ways of liberation.[9]

This type of critical stance, along with its systematic misunder-
standings of Asia, is not, however, unique to Capra and the New Age
movement. Capra is merely one of the more recent inheritors of a tendency in European and American romanticism to idealize the East, and
then to critique the West in terms of that ideal. In the words of one
recent commentator,

> [T]here are actually two "Orients." One is made up of real peo-
> ple and real earth. The other is a myth that resides in the head
> of Westerners. One is an actual cultural area, stretching from
> India to Japan and from Mongolia to Singapore. The other is a
> convenient screen on which the West projects reverse images of
> its own deficiencies.[10]

Although the psychological process at work here is fairly simple,
the images of the Orient which are employed for such purposes turn out

to be the end products of a complex interweaving of psychological and historical forces. In the following sections, some of the factors that feed into the creation of such idealized stereotypes will be analyzed via the specific example of South Asia.[11] Particular attention will be given to the contribution of the Bengal Asiatick Society to the idealization process, and to the line of influence that leads from Calcutta to the American New Age movement.

British Orientalism and the Hindu Golden Age

A useful starting point for this part of our discussion is David Kopf's thesis in *British Orientalism and the Bengal Renaissance*. Kopf argues that the original "picture" of an historical (as opposed to a popular, mythological) Hindu golden age—an idealized India—was the product of British Orientalist scholars associated with the Bengal Asiatick Society in the late eighteenth and early nineteenth centuries.[12] Roughly stated, his position is that the Enlightenment worldview of the Orientalists inclined them to look for an ideal, rational society in India's past:

> The intellectual elite that clustered about Hastings after 1770 was classicist rather than "progressive" in their historical outlook, cosmopolitan rather than nationalist in their view of other cultures, and rationalist rather than romantic in their quest for those "constant and universal principles" that express the unity of human nature.[13]

In a manner parallel to the way in which the early New Age movement of the 1970s would later use the East, the Enlightenment thinkers used the West's own historical past—particularly the Greek and Roman period—as a background against which to criticize their own society. In their hands, the classical period became both a highly idealized reflection of their own aspirations and the very antithesis of everything they detested in eighteenth-century Europe. (This idealization was relatively easy to accomplish, given that their principal sources of knowledge about classical civilization were the great works of literature and philosophy bequeathed to them by the ancients.) One of the consequences of this kind of idealization was that many Enlightenment intellectuals, such as Gibbon, "expressed a profound identification with the remote age of antiquity" so that "the decline of the classical world was not so much a cause of jubilation as it was sufficient reason for despair."[14]

A corollary to this portrayal of Greek and Roman civilization was a cyclical notion of history in which ages of gold alternated with ages of darkness. The idea of an uninterrupted progress of history towards a utopian future had not yet become the axiomatic assumption of think-ing that it was to become in the succeeding century. It is against this intellectual backdrop that the Orientalists' "discovery" of the classical age of India is best understood.[15]

Perhaps equally important for this discovery was a cosmopoli-tanism engendered in part by the universalism of rationalism, and in part by the desire to find societies other than classical, Western civi-lization to use as an element of their critique of eighteenth-century Europe. The Enlightenment thinkers believed, "That far the better part of mankind, during far the greater period of recorded history, has lived (except indeed when oppressed and corrupted by Christian powers) more happily and humanely, under laws and customs more free and equitable, more in accord with natural religion and morality, than the peoples of Europe had done during the centuries of ecclesiastical ascen-dency . . ."[16] A particularly striking example of this iconoclastic use of other cultures can be found in Voltaire's writings; for example, his use of India and China:

> [T]he Christian people have never observed their religion, and
> the ancient Indian casts always practiced theirs; . . . in a word,
> the ancient religion of India, and that of literary men in China,
> are the only ones, wherein men have not been barbarous.[17]

In this passage we see clearly that historical India and China have been supplanted by a highly idealized image of Asia, and that the overriding motivation for adopting the image was to criticize European civilization.

As a final point in understanding this process, it should be noted that many of the ideas of the Chinese, Greeks, and Hindus bore—in the eyes of the Enlightenment—a remarkable resemblance to their own ideas. Lord Teignmouth, for example, when he studied translations of Sanskrit texts, "discovered" that Hinduism is "pure deism."[18] Thus, the pictures of the classical civilizations of the world which emerged in the eighteenth century were shaped by dual projections: (1) they were the reverse image of everything the Enlightenment thinkers disliked in their own societies, and (2) they reflected the Enlightenment's own pet ideas.

While the discovery of South Asia's classical age—not to mention the Orientalist recovery of many traditional Indian texts—is certainly praiseworthy (in spite of the misinterpretations caused by their projec-tions), one should also note that the British Orientalists largely ignored the living Hindus and the concrete Hindu practices which surrounded them. The Orientalist scholars, in other words, preferred "the schematic authority of a text to the disorientations of direct encounters with the human," so that "the Orient studied was a textual universe."[19] Various explanations for this approach could be offered (such as the Protestant bias for texts), but, whatever its source, its upshot was that it produced two Indias: the contemporaneous, living Asia, and the historically distant, classical Asia. Conveniently enough, this dichotomization allowed the British to dichotomize their attraction-aversion response to Oriental otherness: "[T]he 'good' Orient was invariably a classical period somewhere in a long-gone India, whereas the 'bad' Orient lingered in present-day Asia."[20]

The "degeneracy of current Asians" theme became an almost unquestioned tenet in Orientalist discourse, and remained even after the "degeneracy of current Europe" theme disappeared in the post-Enlightenment period. Furthermore, the notion of the "true classical Orient" became a tool in the ideological arsenal of British imperialism "that could be used to judge and rule the Orient."[21] The British, in other words, could rationalize their presence in a country as part of a project to "restore a region from its present barbarism to its former classical greatness."[22] The Orientalist scholars, while not particularly conscious of their contributions to imperialist ideology (though they were fully aware that their scholarship contributed to the practical ruling of India in such areas as law-making), generally shared the imperialist attitudes of their fellow countrymen.[23]

The next stage in the development of the image of India's past was taken by the Indians who themselves adopted the textually recreated golden age as an ideological weapon. Ram Mohan Roy, for example, took over certain Orientalist notions as the basis for his attempts to reform Hinduism.[24] Indian nationalists also found themselves relying on the notions and scholarship of the Orientalists. In response to British criticisms of Indian culture, these Hindus claimed that in the past India has possessed a "social order based upon the teachings of the Vedas which was from some points of view even superior to the advanced social idealism inspired by the dogma of Liberty, Equality and Fraternity of the French Illumination."[25] One significant change which the nationalists made in the Orientalist vision was to portray the foreign invaders as being *responsible for* India's "degenerate" state; in the words of Nehru. "It seemed monstrous to me that a great country like India, with a rich and immemorial past, should be bound hand and foot to a faraway island which imposed its will upon her. It was still more monstrous that this forcible union had resulted in poverty and degradation beyond measure."[26] Thus, the same scholarship which had been used to justify imperialism was later used to attack imperialism—an ironic and perhaps fitting fate for classical Orientalism.

To briefly recapitulate the development we have been examining, we could say that the image of the Hindu golden age—created/discovered by British Orientalists—was used repressively by the British rulers, iconoclastically by the Hindu reformers, and subversively by the Indian nationalists. All three groups had a vested interest in maintaining the vision of an idealized Hindu society situated in a more or less distant past. By an interesting turn of events, this picture of India's *past* became—for romantic Americans in this century—a description of *present-day* India.

Journey to the West

The activities of the Asiatick Society shaped Western perceptions of India in two ways—directly through texts, and indirectly through Hindu missionary activity. The direct influence of the British Orientalists on America began quite early (e.g., Sir William Jones's translation of *Shakuntala* was published in the United States in 1805),[27] but it was not until the transcendentalist movement that interest in things Asian came into vogue.[28] Thoreau, for example, read Charles Wilkins's translation of the *Bhagavad Gita* on a regular basis during his stay at Walden Pond and in some of his later correspondence referred to himself as a "yogi."

The transcendentalists were not so much responsible for confusing classical India with contemporary india as they were responsible for introducing certain themes into the American literary tradition which would later contribute to the New Age stereotype of the East. Emerson, for example, voiced the "materialistic West/spiritual East" idea with respect to Buddhism:

> [I]n the essay "Poetry and the Imagination," he set what he took to be Buddhist ideals against the coarse materialism of an industrial society: "Better men saw heavens and earths; saw noble instruments of noble souls. We see railroads, mills, and banks, and we pity the poverty of these dreaming Buddhists. There was as much creative force then as now, but it made globes and astronomic heavens, instead of broadcloth and wine-glasses."[29]

This aspect of the East-West stereotype would become almost axiomatic in Western thinking about Asia.[30] Thoreau voiced the "ancient wisdom of the East" theme in *Walden*:

> I bathe my intellect in the stupendous Hand [Hindu] cosmological philosophy of the *Bhagvat Geeta*, since whose composi-

tion years of gods have elapsed, and in comparison with which our modern world and its literature seem puny and trivial.[31]

And Walt Whitman voiced the "sensual East" theme in, for example, *Song of Myself.*[32] Whitman, however, unlike later generations of Americans, consciously realized that he was using India as a symbol (in Whitman's case, a symbol for the mysterious, unexplored depths of the soul).[33]

It was not until certain representatives of the Hindu religion began to preach in the West that the idealized (Orientalist-influenced) Hinduism of the Indian Renaissance began to be regularly confused with current Hindu practices. The early stages of this confusion can be seen fairly clearly in the preaching activity of the first well-known representative of Hinduism in the West: Vivekananda.

By a complex combination of events, this eloquent disciple of Ramakrishna became one of the "official" representatives of Hinduism at the World's Parliament of Religions which was held in Chicago in 1893.[34] The picture of the Hindu religion which Vivekananda presented in the West was essentially the religion of the Hindu reformers. In his address to the parliament, for example, he invoked the image of the Hindu golden age:

> [A] Greek historian who wrote about India of that time [during its period of classical greatness] was led to say that no Hindu was known to tell an untruth. . . .[35]

And in one of his later writings, he similarly asserted that,

> [A]t that distant date man was not so civilized as we know him now. He had not yet learned to cut his brother's throat because he differed a little in thought from himself; he had not deluged the world in blood, he did not become demon to his own brother.[36]

and repeated the nationalist idea that evil human tendencies did not enter India until outsiders invaded the subcontinent.[37]

In his speech before the World Parliament, he was careful to point out the compatibility of Hinduism with Western science (an implicit contrast with Christianity, which presumably was not so compatible): "[T]he Brahmin boy repeats every day: 'The sun and the moon, the Lord seated like the suns and moons of previous cycles.' And this agrees with modern science."[38] Vivekananda further denied that contemporary Hindus were polytheists: "At the very outset, I may tell you that there is no polytheism in India."[39] The Orientalist view had been that

Vedic Hindus of the Indian golden age, in contrast to present-day Hindus, had been monotheists. In the above passage, Vivekananda has shifted this assertion to the present tense.

The final Vivekananda passage we wish to examine comes from an interview reported in the *Chicago Daily Tribune* of 20 September 1893:

> Christianity wins prosperity by cutting the throats of its fellowmen. At such a price the Hindu will not have prosperity. Blood and sword are not for the Hindu, whose religion is based on the laws of love.[40]

Such a highly idealized Hinduism does not, of course, mesh very well with the realities of Indian history. Later representatives of Hinduism in America—Vedanta Society successors to Vivekananda, Yogananda, the disciples of Swami Shivananda, et cetera—reinforced rather than undermined Vivekananda's presentation of the Hindu religion. This picture of India gradually filtered out into American culture, and was thus readily available to the fifties Beats, the sixties counterculture, and the New Age movement of the seventies and eighties.

In addition to its forward movement through time, it can also be seen that this image of the East had gradually changed according to the varying needs of the persons and groups utilizing it. Thus, for example, the Vedic Indians of the Jones-Colebrooke model of the Hindu golden age were "outgoing and nonmystical,"[41] while the Indians of Vivekananda's portrayal were profoundly spiritual and mystical. The image of the East underwent further modifications in the hands of the sixties counterculture, the immediate predecessor to the New Age movement.

Like the Orientalist picture of the golden age, the sixties picture was shaped by a dual projection: (1) Asian culture was imagined (for iconoclastic purposes) to be the reverse image of everything the counterculture disliked in America, and (2) Asian philosophies and religions were made to reflect countercultural (and, later, New Age) ideas. The iconoclastic pattern—if not the precise content or style—of, for example, Gary Snyder's deployment of Buddhism is reminiscent of Voltaire's use of China and India, and Emerson's use of Buddhism which were noted earlier:

> The joyous and voluntary poverty of Buddhism becomes a positive force. The traditional harmlessness and refusal to take life in any form has nation-shaking implications. The practice of meditation, for which one needs only "the ground beneath one's feet" wipes out mountains of junk being pumped into

the mind by the mass media and supermarket universities. The belief in a serene and generous fulfillment of natural loving desires destroys ideologies which blind, maim, and repress.[42]

The second aspect of this projection process—the imposition of one's own ideas onto Asia—was clearly illustrated by the Capra passage (cited near the beginning of this paper) about the "unsuppressed sensuality of Hinduism." Capra's assertions in this regard are reminiscent of Lord Teignmouth's "discovery" of "pure Deism" in Hindu Scriptures.

Like the Enlightenment thinkers, the counterculturists did not confine their projections to the East, but instead imposed images of themselves on any and every culture and movement which could be interpreted so as to reflect their own values and worldview. To cite again from Snyder,

At this point, looking once more quite closely at history both East and West, some of us noticed the similarities in certain small but influential heretical and esoteric movements. These schools of thought and practice were usually suppressed, or diluted and made harmless, in whatever society they appeared. Peasant witchcraft in Europe, Tantrism in Bengal, Quakers in England, Tachikawaryu in Japan, Ch'an in China. These are all outcroppings of the Great Subculture which runs underground all throughout history. This is the tradition that runs without break from Paleo-Siberian Shamanism and Magdalenion cave-painting; through megaliths and Mysteries, astronomers, ritualists, alchemists and Albingensians; gnostics and vagantes, right down to Golden Gate Park.[43]

The impulse behind the broad lumping together of civilizations (by the Enlightenment) or of tribes, movements, and other groups (by the counterculture and the New Age) for iconoclastic purposes appears to be essentially the same—namely the desire to demonstrate that one's own ideas are not idiosyncratic, but are rather representative of some kind of world wide consensus (i.e., the desire for some sort of "legitimation"). To conclude with a short summary of the preceding discussion, the mystic East stereotype—especially as employed by the sixties counterculture and its successor movement, the New Age—was the outcome of at least two different processes, one social-psychological and one historical. The social-psychological process, which figured in both the Orientalist production of an Asian golden age and the New Age's adoption of an idealized East, can be outlined as follows: *(a)* rejection of or revolt against one's own culture and society, *(b)* formation of, and identification with, ideas and ideals which represent the polar opposite of the object of revolt, *(c)* projection of one's polarized ideals onto a culture, movement, or figure greatly removed in time or space from one's own culture, and finally *(d)* employment of one's own projected image—in a guise borrowed from another culture—as legitimation, both for one's own "counter-cultural" ideas and for attacks on the rejected culture.

The historical process we traced can be pictured as a stream which split apart after it left the Asiatick Society and then reunited several centuries later in the minds of people like the Beat poets. At the head of the stream was the translation activity of the Asiatick Society and its consequent production/discovery of a Hindu golden age. The first branch entered the United States in the form of the translated texts of the British Orientalists, which were in turn picked up and adopted by American literary figures. The second branch was the golden age notion which was picked up and modified by Indian reformers and nationalists, and then exported by Hindu preachers such as Vivekananda who portrayed contemporary Hinduism in terms of the image of golden age Hinduism. Both the textual/literary strand and the Hindu missionary strand fed into the New Age movement, which in turn produced its own vision of the mystic East.

Chapter 5

How New is the New Age?

——————— Robert Ellwood

It is a commonplace that the New Age is not really new at all. Whether commentators look at it as the revival of ancient wisdom or the resurgence of outmoded superstition, they are well aware that the loosely defined collection of teachings and practices going on by that name are no new revelation suddenly dropped from the sky, but a modern revival—neither the first nor, probably, the last—of a longstanding tradition of what may be called the alternative spirituality of the West.

Indeed, this fits well the movement's own self-conception. The "New Age" idea is eschatological rather than current, similar in this respect to the Aquarian Age of sixties' discourse, an imminent but not-yet-realized era of harmonic convergence and upward spiritual mutation. But, as though to harness all possible strands of psychic energy at once for such a quantum leap of the soul, its preparation required the ingathering of numerous treasures from the storehouses of the past. Thus, the chakras of medieval yoga, Hellenistic astrology, gemstone lore, and even the channeled sapience of Egyptian seers from 40,000 B.C. return to lay the foundation for the third millenium. Like innumerable occult orders and mystical movements of all ages, the New Age compensates for a tenuous hold on the present with claims to an ancient and powerful heritage, and supplements its scattered current clientele with an invisible cloud of witnesses summoned from sunnier days along the banks of the Nile or the Ganges.

More concretely, the New Age is a contemporary manifestation of a western alternative spirituality tradition going back at least to the Greco-Roman world. The current flows like an underground river through the Christian centuries, breaking into high visibility in the Renaissance occultism of the so-called "Rosicrucian Enlightenment," eighteenth-century Freemasonry, and nineteenth-century Spiritualism and Theosophy.

Behind its myriad guises this tradition has a rather compact set of basic themes. These begin with a basically Neoplatonic concept of a hierarchical universe culminating in an impersonal, monistic Absolute which operates the universe through law—though the laws may be little known save to the initiate—rather than caprice, and in which spirit and matter are thoroughly intertwined. The monistic grounding and spirit/matter constituency of this universe make possible, in accordance with Neoplatonic "correspondences," linkages between the human and the cosmic: astrology, mineral power, and quasi-magical manipulation of "energies." Belief that the human being, like all the universe, is not to be understood in some simplistic "ghost-in-the-machine" dualistic way, but as a deep and complex commingling of matter, mind, and spirit in which impulses on the plane can affect the others, undergirds the characteristic faith in "holistic" and "alternative" healing. At the same time, there appears to be a complementary affirmation of the ultimate independence and sovereignty of the spiritual or subtle component, able to make excurses from the mortal coil and even to find fresh fleshly homes. This capacity justifies the typical interest in out-of-the-body travel, near-death experiences, and reincarnation. Finally, the acceptance of detached spirit entities enables the tradition to personify the cosmos by spreading between the impersonal Absolute and the human realm a rich assortment of intermediaries: Masters, Neo-Pagan gods, the revenants of Spiritualism, UFO "space brothers," and the kabbalistic angels of the ceremonial magician.

These themes clearly have a close connection to fundamental motifs of the Neoplatonic program: spirit as the superior and autonomous formative element wedded here below to matter, the microcosm/macrocosm partnership, the laws of "correspondence" with their "as above, so below" ramifications, the "great chain of being" linking heaven, earth, and underworld in a gradated collage of intelligences. These beings may be contacted through theurgy, including mediumship, and by the theatrical magical evocations which form so colorful a part of the tradition.

A very important sociopsychic correlate of this program must also not be forgotten: the idea that such an intricate "inner" template for the universe, many of whose contours hardly reveal themselves to surface observation, is not easily accessible to most humans. Its kenning requires special sensitivity, education, and above all initiation—particular powerful experiences designed to induce inward transformation and, with it, new sight and the impartation of proper gnosis or understanding. True gnosis in turn is understandably conveyed only by those who already have it and is best preserved in fairly small, intensive groups where it is valued.

One important outbreak of this tradition—a resurfacing, if you will, of the gnosis—was in the nineteenth-century Spiritualism in America. At first blush this may seem to some a rather strained example, for the rambunctious frontier ambience of much of what followed the Fox sisters' famous rappings of 1848 is far removed from the studious, Faustian atmosphere of the old Rosicrucianism. Yet, in fact, Spiritualism is a boisterous child of that lineage via Swedenborgianism and Mesmerism plus a touch of Native American shamanism. I will assume some familiarity with the genealogy, noting that the child, legitimate or not, is definitely from the Old World family. Nonetheless, the offspring did not entirely resemble its parents. In its New World incarnation occult blood mutated novel features little seen in the old grimoires, and these qualities are now instructively paralleled in the New Age.

The novelties stemmed from the new setting of Spiritualism, with its ancient theurgy of mediumship and its phalanxes of spirit intermediaries, in the levelling and expansive culture of the new republic. The path had been pioneered by the vogue for Swedenborg in previous decades, typified by the presence of Swedenborgian tracts as well as seeds in the pack of John Chapman, "Johnny Appleseed," as he visited remote frontier cabins. Mesmerism had been likewise democratized, the subject of raucous stage demonstrations and countless amateur experiments. But it took the Spiritualist explosion after 1848 to show the full potential of the young nation's mass media, openness to spiritual experimentation, and sense of a unique destiny that called for ongoing religious definition, to make for a startling, if ephemeral,[1] spiritual movement. This context made Spiritualism an early example of the celebrated "mass culture" of the modern era. It was virtually unprecedented as a widespread religious phenomenon grounded, not on immemorial folk religion nor revivalistic "enthusiasm," but by modern-style reportage in the print media together with do-it-yourself "circles" (newspapers and magazines often ran articles telling readers how to set them up), and buttressed more by scientific than professionally religious endorsements. Apart from a quorum of Universalists and a few Unitarians its leadership was almost entirely lay, often women in a time when their sex had very slim opportunities to exercise spiritual leadership in most established denominations.[2] It was largely a proletarian religious movement in significant alliance with that class's new literacy and sense of a power to make itself heard and, moreover, to remake the world.[3] Early Spiritualism therefore perceived itself as a voice of the "progressive" movements of the time. Through the entranced lips of mediums, mentors from the spirit realm spoke tirelessly and eloquently on behalf of abolition, prison reform, the rights of women and children, and the liberation of the working class from enslavement to capital. The new faith was, it was said, the most scientific of all religions, since it depended not on the dead hand of the past or on the authority of entranced hierarchies, but on empirical verification. It was likewise the most democratic, since mediumship and direct access to the spirits was equally available to all, rich or poor, educated or not, male or female. It was thus aligned with the great forward movements of the time, and indeed was said to have been presented to the world by the spirits only now, when humankind was finally ready for a new progressive vision that had to await the fullness of time. While hints of this progressivist style of occultism could certainly have been detected in the previous century's alliance of Freemasonry and Swedenborgianism with the Enlightenment and finally the spirit of the French and American revolutions, it took the era of Jacksonian democracy to bring the esoteric side of progress out of the lodge hall and into the popular culture mainstream. In a comparable way, the contemporary New Age movement's sanction through esoteric spirituality of an overall optimistic eschatology—one certainly in tension with the mood of demographic and ecological gloom in many quarters as the millenium comes to an end—has brought that hopeful vision within reach of anyone able to buy tapes or read popular books or magazines.

Since time does not allow discussion of all parallels between nineteenth century Spiritualism and the twentieth century New Age movement, I would like to focus on this feature, a progressivist and optimistic eschatology. More specifically, I believe that an interesting parallel can be drawn between an ultimately optimistic, though sometimes torturous, eschatology that is emerging out of the current fascination with the Near Death Experience, and the progressivist strand of Spiritualism, which also held that intimacy with the inner dimensions of death and dying afforded esoteric insight into the veiled future of humankind. Two books that currently offer this perception are Michael Grosso, *The Final Choice*, and Kenneth Ring, *Heading Toward Omega.*[4]

Grosso draws the stark contours of an ultramodern, maybe postmodern, myth, grounded on what he deliberately calls the "Game of Survival." It is a game because "play is basic to all living substance" and "is useful in learning to inhabit new environments."(6)

This play, however, is for very high stakes. On the one hand, "the hands of the Doomsday Clock move inexorably toward midnight."(6) On the other, despite the general fact that the human psyche has never been less prepared for death than now, sounds on the fresh New Age wind hint at a counterpoint to the ticking of the apocalyptic clock. A new spiritual familiarity with death is in the offing as well. A modern art of dying is emerging based on new sciences, above all the findings of psychical research—a project directly linked historically to the old Spiritualism. Grosso points especially to the subsphere of out-of-the-body experiences, which delineate the true relationship of spirit and flesh. The capstone of his arch, however, is the vogue for near-death experiences—the ultimate and most philosophically significant case of out-of-the-body experience—which not only offer the clearest vision of all into inner and postmortem realities, but also limn the shape of humankind's initiation into a world beyond Doomsday.

The near-death experience (NDE) has been much discussed since Raymond Moody's book *Life After Life* brought it to wide public attention in 1975. Essentially, Moody and others since him have collected a substantial body of accounts from persons who reportedly have "died" but been resuscitated, and who, during the "time out," left the body, saw the hospital room or accident scene as it were from above, passed through a dark tunnel, encountered a "being of light," engaged in a "life review," and finally returned to this world, generally a deepened and transformed person.[5]

For Grosso, the NDE represents "the core idea of an archetype of death and enlightenment," and so can be compared to mystical experience, classic mystery rituals, visionary dreams, and the like. Finally, it can, he believes, be pressed "into the arena of collective psychology." (7) Here it can model the corporate death and rebirth of a world as well as of an individual. But even the NDE, Grosso maintains, is only part of the picture: Its vogue is but a "part of a larger class of apparitional phenomena whose function is to assist, reassure, encourage, guide and direct individuals, or groups of individuals, in times of Crisis." (8) These entities are called "Messengers from Mind at Large," and in our day have taken the form of such diverse envoys from above—or within—as UFO beings, appearances of the Blessed Virgin Mary, modern spirit guides, the gods of Neopaganism, and the mysteries of the Shroud of Turin. The parallels to the teaching spirits of the last Century's seance-room Spiritualism are clear.

The world, Grosso avers, is under the spell of a "thanatos conspiracy," pushing it toward death through its arms races, ravaging of nature and primal peoples, and concomitant spiritual suicide. But this very crisis may precipitate a global near-death experience and the intervention of the Messengers. "It is as though a Helping Intelligence would arm us with a vision of an expanded life and direct us on an upward evolutionary path." (241) The characteristic human being may then be represented by the *hibakusha*, the Japanese word for survivors of the atomic bomb. But Grosso also entitles a chapter after the name of a play by Luigi Pirandello, *The Man With a Flower in His Mouth*. The play is about a man who knows he is fatally ill. In this knowledge the smallest things take on a new significance, and a transformation of consciousness takes place. This can happen to the human race, Grosso contends; in the last chapter, "A Morphology of the Apocalypse," he points out that all the Messengers, whether prophetic NDE's, Marian visions, or UFO contacts, are fundamentally Beings of Light, like the spirits in the darkened chambers of old. They tend, like well-known Marian apparitions, to prophecy catastrophe for humanity, but calamity with a bright farther side, like all apocalyptics. For in the end, the Messengers may come from that Brightness beyond the present. They are what Grosso calls ADE's: archetypes of death and enlightenment, his fundamental theme. "If the ADE is a kind of holographic projection of Mind at Large, and Mind at Large has a hand in the evolution of life, the ADE may be a prophetic projection of the next stage in the evolution of the next stage in the evolution of consciousness." (135)

Let us return, however, to the prophetic NDE. That is a major motif of Kenneth Rings's book. He has found in his study of near-death experiences that not a few experiencers report to have gained knowledge of the future through the event, either personal (which he calls a "personal flash forward") or in a "prophetic vision" which embraces the future of the human race. Often there are, as was also the case in the opening experiences of nineteenth-century mediums such as Andrew Jackson Davis and D. D. Home, definite overtones of something even earlier, the classic shamanistic initiation. Thus, one of Ring's experiencers reports, "At one point I had complete knowledge of everything, from the beginning of creation to the end of time . . . [but] I was told [by her guides] that I would remain unconscious for five days so that all the things I had been shown would not resurface, so they could be stored for future reference . . ." (196) Most, however, retained sufficient awareness to give a concrete account of future history. These are characteristically highly apocalyptic in the biblical sense, predicting a time of immense woes followed by a paradisal era, of which the catastrophes were but birthpangs. All this will happen within a hundred years or so; Ring's prophecies operate in a relatively short span, rarely going beyond the commencement of the twenty-first century. The expectation was that during the 1980s there would be an increasing incidence of earthquakes, volcanic activity, and massive earth changes, resulting in disturbances in the weather patterns and food supplies. Those will be followed by world economic collapse, and very great possibility of nuclear war or accident. But these troubles are only transitional; they will usher in a new era of human brotherhood, universal love, and world peace. (197) These changes are usually interpreted religiously, though less as the consequence of divine wrath than, in more of a New Age mood, of blaming them on, as one experiencer put it, "our general ignorance of the true reality." She was informed that "mankind was breaking the laws of the universe and as a result of this would suffer." (198)

These prophecies, published in 1984 and received earlier, obviously have some relation to the realities of the decade. Some prophets claim to have known in advance of the Mt. St. Helens' eruption, predicted the drought which was a part of the latter years of the eighties, and hinted at awareness of the ecological crises connected with the now much-discussed ozone depletion and global warming trends. Yet admittedly the decade has not on the one hand produced apocalyptic catastrophe in the dimensions suggested by the prophecies, and they appear on the other hand to have overlooked the benign signs at decade's end, the great reduction of East-West tensions and consequent decline in the prospect of nuclear war. What are we to make of this?

First, we may note that many of the prophets of nuclear disaster saw it as conditional; as one put it, "If people don't get their act together . . . there is going to be a nuclear war . . ." (203) Nineteen eighty-eight was sometimes cited as the year of greatest crisis in this regard. In this light, Ring presents a theory of alternative rather than deterministic futures associating it with the "manyworlds" model of quantum mechanics—a typical New Age move wherein, often to the disconcertion of orthodox physicists, the mysteries of quanta are made to legitimate psychic phenomena. Yet religious prophecy, from biblical to the modern Marian, always fundamentally addresses the present rather than the future, inditing the message "If sin remains as it is, if conditions remain as they are, these disasters will happen, but humankind can and must repent, and then the hand of the Lord will be stayed." Ring also offers an intelligent though succinct review of psychodynamic, psychiatric, archetypal, "zeitgeist," and spiritual interpretations of prophecy in connection with his cases.

How does all this compare with nineteenth century Spiritualism? As we have noted, the spirit-communication of the last century was strongly connected with radical reform, with abolition of slavery, women's rights, temperance, and the rest of it. Yet, particularly as time advanced, the mood was less apocalyptic than in the near-death experience prophecies we have just surveyed. To be sure, in the years preceding the Civil War, Spiritualists wrote in 1853: "Nothing can avert the universal hurricane of which the murky air has for sixty years (and now each day and hour more emphatically) gives note or unmistak-

able potent," and he proceeds to attribute the introduction of Spiritualism's "facts and processes" at this juncture to "the infinitely wise goodness of the Divine Providence."[6] This association of the coming of the
spirits with the crises and opportunities of the age and with humanity's
evolution to a point ready to accept their direct communication, is typical. But the concept of evolution—the spiritual appropriation of Dar-
winism—is significant. The idea of "progression," both after death and
in the future history of the human race, governed. Andrew Jackson
Davis, the most influential Spiritualist thinker, brought it together thus:
"Spiritualism is the last development of the sublime relations between
mankind and the next higher sphere of existence. It is the grandest religion ever bestowed upon mankind. Under such blessings every being
should aim to become . . . progressive in all directions. Growth is the
central law of our being object of all exertion, as it will be the result of all
experience. Through growth we shall overcome evil with good and
straighten the crooked ways of error and injustice."[7] Again, "The only
hope for the physical and mental amelioration of mankind is based
upon a slow but steady intellectual progress, and this must be the result
of a steady, patient but firm and decided investigation as to the causes
of present evils".[8]

Yet there was a conundrum in the relation of Spiritualism to radical
reform, one which the present New Age movement may also not avoid,
and which its apocalyptic wing may actually better confront. This is
that Spiritualism's commitment to progress rested on a highly optimistic view of human nature and the human future, one which virtually
undercut the "patient but firm" investigation of evil of which Davis
spoke. As defined by the famous Rutland Free Convention of 1858, the
new faith held that "spirit-intercourse is opposed to all despotism,
impurity and sensualism," and favorable to freedom and perhaps even
free love, for the reason that "the authority of each individual soul is
absolute and final." It condemned "the individual, the Church or the
State, that attempts to control the opinions or practices of any man or
woman by an authority or power outside of his or her own soul."[9] This
inner-directedness logically led in the direction of gradualism in reform
and a revulsion against the concept of sin, thereby favoring love—as the
principle which appeals best to the sovereign authority of the individual
soul—over force, and self-condemnation over divine judgment. A message delivered through a medium to the great abolitionist William
Lloyd Garrison in 1858, from the spirit of a certain Nathaniel P. Rogers,
who had apparently gathered to himself a sense of wise moderation
on the other side, said, "While I still loathe the hideous form of slavery,
it appears to me now that gradual emancipation, which must come

through the operation of the love principle upon the hearts of all, is far better than to force the master—even by words—to relax his grasp upon the heart of his victim," for the master himself "then becomes a slave to the power which compels him to release his slave."[10] As Moore incisively points out, this argument for gradualism emerged because "Rogers" no longer believed in sin. Davis, like an increasing number of others of his faith, regarded both sin and evil as illusory, in no way to be regarded as impediments to the sovereignty of the soul and the workings of love in the purity of the heart. The Spiritualist A. B. Child praised the person "who sees no evil" as the one who best advanced the cause of progress.[11] As Moore points out, "Spiritualists envisioned a universe without an avenging God. There was nothing to avenge, for man had never fallen. In the history of the human race and in the lives of individuals, one could never speak of regression—only eternal moral advancement."[12]

The present New Age, caught between a sense of cosmic harmony and a generally more pessimistic if not catastrophist age, veers, as we have seen in connection with near-death prophecies, between extremes of disaster and paradise in typical apocalyptic fashion. It may be that, like Spiritualism before it, as world tensions decline and nothing too bad seems to be happening, it will move toward the reformist gradualism and fundamental ease in Zion which is no doubt the natural estate of those who reject the sinful soul and the vengeful God in favor of innate human goodness, betokened by the Spiritualist's and the near-death experiencer's usually educative, progressivist model of life beyond the veil.

Chapter 6

The Magical Staff:
Quantum Healing in the New Age

——————— *Catherine L. Albanese*

On 6 March 1844, in or near Poughkeepsie, New York, Andrew Jackson Davis experienced what he later claimed to be an "initiatory vision." Earlier in the evening he had been magnetized, and he had felt trouble shaking the effects of the trance. In his room at the boarding house where he lived he sank quickly into sleep, but then a voice roused him and commanded him to dress and follow. Davis was led to Mill and Hamilton Streets within Poughkeepsie, there to behold a vision of shepherd and sheep. Then the scene changed darkly, and Davis fell to the ground unconscious. He awoke and began to run, crossed the frozen Hudson River, and, after further paranormal experience, more running, more sleeping, found himself in a cemetery surrounded by a dense wood. The person he saw now, "of ordinary stature but of a spiritual appearance," told of former-day reflection on "the many physical violations [of natural laws] . . . among the inhabitants of the earth." Prompted by his reflection the visitor had founded a "'medical system'"—on "the proposition, that every particle in the human body possesses a close affinity to particular particles below in the subordinate kingdoms—and that these latter particles, if properly associated and applied, would cure any affected portion or organ of the human frame."[1]

Davis now beheld in Galen's hand (for the visitor was, indeed, the ancient Greek physician) an "elegant cane," symbolically constructed to represent "the complete correspondence between this [his medical] system and Nature." It was Galen's gift to the young Davis, and after Davis received it he turned to gaze on a second figure. This time the cemetery guest, with a head that indicated "a most vigorous and gigantic intellect . . . and a high degree of spirituality," told of visits to "this and other earths" and instructed Davis further on his earthly mission. Emanuel Swedenborg (the spirit being was none other) told Davis that by him (Davis) a "new light" would appear and that the light would establish the "law and 'kingdom of heaven' on earth." Davis subsequently, because of anger and impatience, lost his magic staff but, in another vision, was imparted its metaphysical substance. "Behold! Here is thy Magic Staff: UNDER ALL CIRCUMSTANCES KEEP AN EVEN MIND."[2]

The staff of balance was an appropriate sign for the shamanic journey that launched Davis on a celebrated career as clairvoyant physician, social reformer, leading harmonial philosopher, and major theologian of nineteenth-century American spiritualism. Davis's one hundred fifty-seven lectures, delivered in trance on a New York City stage, were published in 1847 as *The Principles of Nature, Her Divine Revelations, and a Voice to Mankind* and in thirty-four years went through as many editions. His medical diagnoses and recommendations, given under entrancement by a mesmeric operator, provided him early with a source of income and reputation. Moreover, his visionary revelations established a harmonial philosophy that he elaborated throughout his life in numerous nontrance lectures and writings. "Thinking means *thing*-ing," he announced in an adage, while he regularly propounded the materiality of God and spirits. And as the century passed, Davis made his mark as a feminist reformer who fought for equal rights for women and, especially, for marital reform. Reform in marital law and living, he believed, would make the Swedenborgian ideal of perfect conjugal love, of the union of destined soulmates, full reality.[3]

Hence, Davis summed up in his person and career key ideas and practices that formed the popular metaphysical substrate of nineteenth-century American religion. His spiritualism was obvious. But as important, his mesmeric propensities and his Swedenborgian beliefs (symbolized by the Galen and Swedenborg of his initiatory vision) pointed to major sources of a mentality that would endure. In this encodement of a habit of mind and life, boundaries between matter and spirit were regularly transgressed and, more, conflated. Matter became spiritual; and spirit, it was discovered, possessed a refined material form. Humans were more like God than any evangelical perfectionist could suppose. And the perfection of fully achieved form could be known in practical life.

Mesmerism touched the nerve of popular consciousness from 1836, when the French mesmerist Charles Poyen began a lecture tour of New England. Significantly, Poyen emphasized the "magnetized" state in which the entranced subject "awoke," capable of thinking and acting in ways that usually far exceeded normal waking consciousness. Poyen regularly performed somnambulic feats with subjects before public audiences, and Davis's own somnambulism echoed, without an operator, what Poyen had pointed toward. Meanwhile, Poyen inspired a host of imitators who began to purvey their mesmeric talents as more or less regular fare for interested American lyceum audiences. The press was not far behind, and accounts of mesmeric feats and experiences became standard features in newspapers and periodicals of the time.[4]

Behind the striking phenomenon of the magnetized subject lay the theories of the Viennese physician Franz Anton Mesmer (1734-1815), who taught of an invisible fluid that acted as medium for all living things. "Between ether and elementary matter," Mesmer had written, "there exist series of matter succeeding each other in fluidity. By their subtlety, they penetrate and fill all interstices."

Mesmer went on to explain that there was one "among these fluid substances . . . which corresponds essentially and is in continuity with that which animates the nerves of the animal body." Thus, animal magnetism specified the general magnetism of the cosmos; and it followed, for Mesmer, that "everything which exists can be experienced, and that animated bodies, finding themselves in contact with all of Nature, have the faculty of being sensitive not only to beings, but also to events which succeed one another." Moreover, humans could experience "in the universal harmony" certain "'connections'" that "'events' and beings" had with their "'preservation.'" In fact, they could "understand either the 'harmony' or the 'dissonance'" that certain substances exerted on them. It was through this "extension of instinct," Mesmer explained, "that a sleeping man can have an intuition of disease and can distinguish, from among all substances, those which contribute to his preservation and cure."[5]

Mesmer's universal fluid, as specified in the animal body, produced one important source of a habit of mind that eroded the distance between matter and spirit. And Mesmer's vision of universal harmony suggested a connection with clairvoyant modes of disease diagnosis and cure. All the more, Mesmer's vision suggested the empowerment of humans for perfection through the newly found capacity.

At the same time, from a second quarter came another powerful source of the matter-spirit conflation. Emanuel Swedenborg (1688-1772), son of a Lutheran bishop, member of the Swedish nobility, and Extraordinary Assessor in the Swedish Royal College of Mines, from 1745 claimed to make mystical journeys to heaven and hell. His prolific accounts of conversations with angelic beings blended Christian scripture with occult-metaphysical teaching. Swedenborg revived the ancient doctrine of correspondence, of worlds echoing worlds so that "as above, so below." In the universe he acknowledged, nature corresponded to spirit, and a divine influx permeated the natural world. Indeed, Swedenborg named his God "the Divine Human." And as he described the heavenly mansions of his visits, it was clear that they were literally that—mansions—strikingly resembling the homes of the Swedish nobility. Heaven was a sensuous place, alive in a riot of harmonious color and object, sight and sound As the symbol of the divine-human connection, "conjugial love" flourished in the Swedenborgian heaven as the perfected fulfillment of human sexuality.[6]

The Church of the New Jerusalem, founded in England after the death of the Swedish seer, spread Swedenborgian teaching among its American followers. But the New Church, as it was called, represented but a small body of believers. Thus, the spread of Swedenborgian ideas came more informally through a network of print and publication, augmented—we may be sure—by word of mouth. Swedenborg's numerous works were early translated from their original Latin into English and appeared in America. Meanwhile, Swedenborgian periodicals such as the *New Jerusalem Magazine* and the *New Jerusalem Messenger* spread the message of Swedenborgian correspondence—to an influential elite of Boston Unitarians among others. So prestigious a journal as the (non-Swedenborgian) *North American Review* carried an article on "Swedenborgianism" in 1821. And at the popular level, Swedenborgian tracts, such as those distributed by the legendary itinerant Johnny Appleseed (John Chapman), brought Swedenborg's gospel to ordinary Americans. Indeed, as early as 1808 Swedenborg's account of his own initiatory vision had appeared on the front page of at least one newspaper in the state of New York, the Canandaigua *Western Repository.*[7]

Swedenborg's doctrine of correspondence was, significantly, a doctrine of harmony, for earthly and heavenly spheres resonated with each other as did a host of more specific signs and symbols. Hence, both mesmerism and Swedenborgianism agreed in the harmonial model of a universe where the boundaries between matter and nonmatter became fluid. Still further, Davis's "even mind," his principle of balance, was only a translation into moral terms of the harmonial cosmology that his mentors supplied. On the other hand, as the manipulations of magnetic operators and Davis's later self-entrancements suggested, one could "manage" the balance in a way favorable to one's personal plans and projects. Knowledge was power, and control of the mind's power was promised by the mesmerist's skill and even by the implicit theology of the Swedenborgian's Divine Human. For if God was Man in the heavenly realm, it followed that a path might be open for humans to become Gods as they walked the earth.

By century's end, some of these connections had been drawn intuitively by a generation of mental healers who founded mind cure and New Thought. And they had been drawn, in another way, by physiological manipulators who established the new healing persuasions of osteopathy and chiropractic.[8] But even as small armies of mental healers and physical manipulators flourished, the death knell for the nineteenth-century scientific paradigm congenial to their efforts was sounding.

In the nineteenth-century theory of the ether, Newtonian physicists had reclaimed Mesmer's "invisible fluid" on their own terms, postulating a mysterious and unseeable "subtle fluid" or "jelly" that filled all space and all objects and obstructed the motion of none. The ether could carry optical and gravitational effects as well as electrical and magnetic ones. In fact, in a specification as "luminiferous ether" it acted as medium for the transmission of waves of light. It seemed, in short, the invisible glue that held the world together.[9]

By 1895, though, there were serious holes in the ether (or, at least, in the ether theory). In that year, the German scientist Max Planck began research on the radiation of black bodies, research that, five years later, he would assess for the German Physical Society. Early in the nineteenth century, the Englishman Thomas Young had used a double-slit apparatus to show that light was a wave And by 1870 Scottish physicist James Clerk Maxwell argued for an electromagnetic wave theory of light, with light the combination of oscillating fields of electricity and magnetism. Now, in 1900, Planck was presenting results that pointed toward light as a particle phenomenon. Light, he was puzzled to report, was emitted and absorbed solely in discrete packets of energy. Planck labeled the energy packets *quanta*, and in the word and the news of the "misbehavior" of light, quantum theory began to be born. By 1905, Albert Einstein proposed more radically that radiant energy was composed of separate speeding and colliding particles. What followed was the elaboration of a new physics. Einstein's colliding photons became the basis for an elegant theory that took shape over the first three decades of the twentieth century, with a mathematical scaffolding to lend it support.[10]

At the subatomic level, matter—it turned out—was not nearly so solid as it first appeared. If light could act like waves in some ways and like particles in others, electrons had become microchameleons. Matter dissolved into energy and then reconfigured itself as matter, as later research with mass accelerators showed. Moreover, it proved impossible to predict with certainty the patterns of the transformation. The quantum world was one of mathematical probability, as the "unsharpness principle" of Werner Heisenberg in 1927 attested. The action of the experimenter changed the outcome of the experiment, and nature always winked and obligingly altered the show.[11]

The Newtonian world had been stood on its head, and some physicists found the new cosmology an occasion for metaphysics. Werner Heisenberg decided that the Platonic world of forms reflected reality: the smallest units of matter were ideas that could be articulated in mathematical terms. He thought, too, that a "sharp separation between the world and the I" could no longer be possible. The new physics, he explained, was "part of a general historical process that tends toward a unification and a widening of our present world."[12] Amid the speculation, the irony was that the new physics had generously supplied a metaphoric base that could lead some to the reconstitution of the mesmeric and Swedenborgian worlds. If matter and energy were moments in a continuous natural process, phases or appearances of an essential and dynamic substrate of the world, then—for some—body and mind, substance and spirit, could be construed as part of a single continuum. The invisible fluid could emerge as highly visible, and its pulsing, wave-like motion in the old etheric world could be reborn in the vibrating quanta of the twentieth century.

The stage was set for a latter-day synthesis that would make the past its prologue to a dawning millennium. In this synthesis, the blurring of matter and energy at the subatomic level would be linked in principle to the occult romanticism of the mesmeric-Swedenborgian habit of mind. The manipulative potential of minds that could control self and others would be joined to a matter that followed laws of harmony. Thus, acts of harmony would become, simultaneously, acts of power and control. And the world in which these things would happen by the late twentieth century would belong to the New Age.

To evoke the New Age is, in some sense, to reify a mood, a moment, or—in what is perhaps the best description—a language; for the New Age is above all a religious discourse community that elicits certain forms of action. The New Age has no central church or organization. It possesses no authoritative denominational officialdom, no creedal platform, no sectarian tests for inclusion or exclusion. Even given a broad translation as an elastic movement with certain kinds of "spiritual" and aesthetic overtones, its identity is elusive: Mesmer and Swedenborg, spiritualism and quantum theory surely do not exhaust its ideational capital. J. Gordon Melton has dated the movement from 1971 and the Boston *East-West Journal* and, more recently, has traced its origins to England in the 1960s and a series of "light" groups who began to meet and discuss prophetic theosophical writings about a coming New Age.

In the Melton assessment, the appearance of light groups in the United States—linked in an international movement to their British cousins—coincided with changes in the American immigration law in 1965 that opened the way for millions of arriving Asian immigrants, among them spiritual teachers congenial to the emerging gospel of the New Age.[13]

Melton calls the New Age movement a "new revivalist religious impulse directed toward the esoteric/metaphysical/Eastern groups and to the mystical strain in all religions," and in recent work (in this volume) he has stressed its ephemeral nature.[14] On the other hand, Robert Ellwood (also in this volume) has emphasized the continuities of the New Age revival with the alternative spirituality tradition of the West "going back at least to the Greco-Roman world." Ellwood has especially noticed New Age connections with nineteenth-century American spiritualism, that "boisterous child" of the Old World heritage "via Swedenborgianism and Mesmerism, plus a touch of Native American shamanism." He has underlined, too, the Neoplatonic provenance of New Age cosmology with "laws of 'correspondence' with their 'as above, so below' ramifications." And Ellwood has pointed to the initiatory nature of the wisdom the New Age seeks to impart, with understanding the gnostic product of "inward transformation."[15]

Indeed, the transformational program of the New Age has been noticed by other academic observers of the movement. Melton's short list of movement characteristics, for example, begins with the assertion that the New Age's "central vision" is "one of radical mystical transformation on an individual level." And in her recent book *New Religions and the Theological Imagination in American Culture,* Mary Farrell Bednarowski quotes with agreement the identification of New Age groups given by New Age teacher David Spangler: "intentional spiritual communities [which] espouse explicitly the idea of an emerging planetary culture based on human transformation."[16]

Even more, the shift from individual to collective concerns represented in the Bednarowski-Spangler reading is significant. For to miss the social side of the New Age directive of personal transformation is to miss a good deal: it is, in fact, to risk misunderstanding the kind of transformation New Agers seek even for the individual. That said, however, whether for single person or for society, New Age transformation requires specification: it is transformation of a special sort, radical change of a particular kind. And it is the kind of change that is desired, the substantive nature of the sought-after transformation, that tells most about the central thrust of the New Age and about its way of linking personal to larger social concerns. For as New Agers ask the age-old question of spiritual transformation—of "What must I (or the world) do to be saved?"—it emerges as "What must I—and the planet—do to be healed?"[17]

It is no accident that the network of communication that has promoted the message of the New Age has relied noticeably on massage therapists and chiropractors, on bulletin boards in natural food stores and in alternative healing clinics, on ephemeral publications strongly supported by advertisers who purvey one or another form of physical, mental, and/or spiritual healing.[18] And if the New Age is a religious discourse community with a characteristic language that identifies it, a large part of its vocabulary concerns the "universe" (read God?) and its healing "energies," "polarities" and their balancing, "chakras" and their activation, "vibrations" and the need for their harmonization.

Hence, in what follows, I want to suggest that the the discourse and related action promoted by the New Age have emerged as a new healing religion. I want to suggest, too, that a planetary dimension is intrinsic to that healing, even though I will considerably bracket its exploration here. And I want to suggest, further, that the healing religion of the New Age has emerged, in good measure, under the metaphorical sign of the quantum; that the quantum functions, in fact, as a kind of magical staff to assist "even mind" and balance. Indeed, in this context it is symmetrically appropriate to speak of the coalescence of the New Age from linked "light" centers. For the issue of light—at once mystically unifying and scientifically discrete—has captured the mind and imagination of the New Age.

Consider, for example, the quantum discourse of the theosophically inclined physician Richard Gerber. For Gerber, healing begins at the subatomic level with the secret life of the electron. "A cosmic ray— a highly energetic photon of light," he tells us, changes in the presence of a "heavy atomic nucleus." "The photon changes form to become two mirror-image particles. Literally, energy becomes matter." To do this, Gerber explains, "the photon (a quantum of electromagnetic energy or light) slows down. . . . In a simplistic sense, a packet of light has been slowed down and frozen." And again, "when viewed from the microcosmic level, *all matter is frozen light!*" It follows for Gerber that, while "mystics through the ages have referred to us as beings of light," modern science "has begun to validate the basic premise."

In practical terms, Gerber's analysis means that, since "matter is composed of highly complex, infinitely orchestrated energy fields," an "Einsteinian" paradigm of healing should replace a Newtonian one. Enter, therefore, "vibrational medicine," which, he says, "*attempts to interface with primary subtle energetic fields that underlie and contribute to the functional expression of the physical body.*" In more theosophical language, the physical body becomes "a complex energetic interference pattern interpenetrated by the organizing bioenergetic field of the etheric body." And vibrational medicine becomes direct work for the manipulation of energy fields "instead of manipulating the cells and organs through drugs or surgery."[19] What kinds of energy work are there? Gerber's book *Vibrational Medicine* finds answers in acupuncture and homeopathy, in psychotropic healing through flower essences, in crystal healing, and in a series of other modalities.

What is instructive here about Gerber's explanation is that, even as he dissects and analyzes, he also fuses and conflates. Behind Gerber stand the long mystical and metaphysical traditions of West and East with their mutual fascination with the spiritual power of light. Behind him, too, stands the American theosophical tradition with its language of astral and etheric bodies And behind him, finally, stands the mesmeric-Swedenborgian mentality of nineteenth-century spiritualism with its linkage of spirit to matter and mind to physical substance. Thus, the quantum Gerber appropriates has passed through the prism of religious teaching, and it emerges as refracted in sacred ways. Moreover, the quantum Gerber appropriates combines the law of harmony with the law of active manipulation. While bodies should "vibrate" in accord with cosmic laws and resonate to universal natural forces, active intervention to make nature more natural is not ruled out. Harmony, in short, may be helped.

Or consider again, from another medical quarter, a different approach to quantum healing. Steeped in Ayurvedic medicine, holistic physician Deepak Chopra also views the phenomenon of spontaneous remission of disease—as in a "miraculous" cancer cure—in quantum terms. For Chopra the quantum is both, in its popular sense, "a discrete jump from one level of functioning to a higher level" and, in the more scientific usage of Stephen Hawking, the smallest unit "'in which waves may be emitted or absorbed.'" Chopra's quantum is both quantum leap and quantum transmutation; and playing on the metaphorical ambiguity, he can theorize about the creative role of consciousness in healing. In fact, Chopra prefers to think of "bodymind" more than either mind or body, for the body, he explains, "has a mind of its own." Neurochemical events in the brain's life tell Chopra of the subtle process by which immaterial thoughts of fear are translated into the material substance of disease.

Because "at the quantum level, matter and energy come into being out of something that is neither matter nor energy," touching the quantum means touching the primal substrate from which form emerges. "Nature is man's healer, because Nature is man," Chopra pronounces confidently. And he tells us that "the discovery of the quantum realm opened a way to follow the influence of the sun, moon, and sea down deeper into ourselves." "Quantum discoveries," he writes, "enable us to go into our very atoms and remember the early universe itself." Evoking the submicroscopic or "virtual" particle called the quark, Chopra confesses that "its building block may well be merely a vibration that has the potential to turn into matter."[20] In this reading science has once again met the etheric body, and mental power becomes the new invisible fluid that magnetizes belief into bodily change. The conflation of matter and spirit functions to empower the mind to alter form and substance. In sum, Chopra's mind is at once mind as slayer and mind as healer.

Taken together, therefore, Richard Gerber and Deepak Chopra have, each of them, identified one of the two major directions in New Age healing. First, with Gerber, the law of harmony prevails. Healing means harmonizing the energies of the body so that they resonate with larger natural forces and laws, not unlike the harmonial work of Andrew Jackson Davis's Galen. Manipulation occurs—that is what the doctor is for—but manipulative effort means subtle work on the physical-energetic level. It means, in short, removing obstructions that block the full operation of harmonial law. Second, with Chopra, the shamanic law reigns supreme. Healing means journeying into the realm of non-matter in which the subtle forces transmute into material substance. Here, as in the mental journeys of Andrew Jackson Davis, mind and imagination assume hegemony over the harmonial life of matter. The healing shaman, whether self or other, travels to the place of primal energy from which the blueprint for organic life is thought to come.

For both harmonial and shamanic healing, Andrew Jackson Davis's magic staff—the "even mind" of natural balance—holds sway. And for both forms of healing, that even mind is imaged and focused in the quantum. It is, for both, the quantum that functions as cultural and religious broker, exchanging the metaphysical capital of the past for a coin that suits the present And it is, for both, the quantum that cloaks the contradiction between harmonizing (with something larger) and controlling the larger forces, that balances the move from mind to matter and back again.

Even a brief glance at instances of the healing religion of the New Age suggests the power of the quantum metaphor and its effectiveness in modulating from harmonic to shamanic models. And such an exercise points, too, to the ambiguity of the healing that New Agers desire. It is surely personal and deeply intimate. It encompasses individual body, mind, and spirit. But it is also a plea for the healing of the planet and a charter to work in ways that are seen to help the process. As David J. Hufford has written of contemporary American folk medicine, "the environment is considered a candidate for healing along with the individual person." Even more, healing, as it is understood in the New Age, is a work of reconciliation. In keeping with its fusion of matter and spirit (the holistic paradigm), this healing emphasizes a forgiveness that dissolves physical disease, emotional hurt, and the collective distress of society and nature. Healing, in this sense, is different from curing. To experience healing may or may not be the same as effecting a physiological change.[21]

Marilyn Ferguson charts the course for the harmonic model when, in her now-classic *Aquarian Conspiracy*, she points to "the rise of the autonomous health seeker." For Ferguson, in what she calls a "social transformation," the contemporary search for self can become "a search for health, for wholeness." It can become, in short, holistic medicine, "a qualitatively different approach . . . that respects the interaction of mind, body, and environment." How does this "qualitatively different approach" do its work? "Beyond the allopathic approach of treating disease and symptoms of disease," says Ferguson, "it seeks to correct the underlying disharmony causing the problem." The holistic approach assumes the body as a "field of energy within other fields" and adopts a "bodymind perspective," in which the "mind is primary or [a] coequal factor in *all* illness."

If this description seems to blur into the shamanic, the quantum's shadow hovers to merge the models. "We are," announces Ferguson, "oscillating fields within larger fields." And health, with the late nineteenth-century social scientist/poet Edward Carpenter, is "a governing harmony, just as the moon governs the tides." "Health and disease don't just happen to us. They are active processes issuing from inner harmony or disharmony, profoundly affected by our states of consciousness, our ability or inability to flow with experience."[22] Thus, both mental effects (states of consciousness) and physical events (experience) affect the harmony. One may, presumably, begin any place—with body or with mind or with the murky land between—to achieve the result of health.

Framed by this language, forms of palm healing are useful illustrations of the harmonial model. Take, for instance, the initiatory method taught as Reiki. Begun in Japan but come to expression as a largely American movement in the late seventies and eighties, Reiki teaches the use of "universal life-force energy" through a series of special "attunements" to the energy received from a Reiki master. Once the initiatory process is past, though, Reiki is taught as a systematic process of using the hands for healing. Reiki practitioners (those who have undergone initiation) explain that their way of healing "brings the body into harmony by relieving physical and emotional blockages" and that Reiki "heals the cause and eliminates the effects of an imbalance." This is to echo the harmonial vocabulary of nineteenth-century magnetic healing. But magnetic vocabulary shades into the metaphor of the quantum, as, for example, in the words of Reiki master Barbara Weber Ray. In her theoretical guide *The Reiki Factor*, Ray informs readers that Reiki is a "science of light." She quotes Marilyn Ferguson approvingly to the effect that "*everything is process*. The solid world is a process, a dance of subatomic particles." And she argues that "the essence of Reiki is light-energy that transforms us—each according to an individual unfolding process."

Under the sign of Einstein's energy-matter equation ($E = MC^2$), Ray finds light and matter "interchangeable," with light appearing to be "at the heart of all things." "From the distant past to contemporary times," she tells readers,

> religious and metaphysical texts have referred consistently to light as the essence of all things. Einstein's conclusion that the speed of light is the only constant in the universe has had stunning implications for modern scientific investigation. In nature and in the vast universe, the basic substance of all things appears to be energy, and energy in its essence can be described as light.

Ray goes on to identify material form as tightly compressed "molecular structure" that is still a form of energy. "Energy," she says, "in certain forms is highly visible and in other forms is mostly invisible to us." Hence, Reiki becomes a way to direct the flow of life energy for the transformative effect of healing. It is, Ray affirms, "to be claimed by all of us as we progress into mankind's New Age, as we restore our power, and as we learn to heal and whole ourselves."[23]

The move from metaphysics through quantum science to palm healing is not unlike similar practical moves that function as explanation for any number of New Age harmonial healing modalities. Here crystal healing comes immediately to mind because of the prominence of crystals as visual tropes of the New Age and because of the recent analysis by Robert C. Fuller. Summarizing New Age estimates, Fuller tells us that "the healing power of crystals is due to their unique ability to harmonize the physical body with the etheric fields from which spiritual energy ultimately emanates." Gemstones, he notes, are selected because of the resonance between their properties and one's personal "vibrations." And, echoing in different words the idea of the removal of block-age, he notices the motif of purification, necessary to the crystal healing process.[24]

But crystal healing is part of a continuum that graduates into heal-ing with liquid essences of flowers and gemstones and then into more traditional forms of homeopathy. In Kevin Ryerson's channeled work *Flower Essences and Vibrational Healing*, the relationship of all three is examined, and theory is joined to recommendations for practice. Ryer-son's channel Gurudas comments on the links:

> When a flower essence, homeopathic remedy, or gem elixir is ingested or used as a salve they follow a similar specific path through the physical and subtle bodies. They initially are assim-ilated into the circulatory system. . . . The remedy settles mid-way between the circulatory and nervous systems. An electro-magnetic current is created here by the polarity of these two systems. . . . These two systems contain quartz-like properties and an electromagnetic current. The blood cells, especially the red and white blood cells, contain more quartz-like properties, and the nervous system contains more an electromagnetic cur-rent. The life force and consciousness use these properties to enter and stimulate the physical body.

Ryerson/Gurudas goes on to speak of the "attunement between crys-talline properties in the physical and subtle bodies, the ethers, and many vibrational remedies." He teaches an intricate process that ends in "a balanced distribution of various energies at correct frequencies, which stimulates the discharge of toxicity to create health."[25]

It is clear that Ryerson/Gurudas sees differences between the action of homeopathic remedies, flower essences, and gem elixirs. Flower essences, he says, possess more of the life force and are more properly vibrational, while homeopathy utilizes "denser inorganic material" and gem elixirs function in between.[26] All three, though, dance precariously on the border between matter and energy, products of a quantum con-sciousness appropriated through the same inherited metaphysical world that nourished Andrew Jackson Davis. Using matter, in how-ever etherialized form, transmits the energy that effects healing, and the healing that is accomplished is at once physical and spiritual.

By contrast, the shamanic model prescribes that one lead with the mind. In *Creative Visualization*, for example, Shakti Gawain presides over a familiar universe in which the physical world is an energy phe-nomenon. "The scientific world is beginning to discover what meta-physical and spiritual teachers have known for centuries. Our physical

universe is not really composed of any 'matter' at all; its basic component is a kind of force or essence which we can call *energy.*" The things
that "appear to be solid and separate" on "finer . . . atomic and subatomic levels" are "smaller and smaller particles within particles, which
eventually turn out to be just pure energy." As important, "the energy is
vibrating at different rates of speed," and so has "different qualities."
"Thought is a relatively fine, light form of energy and therefore very
quick and easy to change." On the other hand, "matter is relatively
dense, compact energy, and therefore slower to move and change." In
this world of faster and slower vibrating energy, magnetic law reigns
supreme: "energy of a certain quality or vibration tends to attract energy
of a similar quality and vibration." From this perspective, an idea
becomes a "blueprint" that "creates an image of the form, which then
magnetizes and guides the physical energy to flow into that form and
eventually manifests it on the physical plane."[27]

Given the theoretical frame, Gawain's general direction seems clear.
If she acknowledges that "we always attract into our lives whatever
we think about the most, believe in most strongly, expect on the deepest
levels, and/or imagine most vividly," disciplined technique is at hand
to reprogram the mind at these strongest, deepest levels. But for
Gawain, this means more than a simple assertion of will over imagination. Rather, it is a process she describes as akin to learning to sail in the
current of a river, at once moving with the flow and guiding. Thus, creative visualization properly performed requires contacting a "higher
self" and "coming from 'source.'" And "source," Gawain declares,
"means the *supply* of infinite love, wisdom, and energy in the universe. . . . Source may mean God, or the universal mind, or the oneness of all, or your true essence."[28] In sum, Gawain is prescribing an
inward journey, a voyage to the self to unlock its dormant powers of
reconfiguration. In so doing, Gawain is recommending a New Age form
of shamanism.

Even so, just as the law of harmony moves, under the sign of the
quantum, into the law of shamanic control, Gawain's form of shamanism can double back into harmony. "A state of 'dis-ease' in the body,"
she tells readers, "is always a reflection of conflict, tension, anxiety, or
disharmony on other levels of being as well." Hence, physical illness
invites one to "restore natural harmony and balance."[29] All the same,
mind must do the restoring, and its evenness and balance become the
shaman's magic staff.

In fact, this new shamanism is, as Jeanne Achterberg tells us, "the
medicine of the imagination." In a searching analysis that explores the
relationship of shamanism to modern medicine, Achterberg acknowl-

edges a mythic nexus between shamanism and science: "Even with the safeguards of the scientific methods, the descriptions the scientist (as well as the shaman) gives of the imagination and the healing process are myths." Evoking traditional shamanic practice in many cultures, Achterberg tells that shamans "ascend to the sky or descend to the underworld of the imagination." Moreover, "the focus of the shamanic journeying is on obtaining power or knowledge in order to help the community, or on healing." For Achterberg, gaining power and being healed are not discontinuous, for the primary problem in an illness is "the loss of personal power that permitted . . . intrusion."[30]

Hence, the symbolic repertoire of the shaman, the material objects and ritual process that are employed in the context of the journey, are means for the reempowerment of the sick community or the sick individual. And their state as matter or condition as mind are not the issue, Achterberg insists. What is important for the "accomplished shaman" is "well-developed powers of the imagination," with symbols and rituals "necessary to open the healing mechanism for the patient." Linking the shamanic process to the quantum gospel, she explains that "quantum physics studies only the hypothetical construct"; it measures "ghosts" by "quantifying antecedent and consequent events." Therefore, argues Achterberg, "if, as the quantum physicists suggest, the imagination is the basis for all form, all matter, the ghosts may remain." And, in another context, "the distinction between body, mind, and spirit is nil. Body is mind, and mind is spirit."[31]

For some in the New Age, the "ghost" journey of the shaman is the work of a trance channel, who brings healing knowledge and advice to clients from an entity understood as dwelling on a different plane. For others, however, the individual must act more practically to be a shaman, as in the example of anthropologist Michael Harner. As part of his fieldwork from 1956 to 1957 and again from 1960 to 1961, Harner experimented with shamanic practice in the Jivaro and Conibo cultures of South America. His Indian guides gave Harner strong (and dangerous) medicinal plant substances to induce the shamanic state, and Harner became seriously ill in the process. By 1980, though, Harner's *Way of the Shaman* appeared, with its programmatic subtitle *A Guide to Power and Healing*.[32] There was some material about Jivaro, Conibo, and other traditional forms of shamanism in the book but more about neoshamanic practice among contemporary Americans. Here not only were the medicines of the Indians gone, but so was most of their cultural apparatus. In their place was the Harner Method with its insistence on sonic driving (drumming) as a practical technique for shamanic journeying.

"The shaman moves between realities, a magical athlete of states of consciousness engaged in mythic feats," Harner wrote. The shaman stood in the middle, "between ordinary reality and nonordinary reality," a "'power-broker' in the sense of manipulating spiritual power to help people, to put them into a healthy equilibrium." But the shaman, it became apparent, was also a good scientific healer. "Particularly exciting, and implicitly supportive of the shamanic approach to health and healing," Harner told, "is the new medical evidence that in an altered state of consciousness the mind may be able to will the body's immune system into action through the hypothalamus." In fact, Harner ventured, "possibly science will eventually find that the unconscious mind of the shaman's patient, under the influence of sonic driving, is being 'programmed' by the ritual to activate the body's immune system against disease." Significantly, there was a "clarity of darkness" in the shaman's journey with a patient, for "the shaman *sees* the hidden forces involved with the depths of the unconscious, and harnesses them or combats them for the welfare and survival of the patient."[33]

Harner's shaman moves among a stock of simple instructions and techniques, journeying to lower, middle, and upper worlds, meeting power animals and teachers, learning what to avoid and what to carry back as wisdom and knowledge gained. "There is no distinction between helping others and helping yourself," Harner says. Still more, in Harner's reading, "shamanism goes far beyond a primarily self-concerned transcendence of ordinary reality." "It is transcendence for a broader purpose, the helping of humankind. The enlightenment of shamanism is the ability to light up what others perceive as darkness, and thereby to *see* and to journey on behalf of a humanity that is perilously close to losing its spiritual connectedness with all its relatives, the plants and animals of this good Earth."[34]

In so stating, Harner has articulated an assumption that joins harmonic to shamanic models of healing—the belief in social impact and importance that is implicit, and often explicit, in New Age healing. Harner's Center (and now Foundation) for Shamanic Studies has grown more and more to emphasize the presence of shamanism in human cultures throughout the world, even as it has grown to rely increasingly on the tape recorder to supply its sonic drive. The interconnectedness of spiritual practice provides a cue for Harner as it does for so many others in the New Age. Their message is simple: there is only one planet that humans inhabit, and the lack of balance of any one of them affects its well-being. As sociologist Meredith McGuire found for clients of alternative healing in suburban New Jersey, the "ideal of holism" for body and mind predisposes to concern for another form of integration. Going "beyond the sense of bodymind holism," there is "an insistence upon the interdependence of all aspects of the cosmos." McGuire has argued that the insistence on connection is related to a "new mode of individualism," in a world in which "people suffer from the loss of connectedness." And she has suggested that the "middle-class forms of alternative healing" she studied may "represent a statement against the rationalization of body and emotions in contemporary society."[35]

If so, the New Agers among the ill have protested rationalization even as they have embraced the order of scientific metaphor as a source of personal power. Hence, whatever the planetary concerns of New Agers themselves, I have pointed to a New Age healing connection, not with the planet as a whole, but more with a specifically American tradition. That tradition included Mesmerism, Swedenborgianism, and Spiritualism; and the same tradition, embedded securely in its metaphysical base, stretched to incorporate the new scientific language of the quantum. Emphasizing the tradition as it is present in contemporary life, I have by no means attempted a comprehensive survey of each and every mode of New Age healing. But I have argued that, as the quantum language has been spoken by the religious discourse community of the New Age, it has come to represent the Archimedean lever that can move believers to harmonial healing from the physical side or to shamanic performance from the mental. The New Age habit of mind can shift comfortably between worlds, conflating matter and energy (spirit) in an ambiguity that means for flexible forms of healing action and that links individual to collective even in highly self-focused forms of healing.

What must I and all of us do to be healed? New Agers ask. And their answer is clear. Without the benefit of an academic theological tradition and in the lineage of Andrew Jackson Davis, they must grasp the magic staff of balance and make the quantum leap.

PART II

Aspects of the New Age

Part Two contains six chapters that together convey some sense of the broad range of New Age activities and of New Age thinking. Methodologically, the chapters run the gamut from closely argued analytic studies to survey descriptions of understudied phenomena.

Susan Love Brown's "Babyboomers, American Character, and the New Age" focuses on the fact that the great majority of New Agers are also baby boomers, and her analysis examines the continuities between the sixties counterculture and the New Age subculture. Brown calls attention to such things as the parallel between the drug culture's interest in alternate states of consciousness and the New Age's interest in meditation and other consciousness-raising techniques.

Stephen M. Clark's "Myth, Metaphor, and Manifestation: The Negotiation of Belief in a New Age Community" deals with a particular New Age community, Findhorn. His chapter discusses the transformation of Findhorn from a gardening center into a community focused on the "cultivation" of human beings. Clark describes how the "myth of the garden" has continued to shape the community, both as a foundation myth and as a metaphor for the spiritual "growth" of its members.

Suzanne Riordan's "Channeling: A New Revelation?" surveys a selection of material "revealed" through New Age channels. Setting aside the more outlandish pronouncements of the less credible (relatively speaking) channels, one finds that there are large areas of consensus—a consensus which adds up to a coherent worldview. Although most of the elements of this worldview have earlier precedents, the peculiar synthesis one finds in the channeled material is new. The system of thought outlined in this essay has a broader significance than the material to which Riordan has restricted her study because, in the main, it reflects the worldview of those segments of the New Age subculture not following the teachings of the channels.

Glenn A. Rupert's "Employing the New Age" looks at the penetration of the American business community by the New Age in the form of New Age-inspired training seminars. Businesses have found such programs to be remarkably effective at improving the output of their employees. However, while certain techniques can be presented without reference to a particular worldview or value system, the tendency has been to indoctrinate workers into the New Age vision of the world, and this has led to certain problems, such as the negative reactions of employees who belong to traditional religious denominations. Rupert's essay outlines this conflict as well as a select number of particular training seminars, especially those derived from *est*.

Aidan A. Kelly's "An Update on Neopagan Witchcraft in America" examines Neopagan Wicca. While drawing its membership as well as part of its inspiration out of the same subculture and from some of the same traditions as the New Age, Neopaganism has come to constitute a distinct movement which overlaps very little with the New Age. Kelly delineates some of the key differences between the two movements, and surveys some of the more important traits of Neopagan Witchcraft. Of particular interest is his discussion of the dimensions of the movement, which, according to Kelly's estimates, is large and growing.

Irving Hexham's "The Evangelical Response to the New Age" examines the conservative Christian reaction to the New Age. The popularity of a few key anti-New Age books in the Christian subculture has spawned a host of imitators, so that the genre now boasts between 50 and 100 titles. From the status of an unfamiliar term in the early eighties, "New Age" has expanded to encompass almost everything conservative Christians dislike. Hexham, a highly respected analyst of alternative spirituality in Evangelical circles, discusses the genre and evaluates most of these works as poorly researched and superficial.

Chapter 7

Baby Boomers, American Character, and the New Age: A Synthesis

——————— *Susan Love Brown*

New Age religion is characterized by beliefs about the all-pervasive nature of consciousness as a primary force in the universe and the ability of human beings to tap into this consciousness directly. The practitioners of New Age religion are more interested in experience than in doctrine, and belief systems are often amalgams of disparate doctrines based on understanding realized through experience. New Age beliefs draw upon Eastern religious and philosophical traditions, mystical aspects of the Judeo-Christian tradition, and elements of the magic worldview./My purpose in this paper is to show how this particular configuration of elements can be accounted for in the United States. The New Age phenomenon requires closer scrutiny within the context of American culture change and character. I should note at the outset that the examples I use in this paper are based on my own field research at Ananda World Brotherhood Village, a twenty-year-old cooperative, yogic community in northern California.[1] But New Age religion itself is neither confined to religious communities, nor to the yoga practiced at Ananda, nor to the age group to which I will attribute its inception, nor to the United States.[2]

In this light I make the following points: (1) that New Age religion is part of a tradition of religious emergence in the United States that goes back to the seventeenth century and whose elements have been part of the cultural milieu since that time; (2) that there is a generational aspect to New Age religion in the United States without which the extent of its influence and the nature of societal change cannot be understood; (3) that New Age religion is one manifestation of a change in American character that began in the Sixties and is now reaching fruition; (4) that this change beginning in the Sixties involved a shift from a social view of self to a psychological view of self, but now implies a further shift from a psychological model to a spiritual model.

An American Religious Tradition

Alexis de Tocqueville, speaking of Americans in his *Democracy in America*, noted that "certain momentary outbreaks occur when their souls seem suddenly to burst the bonds of matter by which they are restrained and to soar impetuously towards heaven." He also noted that "from time to time strange sects arise which endeavor to strike out extraordinary paths to eternal happiness."[3]

The "strange sects" have been known to appear in the United States, both as transplants from Europe and as native American religious enterprises, as far back as the seventeenth century, arising most often in the form of religious communities and movements. Zablocki notes five distinct periods of communitarian activity in U.S. history, each denoting a response to massive change in Europe or the United States.[4] And along with the formation of communities—both religious and secular—in response to change, Americans have formed new religions, some of which have lasted and become significant within the general American religious context. Mormonism and Christian Science are two examples.

New religious groups employ ideas already existing in the culture to formulate their own specific approach to spirituality. For example, according to Quinn, Mormonism developed within the context of "America's religio-magical heritage" in which ritual magic, divining rods, astrology, seer stones, and treasure digging were common.[5] Many of these same threads have found their way into New Age religion, along with some Eastern religious practices.[6]

Scholars have traced an American interest in the religions and philosophies of the Orient back to the eighteenth century when Benjamin Franklin quoted Confucius in the *Pennsylvania Gazette* and to the nineteenth century in letters exchanged between John Adams and Thomas Jefferson regarding Hinduism.[7] Spirituality with an Eastern flavor was also particularly influential on the New England Transcendentalist Movement (especially Emerson and Thoreau). The World's Parliament of Religions held in Chicago in 1893 introduced Indian Swami Vivekananda of the Ramakrishna Mission and Soyen Shaku (representing Japanese Zen) to the United States.[8]

Paramahansa Yogananda, the guru of the community in which I worked, came to the United States in 1920 to attend the International Congress of Religious Liberals held in Boston and was even a guest of

Calvin Coolidge in the White House.[9] He stayed on to found his own organization, the Self-Realization Fellowship, from which many disciples would come, among them Sri Kriyananda who founded Ananda World Brotherhood Village.[10] Yogananda believed that "East and West should destroy forever narrow divisions in the houses of God."[11] Today, his disciples from Ananda—mostly middle-aged, middle-class Americans—take pilgrimages to India to places Yogananda trod and seek to combine the vitality of U.S. culture with the spirituality of India. According to Yogananda, "India is the melting pot of religions; America, the melting pot of nations."[12] He considered this an unbeatable combination.

So when Eastern ideas began to infiltrate the thinking of young people in the United States in the sixties, what seemed like a novel affinity was in fact the continuation of an old American tradition. The treatment of this affinity as "new" by some critics and supporters of the New Age movement ignores the American cultural and historical context and the continuity of responses to change.

The changes in the sixties that led to a search for "a more satisfying culture"[13] provided some of the people who would come and take up residence at Ananda, which began as a meditation retreat founded by Sri Kriyananda and a few disciples in 1967 and blossomed into an actual community on July 4, 1969.[14] So patterned was the response to change among young people that when word got out that a new "commune" had been formed, Ananda was overwhelmed by visitors, many of whom did not have its best interests in mind. Kriyananda, whose personal efforts kept the community financially afloat in the beginning, reported that "many of this horde were the usual drop-outs, seekers, not for a positive way of life, but for a soft berth. They ate our food, ran up our phone bill, and told us how we ought to be living."[15] Eventually, however, the rigors of life at Ananda separated those who were really interested in following the path of kriya yoga from those who were merely trying to cope with change. In those first years at Ananda members spent time sorting out their main goals. A series of events helped to weed out those who were only temporaries from those who would become the core of the community; among these were: (1) the coming of the first mountain winter; (2) the decision to prohibit drug use (including alcohol) by members or others living on the lands; (3) the pronounced entrepreneurial spirit of the community; and (4) a devastating fire in 1976 that destroyed nearly every house on the land.

Although the community banned drug use, it adopted few other rules, preferring to live by custom—a luxury afforded by common interest and small numbers in those early years. Although not hostile to the outside world (meaning the larger U.S. society), Ananda members were separated from its mainstream by their Indian spiritual names, their clothing, their vegetarianism, their use of language, and their belief system. Ananda was a solution to a problem of being different. Ananda provided its members with what so many young people of that day sought: a path to salvation and a way of belonging.

Ananda is one of the few communities to have survived the seventies and eighties. In surviving as a community, Ananda has served as a repository of New Age religious culture, which burst forth upon the American public consciousness in the Eighties. But not only was New Age religion the product of typical responses to social change, it was also the product of a unique situation. New Age religion was carried by a single generation through which it was incubated and transmitted to other parts of American society. That generation is the baby boom generation—those born between 1946 and 1964.

Generational Aspects of the New Age

I discovered just how generational New Age religion is when I went to see and hear Richard Alpert, a psychologist and confederate of Timothy Leary. Alpert, known as Ram Dass to the New Age contingent, wrote a book, *Be Here Now*,[16] that had been a very influential book among Ananda members.[17] I found out about his visit through the Ananda members I meditated with in San Diego and decided to attend. But I did not take it seriously enough.

I left home at the last minute and hadn't bought a ticket ahead of time. The freeway providing access to the area was jammed, and the parking lot of the Scottish Rite Temple, which is huge, was filled. Everyone who wanted to attend was admitted—some 2,000 people—and what was striking to me about the crowd was that it comprised a single generation. I had also found earlier that the mean age of Ananda members in 1986 was 37.7 years, placing them in the vanguard of the baby boom generation.[18]

The significance of the baby boom generation has been noted by demographers and others studying New Age religion.[19] Its sheer size— one-third of all Americans or about 76 million people—has made a difference between it and all other generations.[20] Baby boomers see the world in a different light, and New Age religion, although it has its roots in the American religious past, is an expression of this. But what was so special about this generation?

Demographer Cheryl Russell sees the baby boom generation as a "freak storm of life" resulting from chance factors. Having babies after

World War II was, in essence, a fad.[21] After the War family and home became the ideal of American life, and there was a lot of social pressure to conform to this ideal. In 1946 women had 100,000 babies per month *more* than they had had the previous year.[22] There were 3.4 million babies by the end of that year. Men and women married younger, and there were more marriages than ever before. Russell notes that marriage itself was unique in this era in that only 32 percent of young women (ages 20-25) were unmarried, compared to the year 1900 when almost all young women were unmarried.[23] While the postwar baby boom in European countries came to a close a few years after the war ended, the U.S. baby boom continued, not peaking until 1957, and finally ended in 1965.[24] But besides simply being a huge generation, baby boomers were also the product of a social environment different from that of their parents.

It is not possible to understand why the baby boom generation and its difference led to New Age religion without understanding the world into which it was born—one in which the United States was rising to power in the world and enjoying economic prosperity. This unparalleled prosperity lasted twenty years.[25] By 1955 the United States had 6 percent of the world population, produced two-thirds of the world's goods, and consumed one-third of those goods. "The ranks of the impoverished were reduced by two-thirds, while the middle class rose from 13 percent of all families to a near majority of 47 percent."[26] According to Strickland and Ambrose, the baby boomers were the "healthiest, best-fed, best-clothed, best-housed generation" to come along in the United States.

This generation was the first to be affected by television. When the first boomers were born there were 8,000 households in the United States with television sets. Two years later (1948) there were 100,000 sets. By 1950 there were 3.9 million, and by 1959 there were 50 million. The baby boom generation was the first to feel the impact of mass communications. Baby boomers were also a highly educated generation— nine out of every ten graduated from high school and half have attended college, compared to only 14 percent of their parents' generation.[27] So baby boomers are more than twice as educated as their parents.

Because of the sheer numbers of babies born, the United States became a child-centered society—baby boomers were raised in a society in which they were the center of attention. Strickland and Ambrose list the following effects of economic prosperity on how baby boomers were raised: they received full-time child care from their mothers; home ownership became possible for both middle-class and working-class families; toilet training was relaxed because of the availability of washing machines and diaper services; children had more physical freedom because of improvements in central heating; the change in work to large-scale corporate organization led to a change in attitude from hard work and self-denial to consumership; a child's concerns were less with adults and more with its own peer group; rather than parents as the sole agents of socialization, there were the mass media and peer-group influences.[28]

More and more, peer-group association and power became an important factor for the baby boom generation, and as it grew up the result was rock music, which provided for the ritual gathering of the young; a separate adolescent culture in high school, in which prestige became important; and the rise of teenage gangs and juvenile delinquency.[29]

While alienation was already present among the youth of the fifties—the "beat generation"—it was to take on a greater significance as the baby boomers came of age in the sixties. Baby boomers, born and raised in prosperity in an exceedingly stable and sociocentric world, would rebel against their parents. This rebellion would not take the form of simple transgression, such as smoking, drinking, and sexual exploration. It would be based on an idealistic view of what society should be, helped along by the assumption of material comfort and psychic well-being that saturated baby boomer reality. I found in my research at Ananda that many members had shared their parents' beliefs about right and wrong but rebelled against the exclusivity and hypocrisy inherent in the parental interpretation of these values.[30]

So the changes in the sixties resulted from an incredible conjunction of events: the postwar baby boom (influenced by an unprecedented period of economic prosperity, a child-centered society with more permissive childrearing practices, and the peer-oriented nature of the generation), and the coming of age of that generation when the United States was trying to solve some of its most serious moral problems (racial segregation, the war in Vietnam, and the inequality of women). Consequently, when the babyboom generation began reaching adulthood, its sheer size meant that the changes it sought were inevitable, and these changes entered the scene not with a whimper but with a bang.

A Change in American Character

It is important to note at the outset that the new values and new models of thinking that emerged in the sixties did not originate with the baby boom generation itself but with the discontented and preceding interim generation whence came its teachers. Baby boomers were merely the vehicle by which change entered into American consciousness. The changes that occurred were radical ones—that is, they represented a fundamental shift in American character. And although it did not seem so to people witnessing events at the time, these radical changes were of an orderly nature in that they did not completely rend the fabric of society.

In one sense the changes that occurred in the United States were inevitable, because of the variation inherent in a pluralistic society and the continuing struggle of people to better their standing in a democratic setting. These changes—of which New Age religion is but one manifestation—are described in different ways by different writers.

Social philosopher and trendwatcher Daniel Yankelovich sees the changes in terms of "new rules."[31] He characterizes these new rules in terms of self-fulfillment. He notes that in the sixties "the search for self-fulfillment was largely confined to young Americans on the nation's campuses. . . ."[32] However, by the seventies, "all national surveys showed more than seven out of ten Americans (72 percent) spending a great deal of time thinking about themselves and their inner lives—this in a nation notorious for its impatience with inwardness. The rage for self-fulfillment, our surveys indicated, had now spread to virtually the entire U.S. population."[33]

Yankelovich describes the shift from old rules to new as a sort of shift in paradigms. The old paradigm (post-World War II) was what he calls "the giving/getting compact." This model or paradigm consisted of the idea that if one worked hard, was loyal and steadfast, one would receive material rewards in return. This was the paradigm of the parental generation. This might involve subordinating one's own needs and frustrations, but the rewards—a good home, family, and job—were well worth the sacrifice.[34]

The new paradigm brought into being by the baby boom generation is the self-fulfillment paradigm, in which material rewards have been replaced by intangible ones—"creativity, leisure, autonomy, pleasure, participation, community, adventure, vitality, stimulation, tender loving care."[35] In other words, the new model places a premium on spiritual rather than material rewards. It is easy to make the connection between the kind of upbringing baby boomers enjoyed and their lack of concern about the immediacy of the material world.

Peter Clecak views the events of the sixties and seventies as "a quest for personal fulfillment within a small community (or several communities) of significant others. . . ."[36] Furthermore, Clecak says, this quest was not confined to a single group of people, and it had two broad themes: "fulfillment through salvation and fulfillment through social justice."[37] What we witnessed, then, was a "democratization of person-hood" which saw all sorts of people—racial and ethnic minorities, the handicapped, the elderly, women, homosexuals—making a bid for their own self-fulfillment. The major values of Americans had changed.

In my own research at Ananda, I found many of these observations verified, especially in the results of the Value Orientation Interviews I conducted on a random sample of the community's members.[38]

In 1961 Kluckhohn and Strodtbeck published the results of value orientation interviews conducted in 1951 among members of five communities in the Southwest.[39] American values, as represented by the dominant orientations of Texas homesteaders, were as follows:

Individualism	(relational orientation)
Future	(time orientation)
Mastery-over-Nature	(man-nature orientation)
Doing	(activity-orientation)

When I conducted value orientation interviews at Ananda in 1986, my results were quite different.[40] Ananda members had the following dominant orientations:

Collateral	(relational orientation)
Present	(time orientation)
Harmony-with-Nature	(man-nature orientation)
Being-in Becoming	(activity orientation)

The radical difference in dominant value orientations itself indicates a motivation for breaking away from the larger society to attempt to form a "more satisfying culture."[41]

But what is distinct about baby boomers in general and New Age religion in particular is the dual emphasis on self and experience, which, at Ananda, finds expression in the quest for self-realization and the practice of kriya yoga.[42] However, what probably played an important part in this particular embrace of self and experience was the new awareness of altered states of consciousness ushered in by the drug culture of the sixties.

The American Turn Inward

The widespread use of drugs by American young people in the sixties, while it led to addiction and a dead end for some, opened up possibilities for self-exploration and self-realization for others, exposing as it did other planes of consciousness. The exploration of consciousness led to a reacquaintance with the mystical elements of religion as well as to curiosity about the spiritual ideas of the East and techniques of meditation through which other states of consciousness could be safely achieved and retained by those who mastered them.

When Nordquist visited Ananda in 1976, he found that 75 percent of those having mystical experiences had used drugs that induced them.[43] And during my visit in 1986, longtime members spoke freely of the fact that they had come out of a drug culture in search of something more. Drug use had become part of the mythology of the past.

Zablocki has noted that 96.4 percent of those people living in communities based on Eastern ideologies had used drugs before joining, compared to 56.2 percent of people joining Christian communities.[44]

Psychology also played a part. There is, for example, a definite similarity between the self-realization of yoga and the self-actualization of the humanistic psychology that developed in the sixties. There is a further link between the altered states of consciousness produced by drugs and those sought through meditation. Thus, the psychological and the spiritual become linked through powerful inner experiences.

Veroff, Douvan, and Kulka reported a shift in the way that Americans viewed themselves between 1957 and 1975.[45] This shift involved moving from a view of one's well-being in the context of one's social roles (the sociocentric view) to a view of one's well-being based on a psychological model. This general tendency to view oneself from a psychological perspective was clearly manifested among members of Ananda in a survey conducted by Nordquist, in which the majority of members (79 percent) said they had joined the community for psychological reasons.[46]

Many authors have noted that New Age religion often serves a therapeutic function.[47] Anthropologists have also made a similar observation about the therapeutic role played by shamans and other religious practitioners in non-Western societies. In the case of New Age religion there can be no doubt that channelers and others serve this therapeutic function as well.

But I suggest that the psychological view of self might be in the process of transforming itself into a broader spiritual model. At Ananda about 70 percent of the members in 1986 said that they joined the community for spiritual reasons.[48] This may reflect the general American trend back to religion noted by Gallup and Castelli.[49]

New rituals and formal rules have made their appearance at Ananda. And, after twenty years, Ananda members are reestablishing connections with the larger society. Many members have comfortably acknowledged or reincorporated meaningful aspects of their childhood religions into their present spiritual practices. Kriyananda (who often uses his birth name of James Donald Walters now) no longer assigns spiritual names, and Indian clothes are mostly reserved for special occasions.

The Ananda community and its spiritual teachings afforded its members a way to reestablish connections with other people and with the universe at large during a time when anomie in American society was at its greatest. In this respect, then, New Age religion represents an age-old solution to a recurring problem, but with a distinctly contemporary configuration. What remains to be seen is whether the New Age configuration can hold it own against the American religious mainstream, which itself has changed significantly in the last thirty years. If so, then the New Age in its religious manifestation might well be a permanent reflection of the change in American character that occurred in the sixties.

Chapter 8

Myth, Metaphor, and Manifestation: The Negotiation of Belief in a New Age Community

—————————— *Stephen M. Clark*

One of the difficulties in studying so-called "New Age religion" is that one hardly knows where to begin. Where is the common thread linking such diverse practices as aura reading, past-life regressions, and crystal healing? As the phrase "New-Age" implies, there is a strong millenarian component to this phenomenon. I question whether individuals who occasionally seek out psychic healers, or read tarot cards, but do not subscribe to the belief that a New Age of spiritual enlightenment is emerging, can be accurately termed New Agers. Many who would call themselves New Agers are akin to churchgoers who are in it for the bingo and not for the worship.

Among the members of the Findhorn community in Scotland, where I lived and worked from 1975 through 1978, the belief in a nascent "New Age culture" is firmly grounded, and the demonstration of its principles is the community's reason for being. Like members of any good millenarian movement, the people at Findhorn have a story to tell, a story about the way things could be, one that is both mythic and metaphorical. Implicit in this story is a set of precepts and beliefs through which the members' perceptions of the world are filtered. I became interested in the way in which both the meaning attributed to the story and the structure of beliefs changed over Findhorn's twenty-eight year history, and in the way in which community members explain these changes to themselves and others.

The story is the tale of the founding of Findhorn, a saga of three people who planted a garden in what they termed "conscious cooperation with the spirits of nature." Findhorn dates its inception at 1962, when the three cofounders, Peter and Eileen Caddy, and Dorothy Maclean moved to a trailer park on the Findhorn peninsula. Peter's background included years of involvement in organizations such as the Theosophists and Rosicrucians, which claim access to esoteric wisdom, teaching that both God and the source of all knowledge are within the individual. Since 1953 Eileen received and recorded messages during daily meditation sessions from what she termed the "still small voice within"; a voice she identified as God's. At first the messages were principally inspirational, couched in a language biblical in tone. Gradually, Eileen began to receive messages, or "guidance" as she referred to it, of a much more prosaic nature: instructions for daily life, advice on which foods to eat and which to avoid, and solutions to specific problems.

The third actor in this drama, Dorothy Maclean, also received messages and guidance during meditation sessions. These three believed they were living their lives in accordance with God's will in the most literal sense. Instructions received in meditation were immediately acted upon. Thus, shortly after moving to the trailer park, when Eileen received guidance that Peter should start a vegetable garden, no time was lost in beginning the project. The creation of the garden was the first in a series of events which would culminate in the establishment of one of the most well-known New Age ventures of the 1970s.

In the actions of these three individuals, and the interpretation of events in terms of their spiritual beliefs, lies the basis for the creation of a mythology which would make Findhorn world-famous and attract thousands of variously curious, confused, and committed individuals. Although there is much to say concerning the establishment and growth of Findhorn as a New Age center, I would like to focus on two aspects of this process—first, the creation and subsequent transformation of the garden story, and second, changes in the way the concept of 'manifestation', the belief that all one's needs are met by God, was understood.

The story of the garden and the elaboration of the "laws of manifestation" evolved in tandem. Shortly after Peter began the garden, Dorothy received instructions in meditation that she was to "feel into the nature forces." Peter, convinced that direct contact with the nature forces might give him answers he needed to his questions about gardening, asked Dorothy to contact the "nature spirits" to this end. Dorothy did so, receiving messages in meditation from these nature spirits, which she characterized as the "indwelling spiritual essence" of the plants. She referred to these nature spirits as *Devas*, a sanskrit word loosely translated as "shining one." Dorothy claimed that the nature spirits were willing to enter into an experiment with humans, an experiment of "man and nature in cooperation." Peter was to be sensitive to the needs of the plants as reported in Dorothy's messages and, in turn, the Devas would both instruct him in gardening techniques—as in this message: "It would be good to turn the remainder of that first compost heap, but the other one is not quite ready for turning"—and would lend their own special talents to making the plants vigorous and healthy.

The vegetables Peter grew on the sandy soil of the Findhorn peninsula were both abundant and healthy. Though Peter was spending ten to twelve hours a day, seven days a week working in the garden, he attributed the garden's success wholly to the help of the nature spirits. Word of this unusual experiment in cooperation with nature spread, and spiritually like-minded people came from Scotland and England to see the garden, some to stay to participate in the experiment.

Central to the unfolding story of the garden was the implementation of a spiritual principle which Peter referred to as "manifestation." Simply put, manifestation is the belief that all one's needs are met by God. That is, there is no need to horde possessions or money, but only to "hold the vision in one's mind of what is needed and trust in perfect faith that no need will go unanswered." Peter's understanding of these laws was corroborated, in typically biblical fashion, by Eileen's guidance. One of Eileen's entries reads: "Consider how I fed the children of Israel with manna from Heaven. Forty years in the wilderness I did it for them. Why should not your every need be met."

In relating tales of those early days at Findhorn, story after story is adduced as evidence of the working of these laws—as when Peter needed but could not afford cement to build a patio outside their trailer and a neighbor came to tell them that a truck had just left a load of cement, in bags slightly damaged by water, in the dump across the road. Or how, just when he needed to start an additional compost heap which required a large quantity of straw, Peter discovered a bale which had fallen off a truck on a nearby road. The belief in manifestation formed a central organizing principle for the activities of the three founders of Findhorn, as well as an idiom within which future community members would evaluate the spiritual health of the community and its individual members, as I will show later.

By 1967, five years after the founders had moved to the Findhorn peninsula, the group had grown slightly to eleven or twelve individuals, all of similar age and background to the founders. The community was small, but the myth of the garden was well established and spreading. There are stories of eight-foot foxgloves, roses blooming in the snow, and most famous of all, forty-pound cabbages harvested from the garden.

As news of this experiment spread, through public talks by Peter, radio interviews, and booklets published by the Findhorn group, the ranks of community members and visitors swelled. By 1970 there were 150 members living in the Findhorn trailer park. The next few years were ones of profound change for the community. Dorothy Maclean left Findhorn to return to her native Canada. Peter no longer worked in the garden, spending much of his time traveling and speaking to other spiritual groups. A formal visitor or "guest" program was initiated, allowing the curious to share the Findhorn experience for a one- or two-week period. Publishing projects were undertaken to disseminate both Eileen's guidance and the story of the founding of the community.

Had Findhorn remained a small group of spiritually like-minded individuals communing with God in private meditation outside a village in the north of Scotland it would warrant little more than a footnote in a study of the New Age movement. However, Findhorn became much more than that. It saw itself as a "center of demonstration," a "university of light" that, to quote Eileen's guidance, would "grow from a group to a village, to a city of light." In its self-imposed role as a center of demonstration of New Age principles, Findhorn invited the scrutiny that would ultimately lead to a transformation in its underlying mythology and in many of its basic precepts.

In the 1970s the newly established guest program hosted from two thousand to four thousand visitors each year, and the community grew in membership. No longer were new members of background, disposition, and age similar to those of the founding members. The 250 individuals who lived in the community at the time of my arrival in 1975 were as varied a group as might be found. Devotees of Bagwhan Shree Rashneesh worked next to followers of Madame Blavatsky and the Theosophist movement. British psychic healers sat in morning meditation with American Ph.D.s in philosophy, Australian trance channelers, and Danish dropouts. The greatest proportion of community members were American, followed by British citizens, Australians, Canadians, and South Africans, with fourteen nations represented in all.

Many came, inspired by accounts of the garden in books published by the community, and were disappointed. By this time roses had restricted their blooming to the summer months, foxgloves aspired to reach five rather than eight fee, and the average cabbage weighed four not forty pounds. It was impossible to ignore the fact that while the garden was beautiful and flourished, the "experiment of man in cooperation with nature" had run its course. The myth responsible for Findhorn's fame was threatening to undermine its credibility and its existence.

Responsibility for the garden was assumed by a man with forty years of experience as an amateur and professional gardener. Whenever he asked the other gardeners to prune or cut back a plant, the response of three-quarters of the gardeners, with care and concern in their hearts for the plans, would be: "No, that hurts them, and we've been asking the Devas to do something about it instead"; or "Maybe they like being close like that." There were two irreconcilable approaches to gardening.

The "laws of manifestation" as championed by Peter were to play an even greater role in exacerbating the various schisms the growing community was experiencing. Some members, quoting Eileen's guidance that the community was to grow into a "city of light," advocated a program of expansion through the purchase of local properties and were willing to go into debt to achieve these goals. Members opposed to this program countered that if expansion was part of God's plan, the money would "manifest"; that to borrow money was simply lack of faith in the "laws."

Even as Findhorn's debt to cover operating expenses increased, some members objected to raising the weekly rates charged to visitors to the community or to increasing the price of books published, on the grounds that, to quote Peter: "If we move ahead in perfect faith, all of our needs will be met." The growing financial debt and dwindling living space made it clear to most members that all of their needs were not being met. While visitors asked what happened to the forty-pound cabbages, community meetings were peppered with seemingly irreconcilable debates on the meaning and role of manifestation for the growing community.

In *The Social Psychology of Social Movements*,[1] Hans Toch discusses the role of selective processing and perception in supporting preexisting interpretations of reality. He argues that belief systems allow their adherents to pay attention to some events, while deeming others unworthy of consideration. In Findhorn's formative years, Peter, Eileen, Dorothy, and the few additional community members were able to interpret every fortuitous event, such as the bale of straw found by the side of the road, as instances of the working of the "laws of manifestation," evidential of divine intervention and proof that they were chosen by God for an important task. Any unpropitious situation, like Peter's inability to find work despite much effort, was reinterpreted, in line with their beliefs, as proof that God had chosen Peter for a higher calling—one that a full-time job would interfere with. For many years community members were able to follow a similar pattern of selective perception and processing of events, especially in relation to manifestation. However, the ideological schism which developed over financial difficulties and the expansion of the community resulted in two conflicting sets of perceptions and posed a danger both to communal unity and to the integrity of one of Findhorn's central tenets.

The dilemma of the garden posed even more difficulty for members. No longer was anyone in communication with the Devas, receiving instructions and cooperation in its management. Although the garden was lush, the spectacular growth alleged by Findhorn's founders was nowhere evident. The very reason most people had journeyed to Findhorn had disappeared. According to Festinger's theory of cognitive dissonance,[2] where mutually contradictory cognitions, perceptions, values, or knowledge are entertained, the individual must act to reduce the dissonance. Festinger argues that this reduction in dissonance can be achieved either by changing the real world so as to modify the data coming in, or by modifying one's perceptions of self and the real world so as no longer to cognize the situation as a dilemma. Members of the Findhorn community tended toward the second solution, choosing to reinterpret their values and beliefs in order to reduce cognitive dissonance about manifestation and the garden.

In the case of their belief in manifestation, this reinterpretation took the form of a one-hundred page "Study Paper" entitled: "The *New* Laws of Manifestation," [emphasis mine] written in 1972 by a respected and influential community member who, it was believed, was able to contact and converse with "higher levels of consciousness." This paper essentially argues that as part of the unfolding of "new age consciousness" the "old" laws of manifestation, of essentially "holding the vision" of what was needed until it became manifest, were being replaced by more appropriate "new" laws. The new laws require that the individual become one with his or her higher self or God essence in order even to know what his or her true needs are. Simply "holding the vision" would no longer do. Community members must act in unison, identifying with the indwelling divinity before manifestation could occur.

This exposition of the new laws neatly sidestepped the issue of whether manifestation worked at all by placing the additional requirement of achieving a "higher state of consciousness" before the laws of manifestation would work. Although this placed community members in the uncomfortable position of personal responsibility for the failure or success of manifestation, it did reduce the dissonance associated with prior failures to manifest perceived needs. The incorporation of this revamped belief into daily practice and discourse took some time. Study groups were formed to discuss the new laws, and there was much casual dialogue on the matter. Within the period of a year, however, this new exposition of the laws of manifestation was the accepted norm.

A resolution to the dilemma of the garden was evoked from within the community out of the very garden story itself. The dilemma was resolved by a subtle shift of focus in the community's understanding of its purpose. In *The New Laws of Manifestation*, the following comments from one of the gardeners regarding the demise of the role of the nature spirits in the garden is indicative of this shift:

> Does this mean that the experiment in cooperation between man and nature is over? Without the assistance of those sensitives who can tune into the nature forces directly, is man once again left alone in the garden? Does the garden have anything now to offer the rest of us, seeking a way to make ourselves and our planet whole? In 1970 when Peter turned his focus toward other areas of the community, the next phase of the garden experiment began. The community is now committed to the growth of *human consciousness* through various work and study programs. (emphasis mine)

Another community member says:

> The founders of Findhorn were not establishing a set pattern that had to be imitated in order to cooperate with nature . . . To place the emphasis on the form of the experiment rather than the essential message would be to miss the point. God, the life, the same life we are expressing. They are in fact within us, and each of us has the power to work with these forces to create Heaven on Earth. Recognizing this and acting upon it is the challenge the gardeners are facing in 1974—the challenge of a change of consciousness.

A shift in values was taking place. In the minds of community members the garden experiment wasn't over, it hadn't failed. The community had simply advanced to the next level in fulfilling its mission. Findhorn had changed from a garden growing vegetables, to a garden growing people.

As part of this shift a new symbol emerged to supplant that of the garden: the "Universal Hall." This building, a beautiful pentagonal auditorium seating six hundred, was constructed over a five-year period entirely by the labor of community members and guests. Instead of the garden, community members proudly pointed to this structure, a new symbol of their unity. The Findhorn garden, however, was not simply to pass out of awareness. The story of the garden was about to achieve the status of true myth, a tale of an Edenic past which, in its telling, is meant to organize and make sense of the present. Nowhere was this more poignantly portrayed than in weekly community get-togethers on Friday evenings. At these times members and visitors alike would perform skits, play music, sing, or otherwise entertain the assembled group. Dozens of times over a three-year period I watched a virtually identical, although independently conceived, performance by the group of visitors that were resident that week. They would wheel around the stage, running about chaotically for a few minutes, then slowly come together at center stage, often resting on their heels in a circle. The music would change to something soft and flowing, and the group would begin to raise themselves in unison, arms first, in a representation of the opening of a flower.

While these performances appeared trite and somewhat amusing to members who had seen it all before, I could not help but be impressed by how successfully the Findhorn story had been transformed. The garden had remained the organizing mythology of Findhorn, a metaphor for the growth, or the flowering, of human consciousness.

Given time, I could have pointed to many other aspects of the Findhorn community that underwent change and reinterpretation: the character of Eileen's guidance and the importance attributed to it, attitudes towards the utterances of psychics or the veracity of so-called occult knowledge, to list a few. Often these changes and reinterpretations were initiated by a perceived incompatibility between belief and reality. Many were the result of the changing concerns and orientation of a membership constantly in flux, where the prejudices and orientation of incoming members have an impact on and alter the beliefs of the existing membership.

My experience at Findhorn underscores the plastic quality of New Age beliefs and the remarkable agility with which individuals are able to modify their beliefs and assign new meaning to their experience. I believe that any truly useful study of New Age phenomena will need to address this issue of plasticity of belief and the meaning those beliefs hold for the individual.

Chapter 9

Channeling: A New Revelation?

Suzanne Riordan

Introduction

If, in the words of James Hillman, "the modern vision of ourselves and the world has stultified our imaginations,"[1] then the New Age movement is a backlash against modernity. For those sympathetic to this ideological reorientation, the pendulum is swinging from a worldview in which there was no place for gnomes, goblins, and angels to one teeming with nature spirits, extraterrestrials, and ascended masters. If the former is dry and sterile in its relentlessly materialistic focus, the latter is wildly imaginative and infinitely suggestive. As traditional peoples have always known, humanity is not alone in the cosmos, and the subtle realms which science and monotheism have ignored are a source of great fascination to these postmodern seekers.

The reenchantment of the world is both cause and effect of the popularity of a form of interdimensional communication currently known as "channeling." "Channeling," for the purpose of this article, is defined as "a process in which information is accessed and expressed by someone who is convinced that the source is not their ordinary consciousness." Although the phenomenon has become associated with the movement in the public eye, and while most New Agers are familiar with the concept, it is of little interest to certain segments of the New Age. Proceeding without the sanction of their peers and despite the ridicule of the media, however, others regularly converse with a cosmic cast of disembodied characters which includes the ghost of John Lennon, an intergalactic space commander named "Ashtar," a "healing-teaching collective composed of energy intelligence that exists on a number of planes concurrently"[2] and "God in the first person."[3]

Channeling is not a new phenomenon. It has been known by other names in many cultures and in many ages. It was the craft of the oracle, the seer, the shaman and the prophet—those who have served as intermediaries between the material realm and the realms of the spirit. With the rise of monotheism, direct contact with the spirit world became suspect unless it was considered to emanate from Yahweh, through one of his chosen prophets. Other sources were referred to as "familiar spirits," and those who consulted with them were considered "defiled."[4]

Nineteenth-century Spiritualism sought to prove the immortality of the soul by demonstrating that communication with the dead was possible. The religious establishment of the time condemned the movement, not because they suspected mediums of fraud, but because the manifestations were considered to be the work of the devil.[5] A century earlier Emmanuel Swedenborg, reporting on his extensive adventures in the spirit world, had cautioned those who might wish to follow his example to exercise discernment: "When spirits begin to speak with man, he must beware lest he believe in anything; for they say almost anything. . . ."[6]

The latest incarnation of spirit contact is being keenly monitored by certain Christian fundamentalists who warn that "to be ignorant of such matters . . . is to be unarmed in an era of increasing demonic activity."[7] The growing popularity of channeling is bound to raise questions our culture has not dealt with since the eclipse of Spiritualism, which, in its heyday, engendered a lively debate among intellectuals as to the authenticity of the phenomenon. The contemporary revival of this practice has, in contrast, met with virtual silence from the cultural mainstream.

In today's intellectual community only "transpersonal" psychologists have taken an interest in determining what is or is not authentic amidst the proliferation of "new religions." Ken Wilber has branded many of these contending ideologies as "pop-mysticism," and he and his colleagues Ecker and Anthony have sought to develop a typology and a set of criteria based on the distinction between "pre-personal" and "trans-personal" states.[8] In an essay on the art of distinguishing genuine from "counterfeit" spiritual authority, John Welwood remarks that "ours is an age in which spiritual deceit and counterfeiting seem rampant," in which "the intense search for ultimate values combined with a certain naivete in matters spiritual has set the stage on which charlatans and false prophets have appeared, strutting and fretting, pouring out words full of sound and fury, but signifying very little."[9] Welwood's discussion fails, like Anthony, Ecker, and Wilber's, to deal with the special problem of channeled material, for which the task of discernment is yet more complex.

Given the extraordinary premise of the channeling phenomenon, one finds it difficult, if not impossible, to determine a priori whether a given source is divine or demonic, subconscious or supraconscious, transcendental or "pre-rational." One of the exponents of "Spiritism" suggested, in his day, that the best proof of the authenticity of "Spirit teachings" is "the concordance that exists between revelations which have been received spontaneously by a large number of mediums not known to each other and located in different places."[10] The incidence of convergence among certain of the contemporary channeled texts is undeniable; this may be due to the fact that most of the channels in question subscribed to what may be considered a "New Age worldview" prior to their first channeling experience. In the case of several of the earliest and most seminal among the contemporary works, however, the channel was not initially sympathetic to the thought system represented by the material that "came through" them. Regardless of their "authenticity" or their provenance, the channeled materials, and particularly those texts which exemplify a convergent philosophy, are a rich source of information about the emerging New Age cosmology.

A survey of the stations on the channeling circuit will reveal quite a bit of static. A bewildering cacophony of cosmic voices babble, gossip, and prophesy on every aspect of human and nonhuman life, offering a myriad of ingenious revisionist (and often mutually contradictory) versions of history, theology, and science, and a profusion of clashing—but equally unorthodox—commentaries on current events. We are told that the secretive summit meeting between Reagan and Gorbachev at Reykjavik was really about sending a joint mission to the "inner earth"; that we are the products of a genetic engineering experiment conducted by the "Nephilim," whose home planet periodically comes into orbit with Earth; that a race of lizards is guarding one of the major "time portals" into our dimension; and that our currently lobed pituitary glands were whole and spherical before they suffered radiation damage in an interstellar war.

In the flood of channeled material which has been published or delivered to "live" audiences in the last two decades, there is much indeed that is trivial, contradictory, and confusing. The authors of much of this material make claims which, while not necessarily untrue or fraudulent, are difficult or impossible for the reader to verify. There are, however, a number of other channeled documents which address issues more immediately relevant to the human condition. The best of these writings are not only coherent and plausible, but eloquently persuasive and sometimes disarmingly moving.

The worldview which is emerging from these channeled documents, though by no means wholly consistent, has a distinctive core which owes much to Buddhism, Vedanta, and New Thought, among other traditions. The synthesis is a fresh one, however, and by its emphasis on the creative potential of the human species and by its promise of a quantum transformation in consciousness, offers hope in an era of disintegrating social structures. For many New Agers, this material rivals the Scriptures of historical religions in its inspirational value.

Our aim will be to examine this body of literature and to identify its salient themes. Perhaps this effort will serve as a preliminary step toward understanding the philosophic underpinnings of the New Age movement and toward defining it in relation to its ideological predecessors and contemporaries.

The Sources

The principal sources whose ideas we shall consider are "Seth" and the posthumous William James, "Emmanuel," "Bartholomew," "Lazaris," "Raphael," "Alexander," "Mission Control," the author of *A Course in Miracles*, and the "angelic beings" whose ideas appear in *Return of the Bird Tribes*, and *Starseed, The Third Millennium*.

"Seth" is an "energy personality essence" who spoke through author Jane Roberts Butts for twenty years. Roberts produced a book or two almost every year from 1970 to 1984 based on her husband's transcripts of taped sessions with Seth. One of Roberts's books, *The After-death Journal of an American Philosopher: The World View of William James* (1978), presumably issued from a kind of gestalt combining Roberts's consciousness with that of the late William James. It was written "automatically" on the typewriter; "the manuscript came with its own title and structure," according to Roberts; "all I did was add chapter headings."[11]

"Emmanuel" appeared to Pat Rodegast in the early seventies, two years after she began to experience "inner visions" during her daily meditation sessions. He appeared then, as he does now, as a "being of golden light." He describes himself as having "been through all of the human manifestations that you are experiencing," and as having eventually evolved to the point "when I could say truly and completely, 'I am one with God.'"[12] He was then "released from [his] reincarnational cycles," and returns now as "the voice of your remembering."

"Bartholomew" is the name Stanford University graduate Mary-Margaret Moore decided to give to "the vast, alive, compassionate, wise energy field" that she tapped into in 1977 during a hypnosis session designed to relieve her back problems. When asked what the voice wished to be called it answered "Anything you want, but remember— the formless has no name, being beyond the realm of name and form." The manner in which this energy wishes to be viewed by his/her/its audience can be inferred from the titles of the three books he has inspired: *I Come As A Brother* (1984), *From the Heart of a Gentle Brother* (1987), and *Reflections of an Elder Brother* (1989).

Jach Pursel is a former insurance salesman who habitually fell asleep halfway through his daily meditation session, until one day in 1974 he began to see things: a forest, a cabin, and, in the cabin, a man. "He was gentle. I was not afraid. He talked to me. I remembered every word."[13] This was the beginning of an ongoing enterprise in which "a spark of love and light" who calls himself "Lazaris" speaks through Jach to individuals in private sessions or to audiences as large as seven-hundred people. During the weekend seminars Pursel sometimes sits in an armchair at the front of the room while members of the audience line up on either side and file by one by one, often quietly sobbing, to receive a healing touch and a hug from Lazaris. When asked how he could know so much about us and our world, Lazaris replied, "we are outside the set of 'all those who have *ever* been physical,' and therefore we are capable of a deeper level of insight about you and your world."[14]

Ken Carey had "gone back to the land" with his family and was living without electricity, plumbing, radio, television, or newspapers when, in the winter of 1978-79, during an eleven-day period, he "received" *The Starseed Transmissions*. While the author is officially "Raphael," the voice shifts two-thirds of the way through the book and declares "I am the Christ . . . I came to you first through the man named Jesus." Carey was told that *Starseed Transmissions* was the first in a series, and many New Age readers eagerly awaited the promised works which appeared in *Vision* (1985), *The Return of the Bird Tribes* (1988), and *Starseed: The Third Millennium* (1991). Carey claims that the 1988 work is based on a series of encounters he had with angels who had been involved in the founding of the Iroquois League and that the most recent transmissions came from a collective of speakers who each entered the discussion whenever it touched on his or her area of specialization.

"Alexander" was named by Ramon Stevens when the entity who had begun to communicate with him in December 1986 through his home computer announced that "names are meaningless."[15] Alexander declares that he has "chosen to communicate with the earth plane at this time both to further my own work and to cast a fond look back at my beloved earth."[16] A 384-page book entitled *Divine Grace* issued from the collaborative endeavor between Stevens and Alexander. It was delivered "as a seamless whole" over a period of about ninety-two hours. It is suspiciously similar in tone and content to the Seth and William James works, which are favorites of Stevens, and may well come to be considered an eloquent update to Jane Roberts's contribution.

E.T. 101, The Cosmic Instruction Manual, is a caustic satire on the state of planet Earth which was channeled by Diana Luppi, a columnist for *The Santa Fe Reporter*. The source refers to itself as "Mission Control," which is the "tactical arm of the extraterrestrial mission to Planet Earth." It claims to be a "post-new age publication" and the "remedial" version of an original manual written for "Planetary Liberation Organization" volunteers, the current edition being "specifically designed for this planetary system—a system which defies all true rationality and has raised dysfunctionality to an art form."[17]

A Course in Miracles is a twelve-hundred-page document which was transcribed between 1965 and 1973 by Helen Schucman, then Assistant to the head of the Psychology Department at Presbyterian Hospital in New York and Associate Professor of Medical Psychology at Columbia University's College of Physicians and Surgeons. After a series of vivid dreams and visionary fantasies, Schucman, who was born Jewish and considered herself an atheist, began to hear an inner voice. One day the voice said: "This is a course in miracles. Please take notes."[18] That night she received what was to become the first page of the first volume, or *Text* of a "course" designed to "remove the blocks to the awareness of love's presence, which is your natural inheritance." The *Course* presents a thought system based on the twin ideas that "nothing real can be threatened" and that "nothing unreal exists." "Miracles" are defined as shifts in perception which allow an individual to relinquish illusions based on guilt and fear. The curriculum includes daily lessons aimed at correcting perceptions based on illusion. Although *A Course in Miracles* is published anonymously, the text strongly implies that its source is the biblical Christ.

The Content

Although from different sources, in terms both of their fleshly vehicles and—presumably—of their otherworldly origins, these revelations echo each other in tone and content. Taken as a whole, this body of literature offers an analysis of the human condition and a set of prescriptions designed to assist humanity in discovering its true destiny. The argument is based on certain assumptions about the nature of reality which the authors present from their presumably enhanced perspective. In essence, they seek to convince us that we are not who we think we are and that much of our suffering can be traced to our mistaken identity; they are here to "awaken" and "remind" us. Their tone is passionate and imploring, sometimes angry, ironic, or admonishing, but more often (and especially in Emmanuel's books) tender and reassuring. In most cases it is respectful, but as a parent would comfort or admonish a well-meaning but misguided child. The style is personal and direct. One of the striking similarities between the documents is the fact that the reader is addressed in the second person: "You believe that," "you forget that," "your sciences tell you that. . . ."

The new oracles have a decidedly egalitarian bent. The grassroots quality of the New Age movement is reflected in the phenomenon of a collection of unaffiliated upstarts speaking with authority of our origins and our destiny, of the nature of the atom and the nature of the soul, and of the relationship between the two. Not only the medium but the message is democratic. Among the themes emerging from this body of literature is a critique both of modernity and of religion for denying "the inherent wisdom and goodness of the Self" and for encouraging dependence on external sources of authority. The antiestablishment flavor of the material is reminiscent of Spiritualism, whose uncompromisingly individualistic proponents "denounced the authority of churches over believers, of governments over citizens, of doctors over patients, of masters over slaves, and, most of all, of men over women."[19]

Among the basic assumptions shared by these disembodied luminaries is that the human flesh and blood experience in time and space is but one mode among many of experiencing consciousness. They take for granted the primacy of consciousness over matter and the immanence of the divine—what Willis Harmann has called "transcendental monism."[20] Much of the channeled material offers an explanation for the fact that the nature of reality is not obvious to human beings.

The thrust of the argument is psychological. Undoubtedly the most prominent theme of the material as a whole is the problematic role which fear plays in human psychology. Various explanations are proffered for this, according to the particular metaphor used to describe the human condition. Humanity is considered to have drifted into a deep sleep, to have severed its connection with its source and fallen under the "spell of matter"—to have forgotten its origins and identity. Most of the sources imply that this even was a necessary sacrifice, a calculated risk taken in the context of a grand adventure, an expedition, an experiment in which a new species is given free will that it may consciously—by trial and error, as it were—develop values compatible with "All That Is."[21]

Several of the authors indicate that the alienation experienced by humanity need not have been so severe. Ken Carey's sources refer to an "unexpected delay in achieving human cooperation,"[22] to the "unexpected strength of materiality's influence on human consciousness."[23] All of the voices acknowledge the suffering which humanity has experienced on this leg of its journey and seek to alleviate or eliminate it. This they presumably hope to accomplish by convincing us of the illusory nature of this reality and by suggesting practices designed to lift the spell, to awaken us from the dream, to remind us of our "vastness" and our divinity (or, at the very least, to broaden our frame of reference).

Segments of the Seth, Alexander, and Ken Carey material, as well the E.T. 101 manual, adopt a polemic and sometimes strident tone. Science, medicine, psychology and religion, government and the military—indeed, modernity and history itself—are all targets of criticism. According to the authors of *Return of the Bird Tribes*, "Historical people have no vision—they turn their perception over to others. They refuse to give credibility to any experience not easily put into words." In healthy, non-historical societies, the oracles maintain, "people are not overly concerned with other people's fantasies."[24]

Several of the oracles identify the alienation of mankind from Nature as one of the primary maladies of modern civilization. In a chapter entitled, "Why Conservatives Hate the Natural World and Love War," Alexander argues that "the core motive of the conservative in your society is fear of impulses" and "a deep and unconscious resentment against the natural order" with all of its unpredictability and spontaneity. "The drooling over the profit potential of a redwood forest," Alexander continues, "is the surface patina on the deeper, unconscious determination to eliminate the daily insult the natural world presents." This, according to Alexander, explains the conservative's "fascination with firepower and the instruments of death" and why the world of finance, "with its balance sheets, interest rates and promptly maturing CDs, is [for the conservative] a welcome haven from the chaos of the rest of human society and of the natural world."[25]

The authors of E.T. 101 take advantage of their position to be blunt and to the point:

> The people of this planet stand in total arrogance, adamantly denying their omnipresence. They declare their separation from themselves, each other, and all life while passing this off as an

act of humility. Humility is not denial; *separation* is denial. And maintaining that separation is the ultimate act of pride.[26]

"Fear is Your Only Enemy"

Despite the marked contrast between its tone and that of the infinitely patient voice of Emmanuel or the more philosophic irony of some of the other authors, Mission Control's logic rests on the same foundation:

> We have noticed that you pretend to value truth on this planet. . . . Meanwhile, all you are doing is paying global lip service to it. . . . You have no idea what truth really is.
>
> How the obvious has escaped you is a tedious story. The abridged version of it amounts to this: You embraced fear. After that unholy act, it has been downhill ever since. Fear is the first lie, the lie that tells you that you are separated from the whole.[27]

According to Mission Control this psychological event is at the root of the repetitiveness of history:

> The true reason for the nauseating up-and-down motion of all human civilizations . . . is that their ideologies, political systems, and social structures have failed to liberate anybody— especially themselves—from the vice-like grip of fear.[28]

Alexander agrees that "Fear is your only enemy" and predicts that its reign is due to end soon:

> Yours is the age of struggle between fear and reason, fear and understanding. The outcome of this struggle, which is *in no way predetermined*, will lead to your world's entering a new age of peace and harmony, or to its destruction.[29]

Portions of the writings we are considering aim to place the contemporary human dilemma within the context of a "history of consciousness." Seth and Alexander, in particular, trace the thought patterns characteristic of modernity to the appearance of the ego, which they would have us believe occurred when Jehovah arose from the "amoral, unprincipled rubble" of the Roman and Greek civilizations.[30]

"An Experiment in Consciousness"

In *Seth Speaks*, published in 1970, the author describes a reorientation of the psyche which occurred with the rise of Judaism and set the stage for the birth of modernity:

> Man desired in one way to step out of himself, out of the framework in which he had his psychological existence, to try new

challenges, to step out of a mode of consciousness into another. He wanted to study the process of his own consciousness. In one way this meant a giant separation from the inner spontaneity that had given him both peace and security. On the other hand, it offered a new creativity, in his terms.[31]

Seth describes the process by which the human ego differentiated itself from the "cosmic whole," thus providing the "inner self" with feedback and with a new perspective. The ego, however, "having its birth from within," and "frightened that it [will] dissolve back into the inner self . . . must always boast of its independence while maintaining the nagging certainty of its inner origin."[32]

According to Seth, this experiment in consciousness found expression in the early Hebrew god who "became a symbol of man's unleashed ego," using thunder, lightning and fire—the forces of nature—to destroy his enemies. The reorientation "necessitated an arbitrary division between the subject and the perceiver—nature and man—and brought about a situation in which the species came to consider itself apart from the rest of existence."[33] The consciousness of the species "had to pretend to dislike and disown [its] source in the same way that an adolescent may momentarily turn aside from its parents in order to encourage independence."[34]

One of the consequences of this orientation, according to this argument, was a polarization of the sexes. Characteristics that were considered female became associated with nature—the source from which humanity wished to distance itself—and this resulted in a civilization in which intellect, knowledge, and fact were divorced from intuition, emotion, and revelation and the latter devalued. This divorce has caused a fragmentation in our sense of identity: we distrust and disown part of our own experience. As we distrust Nature, so we distrust our own nature and our very Source, for, in the words of the posthumous James: "It is impossible to trust God and distrust the self, or vice versa."[35]

"A Fall into the Illusion of Separation"

The authors of *Starseed Transmissions* have their own version of the divorce. They explain that humanity's "fall into the illusion of separation" occurred through "a simple lack of faith," through "a loss of confidence in the absolute perfection of universal design."[36] Cutting itself off from "central control," as it were, consciousness became contracted and fearful and began to defend its individualized identity with "unnecessary and cumbersome ego structures." According to Raphael, we were not "born into sin," but we constantly recreate the barriers to the clarity and direction which are our inheritance by substituting intellectual ratiocination for inner guidance:

> Daily you commit Original Sin; daily you eat of the forbidden fruit, and it is from moment to moment that you keep yourself imprisoned by allowing a dubious rational thought process to come between you and your immediate sensing of God's will. This was the hesitation that led to your initial fall from grace, and it is the same hesitation that keeps you now in a fallen state. There should rightly be no interval between the determination of the need to take action and the implementation of that action. This rational interference is what caused you to stumble in your primal dance of trust with God.[37]

The Ego: Its Affinity for Fear, Guilt, the Intellect and the Past

Raphael contends that human consciousness, like everything in the manifested universe, "from the smallest subatomic particle to the greatest galaxy," has its existence in two dimensions, and is actually continually "flash[ing] on and off" in each one. In the "Fallen" state of consciousness this process continues but unconsciously: "you find yourself trapped with your awareness on one side only, while the actual substance of your being continues to function on both sides."[38] The ego, as this truncated identity, attempts to compensate for its handicap by carrying past experiences into the present and calcifying them into limiting thought-structures. Raphael defines Satan in terms of guilt and fear: "Energized by your past-oriented guilt and your future-oriented fear, he follows you around like some vast cosmic shadow."[39] We are "designed to be filled to the full with the energy and power of Life." Instead,

> Like two enormous rips in the side, guilt and fear allow the precious life-substance to escape, leaving you withered, ineffectual and short-lived, all the while, using your own life-substance to energize everything that you fear.[40]

Emmanuel has his own metaphors for the human experience:

> The truth is that you, as Gods, have agreed to enter into the world of illusion, to know the nature of love from outside itself, thus remembering love within darkness."[41]

This darkness, insists Emmanuel, "needs to be seen, not as a threat, but as an opportunity to love,"[42] for,

One knows love by living without it.
One finds love by realizing one has lost it.[43]

Emmanuel speaks of the "physical earthly plane" as a "school-room" or a "learning situation,"[44] and of "the separation" in terms of "forgetting," but forgetting with a purpose.[45] He refers to our experience as separate and fragmented beings as an illusion, albeit a necessary one:

You promised to remain here in the illusion,
believing the illusion,
until what you have come to accomplish
has been done.
Then you can release it.[46]

As for "the Fall":

In truth, one never "fell" at all.
The Fall is a symbol of human experience.
As a symbol it is the forgetting
of the initial purpose of individuation,
getting lost in distraction,
the intent of the soul forgotten.
How could one leave God?
One *is* God.[47]

Nonetheless, he admits, "each one of you, when you are born, con-tracts a fatal disease. It is fear."[48] This is because "there is a natural fear and resistance when one does not recall one's own Divinity."[49] Echoing one of the principal themes that runs through the channeled material we have chosen to examine, Emmanuel links fear with the past and the intellect: "The moment fear takes hold you are locked into what has been." "Fear is tenacious. The intellect will cling to fear. It has created it."[50] He comments on the "subtle inroads" fear can make in our lives, especially when cloaked in reason: "If you no longer allow fear to step blatantly before you and shout of cataclysm, it will creep behind you and whisper something reasonable in your ear. Be wary of rational thinking, reasonable supposition."[51]

A *Course in Miracles* adopts a different tone, one more dramatic and determined. The *Course* teaches that "the separation," "the detour into fear,"[52] is based on the distorted beliefs that "what God created can be changed by your own mind"; that "what is perfect can be rendered imperfect or lacking"; that "you can distort the creations of God" (including yourself); and that "you can create yourself."[53] With relentless logic, the author of the *Course* seeks to convince us that we live in a nightmare of our own creation, identifying with the separate ego in a vengeful world.

According to the *Course*, the ego is by definition alienated:

The ego is the mind's belief that it is completely on its own.[54]

The ego is guilt-ridden:

If the ego is the symbol of the separation, it is also the symbol of guilt. Guilt is more than merely not of God. It is the symbol of attack on God. This is a totally meaningless concept except to the ego, but do not underestimate the power of the ego's belief in it. This is the belief from which all guilt really stems. . . . The ego is the part of the mind that believes in division. How could part of God detach itself without believing it is attacking Him? . . . The ego believes that this is what you did because it believes that it *is* you.[55]

It is fearful:

The ego is quite literally a fearful thought. However ridiculous the idea of attacking God may be to the sane mind, never forget that the ego is not sane. It represents a delusional system, and speaks for it. Listening to the ego's voice means that you believe it is possible to attack God, and that a part of Him has been torn away by you. Fear of retaliation from without follows, because the severity of the guilt is so acute that it must be projected.[56]

It cannot distinguish the present from the past:

The ego has a strange notion of time, . . . The ego invests heavily in the past, and in the end believes that the past is the only aspect of time that is meaningful. Remember that its emphasis on guilt enables it to ensure its continuity by making the future like the past, and thus avoiding the present. "Now" has no meaning to the ego. The present merely reminds it of past hurts, and it reacts to the present as if it *were* the past.[57]

The ego's investment in the past keeps us locked into a vicious cycle:

The shadowy figures from the past are precisely what you must escape. They are not real, and have no hold over you unless you bring them with you. They carry the spots of pain in your minds, directing you to attack in the present in retaliation for a past that is no more. And this decision is one of future pain.[58]

A Better Way

A Course in Miracles is designed to teach the student to short-circuit the vicious circle created when fear fights its phantasms from the past in the all-too-familiar process described succinctly by Bartholomew: "You get hurt, you hurt them, they hurt you back, and so it goes endlessly."[59]

"Eventually everyone begins to recognize, however dimly, that there *must* be a better way," the author of the *Course* states.[60] This recognition becomes the turning point in the healing process, leading to the reawakening of spiritual vision and to the decision to bring the mind into the service of the spirit. The *Course* teaches that "only the mind can create."[61] Correction therefore "belongs at the thought level."[62] When the mind is in service to the ego it misperceives and miscreates. The fearful world which we experience as a result is but a dream which holds us spellbound. Our salvation from the guilt and fear which consequently plague us lies in taking back the power that we have given this illusion, in awakening to our true identity and in realizing that there is, in truth, nothing to fear.

The fact that we create our own reality does not mean that we are not created by god:

> It is as needful that you recognize you made the world you see, as that you recognize that you did not create yourself. *They are the same mistake.*[63]

Choose Only Love

In the face of the ego's tenacious insistence to the contrary, the student of *A Course in Miracles* is reminded that every encounter with hostility is an opportunity for release from the illusion that life is a "bloody battlefield." If you perceive yourself as under attack from your brother, you are forgetting who you are and who he is. In reality, "when a brother acts insanely, he is offering you an opportunity to bless him. You need the blessing you can offer him. There is no way for you to have it except by giving it."[64] In this situation one can choose love or fear. One can identify with the ego which "always tries to preserve conflict"[65] and choose to counterattack, or one can see through the illusion and respond with love and forgiveness, knowing that, "In reality you are perfectly unaffected by all expressions of lack of love," for Peace is "an attribute *in* you."[66]

According to the *Course*, "no belief is neutral,"[67] and "there are no idle thoughts." Because "all thinking produces form at some level,"[69] every belief, every thought, every action is either loving or fearful.

This idea reappears in Emmanuel's works:

Every moment of your life
you are offered the opportunity
to choose—
love or fear,
to treat the earth
or to soar the heavens.[70]

According to Emmanuel,

Illusion has formed your human world. Your world cannot
return to Light until all parts of it are remembered in the
essence of Perfect Love. . . . As you love, you transform what
had not been loved back into its essence. When the last soul
remembers to choose love, your entire planet will return Home,
and with it every star you see in the heavens.[71]

In Bartholomew's terms,

Your cells have two choices—they can either expand or con-
tract. Safety does not lie in contraction. Something has gone
awry because you have *believed* that *contraction* could make you
safe. Now practice the opposite. Start believing that it is *expansion* that will make you safe, and then be the observer. . . . If
love is "the way," how can you possible think that giving love
under any circumstance could hurt you? It is the love moving
out of your cellular body that keeps you safe. When you choose
extension, *your love has the ability to change your environment!*[72]

Mind Creates Reality

The uncanny echo effect encountered in studying the channeled material is nowhere more evident than in the various authors' discussions of
the New Age dictum: "You create your own reality."
According to Alexander,

You have been given a wondrous creation, the fiction of a physical world, through which to learn lessons available nowhere
else in all the realms of existence. You create the world . . . This
is the lesson of this age. You create your own reality. It is the
final lesson of the earth plane.[73]

The author of *A Course in Miracle* is eager to impress upon us the
importance of consciously controlling our thoughts:

Few appreciate the real power of the mind, and no one remains
fully aware of it all the time. However, if you hope to spare

yourself from fear there are some things you must realize, and realize fully. The mind is very powerful, and never loses its creative force. It never sleeps. Every instant it is creating. It is hard to recognize that thought and belief combine into a power surge that can literally move mountains. It appears at first glance that to believe such power about yourself is arrogant, but that is not the real reason you do not believe it. You prefer to believe that your thoughts cannot exert real influence because you are actually afraid of them.[74]

Bartholomew addresses the same question:

My friends, again and again I ask you to take seriously the power of your magnificent, wonderful mind. You are afraid of your mind, of what it has created, because you believe you have created a separated world that is no longer joined with God. . . . But God only allows the free play of your awareness to create—*within certain limits*. The Divine within you has placed limits past which you cannot go. You are afraid of being responsible for what your mind creates, so you try not to pay attention to your thoughts . . . [but] you go on creating right out of the shadow part of your unconscious. When you really understand this, you can choose to stay in the moment and remember what it is you really wish to create.[75]

Raphael also alludes both to the role human creativity is designed to play when humanity awakens to its divinity and to the limits which have been placed on it in the interim.

It is important that you recognize the creative power of your thoughts, a power far beyond your knowledge. As long as you think negatively, Life will only allow you a token share of consciousness, lest you spread disease. But the moment your thoughts are of Love and Life, the Lord will flood you with His own awareness and you will enjoy the wonder of His perception. You were born to share in His creative power. The stuff of which you are made is so charged with the ability to create that everything you touch comes to life; every thought, every identity, every image.[76]

Lazaris frames the issue of our necessarily (if temporarily) circumscribed power to create in a humorous light, linking it to the [apparent] existence of time:

Though you often treat it like an enemy, time is actually a grand and valuable friend. It is the cushion between the thoughts you think and the reality they create. Time is the net under the high-wire act of life. When you make a mistake, it catches you. You bounce rather than crash. Time gives you a second chance.

Without time, your life would be insane. Imagine for a moment that every thought you think happens *now*! As you are reading these words, an errant thought about sickness or death occurs, and you never even get to finish the sentence . . . As you drive to work you have a stray thought about an auto accident and "you didn't even see them coming." In a business meeting your mind wanders and in the midst of a daydream you vanish! Life would be insane![77]

Prescription: "Trust God," "Go Within," "Live in the Now"

The metaphors are different, the level of analysis varies, but in essence the message is one. The mission of these New Age oracles is to awaken us from the illusion that we are alone and trapped in a cruel world and to remind us of the "Vastness" and our proper place within it. The first step in this process is to love and forgive ourselves, to let go of fear, one moment at a time, and to trust—to trust Nature, to trust God, and to trust our Selves.

Emmanuel assures us that there is nothing to fear in the universe:

Rest yourself
in the reality of God's eternal
and everlasting Presence
and know
that there are plans deeper,
there is consciousness wiser,
loving hearts far more powerful,
than any that walk your earth.
I bless you
with the awareness
of your eternal safety.
You are safe. You are safe.
You are infinitely safe.
Oh, my dears,
if I could only make it possible
for you to experience the loving, gentle kindness
of the universe,
the balance, the fairness,
the sweetness and the joy,

there would never another moment of fear
in your entire lives.
And this is true.[78]

Emmanuel teaches that enlightenment is letting go of fear, that, without fear, "your life would appear to you as it truly is; a wondrous adventure, excitement, delight, creation,"[79] for "suffering is not the way to Light and to Heaven. Pleasure is," and "if you judge pleasure in the context of the illusion then you lose the pleasure and it keeps you in the schoolroom longer.[80] According to Alexander, "Divine Grace," which is "the blessed bed of love and intent . . . on which your existence rests" is "raucous, exuberant, vital, active and inquisitive . . . char[ging] head-long into physical expression with joy and abandon."[81] And so are we urged to celebrate life and to explore a myriad of opportunities for growth, expression, and fulfillment.

We are enjoined to wean ourselves from the habit of listening to others, to "take our power back" from all the external sources of author-ity to which we have given it.[82] We are encouraged to turn our gaze within, to meditate, to "turn our face to the divine," to "pray without ceasing,"[83] and to explore those "greater dimensions of [our] being" through our dreams.[84]

Alexander, Raphael, Seth, and Bartholomew emphasize the need to acknowledge all feelings and impulses. "It is very important," Seth insists, "that you understand the true innocence of *all* feelings, for each of them, if left alone and followed, will lead you back to the reality of love."[85] According to Alexander, impulses are "the constant telegrams from the depths of your very being, your Divine Grace, asking for respect and consideration."[86] He warns of the danger of repressing them: "Impulses have a bad name in your time. You have been taught that they are untrustworthy urgings from Hell or the id, to be ignored, repressed, stomped out of consciousness lest you accede to them and commit unspeakable atrocities."[87] In reality, the channeled voices insist, the individual's "natural inclinations and learnings" are the "built-in impetus and guidance" which is our heritage.[88] According to the posthu-mous William James, "science, religion and psychology have unfortu-nately, with the best of intentions, muddled that inner knowledge and separated man from the practical use of inner direction."[89] Having sought nourishment first from "the frosted confections of packaged faith," and then from the scientist's "plain doctrines—the new bread and butter for the masses," humanity found—or so argues James—that "neither nourishment greatly nourishes."[90]

James's prescription is to throw away all theories that tell us not to trust our own spontaneous, creative impulses, and to "ride the thrust" of our own desire until we are lifted "into communion with that far vaster desire and power" where individual desire is not annihilated, but "activated" at a higher level.[91] Most of the channeled sources agree with James that by learning to trust those wider dimensions of our own consciousness, by cultivating the habit of "listening to the heart," and "living in the Now," we become receptive to the hints and suggestions, to the shouts of encouragement coming from a "dimly sensed" "symbolic grandstand" on another level of being. Bartholomew assures us that "you are not on this journey by yourself," that "you have no idea of the amount of help waiting to rush in when humility is present and the plea is made, 'Teach me.'"[92]

"All That Is," in the words of Alexander, "does not cut you loose in a cold, dark universe but forever cushions your life with the eternal flow of Divine Grace."[93] Furthermore, "it seeks not to impose its values on you but to set you free to learn, through your experience, that you are happiest when you live by its values."[94] "In choosing to do God's will," affirms Raphael, "you will discover the only true freedom."[95]

The vision which the new oracles hold for humanity seems to be two-fold. For the duration of the earth experience, they presage a mass "awakening" by that portion of humanity which is ready to make the leap, and an unprecedented creative collaboration between spirit and matter.[96] When the spell is lifted, according to Ken Carey's sources, "the world becomes your paint and canvas," for "the true human is designed to aid the development of all life forms, drawing out their ever-expanding capacities to provide always fuller revelations of that which lies in the heart of God."[97] When this happens, they assure us,

> You will remember the songs that call forth root and tree, flower and cloud, leaf and stone; but more than this . . . you will remember how to sing the songs that only awakened humans can sing, songs that will bring metals up from the ground, songs that will attract elements, minerals, materials, from across great distances, through the power of their true names.[98]

In time this will yield to a homecoming in which "you will dissolve your planet back into Light, which, in truth, it never left."[99]

Conclusion

Against the background noise of a disintegrating cultural consensus, New Agers are crafting a polyphonic revelation proclaiming that the time has come for humanity to be delivered from its self-imposed prison. If healing is the principal agenda of the New Age, as Albanese and Lucas have argued,[100] the new oracles would suggest that it involves a radically new self-definition and a conscious reidentification with the Whole. The channeled sources offer a detailed diagnosis of the ailment which afflicts the modern psyche. It is guilt (self-loathing) and fear. Its etiology is the repudiation by an adolescent consciousness of its cosmic parent, the ego's denial of its divine source. The oracles' prescription is a reconciliation with Self and Spirit, a "reawakening" from the illusion of separation—a "remembering" of one's own divinity, of one's participation in Its wondrous creativity.

On the one hand, the new cosmology is a radically democratic one. It is the creed of the mystic; "Follow your own heart to God." It urges humans to stop giving their power away and asserts that "you create your own reality." It declares just as unequivocally, on the other hand, that "you do not create yourself" and thus points to a cosmic hierarchy. The individual has free will but is fulfilled only when consciously choosing in alignment with Spirit. Until he/she creates in accordance with the Divine Plan, his/her creations are "miscreations," left on the drafting table, as it were, as part of a learning experience. According to New Age oracles, the earth experience is but "an adventure in consciousness" designed to gestate "a fully conscious participatory species"[101] or a schoolroom in which God's children are discovering who they are by discovering who they are not.

Some of the channeled sources claim to be graduates of the human schoolroom, elder brothers who return to provide solace and encouragement;[102] others refer to themselves as "angelic messengers . . . ordained at the inception of the human project to awaken you when the time was right."[103] In several cases, the voice appears to be that of the biblical Christ.[104] The sources take great pains to emphasize their essential commonality with humanity, depicting themselves in some cases as the parts of ourselves who agreed to stay on-board the ship to monitor our plunge into forgetfulness.[105]

There is a certain paradox inherent in the phenomenon of voices from on high cautioning "slumbering" humans against seeking a higher authority than their own hearts. When a godlike messenger appears to remind us that we, too, are Gods, the temptation is to become awed by the messenger and to miss the essence of his teaching. Several of the oracles comment on the unfortunate consequences that ensued when Christianity encountered this challenge.[106]

The New Age oracles seem determined to help present-day seekers avoid this pitfall by speaking through individuals who are acting in collaboration with anonymous, invisible counterparts. The emphasis is necessarily on the teachings themselves, teachings which, for the New Ager, have implications as revolutionary as those of the biblical Christ. As the late Joseph Campbell remarked toward the end of his life: "Now, it's not a nice thing to say, but it's not good for institutions if people find that it's all within themselves."[107] Or, as Lazaris put it: "That reality is a self-generated illusion is the greatest liberating concept in your world today. Knowing that we either caused it or allowed it is a grand source of power—liberating power."[108]

This is the quintessential heresy, for it defines humanity not as inherently sinful, but as sovereign and creative children of God who have chosen, in the name of adventure and exploration, to sacrifice—for a time—their divine identity and don the costume of a limited creature. The new cosmology is equally antithetical to the self-definition of "modern" man, whose existence is predicated on his independence from the divine parent, and to that of the Fundamentalist Christian who sees the human predicament as defined by sin, and not "the illusion of the separate ego."[109] It challenges Eastern religion's dismissal of individualism and desire, and enjoins the more mainstream Christian to take seriously Jesus' promise that we, too, would someday heal the blind and raise the dead. It insists that trusting Self and trusting God, that being true to one's own heart and serving the All, are necessary conditions one for the other. "Repentance," according to Ken Carey's angelic partners, "is a doorway, not an abode; it is of value only when it inspires healthy change and passes on into a state of restored self-acceptance." For "to value yourself less than God values you is not humility, it is price of a most destructive nature."[110]

The new cosmology posits a friendlier universe than that of the Fundamentalist and one with a great deal more soul than that of the scientist. Indeed, the effusive optimism of many of the new oracles contrasts dramatically with mainstream society's sober assessment of humanity's future. Their vision of mankind's relationship to the cosmos is rooted in a set of epistemological assumptions radically divergent from those of modernity. For the New Ager the point of power is within; vast realms of information are available to the individual who forsakes an exclusive reliance on the five senses for revelation—be it intuited, dreamt or channeled. As a methodology, revelation poses a challenge to logical deduction and the repeatable experiment—to any system which circumvents the inherent, inner guidance which the new cosmology posits. As a bridge between Creator and created, between the mystic and the Mystery, it dispels the alienation of a humanity which has forgotten its connection with the Whole. If a fear born of the illusion of separation is the central problem in the thought system of the new oracles, and if "revelation induces complete but temporary suspension of doubt and fear," as *A Course in Miracles* declares, then, in a very literal sense, for those New Agers who are inspired by channeling, the medium is the message.

Chapter 10

Employing the New Age: Training Seminars

———————————————— *Glenn A. Rupert*

> We look within to find our own individual self and universal source. That source has been called the inner self, the Self, the hidden mind, the divine spark, the Divine Ego, the Great I Am, God, and Essence. Some say that the very purpose of human existence is to get acquainted with your own essential qualities and express them in your daily activities. Whether it is the purpose of life or not, it is a fine definition of personal creativity: living every moment from your essence.

The above passage is not quoted from a book on metaphysics, Eastern philosophy, or one authored by Shirley MacLaine. It is from *Creativity in Business*, written by Michael Ray, a professor at Stanford Business School.[1] Ray has taught a course of the same name for several years. Its purpose is to teach students how to use New Age metaphysical teachings to increase their creativity in a business setting. The contents of the book include meditation techniques, yoga exercises, and even specific instructions on how to contact a personal "Spirit Guide."[2]

Creativity in Business is a clear example of how the American business community is becoming more and more receptive to New Age practices when used to increase productivity and efficiency. In July of 1986 officials from IBM, AT&T, and General Motors met in New Mexico to discuss how metaphysics, the occult, and Hindu mysticism could possibly aid businessmen in an increasingly competitive marketplace.[3]

Even the U.S. Army has joined in. The slogan "Be All You Can Be" is a direct result of a commission established to explore the possibility of creating a "New Age Army."[4] Interest in New Age training methods became so significant in the armed services that in 1984 a project was undertaken by the National Research Council which would investigate these phenomena in detail. Their final report, published in 1988, concluded that there is "no scientific justification from research conducted over a period of 130 years for the existence of parapsychological phenomena," and recommended no further funding for such projects.[5] Proponents of these programs have been outraged at the NRC's findings and have heavily contested the 1988 report.[6]

The most popular vehicle for implementing these beliefs in the workplace has been different training seminars, easily available to any interested company. Over the past decade GM, Lockheed, Scott Paper, and a host of other major corporations have paid for their personnel to attend seminars which, many critics argue, rely upon unconventional religious beliefs to maximize participants' productivity. The trend is undoubtedly significant; it has been estimated that American corporations collectively spend about $4 billion per year on New Age seminars.[7] What exactly are these seminars, and what is their appeal?

Many of the doctrines of these groups are taken from the New Age movement. According to the *New York Times*, "One concept commonly transmitted in the sessions by 'human potential' groups is that because man is a deity equal to God he can do no wrong; thus there is no sin, no reason for guilt in life."[8] Beliefs such as this obviously cross the line from the secular to the spiritual.

Some of the seminars in question are more "religious" than others. Two of the most prominent, Lifespring and Transformational Technologies, are similar to *est*, a self-help seminar of the seventies. Like their predecessor, they maintain a purposefully secular appearance, although many underlying religious beliefs show through. Insight Seminars, part of the California-based Movement for Spiritual Inner Awareness (MSIA—pronounced "messiah"), has a more visible emphasis on spiritual growth. Both WISE and Sterling Management, subsidiaries of the Church of Scientology, have distinct religious overtones. Beyond these few major organizations there exists a host of smaller-scale operations which also rely on a spiritual or religious foundation. Whether or not these seminars are a part of the New Age movement is open to debate. However, all of the abovementioned organizations are based upon beliefs which are clearly identified with the movement.

The Seminars

In the 1980s big names such as Boeing, Lockheed, and General Electric attracted attention to human potential seminars. In the 1970s celebrities such as John Denver and Cloris Leachman spotlighted Erhard Seminars Training, known as *est*. In many ways, the roots of the corporate seminars lie with *est*, so a discussion of that seminar is fitting. Founded by Werner Erhard (born Jack Rosenberg) in 1971, *est* gained tremendous publicity, both because of its many celebrity disciples and for the extreme methods used to make trainees face their fears. *Est* quickly built a loyal following, which soon became its most valuable marketing asset. Promised life changing experiences, uncounted numbers of people enrolled in the seminar. It was dissolved by Erhard in 1984, after enrollment had all but disappeared.

According to a prominent psychiatric journal, the training consisted of "psychoanalytic theory, Jungian psychology, transactional analysis, and Eastern philosophy."[9] The eventual goal of the training was to solve the participant's problems by making him or her "get it." "Getting it" was described as overcoming whatever was holding him or her back, or causing the problems. Dramatic procedures were held to be the only reliable system to make the trainee realize what that problem was. Once the problem was identified, *est* philosophy was introduced to overcome it.

Essentially, *est* subjects were taught that each person individually creates his or her own reality. Consequently, each person is entirely responsible for the circumstances in which he lives. The key to successful living is to alter your reality so that you are able to succeed or be happy. That is "getting it."

The methods used by *est* trainers were considered by many to be excessively confrontational. Throughout the training, subjects were deprived of sleep, alcohol, tobacco, and regular bathroom use. Although these may seem to be extreme measures, they were used to show the participants that they need not be dependent upon any of these "necessities." The *est* trainees were also put through several confrontational exercises which forced them to face their greatest fears (inadequacy, fear of rejection, etc.).[10]

An organization which is quite similar to *est* is Lifespring, founded by former *est* trainer John Hanley in 1974. Both Erhard and Hanley began their careers at Mind Dynamics, a training organization which also used draconian methods to force its subjects to face their fears.[11]

Although Hanley rejects the assertion that his program is a duplicate of *est*, certain similarities are striking. Both use authoritarian trainers who enforce numerous rules upon the trainees. Both require applause after any of the trainees "share" with the group, and both emphasize feeling and action, rather than ratiocintion. In addition, the alumni of the two programs are fiercely loyal and recruit heavily, making marketing expenses unnecessary.[12] Interestingly enough, Lifespring graduates have long praised the organization with statements such as "it changed my life," but have never been able to say specifically how it did so.[13]

Lifespring began as *est* did, by catering to individuals as a human potential seminar. However, Hanley has recently been trying to expand the appeal of Lifespring to business as well. In the past, Lifespring has offered courses to corporate employees, but Hanley is not satisfied with his limited appeal to businesses. He has been trying for ten years to adapt Lifespring to a corporate environment, but has had only limited success.[14]

Despite Lifespring's limited success in dealing with business, other training programs have flourished. After Erhard dissolved *est* in 1984, he created two new organizations: the Forum, again targeting individuals, and Transformational Technologies Inc., created specifically to train corporate managers. Transformational Technologies is not a seminar per se, rather, it is a licensing firm which commissions other companies to train managers. The price for a franchise is currently $20,000, plus 8 percent of all receipts. There are currently over fifty licensees which pulled in over $15 million for Erhard in 1986. To date, TTI's licensees have trained employees from GM, GE, Procter and Gamble, TRW, Lockheed, and numerous others.[15] In addition, Erhard has been working with Soviet managers and educational leaders since 1981, at the invitation of the Soviet government and with the approval of the State Department.[16]

Although Erhard denies that there is any *est* left in TTI, he and his staff are ambiguous about exactly what TTI is. For example, Erhard's friend Jim Selman, who actually runs TTI, said that "when we talk management technology, what we are talking about is a rigorously tested and challenged body of distinction for having access to whatever the phenomenon of management really is."[17] In an interview with *Industry Week* concerning TTI, Erhard alluded to his estian philosophy by stating that "if you want a breakthrough in people's actions, you have to alter the way the world occurs for them."[18] Exactly how much of *est* is left in TTI is a mystery, but Erhard's past philosophies should not be overlooked.

A more obvious example of a "New Age" training seminar is Insight Seminars, part of the Movement for Spiritual Inner Awareness. The California based MSIA was founded by John-Roger (Hinkins) in the early seventies. John-Roger is the self-proclaimed carrier of the Mystical Traveller Consciousness, a spiritual entity that has purportedly come in many incarnations to bring man closer to his divine potential. MSIA is a New Age organization which launched Insight Seminars in 1978.

Russell Bishop was a trainer with Lifespring and an MSIA minister before he left Lifespring to start Insight Seminars for John-Roger. According to Bishop, Insight was developed from "standard curriculum in education" to "work with people on the practical day-to-day stuff of life . . . the intention was to do a very basic practical seminar, devoid of spiritual or religious intent."[19]

In practice, however, great difficulty arose in divorcing Insight from its spiritual heritage. Immediately preceding the first Insight meeting, John-Roger called a meeting with ministers to tell them of a meeting in Hawaii from which he had just returned. It was a "four-day meeting up on a high mountain peak . . . called through the Traveller Consciousness. . . ." It was attended by "the spiritual hierarchy of the planet," which included Jesus, Krishna, and other "ascended masters."[20]

He told his ministers that the new Insight program would provide them with an opportunity to "look at the teachings of the Traveller . . . in a different perspective." At the beginning of each Insight training session, the trainers and assistants would purify themselves and the room by "calling in the Light," repeating the following:

> Father-Mother God, we ask just now to be placed in the light of the Holy Spirit, through John-Roger, the Mystical Traveller, Preceptor Consciousness, and we ask that only that for which is for the highest good be brought forth.

According to a former Insight trainer Michael Hesse, "What we were doing in Insight was trying to spread the Traveller's message. . . . Anyone who got involved quickly learned that there was a spiritual side."[21]

Since its inception, Insight Seminars has grown considerably. It has now been split into Insight I, II, and III. Each level progresses further into John-Roger's mystical teachings. To date, well over fifty thousand people have participated in Insight training. Philip Lippincott, president and CEO of Scott Paper, has been captivated by John-Roger's teachings, and has offered the insight training to all employees at company expense. Some of the other companies which have sent employees include Lockheed, McDonnell Douglas, Chemical Bank, and the U.S. Social Security Administration. In the words of an Insight graduate, "it gave me a sense of purpose and clarity about my life. . . . It was magical, an incredible high." At $450 per person tuition, it ought to be.[22]

Never a stranger to controversy, the Church of Scientology has also sought to capitalize on this current trend in employee training. Considered by many to be a New Age cult, L. Ron Hubbard's organization teaches that humans are descended from a race of gods named "Thetans," and have digressed from that state because negative "engrams" (bad memories) have become imprinted on their personalities. According to Hubbard, these engrams must be removed through certain Scientology procedures. It is only after such treatment that humans can realize their full, entirely divine, potential.

Insofar as maximizing human potential is concerned, Scientology doctrine is essentially the same as that of the seminars examined above. If fears and inhibitions are confronted and dealt with, thus removed, performance should be significantly enhanced. This is what est and the others seek to accomplish, and this is what Scientology claims to do as well.

The Church of Scientology oversees two organizations which train corporate employees: WISE and Sterling Management. WISE is a nonprofit organization which claims to have Volkswagen as a customer. Sterling Management is a fledgling consulting firm which has only served smaller companies so far.

Interestingly enough, before Werner Erhard founded est, he was a member of this religious organization. In light of this, similarities in the techniques used by est and Scientology seminars are all the more striking. Two of these are known as "bullbaiting" and "confronts." When a participant is bullbaited, he or she must remain expressionless while other trainees and instructors harass him with taunts and insults. A confront consists of two subjects who are forced to stare unflinchingly into each other's eyes until released. Not everyone responds positively to these exercises.

In 1987 employees of Megaplex, an Atlanta answering service, were encouraged to attend a Scientology seminar at company expense. According to one employee, the seminar began as a normal management course, but soon plunged deep into the doctrines of Scientology. This, coupled with the dramatic training methods used, caused a hostile reaction to the training. This employee quit almost immediately after the conclusion of the training, realizing that rejecting the training would mean that she would have no future at this company. Another Megaplex worker described the seminar as "one of the most traumatic experiences of my life. It was essentially brainwashing." But their supervisor disagreed. According to him, profits went up "phenomenally." He also stated that he would continue to urge employees to attend the training.[23]

Benefits and Dangers

The incident at Megaplex raises the question of what the advantages and drawbacks are for a company that decides to send its employees to a human potential seminar? The potential advantages consist of more productive and motivated employees, resulting in greater efficiency and higher profits. The risks taken by the company consist of possible psychological harm to the participants or infringement of personal religious beliefs, either of which could result in lawsuits or dismissal of the worker who was sent for training in the first place.

Although *est* never significantly trained employees at companies' expense, far more psychological research has been done on it than on any of the more recent seminars. Much of this work was conducted on participants who claimed to have been psychologically harmed by the est training.[24] Lifespring, which uses nearly identical methods and teachings, has been in court quite frequently. Since it was founded in 1974, Lifespring has dealt with over thirty lawsuits, or about two per year. Almost all of these have claimed that the training caused severe psychosis, and six have claimed that trainees died as a direct result of the training. Most of these suits have been settled out of court, for as much as $500,000 each. Legal expenses constitute Lifespring's most significant expense at $1 million per year, small considering that the organization grosses over $24 million in an identical time period.[25]

Although the lawsuits mentioned above have been filed because of the alleged psychological dangers of human potential seminars, the primary obstacle to the seminars' widespread use in business has to do with religious freedom. Several legal battles have ensued over the religious contents of these seminars as well. Soon after Steven Hiatt, an employee of Walker Chevrolet in Tacoma, Washington, refused to participate in "New Age Thinking to Increase Dealership Profitability," he was fired from his job. Hiatt said that he refused to participate because the seminar stressed self-will rather than God's will. Hiatt's former employer claimed that he was let go because of job performance, not because of the seminar. In a similar case in Georgia, William Gleason, former manager of human resources at a Firestone Tire and Rubber Co. plant, refused to implement a seminar which he said constituted a form of "secular humanism." Firestone has since reached an out of court settlement with Gleason.[26]

The best known example of resistance to human potential training occurred in 1987 in California. Pacific Bell, the telephone company which services the San Francisco area, sought to revise its image and performance by training all employees at Leadership Development, a training program founded by Charles Krone. In the past, Krone has also trained employees for Du Pont and Scott Paper. Krone has claimed "to make people rethink the way they think, and hence arrive at new ways of solving problems." As part of his training program, Krone developed his own vocabulary. It is indecipherable to outsiders, since it applies specifically to his philosophies, based on the teachings of Armenian mystic Georges Gurdjieff. In his two years of working with Pac Bell, Krone certainly left his impression. In the 1987 statement of principles of the company, "interaction" was defined as:

> the continuous ability to engage with the connectedness and relatedness that exists and potentially exists, which is essential for the creations necessary to maintain and enhance viability of ourselves and the organization of which we are a part.[27]

Upper level management was very satisfied with the results of the training. Meetings gained a better sense of direction, relations between managers improved, and productivity in company operations increased by 23 percent.[28]

Although Pac Bell was not directly confronted by its employees, resentment towards the training mounted. Between the obscure jargon, the Krone representatives who sat in at meetings to make sure agendas and note-taking procedures were followed, and the pressure to adapt and fit in to the new way of thinking, Pac Bell workers had had enough. After a story about the discontent broke in the San Francisco *Chronicle*, the Public Utilities Commission began a full-scale investigation. Guaranteed anonymity, employees aired their grievances.

Originally, Pac Bell had planned to spend $147 million on the Krone training, while passing the expense along to the rate payers. After the PUC investigation, only $40 million had been spent, $25 million of which was charged to the stockholders. Pac Bell quickly stopped the training. As a result of the fiasco, the company president took an early retirement and the main proponent of the program, Vice President Lee Cox, was demoted to a subsidiary.[29] The image of the company was certainly transformed, but not as intended.

As with any investment which businesses must consider, human potential seminars offer numerous benefits, but also present many risks. In several instances, companies have demonstrated improved performance after their employees participated in these types of training sessions. The fact that corporations spend astronomical sums to train their employees demonstrate that businessmen consider these seminars a risk worth taking.

However, controversy has always surrounded them, from the

infancy of est to the disaster of Pac Bell's "Kroning." Some people have been psychologically harmed, and many have successfully sued these training organizations and their employers, especially if attendance has been required. Also, many of these seminars are based in distinctly religious doctrines, which may infringe upon the First Amendment rights of an employee required to attend. In short, the benefits offered by these programs may not be worth their long-range cost.

Chapter 11

An Update on Neopagan Witchcraft in America[1]

——————— *Aidan A. Kelly*

The Neopagan movement in America and other English-speaking nations parallels the New Age movement in some ways, differs sharply from it in others, and overlaps it in some minor ways. Comparing and contrasting these two movements, which are roughly the same size, will help clarify the nature of the New Age movement as such.

The Neopagan Witchcraft movement in America is a new religion that, like almost all new religions, claims to be an old religion. It does, as one might expect, emphasize the reality and learnability of magic (or at least parapsychology) as one of its central concepts; but in almost every other way it is a surprise to anyone who comes from the study of "witchcraft" in some other context. I have demonstrated[2] from the available evidence, which is copious, that the religion actually began in September 1939 on the south coast of England, as an attempt to reconstruct the medieval Witchcraft religion described by Margaret Murray. The founding members included a retired British civil servant, Gerald Brosseau Gardner; a locally prominent homeowner and socialite, Dorothy Clutterbuck Fordham; probably Dolores North, later known for her regular column in a British occult magazine similar to *Fate*; the occult novelist Louis Wilkinson; and probably others in the occult circles of London and southern England.

Gardner took over leadership of the group, perhaps by default, around the end of World War II, and began developing it in a direction that would better meet his own sexual needs. At this point the religion began to take on characteristics typical of many libertarian movements of the past, especially a focus on sexuality as sacramental, which it has retained ever since. (In fairness to all I must stress, however, that this emphasis on sexuality remains theoretical and inspirational, not something expressed in practice.)

136

Gardner began writing and publishing in the late 1940s and 1950s, and his books have been primary documents of the movement ever since. After Doreen Valiente was initiated in 1953, she threw her excellent writing skills into the service of the movement and produced the text of the *Book of Shadows* (in practice, the liturgical manual) that is essentially the one now used by the movement throughout the world. She has described her contributions modestly but accurately in her recent *The Rebirth of Witchcraft*. During this period, the Craft began to assimilate the *White Goddess* theology of Robert Graves, who revived many theories about a matriarchal period in European prehistory, theories that had long ago been discarded by scholars as inadequate to deal with the known facts.

The Craft continued to grow steadily in England. Gardner initiated a great many new priestesses from 1957 until his death in 1964, and these carried on the Craft enthusiastically. Raymond Buckland, after a long correspondence with Gardner, was initiated in 1963 in Perth, Scotland, by Monique Wilson (Lady Olwen), from whom much of the Craft in America descends, since Buckland brought the Craft back to the USA and, with his wife Rosemary as High Priestess, founded the New York coven in Bayside, Long Island. Almost all the "official" Gardnerians in America are descendants of that coven.

However, these "official" Gardnerians are now a very small fraction of the whole movement, largely because they operate according to a fairly strict interpretation of the rules that were gradually established by the New York coven in its steadily expanding text of the *Book of Shadows*. Most American Witches, being spiritually akin to anarchists, libertarians, and other proponents of radical theories, regard the Gardnerian concept of "orthodox Witchcraft" as an oxymoron and practice the Craft much more flexibly, using whatever they like from the Gardnerian repertoire and creating whatever else they need from whatever looks useful in past or present religions. Many of these claim to descend from some other "tradition" of Witchcraft independent of Gardner, but such claims are almost entirely historically specious. The rare exceptions are the few individuals, such as Victor Anderson (from whom Starhawk derived most of her information), who had practiced a pre-Gardnerian, folk-magic type of Witchcraft, but that was so different from Gardnerianism, in both praxis and theology, that they can be considered to be the same religion only by a great stretch of the imagination.

Since the late 1960s, enough information on the theory and praxis of Gardnerian-style Witchcraft has been available in books that any small group who wanted to could train themselves as a coven. Those who did so could be, and were, recognized as members of the same religion when they later met other Witches; and more and more covens began this way as more and more books because available in the 1970s and 1980s. We have now reached a stage where an attempt to diagram the proliferation of Craft covens and traditions resembles a jungle.

The Neopagan and New Age movements share so many characteristics that one might expect their members to feel a certain amount of kinship, but in fact they do not. Both, for example, are extremely interested in developing personal psychic abilities as much as possible. However, New Agers eschew the terms "magic" and "witchcraft." New Age bookstores almost never have sections labeled "Magic" or "Witchcraft." Instead, books on magic are shelved with works on spiritual disciplines, such as Yoga; and books on Neopagan Witchcraft are shelved with books on "Women's Studies."

Second, many typical New Age assumptions about religion are generally rejected by Neopagans. Many New Agers assume, for example, that all religions are ultimately the same; that spirituality is best learned by sitting at the feet of a master teacher or guru, preferably from one of the Eastern religions; and that a new world teacher or messiah will appear to usher in the New Age. Neopagans, in contrast, like the Craft specifically because it is so different from the Puritanical, world-hating Christianity that continues to be prominent in American culture. Most Neopagans believe in karma and reincarnation; but they reject the dualism of the Eastern traditions, and consider the guarantee of rebirth to be the *reward* for their spiritual practices. They generally believe that they are practicing an ancient folk religion, whether as a survival or a revival; and, being focused on the pagan religions of the past, they are not particularly interested in a New Age in the future.

They also generally believe that many religions are radically and irreconcilably different from each other; that the "reformed" religions (especially the monotheistic ones) established by Moses, Jesus, Mohammed, the Buddha, and similar figures were NOT an improvement over the folk religions that they replaced; and that if there were a single worldwide religion in the future, it might very well repress human freedom even more than the Roman Catholic Church did in Europe during the "Burning Times." Hence, Neopagans are not at all receptive to teachers and teachings from the monotheistic religions nor to any from the East, with the possible exception of Hinduism, which is seen (whether accurately or not) as an "unreformed" polytheism similar to that of the Greco-Roman world; Neopagans tend to be especially interested in Tantric traditions, since these can easily be seen as a type of magic parallel to that developed in he Western occult tradition.

Neopagans also generally tend to be extremely antiauthoritarian (whatever the reasons in personal backgrounds might be), and so are not at all inclined to accept the personal authority of any guru. The authoritarian structure of the official Gardnerian Witches in America might then seem to be anomalous, but it alone is a reason why there are at least ten times as many Gardnerian-imitating Witches as official Gardnerians in the Neopagan movement.

Neopagan Witches also operate with an ethic that forbids them to accept money for initiating anyone or for training anyone in the essential practices of the Craft as a religion. Neopagan festivals have grown into national gatherings, often of several thousand people, during the last decade, but they have remained quite inexpensive, since no one is attempting to make a profit from them. As a result of this ethic, Neopagans look upon the "Psychic Fairs" and "New Age Expos" with open contempt and tend to consider most New Age gurus to be money-hungry frauds who are exploiting the public by charging exorbitant fees for spiritual practices that can be learned for free within a Neopagan coven. This attitude does not, of course, encourage New Agers to look kindly upon Neopagans.

There are, nevertheless, a minority among the Neopagan Witches who consider themselves to be members of the New Age movement as well. This minority tends to consist of the Witches who understand fairly clearly not only that the Gardnerian Witchcraft movement is a new religion, but also that this newness makes it the potential equal of every other religion in the world, since every religion begins as a new religion at some time and place. If the Craft is a new religion, then it can be understood as contributing to the spiritual growth in the modern world that is leading up to the New Age, whenever and however that might begin.

For scholars, the Craft is even more difficult to study than most new religions are because of its custom of "secrecy" (actually, privacy): there are no central registries for covens, and many covens still do not let their existence be known to anyone except their own members. Nevertheless, by dint of diligence and ingenuity, one can get a fairly reliable assessment of the nature and size of the movement. For the sake of manageability, I take as my starting point the data presented by Margot Adler in the second edition of her *Drawing Down the Moon*, which is the only competent journalistic investigation of the movement to date.

Size of the Movement

How large is the Neopagan movement now? We can estimate its size by four independent methods.

First, because almost all members of the movement are avid readers (see later discussion), we can estimate the movement's size from the sales of certain key books. For example, extrapolating from the sales of the Llewellyn reprint of Israel Regardie's *The Golden Dawn*, Gordon Melton arrived at a figure of 40,000 serious adherents (essentially, members of covens) in the early 1980s. Similarly, Adler's *Drawing Down the Moon* and Starhawk's *The Spiral Dance* had each sold about 50,000 copies by the end of 1985.

Second, we can extrapolate from festival attendance. Even limiting the category of festivals to those that last two days or more (in contrast to local Sabbats—the "traditional" Witch gatherings on the solstices, equinoxes, and Celtic cross-quarter days—which tend to be one-day affairs), there were 44 such annual festivals in 1986, and are closer to 100 now. Attendance can differ widely, but all reports estimate average attendance at between 100 and 200. Adler reports that the responses to her 1985 questionnaire showed that less than 10 percent of American Witches attend festivals at all. *Harvest* magazine learned from a survey of several hundred of its readers in 1986 that, of the readers who attended festivals: they attended an average of two festivals a year; a third of them belonged to covens; a third were solitary Witches; and a third were Neopagans, but not Witches (i.e., did not consider themselves to be initiated or "ordained"). We can therefore carry out some rough calculations, as follows: Total annual attendance at festivals: 5,000 to 20,000; divided by average attendance of two festivals: 2,500 to 10,000; only a third are members of covens: 833 to 3,333.

Only 10 percent of all Witches go to festivals, but covens probably average ten members; so the number of covens would also range from 833 to 3,333, and the number of individuals who consider themselves to be Witches would range from 8,330 to 33,330, plus perhaps another 10 percent for the solitaries, giving roughly 9,000 to 36,000.

Around each coven there tends to be a circle of other people who are somewhat less involved: friends who come to Sabbats, students in study groups, and other noninitiates who are following Neopaganism as their primary spiritual path. The ratio can and does range widely, but a reasonable estimate would be about 100 such Neopagans for every coven. This gives an estimate for the total number of Neopagans in America of between 83,000 and 333,000.

Third, we can extrapolate from the sizes of the mailing lists at the two national contact centers for the Neopagan movement. Valerie Voigt, coordinator of the Pagan, Occult, and Witchcraft Special Interest Group of American Mensa, has between 6,000 and 8,000 "contact cards" in her files. Some percentage of these represents individual "seekers" looking for a coven to contact, and some unknown percentage of covens is not represented here at all, but Valerie estimates that many or most of these cards are the contact persons for covens; if we suppose that "many" means a third, this would give 2,000 to 4,000 covens in America. Similarly, *Circle Network News* has a circulation of about 15,000; even if (as a guess) only 10-20 percent of these are coven subscriptions, that would still indicate 1,500 to 3,000 covens in America.

Fourth, I have been building up a database of the covens, groves, periodicals, and High Priestesses whose existence I have been able to discover for some years now, trying to get a more direct estimate of the size of the movement. After regularly consolidating entries, winnowing out duplications, and deleting dubious data, I have ended up recently with almost 800 entries; and even if these were all functioning covens, this still looks low in comparison to the preceding estimates. However, if I focus on a locale for which I have reliable firsthand information, so that I am reasonably sure that I have heard about the existence of almost all the Craft covens in that locale, then I can get an estimate of the average number of covens relative to total population. One such locale is the San Francisco Bay area, for which I find an average of 1.1 covens per 100,000 population. Looking at, say, St. Louis, Missouri, where I know the Craft has been growing since the late 1960s, I find a much lower ratio, which is almost certainly the result of my having incomplete data. There are around twenty other metropolitan areas where the data give a ratio approaching that for the San Francisco area; thus, the latter is not an anomaly. Hence, if we can extend the ratio for the San Francisco area to the entire country (that is, if the ratio is the same in rural as in metropolitan areas), we would get an estimate of about 3,000 covens in America, and hence again of about 300,000 practicing Neopagans.

To give some perspective on the preceding numbers, let me note that Adler points out that there are only 40,000 Quakers and about 180,000 Unitarians in the USA. Hence, the Neopagan Witchcraft movement is no longer a tiny "cult." Still, one may ask why, if the Craft is that large, it is not more obvious on the American scene. I can offer several reasons.

First, the emphasis on secrecy in the Craft, now the largest component of the overall Neopagan movement, has created a barrier against blatant publicity seeking; no such barrier exists for most New Age movements, which tend to be only 1-10 percent of the size of the Craft movement.

Second, newspapers normally report only bad news, not good news. Except for minor stories about harassment, Congressional bills, and the like, the Craft has been doing little except growing quietly, healthily, and creatively, none of which attracts the interest of reporters.

Third, the Neopagan movement does not produce the kind of flashy, powerful gurus who would attract the attention of reporters. "Power-tripping" is discouraged by the Craft ethic against charging money for performing initiations, by the emphasis on secrecy, and by the generally egalitarian and antiauthoritarian ethos of the movement. Even relatively famous and politically active Craft priestesses like Z. Budapest and Starhawk are personally quiet-living, level-headed, modest, and sensible people.

To close this section, let me note that the Craft movement is growing both absolutely and relative to the overall Neopagan movement. In the mid-1970s, the Witches were only one of many varieties of Neopaganism. In the mid-1980s, Adler observed, "Wiccan organizations have come to the foreground as the primary form of Neopaganism in America, and these organizations now dominate the discussion." The Craft thus seems to be meeting the religious needs of the Neopagan movement much better than the other forms of Neopaganism had been.

Let us therefore next look to see what these "Wiccan organizations" are.

National Organizations and Events

A National Church for Witches. A standing joke among Neopagans is that trying to organize a national church for Witches is a lot like trying to get anarchists to get together to elect someone as Anarch. Despite the inherent difficulty of such organizing, the need for a national umbrella organization has been obvious to Neopagan Witches for the last twenty years, and there has been a certain amount of success in creating one. Nevertheless, there is still no single organization that serves as a national church for the Neopagan Witchcraft movement.

Adler lists a dozen nonprofit religious corporations, most with interstate or national membership, and at least twice as many similar but unincorporated not-for-profit associations. However, almost all of these function in practice as local coordinating councils, not as national bodies. The only body that was designed to be national in scope is the Covenant of the Goddess, which was incorporated in California in 1975; it is able to function because its structure is based on the principle of the autonomy of local congregations (adapted from the charter of the United Church of Christ, and which the founding delegates agreed on as the cornerstone of the Covenant). Its membership peaked at 70 to 80 covens in the mid-1980s (that is, at only 2-5 percent of all the covens in America), and its leaders are currently considering how to inspire it to begin growing again.

Part of the difficulty that COG faces is that it is hard to persuade covens that membership will confer benefits that are worth the hard work at the annual meetings of hammering out consensus agreements on policy in a gathering where opinions range across a spectrum as broad as that from the Orthodox to the Reconstructionists in Judaism. Hence, there have recently been attempts to create a church structure that is less diverse and therefore, perhaps, more viable in practice. One of these is the New Wiccan Church, which admits only covens that hew fairly close to Gardnerian orthodoxy; it now has branches in four states.

Seminary Training. The Craft movement has evolved far enough that the need for formal seminary training is beginning to be felt fairly widely. For one thing, many Wiccans would like to serve as chaplains in prisons, hospitals, and the military, but find that route is closed to them as long as they lack the normal academic credentials that, say, Protestant ministers usually have. At least two Wiccan seminaries have been founded during the last decade, one in New Hampshire, one in Wisconsin. One difficulty here is that Craft training and ordination now takes place, in most Craft traditions, only within covens and under oaths of secrecy. It is not in the least obvious how these procedures could be transformed and transferred to an academic classroom.

Curiously, most professional training of Neopagan Witches takes place in Unitarian seminaries; dozens of Wiccan Priestesses have graduated from Unitarian seminaries during the past decade. As a result, despite the growing dismay of the more conservative Unitarians, there has started to be a significant overlap of membership between the Craft and the Unitarian Universalist Association. The Covenant of Unitarian Universalist Pagans was founded about 1985, and in 1990 had sixty chapters throughout the United States. William Schulz, President of the national UU Church, has written that there has been "a religious revolution" in the UU Church, and that, "to put it in symbolic terms, Ashtar, the Goddess, has been issued invitation where formerly only Lord Jehovah dared to tread." Adler goes on to say, "the Unitarian Church remains one of the only places that Pagans and women involved with Goddess religion can enter the organized ministry."

Festivals have proliferated since the very first ones in 1977. Adler listed more than fifty in 1985, and the number is now approaching one hundred. To these gatherings, which may last up to a week, come Neopagans and Witches of all varieties and traditions from all over the USA, Canada, and elsewhere, although the majority of attendees at most festivals are local. This phenomenon has further decentralized the Craft, making it more accessible to people in general. There are now many

Neopagans whose primary activity consists of attendance at national and local festivals, who do not belong to a coven, and who are not subject to the authority of a High Priestess. In this sense the festivals are one force (among others) working toward creating a genuine laity in the Neopagan Craft movement, which in the past had sometimes seemed to be all chiefs and no braves. "Festivals have completely changed the face of the Pagan movement . . . have created a national Pagan community, a body of nationally shared chants, dances, stories, and ritual techniques. They have even led to the creation of a different type of ritual process—one that permits a large group to experience ecstatic states and a powerful sense of religious communion."[2]

Public Sanctuaries and Temples. Another trend in the Neopagan movement is toward the establishing of sanctuaries and temples. There are a small but growing number (now about a dozen) nature sanctuaries: land permanently dedicated to be used only for worship of nature deities. These are not open to the general public,[2] but can be used by visiting Neopagans and friends who have been properly vouched for. The major use of the land is for Sabbats during warm weather, but the sanctuaries tend to be available also for any uses compatible with the Neopagan ethos, e.g., for spiritual development retreats. Some of the groups who maintain such sanctuaries have recently begun attempting full-scale reconstruction of Greek, Roman, or other ancient pagan religious observances.

The temples, in contrast, are actually what most Americans would call a church: a building dedicated for use as a place of worship and where there is a weekly liturgy (usually on Friday or Saturday night, rather than Sunday morning) to which anyone can come simply by walking in. This is considered a radical innovation, and not necessarily a welcome one, by many in the Craft. To see why it is radical, consider the preexisting situation. The esbat of a coven is utterly private; in order even to hear that an esbat is going to occur, you need to know members of a coven well enough that you could be considered for membership yourself, and you could be invited to an esbat only with the permission of the coven's reigning elders. The rules for a coven's own Sabbat celebration are not much different. These coven activities often resemble a "floating craps game": you must be accepted as a member even to hear when and where the next meeting will occur.

Some Sabbats are more public. Such a Sabbat might be held in a rented hall or out in a park, many more friends would be invited to it, it would be mainly a gathering of the local covens, and it would typically (these days) be sponsored by the local Neopagan association to which the various covens belong; often one member coven will take responsibility for creating and carrying out the liturgy at a Sabbat, and this task will rotate through the local covens each year.[3] But these "open" Sabbats are not advertised, and to be invited to one, you must already be in contact with the sponsoring network. Similarly, the national festivals are not advertised except through the network of Neopagan publications, which are normally available only by subscription, though a few are beginning to be sold through bookstores.[4]

Hence, being able to look up a Neopagan Temple in the Yellow Pages, and simply walk in and participate in the weekly liturgy, is a vastly different experience from that of most Neopagans so far—so much so that a lively theological debate is going on in periodicals and at conferences about whether such Temple liturgies can be considered a kind of Craft liturgy or not. A well-attended conference, sponsored by the Aquarian Tabernacle Church in Seattle and devoted to debating the usefulness and acceptability of such public worship, was held just before the annual meeting of the Covenant of the Goddess, in the Seattle area, in 1990.

In any event, the Neopagan Temples[5] seem, even more than the festivals, to be creating a Neopagan laity: people who consider themselves to be members of the religion, but not clergy, and who therefore do not call themselves Witches. And whatever the word "witch" might mean to others in other contexts, it is clear that, to the members of the Neopagan movement, a Witch is a Neopagan clergyperson; and they do not use the word "Witch" with any other meaning.

Demography

Religious Background. Neopagans are not very different from the overall U.S. population in religious background; yet, the noticeable differences seem quite significant. Melton's figures from 1979 give:[6]

1. National: Protestant, 66.2 percent; Roman Catholic, 26.2 percent; Jewish, 3 percent; other, 4 percent.
2. Neopagans background: Protestant, 42.7 percent; Roman Catholic, 25.8 percent; Jewish, 6.2 percent; other, 25.3 percent.

Adler's 1985 sample, though small and not random, gives essentially the same distribution for Neopagans' background. We can see that Witches are *not* largely ex-Roman Catholics; many have guessed that Catholics' supposed love for ritual would draw them to the Craft, but this turns out to be dead wrong. In contrast, Witches are twice as likely as the general population to be from a Jewish background. Hence, in New York City (which is a third Jewish to begin with), the Craft movement could easily appear to an outsider to be a Jewish subculture, and Craft in-jokes about Hasidic Witches are not far from the mark. The fact is that Rachel's daughters are once again offering cakes and wine to the Queen of Heaven; and if the Jewish community wishes to stop this trend, it will have to offer genuine equality to women, for that is the central issue. There is even a significant movement to create a pagan or polytheistic Judaism—or to recreate it, since its proponents point out that such a "Judaism" clearly existed in the kingdoms of Israel and Judah before the reform of 621 B.C.E. that created Judaism as the state religion of Judah. "Polytheistic Judaism" may look like an oxymoron to those who define Judaism as monotheistic, but it is inherently no stranger a proposal than is Humanistic (nontheistic) Judaism, which seems to be flourishing.

Finally, Witches are more than six times as likely as the general public to be from a nonmainstream religious background; that is, a large fraction of them are from families whose background is in churches that in their own youth were attacked as being "cults." These would include Mormons, Spiritualists, Theosophists, New Thought, and other native American new religions. It may be that many who checked off "Protestant" on the questionnaires are actually from New Thought backgrounds, since the New Thought churches are no longer controversial.

Occupation. Conventional wisdom assumes that new religions attract only poor, weak, stupid, powerless, and generally socially unacceptable persons. My evolutionary model (see the beginning of "Theology and Sources of Recruiting Strength" below) proposes that new religions are created by precisely the same sort of persons who exercise creativity in all other fields, i.e., middle-class intellectuals, and that is what we find from Adler's data:

1. Of 195 responses to Adler's question on occupation, 94 are professional, another 38 in white-collar business positions.
2. Almost all are avid readers: hence, almost all are within the top 20% of the US population in literacy. (In fact, there is a very large overlap between Neopagans and science-fiction fandom.)
3. Of 195 responses to Adler's question on "How did you get to the Craft?" 115 mentioned books, reading, classes, or other intellectual pursuits.

Geographic Distribution. Even though Neopaganism considers itself to be a nature religion, its regard for nature is much more akin to Romanticism than to ancient paganism. It is far easier to be romantic about cows if you don't own any. Neopaganism appears to be a religion of city people, and of what Spectorsky labeled exurbanites: people who have moved from the city out into the country for noneconomic reasons. Furthermore, in my evolutionary model, we would expect to find people who create new religions to be much more prevalent in cities than in rural areas for precisely the same reasons (which I need not detail here) why creative people in all fields prefer cities to small towns and rural areas. If so, we would expect to find a positive correlation between population and the number of Neopagan groups; and this is, in fact, what we do find.

For example, if we look at the Neopagan journals and organizations listed by Adler, we find that 70 (or 65 percent) of the 108 journals, and 41 (or 62 percent) of the 66 organizations, are concentrated in the Boswash strip, around the Great Lakes, and in California, just as the general population is, and that the rest of the journals and organizations are spread fairly evenly over the rest of the country. In my own database of almost 800 entries (which you can examine in the last Appendix in my 1991 book), I find precisely the same pattern. That is, there are now Neopagan Witches in every state, including the "Bible Belt," where they are simply somewhat more secretive than in metropolitan areas.

Theology and Sources of Recruiting Strengths

In March 1986 I hypothesized that the creating of new religions is neither unusual nor pathological, but the ubiquitous normal state; that is, people create new religions whenever they are free to do so, in order to meet religious needs not being met by the current established churches. This hypothesis, like hypotheses about stellar evolution, cannot be tested by direct experiment; but it can be tested against the predictions that follow from it. Some of these, such as the fact that Neopagans tend to be middle-class intellectuals living in cities, have already been mentioned.

Freedom and Diversity. Adler comments that her book "is grounded in the view that reality is multiple and diverse. . . . Polytheism always includes monotheism. The reverse is not true." But, in fact, although almost all monotheistic church hierarchies have excluded polytheism, not all have; and monotheism as such need not, paradoxical as that may seem.

The quintessential question of Greek philosophy was whether the ultimate reality is one or many. The answer of Judaism, once monotheism had been invented by the Second Isaiah, is that God is both one and many, and the Books of the Law and the Prophets were created from that perspective. That is, until Judah was forced to adopt a confrontational theology by the Seleucids (after 198 B.C.E.), Jewish thought about the "gods" of other peoples was not that they were unreal or evil, but that they were the angels of the One God, in whose name they administered the Earth; and they believed other peoples' theologies to be wrong only in not correctly reflecting the arrangements of the Court of Heaven, in which court Satan served as the prosecuting attorney, as in the Book of Job. That there were a great many ways of being Jewish, all acceptable to other Jews, down to the middle of the first century C.E., resulted from this polyvalent theology.

The major loss to Judaism that resulted from the destruction of Jerusalem was, I believe, the loss of this ability to tolerate diversity. For the next 1,900 years, the two surviving forms of Judaism (the one we call Judaism and the one we call Christianity) emphasized only the oneness of God. The Neopagan movement is not alone in recognizing, but is almost unique in emphasizing, God's manyness: He is both singular and plural; they are both male and female. (If you doubt this, I invite you to look again closely at the names of God in Genesis 1-3.) Hence, a major strength of the Craft movement is its reemphasis of both theological and social pluralism; and the Jewish Witches who are attempting the recreation of a polytheistic Judaism are operating from this strength, not from a whim.

Theological Maturity. Partly because of writings by myself, Bonewits, Russell, and others, and partly because of maturity in the movement, Neopagan Witches are much less likely now than they were twenty years ago to believe that the Gardnerian foundational myth is literal history. The myth is essentially the story that Gardner was initiated into one of the last surviving covens in England, one that had preserved a pagan religion from the Middle Ages and ultimately, from the Stone Age. The newer or younger members are more likely to believe in the myth literally, but that is a pattern true of recent converts in all religions, not something peculiar to Neopagans. Feminist Witches are more likely than other Neopagan Witches to believe literally in some form of this myth, but among them also the decline of simplistic beliefs is evident from their writings.

Play and Paradox. A major reason for the strength of the Craft is that it has so far been able to maintain a dynamic balance between tradition and innovation. Indeed, the more conservative among the "official"

Gardnerians have been quite upset by recent revelations by Valiente and by myself of just how innovative Gardner was. As Adler says, "The Pagan community is one of the only spiritual communities that is exploring humor, joy, abandonment, even silliness and outrageousness as valid parts of spiritual experience." Although in their liturgical experiments Witches often reinvent the wheel, they also very often improve the wheel, in my experience. If the Vatican succeeds in its apparent plan to discourage liturgical experimentation among Roman Catholics, then the Witches will have that much less competition.

Men's Spirituality is another area in which the Neopagans are giving the mainstream religions some competition. Although Gerald Gardner was as homophobic as many Englishmen of his generation, and revealed that homophobia in some of his writings, the Gardnerians, like the Neopagan movement in general, accept gay men and women as full members with all the rights anyone else has. The First Officer (President) of the Covenant of the Goddess in 1986-87 was Michael Thorn, a gay man who heads an all-male gay Gardnerian coven in New York City.[7] The Craft gains great strength from the brilliant and competent people who are driven away from the "mainstream" churches because of their sexual orientation.

However, an even greater importance of this openness is that it has given rise in Pagan circles to a great deal of innovative discussion and work—deep psychological work—about Men's Mysteries, about male roles and expectations, about how to break free from the cultural stereotypes that threaten the health and sanity of all men in Western society. No work of equivalent importance was going on in any other context before the recent burgeoning of Robert Bly's influence, and I am not willing to assume that Bly has overtaken Neopagan thought on this topic.

The Divine as Feminine (which is not the same issue as divine plurality) is a topic on which some excellent theological work[8] is being done, but very little practical work, outside of the Neopagan movement. A major attraction of the Craft is its focus on the concept of the Goddess. I suspect the Craft is soon going to be challenged in this arena by the growing population of Hindus in America. I see no evidence that mainstream Christianity is attempting to deal with this topic. Only Andrew Greeley deals with it in a way that reaches the public, that is, in his novels, but he is a voice crying in the wilderness and a prophet without honor in his own country.

Mystical and Other Experiences. Historically mystics have been mistrusted by administrators; St. Teresa was canonized because of her adminis-

trative abilities, not because of her altered states of consciousness. But it
has now become clear that altered states are far more common than
almost anyone had previously thought. It is again Andrew Greeley who
has thrown down the gauntlet.[9] His research reveals that among Americans in general:

1. 60 percent reported ESP experiences;
2. 60 percent reported déjà vu experiences;
3. 25 percent reported clairvoyance;
4. 25 percent reported contact with the dead;
5. 20 percent reported out-of-body experiences;
6. 32 percent reported religious ecstasy.

Again, I see no evidence that mainstream churches are even pretending
to deal with such data or to meet the needs that are thus revealed. The
various magical religions, which train people in how to use and benefit
from such abilities and experiences, and of which the Neopagan
Witches are now the most important and fastest-growing, are thus being
left a clear field to walk away with whatever prizes there are to be won.

Social Service

Twelve-Step Program Involvement. A new mark of maturity in the Neopagan movement is that its members are becoming aware of the need to
provide the kinds of social services for themselves that other churches in
America routinely help provide. For example, problems of alcoholism,
substance abuse, and related kinds of compulsive behavior were just as
common among Neopagans in the 1970s as among any other group of
middle-class Americans, but there were no programs to deal with these
problems. The Twelve-Step programs—that is, Alcoholics Anonymous
and the dozens of other Anonymous fellowships patterned after it—in
theory define themselves as not being allied with any church, denomination, etc., as being open to people of any sort of religious persuasion.
But in historical fact, AA grew out of the Oxford Groups, which were an
Evangelical Christian fellowship, and in practice the vocabulary in
almost all Twelve-Step meetings is that of middle-American Protestant
Christianity, a vocabulary that people attracted to Neopaganism rarely
understand and always dislike.

In the late 1980s, various Neopagans who were aware of these problems, and who knew that AA functions quite well in non-Christian cultures around the world, more or less simultaneously began Neopagan
Twelve-Step meetings in many locations around the United States. It is

now common at festivals for a daily Twelve-Step meeting to be announced among the scheduled events. I anticipate that a national Neopagan Twelve-Step network will soon crystallize, and plans for the writing and publishing of Twelve-Step books written in a Neopagan vocabulary are in the works.

Involvement in Politics, Ecology, etc., is also a relatively new development, as Adler comments. Some of it stems from Starhawk's influence, some from the Feminist Witches, but it represents a maturity that simply did not exist in the 1970s. More and more Witches are realizing that their religious rights are guaranteed by the First Amendment, just like everyone else's, and so are becoming willing to speak out as identified Witches on questions of public policy, especially ones on which the Witches have their own views. There are indications that the Neopagans in some areas are beginning to forge a political alliance with the Greens, and I would expect the pressure they exert to begin influencing Democratic Party platforms within about a decade.

Ecumenical Contacts are also beginning to take place, within the ecumenical graduate seminaries, and on local Interfaith Councils, which I know has happened in Berkeley, Seattle, and New York. Pagan student groups are being formed on college and university campuses around the country, often sponsored by faculty members who are themselves Neopagan or at least understand what the movement is about. Craft spokespersons try to keep in regular contact with local police forces, to offer help when possible, but especially to educate the police about the nature of the Craft and emphasize that it is not "Satanic."

Let me conclude by emphasizing that I think the Neopagan Witches, for reasons indicated above, are rapidly going to become more and more visible, and more and more important, on the American scene, and that they are going to successfully challenge many long-standing assumptions of American society.

Chapter 12

The Evangelical Response to the New Age

—————————————————— *Irving Hexham*

Introduction: "There's No New Age"

Evangelist and writer Francis A. Schaeffer comments in his book *The Church at the End of the Twentieth Century*: "The evangelical church seems to specialize in being behind."[1] He explains that, in his experience, Evangelicals tend to catch on to an idea or concern some twenty to thirty years after it becomes popular in the secular world. In light of Schaeffer's comments it seems appropriate to begin by describing my own experience and involvement with both Evangelicals and the New Age.

In 1971, after completing an M.A. on the New Age Movement in Britain,[2] I approached several Evangelical publishers with a proposal for a book on the New Age. Without exception they told me that my subject was obscure and of no significance. Following these rejections I attempted to publish an article on the New Age in several Evangelical journals. Once again my work was rejected, and doubts were expressed about the accuracy of my observations.[3]

From the mid-1980s in North America, however, "the New Age movement" became a central Evangelical concern. This resulted from the appearance of alarmist Christian books, the publication by Benjamin Creme of a full page advertisement in seventeen major American newspapers proclaiming "the imminent appearance of the Christ (Maitreya) in 1982"[4] and the televising early in 1987 of "Out on a Limb" which told the story of actress Shirley MacLaine's spiritual pilgrimage.[5] Nevertheless, when I lectured at a Theological College[6] in London, May 1987, I was told by enthusiastic ordinands that "the New Age movement may be a fad in America but it won't catch on here." The students went on to vehemently deny that anyone in Britain was reading Shirley MacLaine's *Out on a Limb*.

Immediately after the lecture I visited Foyles Bookshop in central London where the sales lady told me that the prominently displayed *Out on a Limb* had been a bestseller for months. A year later British Evangelicals appear to have woken up to the New Age movement[7] as a result of reading various books published by American writers.[8]

These personal anecdotes illustrate the truth of Schaeffer's observations and raise serious questions about the Evangelical subculture. Many Evangelicals like to think of themselves a "prophetic" minority guided by the Bible to stand "outside" or "above" secular culture. In reality the majority of Evangelicals are more like timid sheep who only dare embrace an issue when they are sure they have the approval of the secular world.[9]

Evangelical Awareness of New Age Thought

The first Evangelical author to write about what was to become the New Age movement was, in fact, Francis Schaeffer. An acute observer of cultural trends, he correctly identified the cultural drift of contemporary Western society and sought to alert Evangelicals to what he saw as a threat to their faith.[10] Although his books became bestsellers, the Evangelical establishment chose to ignore Schaeffer's warnings, and many Evangelicals actually found him an embarrassment.[11] Unlike upwardly mobile Evangelical academics,[12] he never held a college appointment and was not looking over his shoulder for the approval of secular colleagues.[13] Rather, he contented himself with being an evangelist and Christian intellectual.[14] As a result his acute awareness of the structure of New Age thinking went unheeded.

Actually, Schaeffer had two advantages over later critics of the New Age. First, he had a profound, if intuitive, grasp of modern culture resulting from years of interaction with secular European intellectuals. Second, he drew upon the rich philosophic resources of the Dutch neo-Calvinist tradition.[15] This tradition provided him with a complex theoretical framework and view of history[16] that gave his hearers tools to interpret their world.

Building on Herman Dooyeweerd's analysis of Western thought, Schaeffer saw modern society locked in a bitter intellectual conflict between the ideal of science based on a mechanistic worldview, and the Romantic notion of free personality which, Dooyweerd argues, leads to anarchy. Schaeffer argued that this intellectual conflict would be resolved by a new cultural synthesis which completely separated questions of science and technology from questions about the meaning and purpose of human life. This development, he argued, would leave governments free to control society through technology while intellectuals, who ought to lead the resistance against these developments, would escape into a mysticism which freed them from political involvements. As a result, Schaeffer predicted and feared the emergence of a technological elite which would manipulate society[17] using religious mysticism[18] to provide a sense of transcendence based on pantheism.[19] No later Evangelical critics of the New Age have advanced on these basic concepts, although many have used them in a debased way.

The New Age Scare of the 1980s

The first Evangelical to publish a book explicitly dealing with New Age themes was Gary North whose *None Dare Call it Witchcraft* appeared in 1976.[20] At the time he did not mention the New Age movement by name. In 1988 North took what was, for him, the unusual step of reissuing a revised version of his book under the new title *Unholy Spirits: Occultism and New Age Humanism.*[21] In a footnote he explains he did not mention New Age thought in his original book because Christians were unfamiliar with the term.

Constance Cumbey and Dave Hunt, however, deserve the credit for awakening the Evangelical subculture from its dogmatic slumber to the existence of the New Age movement in 1983. Cumbey begins by drawing attention to the widespread influence of the New Age in her book *The Hidden Dangers of the Rainbow: The New Age Movement and the Coming Age of Barbarism*[22] but quickly loses academic credibility by her conspiracy theories, which seek to identify the New Age movement with a plot masterminded by Benjamin Creme, Theosophy, and Nazism.[23] Similarly, Dave Hunt, in *Peace, Prosperity and the Coming Holocaust: The New Age Movement in Prophecy,*[24] made equally apocalyptic claims warning Christians against the dangers of the New Age movement.

The first really serious, semischolarly Evangelical critique of the New Age movement was Douglas Groothuis's best-selling *Unmasking the New Age: Is There a New Religious Movement Trying to Transform Society?*[25] An essentially descriptive book, Groothuis attempts to give an overview of the New Age movement and Evangelical critique. This was followed two years later by a sequel, *Confronting the New Age: How to Resist a Growing Religious Movement,*[26] which adds little to his earlier discussion. More recently he has published *Revealing the New Age Jesus.*[27] Essentially, Groothuis outlines the basic beliefs of the New Age movement and then offers biblical objections.

The Band Wagon Effect

Following the publication of Groothuis's *Unmasking the New Age*, a host of copycat titles appeared.[28] Many of these claimed to be written by people who had worked within the New Age movement before their conversion to Evangelical Christianity, and are, in effect, testimonies. They follow a similar pattern: ensnarement by the New Age, gradual disillusionment, and conversion, followed by a desire to expose the evils of the movement. Few pretend to scholarship, although most throw in a few academic-sounding examples to add authority to their case. Needless to say, most of these books are sensational tracts with little real value.[29]

A different, and one of the better Evangelical, approaches to the New Age is found in the Berkeley-based Spiritual Counterfeits Project book *The New Age Rage: A Probing Analysis of the Newest Religious Craze,*[30] edited by Karen Hoyt. It contains a collection of essays examining various New Age beliefs. Written in an academic style, it is more scholarly than most Evangelical books on the subject yet, despite its academic tone, the book lacks rigor. As a result, it tends to be too academic for the average Church member but not scholarly enough for use in universities.

By far the best Evangelical work on the New Age is Russell Chandler's, *Understanding the New Age.*[31] Written by a highly successful Los Angeles journalist, it is both entertaining and accurate. It gives an excellent overview of various New Age groups, leaders, and movements, with perceptive comments. The major weakness of the book is that it is essentially descriptive and never really comes to grip with New Age claims.

Elliot Miller's *A Crash Course on the New Age Movement*[32] is hardly a crash course. Rather, it is an extended critique which supplements Chandler's more descriptive work. The book is easily readable and presents a balanced assessment of New Age views with Evangelical criticisms. The greatest value of this book is "Appendix B: Constance Cumbey's New Age Conspiracy Theory: A Summary Critique." For anyone troubled by Cumbey, Hunt, or similar conspiracy theorists, this section of the book alone makes it worth buying.

Easy reading, however, is the only justification for Walter Martin's *The New Age Cult.*[33] But, as the average Evangelical Christian book caters to people with a ninth grade reading level, Martin's book serves a purpose. It also caters to the Christian who doesn't want to be bothered with details yet has a vague curiosity about New Age religion.

Finally, there are a number of Evangelical books which adopt an academic style to concentrate on a single aspect of the New Age movement. The most extensive of these is David K. Clark and Norman Geisler's *Apologetics in the New Age: A Christian Critique of Pantheism.* Other works critiquing specific aspects of New Age beliefs include *The Reincarnations Sensation;*[34] *Reincarnation: A Christian Appraisal;*[35] *Faith Misguided: Exposing the Dangers of Mysticism;*[36] and *The Holistic Healers: A Christian Perspective on New-Age Health Care.*[37]

Evangelical Fiction and the New Age

Many of the more popular Evangelical books on the New Age are more akin to fiction than serious scholarship. It is not surprising, therefore, to learn that by far the most popular Evangelical book on the New Age is a novel by Evangelical author Frank E. Paretti. His surrealist work *This Present Darkness*[38] has sold over a million copies and is rumored to be under consideration as a major motion picture.

The book itself, which can perhaps be described as sanctified Stephen King, presents a simply written adventure yarn with cosmic dimensions. The novel is set in a small American town that has become the center of a vast New Age conspiracy to control the world. The heroes are two journalists and a local fundamentalist minister. The journalists unwittingly discover the plot, eventually expose it, and the perpetrators are brought to justice. The fundamentalist minister and his congregation do spiritual warfare, in medieval style, with angels and demons.

Significantly, the evil genius is a female professor of psychology who regularly meditates to enable her to communicate with evil spirits. Thus, various Fundamentalist[39] bogy men—feminism, secular higher education, skeptical journalists, psychology, and the New Age movement—are lumped together and exposed.

In itself the book is essentially harmless and a good read for people who want a mild form of horror story. What is alarming is the way it has helped create new social boundaries for many evangelical Christians who escaped from a restrictive fundamentalism during the 1970s and 1980s.[40] Opposition to the "New Age movement" and anything which is identified as being connected with it, such as ecology, support for nuclear disarmament, or even meditation, has replaced older social taboos like the cinema, makeup, and smoking as the criteria used to identify "true" from "false" Christians by many evangelical church members.[41]

Yet, because of the book's emphasis on prayer and spirituality, its role in creating and maintaining these new social boundaries is usually overlooked by Christians. Nevertheless, the way the book portrays its villains as "enemies of the faith" confirms existing stereotypes and creates new boundaries which are as restrictive as those abandoned in the 1970s and 1980s.[42] As a result this book has unwittingly had a very negative effect on the outlook of numerous evangelicals by labeling many contemporary social movements and institutions as either demonic or potentially evil. At the same time it needs to be noted that, frequently, New Age writers present the mirror image view of Christianity as a spiritually dead, bigoted, and intolerant movement opposed to both the intellect and true religion.[43]

Finally, it is disturbing to see the way Frank Paretti has become a popular and oft-quoted authority on the New Age and related religious issues among Evangelicals, even though his actual qualifications in religious matters are minimal.[44] This, more than anything else, underscores the intellectual poverty of contemporary Evangelicalism.

The Strengths of Evangelical Critiques
of the New Age

Schaeffer's early criticism of what became the New Age movement remains the best Evangelical apologetic and analysis of New Age thought in print. Although he wrote in a very general style, he grasped the forces at work in modern culture and saw how intellectual ideas filtered down to the man in the street. If Evangelicals had taken note and built on the foundation Schaeffer laid, they would be in a much stronger position than is the case today.

It was Cumbey and Hunt, however, who began the Evangelical fascination with the New Age by exposing many of the wilder statements made by New Age apostles. In doing so they made some good points about the implications of New Age thought for Western society and set the tone for later discussions.

Groothuis and the better Evangelical writers have followed this lead in exposing many of the sillier aspects of the New Age. In this way Evangelical writers have provided a real service to the public in alerting people to the great influence some New Age thinkers have had on the educational establishment and various caring professions.

There can be no doubt that many dubious practices and strange stories with pseudoreligious or spiritual themes have entered school curricula and textbooks. Yet, parents rarely examine their children's textbooks or question school on the curriculum, preferring to trust that teachers know their job. Unfortunately, especially in subjects like social studies, teachers often do not know their job and are attracted to the latest fad. Thus, infiltration of New Age ideas into education is dangerous not because it is New Age but because it represents an unscientific ethos which has a detrimental effect on scholarship.

Similarly, many so-called holistic health practices and modern therapies, which are a reaction to scientific medicine are pure quackery. This is not to say that some things like herbal medicine, attention to nutrition, and various forms of exercise do not have a place in modern society. They do. But as with all things, they must be approached with care, and not uncritically as the New Age tends to do. Therefore, by drawing attention to the widespread uncritical acceptance of these ideas and practices, Evangelical authors have served the public well.

The Weaknesses of Evangelical Critiques of the New Age

Despite all their efforts there are major weaknesses in Evangelical critiques of the New Age. The major ones are as follows:

First, there is a tendency among Evangelical writers to misuse footnotes. As a result many Evangelical books use quotations from known Evangelical writers to add authority rather than information. Such a use of authorities is fallacious. But, the abuse of footnotes goes even further. A surprising number of Evangelical writers seem to think that footnotes in and of themselves make a work scholarly, when, in fact, it is the quality of the footnote that really matters.[45]

As a result it is common practice for Evangelical books to give a footnote which, instead of actually citing the primary source, simply notes a secondary source said to contain the original. Thus, in *What is the New Age? A Detailed Candid Look at This Fast Growing Movement*, instead of quoting directly from the *Confessions of Saint Augustine*, Michael Cole cites Augustine "as quoted" in *The History of Christianity*, published by Lion Books.[46] Other writers in the same book repeatedly indulge in the same technique.[47] It never seems to occur to them that the authorities they are referring to may have been misquoted by the secondary sources they are using. Such lack of care makes their work of dubious scholarly value.

Second, because of their unscholarly methods, it is very difficult to know if one can really trust what many Evangelical writers say. For example, in their best-selling book *The Seduction of Christianity: Spiritual Discernment in the Last Days*,[48] Dave Hunt and T. A. McMahon find New Age influences behind many successful Christian ministries which they dislike.[49] Thus, they repeatedly misquote Korean Church leader Yonggi Cho[50] and say things like "Cho commends the Japanese Bud-

dhist occultist, the Soka Gakkai, for performing 'miracles.' . . ."[51]
In context, what Cho actually says is: "in the Orient I have real trouble preaching about the miraculous power of God, for in Buddhism monks also have performed fantastic miracles. . . . In Korea . . . when attending the Japanese Sokagakkai, many are healed—some of stomach ulcers. . . . So naturally we Christians . . . have real difficulty in explaining these occurrences. . . ."[52] After outlining the problem of preaching Christianity in an Oriental culture, Cho then explains his understanding of non-Christian miracles by saying, "The Holy Spirit said to me, 'Look at the Sokagakkai. They belong to Satan.' . . . The Holy Spirit showed me that it was in this manner that the magicians in Egypt carried out dominion over various occurrences just as Moses did."[53] Quite clearly, read in context, Cho *is not* commending Soka Gakkai or the occult. From Hunt and McMahon's use of Cho's book it is unclear, therefore, whether they deliberately distort their evidence or do not know how to read a text.

Third, many Evangelical authors accept the fantastic claims of New Age advocates far too easily. Thus, Gary North is prepared to believe in the reality of phenomena such as "Kirlian Photography" which claims to capture the "human aura" on film.[54] He is equally credulous about "spontaneous human combustion"[55] and a whole range of other occult claims which ought to be treated with the utmost skepticism.[56]

Fourth, Evangelical authors often create guilt by association. Thus, Dave Hunt and T. A. McMahon say that "Since reincarnation is a basic belief to witchcraft, it is not surprising that it is *amoral*."[57] (Emphasis added.) Believe in reincarnation may be faulted in many ways, but it is not necessarily "amoral" or associated with witchcraft. Nor should witchcraft be automatically associated with sorcery and evil. Popular western ideas about reincarnation are sometimes held by people interested in witchcraft who *may* also be amoral. But, it cannot be assumed that belief in reincarnation involves witchcraft, and it must be recognized that belief in reincarnation can lead to high moral standards.

Fifth, there is a strong tendency towards reductionism among Evangelical critics of the New Age. For example, Groothuis explains New Age thought under the headings: "1. All Is One . . . ; 2. All Is God . . . ; 3. Humanity Is God . . . ; 4. A Change in Consciousness . . . ; 5. All Religions Are One . . . ; 6. Cosmic Evolutionary Optimism. . . ."[58] These ideas, which boil down to monism, pantheism, relativism, and evolutionary philosophy, are central to Evangelical critiques.[59]

Sixth, despite the importance Evangelicals place on the concepts they use to identify New Age ideas, no Evangelical author I have read takes the time to adequately define his or her terms. Monism, for example, is loosely used as a bogy word. No one seems to realize that, depending on one's definition, Christianity can be seen as a form of monism because it claims all things are created by One Being: God.[60]

Seventh, in taking a strong stand against the use of certain words, Evangelical writers do not seem to recognize that many of the alternatives they prefer are equally problematic for orthodox Christianity. For example, in rejecting monism Groothuis and others identify Christianity with pluralism. In doing so they fail to recognize that pluralism was promoted by Bertrand Russell in his rejection of Christianity. Russell says he embraced pluralism because "the universe is all spots and jumps, without unity, without continuity, without coherence or orderliness. . . ."[61] Is this what Evangelicals mean by pluralism?

Finally, along with a tendency to intellectual reductionism goes the desire to force opponents into a preconceived theoretical framework. This is most clearly seen in Clark and Geisler's *Apologetics in the New Age*.[62] In the "Introduction" the reader is told "Pantheism is a multiform world view that needs to be understood and evaluated. This is especially true in its New Age manifestations. . . ."[63] And "we will explore the basic world view of pantheism examining the views of its greatest defenders. . . ."[64]

They then say "*Pantheism* etymologically means 'All is God' . . . the key idea [is] that all of reality is one. (This is called 'monism'.) Anything real is interrelated with everything else that is real. There may be many levels of reality, but in the final analysis, all reality is unified ontologically, that is, in its being. There is no infinite contrast between an eternal Creator and a temporal creature. The ultimate reality, God, alone is real. Insofar as we are real, you and I, are part of God.[65] . . . A modern version of Stoic pantheistic philosophy is the New Age movement."[66]

On the basis of this definition, five chapters are devoted to the work of D. T. Suzuki, Shankara, Radhakrishnan, Plotinus, and Spinoza whom, they claim, contributed to the creation of New Age thought. The problem is that, with the exception of Spinoza, it is highly debatable whether any of these figures were pantheists.[67] Certainly, the central teachings of these men, other than Spinoza, do not fit the definition of pantheism given above. Indeed, as they admit, Suzuki explicitly denied he was a pantheist.[68] So did Radhakrishnan;[69] and while Shankara's nondualism may be unfamiliar to Western readers, it is certainly not pantheism.[70] Plotinus is more difficult to categorize, but the general opinion of Plotinus scholars is that he was not a pantheist.[71] Surprisingly, such figures as Marcus, Aurelius, Scotus Erigena, Giordano Bruno, Jakob Boehme, Goethe, Lessing, Fichte, and Hegel, all of whom can be plausibly represented as pantheists, are not mentioned in the text.

Clearly, most of the Evangelical authors discussed, and I have restricted my comments to the better Evangelical critiques of the New Age, take the easy way out by attacking men of straw. I have read no Evangelical critique of the New Age which even begins to approach the depth of Robert Basil's *Not Necessarily the New Age: Critical Essays*,[72] a secular book published by American skeptics.

Evaluating Evangelical Critiques of the New Age

Some Evangelical writers, like Chandler, make no claim to serious scholarship, preferring to remain in the realm of serious journalism. Such books serve an important function and are to be commended. Others, like the work of Cumbey and Hunt, are the products of conspiratorial theories which, although they sometimes contain insights into obscure aspects of the New Age movement, are very poor scholarship. Finally, there are works written for readers with a college education such as those of Groothuis, the Spiritual Counterfeits Project, and Christian academics like Clark and Geisler. These latter works claim to be serious scholarly critiques of New Age thought and must be evaluated as such.

In general it can be said that Evangelical critiques of the New Age are popular tracts written in a simplistic style. They are characterized by reductionism, lack of definition, and poor scholarship. They draw upon a limited range of sources and frequently appeal to the authority of other Evangelicals or writers like C. S. Lewis and G. K. Chesterton.[73]

As readers will gather, I am not overly impressed by Evangelical writers on the New Age movement. Anyone who doubts the appropriateness of my reaction should visit his or her local New Age bookshop. There one will find a large collection of well-written, often highly complex books. Some are, of course, sheer trash. But others reflect careful scholarship. After this expedition one ought to continue on to the local Christian bookstore. My bet is that one will find more obvious trash at the Christian than the New Age bookshop. But I have a more serious complaint.

Early in 1990 I selected a number of random passages from bestselling New Age books currently on sale. I then did the same thing for Christian bestsellers. After this I subjected both sets of readings to computer analysis using the Rightwriter program.[74] This includes a readability index which uses the Flesch, Flesch-Kincaid, and the Fog formulas as a basis for analysis. The results showed that while the average New Age book required a "grade 14" reading level, Christian books were written at "grade 9" level.

I realize the weaknesses of using a computer program to analyze readability in this way. Nevertheless, the results of my experiment leave me very uncomfortable. Such a big discrepancy between Evangelical reading levels and those of people frequenting New Age bookshops does not augur well for the future of Evangelical Christianity. This readability gap suggests that Evangelical apologetics are likely to have little impact on anyone really committed to New Age thought or even on someone who reads both points of view. It also suggests that, because Evangelicals are relatively ill educated, they will have an increasingly diminished impact on modern society, which is a "knowledge society."[75]

One major weakness of Evangelical writings on the New Age deserves close attention. Evangelical writers seem unable to recognize and adapt to the reality of cultural and religious pluralism in modern society.[76] As a result they tend to identify all religious change, especially if it involves Eastern religions, with the New Age. Yet, in many instances the phenomena they are reporting represent ancient religious traditions which exist independently of the New Age movement.[77] This failure to understand modern culture reflects the narrowness of contemporary theological education which, in general, leaves ordinands totally unprepared for meeting people of other faiths.[78] Fortunately, with the publication of Terry Muck's *Alien Gods on American Turf*[79] the situation is beginning to change for the better.

Finally, it seems clear to me that Evangelical paranoia over the New Age functions to define boundaries and replace older, more traditional disincentives, such as not attending cinemas, women refusing to wear makeup, and total abstinence. This aspect of the encounter between Evangelicals and the New Age would be a fruitful subject of a sociological investigation but is beyond the scope of my paper. At the same time, Peretti's book *This Present Darkness* draws attention to the entertainment value of New Age apologetics and the fact that having a visible opponent which can be readily identified adds much needed drama to church life.[80]

The danger of this situation for Evangelicals themselves is that when Evangelical students enter the university, they are often unprepared for serious academic study. As a result I have seen many enthusiastic Evangelicals, suckled on Dave Hunt and even Douglas Groothuis, who were totally unteachable until the day they quite suddenly "lost their faith" and renounced their Evangelical roots. The tragedy is that such people thought they knew their Evangelical heritage when, in fact, their minds were prematurely closed by easy answers and quick solutions.

Thus, the contemporary Evangelical encounter with the New Age is one which has serious implications for the future of Evangelicalism. Indeed, I would argue that the failure of Evangelicals to address this issue and the related issue of religious pluralism could spell the death knell of Evangelical Christianity as an intellectually respectable force in North America and even Britain.

PART III

Comparative Studies

Section Three contains three chapters that view the New Age in terms of comparisons to certain other phenomena. Specifically, the first two essays work with a comparison between the New Age and women's spirituality, while the third compares the New Age movement with Charismatic/Pentecostal Christianity.

Mary Farrell Bednaroski's "The New Age Movement and Women's Spirituality" is a point by point comparison of the New Age with Women's Spirituality. Both movements, for example, critique established Western religions and mechanistic science, and both aim to resacralize the cosmos as part of the transformation of human consciousness and the transformation of society's institutions. The New Age, however, tends to conceive of the sacred in impersonal, monistic terms—a marked contrast to the Women's Spirituality movement which pictures the sacred as feminine and pluralistic.

Shoshanah Feher's "Who Holds the Cards? Women and New Age Astrology" presents results from a survey of participants at an astrology conference that was held in 1989. Feher finds that astrologers can be distinguished into two categories, New Age and non-New Age. Non-New Age astrologers focus on the prediction of events whereas New Age astrologers focus on astrology as a tool for personal transformation. She also finds that while non-New Age practitioners tend to be constituted by an even balance of males and females, New Age practitioners are overwhelmingly female.

Phillip Lucas's "The New Age Movement and the Pentecostal/Charismatic Revival" is, as the title suggests, a comparative study of the New Age and Charismatic/Pentecostal Christianity. Lucas finds that, in spite of surface dissimilarities, the two movements share certain basic themes and emphases at the level of deep structure. The study is particularly useful for the thoughtful manner in which it sets both movements in the context of William G. McLoughlin's work on cycles of revival and Anthony F. C. Wallace's work on revitalization movements.

Chapter 13

The New Age Movement and Feminist Spirituality: Overlapping Conversations at the End of the Century

———————— *Mary Farrell Bednarowski*

In *Emergence; The Rebirth of the Sacred*, David Spangler identifies four levels of the New Age movement. The first he identifies as the "commercial," which uses the label "New Age" as a marketing ploy—New Age shoes or food or awareness techniques. The second is the level of "glamour," which includes those manifestations best known to the media and to popular culture. This level Spangler describes as "populated with strange and exotic beings, masters, adepts, extraterrestrials. It is a place of psychic powers and occult mysteries, of conspiracies and hidden teachings." The temptations at this level are to ego fulfillment and withdrawal from society.[1]

The third level of the New Age is concerned with change, the kind of paradigmatic change that Marilyn Ferguson chronicles in *The Aquarian Conspiracy*—emerging new forms of government and politics, business, education, gender roles, science, religion, and psychology.[2] The fourth level of the New Age is devoted to a redefining of the sacred and the resacralizing of the earth, of humankind, and of everyday life. Spangler calls it "an awakening of the consciousness that can celebrate divinity within the ordinary and, in this celebration, bring to life a sacred civilization." On this level, says Spangler, the New Age movement is "fundamentally a spiritual event, the birth of a new consciousness, a new awareness and experience of life."[3] The primary concern is with a global transformation of thinking and living. It is at the third and, particularly, the fourth level of the New Age movement that there are convergences of cultural critique, rhetoric, values, and spiritual and political agendas between New Age thinking and Women's Spirituality.

In its various and multiple manifestations, the Feminist Spirituality movement is no easier to define than the New Age movement. It is a part of the contemporary women's movement that cuts across many boundaries. Its adherents and interpreters may be witches or goddess worshippers or both. They may be working within the established religious traditions. Many are academics in the fields of religious studies and theology. Others are engaged in counseling, or alternative healing therapies or various occult arts, such as astrology. There are also women who would claim membership in both the New Age and Feminist Spirituality movements .

The central concerns that hold such diverse persons in some kind of community (although not without many basic disagreements) are the articulation of concepts: concepts that offer women perceptions of why things are the way they are and how they might be otherwise; that adequately describe women's experiences of the sacred as they have been different from men's; that offer insights from women's nature and women's experiences as they are understood to be revealing of the workings of the universe and thus revelatory at a cosmic level; and that move women to action—political action, defined broadly—on their own behalf and, by implication, on behalf of the rest of the planet.

Like the New Age movement, the Feminist Spirituality movement is engaged in the tasks of resacralizing the cosmos and transforming of human consciousness and society's institutions. In their similarities these two movements offer insights into an alternative worldview that has persisted in American culture for several centuries and that seems to be increasingly emerging into the mainstream at the end of the twentieth century. In their divergences—over such issues as whether spirituality must be earth and body-bound in order to be authentic, or whether change is first and best effected by the transformation of individuals or of societies—there are insights, likewise, into ultimate issues that are ongoing in any form of spirituality in American culture.

Among the most striking similarities between the two movements is their critique of the established Western religious traditions and of Newtonian science as the primary desacralizers of the cosmos and of American culture. According to New Age thinkers and feminists, Judaism and Christianity espouse a deity who is male, transcendent, and "other." This is a static deity, omnipotent, omniscient, omnipresent, static, unchanging in his perfection. This God has created the world but does not inhabit it, for the creation, along with humankind, is fallen. At the center of creation, at the center of human existence, there is brokenness rather than wholeness, sin and estrangement rather than creativity. To be saved means salvation from the world, from the body.

And, in order to be saved one must repent of one's sinfulness, one's very humanness. Saving power can come only from without. In an ironic twist, however, humankind, even in its fallen state, has been elevated as the height of creation and different from it. The result is alienation from the rest of the cosmos as well as estrangement from the divine.

New Age thinkers and interpreters of Feminist Spirituality further accuse the established traditions of reserving the province of the sacred for themselves, meting it out only through prescribed rituals and institutionalized experiences, offering access only through priestly intermediaries. Fearful, particularly, of ongoing revelation and of mystical experiences that cannot be controlled, the established religions find a variety of ways to maintain their power over the sacred.

Women intensify and focus these critiques on women's issues by pointing to those various and numerous religious writings that depict women as even more fallen than men, more fleshly, more trapped in matter. Thus, women are not only more susceptible to sin; they are objects of temptation as well, for they pull men down into matter—into the nonsacred. In addition, the established traditions have reserved positions of spiritual leadership for men and have defined spiritual leadership in ways that are hierarchical and excluding.[4]

New Age thinkers and women in the Feminist Spirituality movement have been equally hard on Newtonian science, the science of modernity. Newtonian science, they say, is a science of parts rather than of wholes, of analysis rather than synthesis. It is a materialist science that, by its very method, denies the reality of the transcendent, whether defined as spirit, soul, mind, consciousness, psyche, or the "more" in human experience. The result is spirit alienated from matter, and, as David Griffin points out, a consequent devaluing of nature: "No intrinsic value can exist within nature, no value of natural things for themselves . . . no internalization of divinity can occur." And, again, as in the case of religion, the result is the draining of the divine life from the cosmos and the estrangement of the realities of human consciousness from the study of nature: "Human life was rendered both alien and autonomous ."[5]

The double critique of religion and science dictates that the primary task of the New Age movement and Feminist Spirituality is the resacralization of the cosmos and the reimaging of the sacred. Resacralization requires the reinfusion of the sacred into the universe. For this to take place there must be a redefining of the very nature of the sacred. It cannot be contained solely within the transcendent being of the God of the Bible. Nor can it dwell, by divine flat, only within certain aspects of the universe, traditionally defined as soul or spirit or, more recently, consciousness or psyche.

New Age thinkers tend to conceptualize the sacred in impersonal terms in order to do away with what they see as the limitations of traditional anthropomorphic, primarily male depictions of deity. The divine life emanates from the One, the Absolute, the ultimate, impersonal source of both spirit and matter that spills itself out into the many and reintegrates the Western dualism of spirit and matter. Much of the imaginative impetus for reimagining the sacred comes from the sciences, particularly from the "new physics," the universe of the quantum. Not only, according to New Agers, does the new physics offer us more coherent descriptions of our expanding knowledge of the natural world; it gives us more compelling ways to envision the divine indwelling of nature. In *Facing West from California's Shores: A Jesuit's Journey into New Age Consciousness*, David Toolan explores the possibility opened up by the new physics that the cosmos is alive rather than inert. "Do we know," he asks, "that matter is dead, that the physical universe doesn't pulse and breathe, doesn't heat up and cool down, communicate, circulate, and break with the past like a human being does?"[6] In his interpretation of the reenlivening of matter, Toolan makes particular use of the work of the theoretical physicist, David Bohm.

An often-cited source in New Age literature, Bohm speaks of the concepts of postmodern science and the new physics as undergirding his theory of "unbroken wholeness." Bohm attempts to show in his technical writings the reality of the "holomovement," an understanding that "the whole universe is *actively* unfolded to some degree in each of the parts." The parts are internally related to each other and to the whole. Bohm's theory refutes the assumption of Newtonian science that the parts are only externally related to each other and to the whole.[7]

Toolan acknowledges some of the objections to Bohm's work by scientists and by other New Age spokespersons such as Ken Wilber. Wilber has criticized some Bohm enthusiasts as leaping too quickly to embrace what he sees as a kind of pantheism that is reductionistic in its blending of physics and mysticism.[8] Toolan holds, nonetheless, that Bohm is both scientist and "poetic ontologist." Without reducing separate realities to each other, Toolan insists, one can speculate on the relationship between the quantum world and the divine life that permeates the universe. Such speculation leads to new kinds of God-language more appropriate for the realities of the universe that has been revealed by the new physics: "If you know what you are doing at the reflective level, 'quantum action' can stand for the polynomial God who transcends all names, who resists all systematizing closure."[9]

Feminist Spirituality shares in the concern of the New Age movement to re-imagine the sacred. It is the Goddess who is the primary vehicle in this enterprise, for her indwelling presence not only restores life to the universe; she infuses it with the particular qualities of the feminine which have been lost to universal consciousness through the dominance of patriarchal religion and mechanistic science. The Goddess is an image of growing versatility and popularity in women's literature from a variety of religious traditions, including Neopaganism, Wicca, and theologies emerging from Judaism, Catholicism, and Protestantism. She emerges in two major manifestations: the Goddess in history, which refers to the goddesses of ancient matriarchies,[10] a concept often used in conjunction with political issues; and the Goddess Within, a reference to the indwelling of the divine within the human, particularly the feminine, psyche.

At one level, the Goddess bears an affinity to the One or the Absolute as a depiction of the divine in the New Age movement. She is the One that unites the many. But, very quickly, the multiple nature of the Goddess emerges.[11] She has innumerable manifestations and functions. She sacralizes the earth and nature, natural functions, female body functions, the interior of the human, particularly the female, psyche. She sacralizes the ordinary. "You wear your mythology as easily as a housedress," says one poet of the goddess Isis.[12] She is tied to the different phases of women's lives—the maiden, the bride, the mother, the widow, the crone.

This multiplicity of forms in which the Goddess appears helps to mitigate any tendency in Feminist Spirituality to anthropomorphize the divine. This effort is made to alleviate fears about Mother God simply replacing Father God and in so doing reifying all those qualities that are ascribed by the culture to women and devalued. There is, perhaps, a fine distinction between the Goddess who is anthropomorphized and the Goddess who is understood as somehow "personal," but it is the latter trait that interpreters of Feminist Spirituality insist upon. Interpreters of Feminist Spirituality find different ways to lessen what they consider anthropomorphizing tendencies in regard to the Goddess. Merlin Stone speaks of the Goddess as "the actual organic process, the flow, the changes, transitions, and transformations that the person, tree, or river go through."[13] Nelle Morton, a Protestant theologian, speaks of the Goddess as "metaphor." "When I speak of the Goddess as metaphoric image," she says, "I am in no way referring to an entity 'out there' who appears miraculously as a fairy godmother and turns the pumpkin into a carriage."[14] Many feminists speak of "experiencing" the Goddess rather than "believing" in her.

However they re-image the sacred and whatever sources they draw upon to do so, New Age thinkers and interpreters of Feminist Spirituality understand the sacred as immanent within the natural world, the body, the psyche. To perceive the divine as immanent counteracts the fear that we are alone in a lifeless universe leading lives that are meaningless in any cosmic sense. Immanence, likewise, implies that the sacred aspect of reality is accessible. We may find the divine within ourselves, within each other, within nature. "The knowingness that resides within each of us," says Shakti Gawain, a particularly popular interpreter of the New Age, "can be accessed through what we usually call our intuition. By learning to contact, listen to, and act on our intuition, we can directly connect to the higher power of the universe and allow it to become our guiding force."[15]

It is the insistence on the immanence of the sacred that fosters the primary value shared by both movements: radical, ontological interconnectedness, interrelatedness. Many interpreters of Feminist Spirituality, in fact, insist that interrelatedness is a particularly feminine value, but one that has been denigrated by both men and women. "We are afraid to drop our illusion of separateness," says Corinne McLaughlin in an article written for a Theosophical journal, "and see our interconnectedness, which is the feminine perspective. The feminine within each of us is the soul of earth—our deepest roots as humans."[16]

Whether or not interconnectedness is specifically connected to the feminine, it is difficult to overestimate the power of this concept in the New Age and Feminist Spirituality movements. Used in combination with "immanence," the word has an almost talismanic effect, a way of immediately invoking the outlines of a universe of relationships and correspondences that is perceived as alternative to those of the established religious traditions and Newtonian science. To think in terms of a new kind of universe, a new worldview, is to espouse new values, say New Agers and those who embrace Feminist Spirituality.

In his nontechnical writings, David Bohm speaks in terms of the values that emerge from a more holistic way of thinking about the universe. He maintains that the way we envision the world is a crucial factor in our consciousness and our being. "If we think of the world as separate from us," he says, "and constituted of disjoint parts to be manipulated with the aid of calculations, we will tend to try to become separate people, whose main motivation with regard to each other and to nature is also manipulation and calculation." Conversely, if we respond intuitively and imaginatively to an understanding of the world and feel at one with it, we are more likely to feel "genuine love" for the world than to want to manipulate it. "We will want to care for it, as we would for anyone who is close to us and therefore enfolded in us as an inseparable part."[17]

To "genuinely love" the world, to value it, is to want to tell its story. Just as women claim that their stories have been excluded from the story of humankind, Thomas Berry claims that we have failed to tell the story of the universe. Berry is a Catholic priest and director of a research center in New York dedicated to seeking out viable modes of human existence on earth. His work has appeal for both the New Age movement and Feminist Spirituality. He is best known for his insistence on the need for a "new story," a cosmic story, if we are to meet the needs of the human community and the planet at this time in history. Up to this time, says Berry, neither the story of religion nor the story of science has been sufficient to convey the totality of how the universe came into being and how human beings fit into it. "We are in trouble now because we do not have a good story. We are in between stories."[18]

If the divine dwells within every part of the universe and if every part is, in turn, related to the whole, then, to be sufficient, says Berry, the new story has to be of the whole universe. Thus, along with what is conveyed by science about the physical dimensions of the universe, the new story will convey a spirituality that Berry claims was manifested by the universe from the beginning: "the unique and irreplaceable qualities of the individual and inseparable bonding with every other being in the universe. These constitute the ultimate basis of a functional spirituality for the human community just as they constitute the functional cosmology of the human community."[19]

Brian Swimme, a physicist and cosmologist who has been greatly influenced by Berry, goes even further with the insistence that the cosmic story must be told. In *The Universe is a Green Dragon*, Swimme sees the end of the twentieth century as a particularly pivotal time in the history of the planet, because in the new physics, science has discovered mystery and been transformed by the encounter. For Swimme, the recent discoveries of science about the origins and nature of the universe offer "primary revelation" and the chance to tell the kind of cosmic story Berry calls for. These discoveries reveal that "our ancestry stretches back through the life forms and into the stars, back to the beginnings of the primeval fireball. . . . For the first time in history," says Swimme, "we can agree on the basic stories of the galaxies, the stars, the planets, minerals, life forms, and human culture. "[20] Against the backdrop of the cosmic story, the individual stories of spiritual traditions, different periods in human history, and various tribes and cultures do not lose their importance. "Rather," says Swimme, "the story provides the proper setting for the teachings of all traditions, showing the true magnitude of their central truths."[21]

David Spangler offers another version of the cosmic story when he speaks in term of a planetary culture. Spangler echoes Berry's and Swimme's insistence that this is not a culture that subsumes all differences, since it will exist "side by side in a complementary way with the different historical cultures both enriching and being enriched by them."[22] The planetary culture will be based on what Teilhard de Chardin described as an organic unity, one in which individual differences are intensified rather than fused into one substance.[23]

Women in the Spirituality movement voice the concern that women's stories not be left out of the cosmic story as they have been in the past. Very early in the women's movement, the telling of individual women's stories and the search for patterns in their stories became a dominant way to seek out emerging paradigms of women's experiences. These experiences have been different from men's and are considered worthy of a separate telling in the recounting of history and in the interpretation of religious traditions. "We looked for the fragments of women's stories," says Terri Hawthorne in telling her own story of discovering the Goddess of History and the Goddess Within in a women's art collective in St. Paul, Minnesota. "We read alternative commentaries on scripture, and old documents for the stories that had been deleted. We broadened our fields to include archaeology, anthropology and art history. And we began to employ our imagination and collective memories, to use group discussions, meditations and rituals to 'remember' our heritage."[24]

Many women in the Spirituality movement claim that it is, in fact, specifically by the incorporation of women's stories into the cosmic story and by the acknowledged reemergence of the feminine principle into the universe that the New Age vision of a planetary culture can come about. Corinne McLaughlin attributes the kind of cultural fragmentation we experience at this time in history to the very absence of the feminine principle in human consciousness. "The feminine awareness is the ground of being," she says, "providing the essential background for the foreground of life's activities . . . so women today are mediating the voice of the planet that seeks planethood—and unity of the human family."[25]

In spite of widespread sympathy for the concept of a planetary culture, the rhetoric of the Feminist Spirituality movement does not linger long at the cosmic and global levels; it moves fairly quickly to the political. There is a widespread assumption that the emergence of the feminine principle—the Goddess—will foster alternative kinds of political systems, particularly if global emphasis is on interconnectedness rather than on "power over, hierarchy and dominance." Conviction that there are other ways of organizing ourselves is a persistent theme in much of Women's Spirituality. And the place to look for models is in those societies where interrelatedness has been the primary value: paleolithic and neolithic cultures and "from some contemporary indigenous peoples, who live in peaceful, egalitarian ways."[26]

A reinterpretation of the meaning of "power" is an important part of the discussion about alternative political systems in the New Age movement and in Women's Spirituality. One of the most prolific writers on this subject is Starhawk, a feminist witch. Her espousal of an occult worldview places her, also, within the New Age community, although she is critical of what she sees as the New Age tendency to be too optimistic about the myth of progress and to underestimate badly what is required to heal the various wounds of the planet. In her earlier writings and in her most recent book, *Truth or Dare: Encounters with Power, Authority, and Mystery*, Starhawk puts forth the concepts of "power-from-within" and "power-with" rather than "power-over." "The language of power-over," she says, "is the language of law, of rules, of abstract, generalized formulations enforced on the concrete realities of particular circumstances." Power-from-within emerges from a view of the world as a living being with all things interrelated and therefore, all of them valuable. Starhawk denies that immanent value necessarily means innate goodness, and she offers the concept of power-with as a bridge between power-over and power-from-within. Power-with "can recognize inherent worth, but can also rate and compare, valuing some more highly than others."[27]

Starhawk applies her reinterpretation of the meaning of power to the subject of ecofeminism, the branch of Feminist Spirituality that combines feminist and environmental concerns and is based on the conviction shared by the New Age movement that "we are all a part of the organic flow of life."[28] In an essay called "Feminist, Earthbased Spirituality and Ecofeminism," she describes ecofeminism as a spiritual movement because it is involved in a transformation of cultural values. It is not a movement that requires goddess worship or ritual or a belief system. What it does require, on the broad level of cultural values, is a shifting from the metaphor of "battle" as the underlying cultural paradigm to that of "birth." Thinking of universal relationships in terms of war, says Starhawk, reinforces the tendency to organize society in terms of hierarchical structures that pit people against each other as enemies. When birth is the underlying metaphor, "the world shifts. The cosmos becomes a living body in which we all participate, continually merging and emerging in rhythmic cycles."[29] Not only does the birth metaphor suggest different ways of organizing society; it necessitates and reinforces the participation of women at all levels.

Starhawk's insistence that an ecofeminist spirituality must be "earth-based," points to a place where much of Women's Spirituality and New Age thinking diverge. In a reaction against what it has criticized as the otherworldly emphasis of traditional Christian spiritualities, Feminist Spirituality makes the claim that, however the sacred or the transcendent is defined, its home is the earth and the body. "The life of the spirit, or soul, refers merely to functions of the mind," says Charlene Spretnak, a well-known interpreter of ecofeminism. "Hence spirituality is an intrinsic dimension of human consciousness and is not separate from the body." Spretnak denies that "self denial," which usually meant "body-denial" in Western spirituality, is not a good basis for moral conduct. She offers, instead, the body-affirming spirituality of the Goddess as an impetus for the vision of ecofeminism.[30]

At another point of departure, New Age thinking is more likely than Women's Spirituality to be concerned with nonearthly beings or other realms of reality, although at Spangler's third and fourth levels there is an evident sophistication that goes beyond popular concepts of the supernatural. If women in the Spirituality movement are more inclined to speak in terms of interrelatedness with the earth and with natural processes, New Agers often refer to relationships with other planes of existence. In *Emergence*, David Spangler writes of his relationship with "John," whom he identifies as a spiritual being who "lives in the world I briefly touched when I was seven, a world defined by the connectedness and interrelatedness of things, in which the loving spirit of God is everywhere present."[31] Spangler thinks of his communication as offering him a connection with a different part of the universe, but takes care to say that it is "no substitute for communion with the sacred."[32]

Carol Parrish-Harra, another New Age writer and founder of a community in Tahlequah, Oklahoma, interprets her life of spiritual seeking in terms of her access to other dimensions of reality. She understands herself as a "walk-in," one whose body became inhabited by an older soul in a near-death experience during childbirth.[33] While much of Parrish-Harra's rhetoric is compatible with that of Feminist Spirituality, her language of "higher selves," souls "inhabiting" bodies, and messengers from more spiritual realms is not the language of most, particularly earth-based, Feminist spirituality. Other examples of the differences in emphases between New Age thinking and Feminist Spirituality can frequently be found in contemporary Theosophical literature. In writing of "the veiled mother of the world," Corinne McLaughlin espouses many of the themes of Feminist Spirituality, including the need to resacralize matter, as noted above. But she herself makes distinctions between what she has to say and what at least some other women have to say, since she wants to connect "with the Divine Mother in the earth *and* in the heavens," and to add "a dimension that is often left out by those who see the Divine Mother as purely an Earth Mother."[34]

The foregoing give some clues as to areas in which the New Age movement and Feminist Spirituality disagree, particularly in regard to the ontological realities that must be taken into consideration in formulating spiritualities that will save the earth and its human and nonhuman inhabitants from war and ecological disaster. There are other areas, as well, that might be explored fruitfully, among them the various interpretations of Eastern religious traditions as they have been appropriated by the New Age movement and by feminist spiritualities— whether the doctrine of karma, for example, offers liberation from what has appeared to be the capricious meting out of justice and good fortune in the established traditions; or, whether, it is just as punitive a way of asking the oppressed to wait for another lifetime for their sufferings to be redressed. There is also work to be done in interpreting how contemporary women's spiritualities respond to the positive thinking movements of the nineteenth and twentieth centuries that have traditionally appealed in greater proportion to women. Many feminists claim that optimism about changing circumstances by changing consciousness is a privilege of class. A third area of difference to explore involves the tendency of the New Age movement to speak in terms of spiritual hierarchies in spite of the accompanying rhetoric of immanence and interrelatedness; this is in contrast with the antipathy that many women's spiritualities exhibit over any kind of hierarchical thinking.

In spite of all the qualifications and reservations that rightly need to be made about such a broad comparison as forms the basis for this essay, there remains the fact that the New Age movement and various kinds of women's spiritualities operate out of similar worldviews—a holistic universe in which all parts are valued and internally related to the whole and to each other. These overlapping worldviews of relationships and correspondences are not so different, moreover, at least in spirit, from that of the contemporary ecology movement.

For many reasons the similarities are not surprising. Both movements emerged from the late 1960s and early 1970s. They attribute various kinds of cultural malaise—desacralization, ecological and nuclear disaster, class, race, and gender warfare—to the same cause: the dualisms between spirit and matter, male and female, science and religion, thinking and feeling, that they see as having been fostered by Newtonian science and the established religions. Both have obvious ties to the nineteenth-century alternative spiritualities that Robert Ellwood describes in many of his writings, including the essay in this volume.[35] Both movements, likewise, tend to turn for inspiration more to the ancient past—to the goddess matriarchies, the first several centuries of the Common Era, the Renaissance—than to the recent past.

To look at these two movements together provides some of the broad outlines of alternative spiritualities in American culture as they are responding to contemporary issues, both religious and scientific. Taken together, they also provide perspectives on each other. At a broader level of cultural interpretation, however, these movements suggest that American culture is by no means finished with those questions of an ultimate nature that have traditionally been asked within the boundaries of specific religions and in traditional theological language. These questions—about the nature of reality and divinity and creation, about the place of human persons, male and female, within the cosmos, about how to counter injustice—are now being addressed and answered, to the satisfaction of many, in other parts of the culture. Perhaps they always have been, and studies such as this are only making that fact more clear, rather than bringing to light a new discovery.[36]

Chapter 14

Who Holds the Cards?
Women and New Age Astrology

——————————— *Shoshanah Feher*

Introduction

Astrology is often thought of as a form of fortune telling. Many assume that predictive questions such as: Will I ever fall in love? Will I win the lottery this month? are of central concern to astrologers. Despite this conception, not all astrologers are interested in prediction. This study examines the difference between those practitioners of astrology who utilize their craft as an instrument for predicting future events and those who speak of it as one tool among many in a spiritual quest. I propose that the difference between the two types of practitioners of astrology corresponds to whether or not they identify themselves as members of the New Age movement.[1]

Of central concern in this paper is the way in which gender manifests itself in the New Age movement. I will argue that women are more likely than men to identify themselves as members of the New Age movement. Further, I posit that women's identification with the New Age movement occurs because women's worldview is consistent with that of the New Age.

Prior to the publication of this anthology, very little has been written about astrologers or the New Age from a social scientific perspective. Obviously, then, women's involvement has not been carefully studied. We know, however, that women's experiences have led them on spiritual paths that differ from men's.[2] This is in great part due to women's understanding of the world, which tends to be more wholistic and integrative than men's.[3]

Methods

The data on which this paper is based were collected at The United Astrologer's Congress in New Orleans, Louisiana, 1989 (UAC 1989). The congress was chosen as the site for administering the questionnaire because it attracted a large number of people interested in astrology at every level of expertise.

The questionnaires were distributed to approximately 600 attendees, 383 of whom completed the survey. The respondents answered questions ranging from general involvement in astrology to demographic characteristics. They were also instructed to answer a series of questions designed to assess the nature of the astrological services they provide or, conversely, seek. The use of a questionnaire enabled the participation of a large number of people involved in astrology.

To supplement the survey data, I conducted personal interviews. In this paper interviewees are referred to by fictional names. These interviews helped to flesh out areas that were limited by the questionnaire and to develop a better understanding of astrology and the New Age movement.

It is important to keep in mind that the respondents in this study are a select group, namely those with sufficient interest in astrology to attend an astrology conference. One might therefore argue that this data is not generalizable to the population at large. Nevertheless, the study based on this sample of astrologers has provided interesting insights about gender in astrology and the New Age movement.

Results

One of the most interesting results of this study is finding that two distinct groups exist among astrologers: New Age astrologers and non-New Age astrologers.[4] The difference between the two groups is based primarily on the role that astrology plays in their lives: whether astrology is part of a worldview or is perceived as a predictive tool.

The difference between those respondents who identify with the New Age and those who do not stems from an analysis of several characteristics. These characteristics are: the respondents' religious identity, what they believe the purpose of astrology to be, their involvement in other esoteric teachings, their social networks, and their demographic characteristics. In this section, I will explore these six areas in turn.

In terms of current religious identity, New Agers are more likely to consider themselves religious "others" than are non-New Agers. While they consider themselves religious, they do not identify with mainline religion. Non-New Agers either identify with mainline religion *or* are not religious. This is particularly interesting in view of the finding that there is no significant difference between New Age and non-New Age astrologers when it comes to the religions in which they were raised: proportionally, both were raised in the same religions. The New Age movement seems to encompass a spiritual outlook, an "other" way of expressing spirituality. By identifying with "other" religions, New Agers maintain a spirituality while turning away from traditional Western religion. Those interested in astrology independent of the New Age are so without necessarily being "spiritual" and identify somewhat with mainline religion, or more frequently with none.

Another way in which the difference between astrologers who identify with the New Age and those who do not is evident is in their views of astrology's purpose (see appendix). Both New Agers and non-New Agers are likely to think of astrology as a healing art or as a psychological tool. However, more New Agers than non-New Agers put astrology in this category. Astrology, then, is experienced as a therapy—it deals with the mind (psychological tool) and the body or spirit (healing art). In a similar vein, New Agers are more likely to believe that astrologers should be primarily concerned with counseling people rather than with forecasting future events or trends. They are also more likely to be influenced by metaphysical religion and are overwhelmingly more involved in other esoteric teachings than non-New Agers. New Agers are more likely to label themselves professional astrologers, and more of them professionally practice other esoteric teachings. In looking at New Age astrologers, one sees that these respondents emphasize the counseling aspect of astrology rather than its predictive powers.

Non-New Agers, by contrast, are more likely to use astrology for predictive purposes, their adherents wanting concrete, tangible answers to specific questions. For instance, UAC 1989 classes fitting this description dealt with finance. An astrologer whose interest is in business or the stock market might be an example of the non-New Age astrologer. For these people, astrology is a divinatory craft.

For New Agers, astrology informs the way they view the world; it is an integral part of their spirituality, explaining the apostasy of their childhood religion and the current identification with an "other" religion. Concerned with the transformation process, New Agers are likely to have an interest that extends beyond the client-professional status. Therefore, they are also likely to engage in other esoteric teachings and to have friends who are involved in astrology, in this way approaching a life-style enclave.[5] For non-New Agers, social networks may be independent of astrology, since astrology does not inform their worldview or meaning system. And, because it is a divinatory technique, they may not feel the need to do astrology professionally but are comfortable leaving it to the "experts."

Those involved in the New Age not only are part of a larger spirituality, but also form a community of sorts. Geographically, they tend to live in similar areas. Consistent with Stark and Bainbridge's findings on cults, New Agers are most likely to live in the Pacific and Mountain regions as well as the South Atlantic area, specifically Florida.[6] Non-New Age astrologers are more evenly distributed across the country. Not only do New Agers cluster in terms of regional area, but their friends are more likely to read astrological charts than non-New Agers' friends (see appendix). In this way New Agers have developed social networks which enable them to form a community of like-minded people. Given the emphasis on astrology as a counseling tool and the involvement in other esoteric teachings, one sees that, for many, astrology is subsumed under the umbrella of the New Age. Astrology, then, is one among many teachings. It is a tool which can be used in conjunction with other esoteric "tools" in the transformation process.

Astrology takes on a spiritual dimension and is fueled by the study of metaphysical religion and other esoteric teachings when combined with the New Age. In speaking of how astrology fits into the larger process of the New Age movement, Harvey explains that, having been interested in the transformation process for years, he finally found astrology to be "a very powerful tool in the process of searching for self knowledge." Another informant, Gary, takes this idea one step further and says that it is impossible to do astrology seriously without being "an advocate of the perennial philosophy." Without this idea, Gary says,

> one is almost forced into a deterministic model because if you don't accept the idea that individuals are a consciousness that is continuous, that's evolving over time, that has no particular beginning and perhaps no particular end . . . you're more or less forced to consider that the individual in the context of one life is somehow determined by these astrological forces or configurations external to his or her consciousness.

Thus, Gary is differentiating between a New Age and non-New Age approach: those people who see astrology as part of a larger spirituality versus those who do not. For those who view astrology as independent of reincarnation or any other esoteric teaching, astrology becomes necessarily predictive. If, however, one believes in "perennial philosophy," then astrology is not deterministic but rather helps in the expression of the individual's consciousness.

The most striking characteristic differentiating New Age from non-New Age respondents is sex. The table below, drawn from the UAC study, shows that more women than men identify with the New Age movement.

The Relationship Between Sex and New Age

	Sex	
	Male	*Female*
Percent New Age	62	83
	(n = 92)	(n = 266)

p = .000

The question is: why are women more likely than men to identify with the New Age? Theories focusing on this issue center around two themes. One is that the New Age, unlike mainline religions, gives women a voice and in so doing allows them to move out of their traditional roles. The other theme is that there is something in the ideology of the New Age that particularly appeals to women. I will look at these two possibilities in turn and then speculate about the relationship of the New Age to feminist spirituality.

Discussion

The New Age Gives Women a Voice

Traditionally, women's voices have been silenced in mainstream religions. Because these religions have been male dominated,[7] the experiences of women have not been heard.[8] The New Age movement, however, has allowed women to break away from male-centered ideology and religious institutions.

In his study of astrology in France, Fischler theorizes that women turn to astrology as a result of modernization and its accompanying crises.[9] Women have been kept apart from the "political community" and have only recently begun leaving their traditional position as housewives.

Fischler's historical analysis of why women are attracted to astrology fits in with Gary Ward's analysis of women in New Thought.[10] New Thought, he states, has traditionally attracted disproportionately high numbers of women due to both the movement's content and organization. As one Christian Scientist wrote in the 19th century, ". . . in this movement woman's real voice has been heard for the first time in the history of the race."[11]

Both Fischler's account of astrology and Ward's of Christian Science explain women's turning away from traditional Western male-biased religion and towards an expression that fits with their lives—via the ancient craft of astrology or the relatively new response of sectarian Christianity. Because traditional religion is defined by men,[12] women have not had a voice.[13] In stifling the female voice, new spiritual expressions have arisen. Women have sought out old nontraditional religious expressions or developed new sectarian places and positions to fully express their faith.[14] The theologies of both these types of movements get away from God-as-a-man imagery and incorporate women. As a result, there has often been a high degree of female leadership in these churches.[15] Whether in leadership positions or not, women have protested against the prevailing structures and have worked to create an alternate reality. Harvey believes that the astrologer is an example of someone who creates an alternate reality. The astrologer, Harvey states, uses a different approach than the fundamentalist Christian to answer the same existential questions:

> The astrologer has more alternatives in terms of what he's willing to look at than the fundamentalists. If the fundamentalists say, 'I need a rope to hang on to, I need someone that I can put my trust in, God or the Church, or whatever it is, because I don't want to figure out what I'm supposed to do myself.'

According to Harvey, in the New Age movement the relationship to God is direct. It is a nonhierarchical system, unlike mainline religions. With men to mediate between women and their spiritual experiences, traditional Western religion has not made room for women in its structure. Therefore, some women have begun to reform their mainline traditions or, in the case of the New Age, to look elsewhere. New Age astrology, then, provides women with a new arena in which they have a voice.

The New Age Appeals Ideologically to Women

There are ideological aspects of the New Age which, I propose, are inherently appealing to women because they relate directly to women's experiences. Self-identified New Agers talk about women having intuition, a characteristic held in esteem by New Agers; astrologers "require lots of intuition, a lot of men don't open up to that space" (Brian). Another informant elaborates, "Women tend to have more of an emphasis on right brain kind of activity, this requires a big intuitive kind of component, you can't do astrology just with your head. So in that sense, they're naturals at it" [Harvey]. Men, as Brian points out, generally "don't open up to that space" because, for them, knowledge depends on a clear and distinct determination of the boundaries between self and world.[16] Men's consciousness is founded on the differentiation of pairs of opposites. And while men are dualistically categorizing the world, women are attempting to restore wholeness and balance to the institutions of society and to reintegrate spirit and matter, mind/soul and body. This "dualistic" nature of men[17] is deemed both "unnatural" and antagonistic to women's nature[18] and to women's psychological[19] and moral development.[20]

Some theorists argue that "the awareness of oneness and openness to new sources of power . . . is a Wholistic understanding of the world"[21] and is a form of spirituality that is specific to, or inherent in, women. The New Age, in its emphasis on oneness with the universe and healing therapies, is therefore feminine in content. The New Age relies on being receiving, encompassing, global, wholistic, nourishing—all of which are terms traditionally used to describe women. Brian, speaking of a woman astrologer friend of his who introduced him to practicing astrology professionally, says, "she was a housewife but just an incredible counselor, totally untrained but just so nurturing and really had a fine grasp of astrology."

Unlike women, men are "conditioned more into some kind of self-reliance sort of space" (Brian), unable to go and ask for help outside of themselves (Harvey, Brian). Women, on the other hand, are not only "receivers" but "givers": an important characteristic of the New Age astrologer who carries out counseling activities. As Janet put it, "Women . . . want to help people with counseling and they can do that because they can give more empathy than men." In their travels, Rennie and Grimstad noticed that women all over the country, are becoming

> sensitized and receptive to the psychic potential inherent in human nature—and they are realizing that women in particular are the repository of powers and capabilities that have been suppressed, that have been casualties of Western man's drive to technological control over nature. It is as if [women] have recognized an even deeper source of female alienation and fragmentation than the sex role polarization which has so effectively limited women's lives—the mind/body dualism progressively fostered by patriarchal culture.

The phenomenon Rennie and Grimstad discuss might be subsumed under, or overlap with, the New Age. In either case, it is clear that the New Age is an integrative view of the world, since it emphasizes transforming people spiritually to make them aware of their oneness with the universe. This wholistic approach is traditionally female. And astrology is a tool which fits into the transformation process and is integrative in its emphasis on unity with the heavens. "Astrology . . . [is] a key to understanding the self in harmony with the Universe and the cyclic nature of time."[23] Astrology empowers, since a woman's "birth chart is a set of instructions about how she can work toward self-integration."[24] However, often astrology has become a predictive tool or, as Janet points out, a business which is "very male-oriented." Minerva agrees, stating, "we see patriarchy misuse [astrology] as a fortune-telling amusement." Brian notes that his misgivings over astrology stemmed from his discomfort with traditional astrology's dualism where things are either good or bad. In viewing astrology in a broader, philosophical, humanistically-informed perspective, he felt more comfortable:

> This humanist, or transpersonal approach is an approach beyond yourself . . . it's to begin to live life as part of the whole . . . it's not: When's this man going to come into my life? . . . When is my career going to happen?

Brian and Janet both see that astrology is often deterministic and tends toward fortune telling. They, however, are not interested in astrology at this level. They are interested in astrology inasmuch as it is a way to better understand themselves and their surroundings. Using astrology as a tool, they are able to give the world meaning in a new and different way.

The literature indicates that men and women view the world in different ways. Men are generally dualistic and deterministic, whereas women have traditionally been described as integrative and empathetic. The New Age emphasizes the latter traits and is therefore likely to appeal initially and primarily to women.

Feminist Spirituality

Many feminist theorists believe that women must look toward alternative religions. As Daly writes, "accepting the wholeness that includes psychic awareness and exploration takes feminist consciousness into an entirely new dimension—it amounts to a new definition of reality."[25] Daly believes women must get beyond the Judeo-Christian understanding and make "qualitative leaps" in their transcendence. The women's movement is essentially about relating to others and the environment in a new way. However, women will be unable to change their relationships within the confines of traditional religion.[26] The dualistic nature of traditional religion has separated the individual from God, and has therefore alienated women from their aspirations. By putting the "Source" outside of themselves, traditional religion encourages its adherents to look away from themselves to some external authority.

The New Age encourages people to look away from external authority and within themselves.

The New Age may be considered by some to be a feminist spirituality: women are empowered by a spiritual relationship which is not determined by men. In this way, women's spirituality is empowering. It allows women to take control of their lives. An historical example is Mary Baker Eddy, the founder of Christian Science, who provided women with new ways to be active and even independent in the economic sphere. Wherever there are feminist communities, women are reexploring psychic phenomena that advocate personal control: astrology, Tarot, prepatriarchal forms of religion, goddess-centered philosophies, ESP, etc.[27] Astrology, for example, allows women to look within themselves by helping to:

> develop a new understanding of our universe and how we operate in it. . . . This knowledge is power, power enabling a woman to sense her own uniqueness, to become aware of her strengths and weaknesses, and to take control of her own identity. . . . To claim her own definition—that these qualities, whatever they may, are her own and can be changed or controlled by no one but herself—is real empowerment.[28]

This is a new reality for women who have been controlled by others in our society. Gary talks about how astrology enables people to take responsibility for their own lives and that therefore,

> . . . just giving people information based on their chart is not necessarily helpful and in fact it can be counterproductive because there's an implication that the responsibility for their problems is somehow outside themselves, in the position of the planets, etc.

Although it can be argued that the basic underlying theme of the New Age is feminist, I would like to point out that, from a sociological perspective, it has an antifeminist current. While empowering, the New Age is an individualistic movement which does not account for social structure. In other words, it places responsibility on the individual without acknowledging that there are larger, structural issues which may leave women frustrated and yet more alienated, despite their newfound empowerment.

Conclusion

In this study, it has become clear that those astrologers who identify with the New Age are a different type of adherent to astrology than those who do not. New Agers are likely to practice a variety of esoteric teachings, astrology being one more tool in their spiritual quest. For non-New Agers, astrology is more likely a predictive craft, independent of spirituality.

Among those involved in the New Age, women are overrepresented. In this paper I have tried to posit some plausible explanations for this. I have argued that, unlike traditional religion, the New Age has given women a voice. I have also argued that the New Age appeals to women because it values traits that have been traditionally attributed to women (e.g., intuition, nuturance, etc). And that, perhaps, New Age astrology is a feminist spirituality.

However, when movements draw only on women, it is a sign of their failure to penetrate into the social mainstream.[29] Success lies in male involvement, not only because it helps perpetuate the movement but, more importantly, because it legitimates it. Thus, as long as women enjoy less status than men, astrology and the New Age movement will not be highly regarded by society at large.

Appendix

The Percent of Respondents Within Each Group
(New Age and Non-New Age) who:

	New Age	Non-New Age
See Astrology as A Healing Art	92	81
See Astrology as A Psychological Tool	99	94
Are Influenced by Metaphysical Religion	61	20
Professionally Practice Other Esoteric Teachings	25	7
Self Identify as Professional Astrologers	61	47
Have Friends Who Read Charts	55	39
	N = 283[30]	N = 81

p = .01[31]

Chapter 15

The New Age Movement and the Pentecostal/Charismatic Revival: Distinct Yet Parallel Phases of a Fourth Great Awakening?

——————————— *Phillip C. Lucas*

Introduction

In her address delivered to the centennial celebration of the American Society of Church History (1988), historian of American religions Catherine Albanese sought to identify the broad outlines of an emerging, ethnically (that is, characteristic of America as a *nation*) American religion. In the concluding portion of that address, she briefly highlighted a series of rather startling convergences between the New Age movement and Christian fundamentalism. The convergences she identified included each movement's focus on personal transformation, healing, direct spiritual experience, the reality of continuing revelation, a peculiarly American species of religious materialism, and a democratized spirituality that "fell forward" into visions of the millennium.[1]

I became interested in probing these convergences within a phenomenological framework and observing how they were manifested in each movement's characteristic rituals, cosmology, institutions, spiritual practices, attitude towards contemporary society, and doctrines. Did significant convergences or parallels really exist between such seemingly different religious movements? If so, what light did this shed on the religious character of the American soil from which they sprang?

At the same time, in obedience to what Ninian Smart has called the "contextual imperative,"[2] I wanted to examine the parallels and convergences between the two groups in the context of the socio-historical period within which they both rose to prominence, the 1960s and 1970s. Were there particular societal conditions during this period of which the New Age movement and the fundamentalist resurgence were two manifestations? Were these movements two alternative strategies created to address a shared experience of socio-political crisis? Additionally, were these two movements possible harbingers of an emerging national religious synthesis?

As I began examining the primary sources, conducting oral interviews, engaging in participant observation of worship services, and analyzing recent sociological survey data bearing on each group's belief systems, it became clear that the groups clustered under the fundamentalist umbrella evinced significant differences in lifestyle, worldview, attitude toward ecstatic experience, and liturgical practices. I discovered that the two groups under this umbrella that most clearly converged with the New Age movement in the way Albanese had suggested were the Pentecostals and the charismatics. As a consequence, I decided to narrow the focus of my examination to the parallels, convergences, and *contrasts* between these two movements and the New Age movement.

The most promising socio-historical perspective I found from which to view both the contrasts and the convergences between New Agers and Pentecostals/charismatics was that advanced by William McLoughlin in his influential essay *Revivals, Awakenings, and Reform*. McLoughlin's thesis is that American culture periodically renews itself by what he terms "great awakenings." These are periods of between thirty and forty years when a fundamental reorientation takes place in our belief or value system, ethical norms, and institutional structures. When the period has ended, those values, norms, and institutions have become better adapted to actual social and environmental conditions.[3] According to McLoughlin, the period 1960-1990 saw the beginning of America's Fourth Great Awakening.

In a schema developed through Anthony F. C. Wallace's 1956 essay "Revitalization Movements," McLoughlin argued that during the early stages of a great awakening, the major institutions of society, i.e. churches, schools, police, courts, jails, and government, begin to malfunction and lose their legitimacy in the eyes of a growing number of individuals. As society moves into a period of cultural distortion (when the routine "mazeways" become blocked and out of touch with contemporary needs), a revivalist, traditionalist movement characteristically arises that blames the societal crisis on a collective failure to adhere to the traditional beliefs, mores, and values of the culture.[4] This movement awaits God's apocalyptic retribution on society and advocates a way of life that is essentially a return to the "basics," to the purity and vitality of an idealized time of beginnings. Throughout this essay, I will probe whether the Pentecostalist/charismatic movement can best be understood as one part of the Fourth Great Awakening's revivalist, traditionalist phase (which, to be sure, includes the larger fundamentalist resurgence).

In the middle stages of a great awakening, prophetic movements arise which advance new sets of religious and social norms for individual and group behavior. The leaders of these widely dispersed movements then begin to attract the more flexible (usually the younger) members of the society, who are willing to experiment with new economic, political, and familial arrangements (sometimes in a communal context), as well as new sexual mores.[5] The ideological reorientation that McLoughlin believes is occurring during the Fourth Great Awakening includes "a new sense of the mystical unity of all mankind and of the vital power of harmony between man and nature," an image of God that is life supporting, nurturing, and more immanent than transcendent, and an ethic of cooperation, service and mutual care.[6] This essay will also consider evidence which indicates that the New Age movement, in significant ways, articulates these ideological reorientations and thus represents the progressive, future-oriented, experimental phase of our current great awakening.

McLoughlin's "multi-phase" framework, if it proves solid, will help to explain the contrasts between the two movements. But what about the convergences and parallels? I will attempt to understand these as rooted in the fact that both movements draw on a shared American heritage of beliefs, experiences, myths, and traditions. One of the most important of these is the old revivalistic belief that "God has yet further light to shed upon his revelations."[7] The others include, in McLoughlin's list, individualism, pietism, perfectionism, and millenarianism.[8]

I will also attempt to show that each of these movements offers solutions to a common problem: the crisis that American society has faced as a result of the profound socio-cultural disorientation of the 1960s and 1970s. The two movements can then be viewed as in some ways distinct, and in other ways generic, moments in a greater pattern of societal revitalization. Both will be seen to share in the larger awakening's desire to transform both the individual and society. In addition, their underlying structures of thought will be seen to manifest in parallel ways two characteristic themes that McLoughlin identifies as areas of emphasis during a great awakening.

One of these themes is the emphasis on the immanence of the divine as opposed to its transcendence. During awakenings God is felt to be present again in the world—in visions, in sacred utterances and revelations, in charismatic spiritual leaders, and in the natural environment.[9]

The second theme is that of a great battle between the powers of evil and the powers of good that ends in the cleansing of all darkness and disharmony from the world and in the appearance of a transformed humanity.[10] This theme ties into part of America's cultural mythos: the belief that we are a chosen people, a new Israel ordained by God to lead the world (through virtuous living) into a glorious era of peace, prosperity, brotherhood, and equality.[11]

Defining "New Age Movement," "Charismatic," and "Pentecostal"

Before I can begin my analysis, it is necessary to delineate what I mean by the New Age movement, as well as by such terms as *Pentecostal* and *charismatic*.

My reading of the primary materials and of studies by scholars such as Catherine Albanese, Gordon Melton, Robert Ellwood, and Mary Bednarowski has led me to identify the New Age movement as an American social and religious phenomenon that has four major distinguishing characteristics. First, there is the belief that the earth and its peoples are on the verge of a radical spiritual transformation. This transformation will occur at the level of human consciousness and will entail a dawning awareness of the oneness of the human family and the intimate relationship that exists between the human species and the entire fabric of the natural world. Second, there is the eclectic embrace of a wide array of healing therapies as well as spiritual beliefs and practices. These include, among others, yoga, various forms of meditation, crystal healing, macrobiotics, reincarnation, the Western esoteric tradition, tantra, and trance channeling. Third, the New Age involves the adoption of an ethic of self-empowerment, which focuses on the realization of individual goals and aspirations as a prerequisite for efficacious societal transformation. Fourth, there is the desire to reconcile religious and scientific worldviews in a higher synthesis that enhances the human condition both spiritually and materially.[12]

The New Age movement has its roots in the many alternative religions that have emerged and spread in this country since the mid-1800s, especially Swedenborgianism, Spiritualism, New Thought, and those movements that have attempted to harmonize Western and Eastern religious traditions, such as transcendentalism and Theosophy.[13] The movement is hard to pin down in quantitative terms, because it has no central organization whose membership can be counted and because there is no definitive way of delimiting its boundaries.[14] Its breadth can be observed, however, in the various directories, journals, and "networking" publications it produces. Even a rough count of New Agers is complicated by the facts that a wide variety of beliefs and practices are commonly situated under the New Age "umbrella" and that there are many persons who identify themselves with particular denominations and who nevertheless subscribe to many of these beliefs and practices. For example, in a new and yet unpublished sociological survey conducted by Wade Clark Roof and Phillip Hammond, 27 percent of Roman Catholic, Greek Orthodox, Episcopalian, and Lutheran respondents indicated a belief in astrology, and 31 percent of these same respondents indicated a belief in reincarnation.[15] However, even if the movement cannot be measured accurately in quantitative terms, it is clear that it has made a significant impact on American society over the last twenty years and is steadily growing in influence and in media exposure.

A word need now be said concerning this paper's use of the two related terms, *Pentecostal* and *charismatic*. By Pentecostal, I refer to those American denominations—including the Assemblies of God, the United Pentecostal Church, International, the Church of God (Cleveland, Tennessee), the Church of God in Christ, the International Church of the Foursquare Gospel, and the Pentecostal Holiness Church—that were formed at the beginning of the twentieth century as a result of doctrinal and liturgical controversies within the Holiness movement.[16]

These controversies eventually resulted in the emergence of churches that placed primary emphasis on the doctrine of charismatic gifts following a "baptism of the Holy Spirit," and on spontaneity of emotional expression during worship. After slow expansion through their first forty-five years, these churches began growing rapidly during the 1960s. The Assemblies of God alone have experienced a growth rate of about 400 percent between 1965, when it numbered five hundred thousand members, and 1985, when it numbered two million.[17]

By the term *charismatic* I refer to the movement that began in the late 1950s and early 1960s when members of non-Pentecostal denominations began experiencing a Pentecostal-type "baptism of the Holy Spirit." Those experiencing the baptism for the most part did not join classical Pentecostalist churches but rather sought to renew their own denominations from within. This renewal gained national publicity in the 1960s and spread to such mainstream denominations as Roman Catholicism, Lutheranism, Episcopalianism, and Methodism.[18]

The Pentecostal and the charismatic movements have mushroomed into the largest Christian movement of the twentieth century. A Gallup

Poll taken in 1979 showed that 19 percent or 29 million adult Americans identified themselves as "Pentecostal" or "charismatic" Christians.[19] As documented in David Barrett's 1988 report on the movement, there are now over 176,000,000 Pentecostals and 123,000,000 Protestant and Catholic charismatics worldwide. In North America alone, Barrett documents 22,550,000 Pentecostalists and 43,212,000 charismatics.[20]

Invisible Realms of Sacred Power and Experience: A Parallel Rediscovery

The first of the parallels I wish to consider concerns what may be termed each movement's attempt at *rediscovery of invisible realms of sacred power* and each movement' s emphasis on *ecstatic, emotional experience* of this power. In the Pentecostal/charismatic movement this experience occurs generally in its participant-oriented worship, with religious emotions being freely expressed through upraised hands, dancing, and spontaneous shouts of praise. This behavior is in sharp contrast to the more restrained worship of mainline churches.

In contrast to the skepticism regarding the supernatural that has prevailed in mainline religious culture since the upheavals of the 1960s, Pentecostals and charismatics believe that the Holy Spirit intervenes directly in their daily lives, performing tangible miracles. These manifestations of divine grace begin with the foundational "baptism of the Holy Spirit," which Pentecostals believe endues them with the same spiritual gifts as were given to the early Christian community. When a person experiences one or more of these gifts, s/he understands s/he has received the "second blessing" and has visible evidence that the Holy Spirit is now intimately at work in his or her life. These supernatural gifts include the ability to prophesy, to speak in foreign tongues, to interpret these tongues, to sing in the Spirit, to utter words of wisdom, to discern spirit entities, and to exorcise demons.

The late humanistic psychologist and father of the human potential movement Abraham Maslow spoke of the spiritual vacuum created in the believer's life when subjective religious experience is forgotten or devalued in a tradition and replaced by a dry, external set of behaviors, dogmas, and forms, devoid of feeling and intensity.[21] More than one commentator has attributed the popularity of the Pentecostal/charismatic movement to its ability to transcend dry formalism and to mediate continuing encounters with divine power for its adherents.[22]

The New Age movement, too, is strongly oriented to experiential encounters with sacred power. Many of those who participate in this movement were part of the counterculture generation of the sixties, who left the mainstream churches in droves because of what they perceived as rigid moralism, verbalism, and general inability to mediate ecstatic spiritual experience. They turned to the mystical, experience-centered new religious movements where transformative contact with sacred power was offered through such spiritual practices as yoga, meditation, chanting, and sacred dance.

Many New Agers accept the existence of a universal energy that differs from more common forms of energy like heat and light. This universal power is believed to undergird and permeate all existence. It goes by many names including *prana, mana, odic force, orgone energy,* and *ch'i*.[23] The Pentecostal/charismatic movement's concept of the Holy Spirit is in some ways analogous to this. It is the divine force moving behind the miraculous events of healing, prophecy, glossolalia, and exorcism. It is the point where God's sacred power enters the human realm and manifests itself tangibly to human agents.

The main difference between these concepts lies in how they are conceived in cosmological and theological terms. As befits the traditionalist character of the Pentecostal/charismatic movement, this sacred power is conceived of within a strict, biblical paradigm. It is the Holy Spirit, the Spirit of Truth sent by Christ to comfort and enlighten all true Christians. The experience of the Holy Spirit is conceived of as a supernatural event, an intervention of divine grace in human affairs. Just as the Holy Spirit had "spoken through the prophets" in Old Testament times to reawaken Israel to the responsibilities of its covenant with Yahweh, so now also, Pentecostals and charismatics believe, God is pouring out the Holy Spirit on his elect to reawaken them to their divine calling in Christ. Pentecostals/charismatics accept the traditional Christian dualisms of spirit and matter, heaven and earth, natural and supernatural. Their experience of the Holy Spirit is thus a divinely given pretaste of the heavenly realm where they will spend eternity after physical death.

For New Agers the sacred power they experience is conceived of, according to Albanese, as a *natural* energy that permeates, not only the physical body, but the entire created cosmos. It is believed to follow natural laws, like electricity, and to be wholly impersonal. The energy is, in fact, matter vibrating at a higher rate of vibration than the matter we see in physical forms. It is part of a subtle realm of vibration that permeates the natural world and, in a sense, sustains all natural forms with their essential life force. It is not God's supernatural intervention that makes an experience of this power available, but rather (as befits the pragmatic, science-affirming, and experimental character of the New

Age movement) specific spiritual practices and methods that put a person in harmony with it and thus allow the person to act as its conductor and receptacle. This energy can be exchanged freely in interpersonal relationships through sexuality (i.e., in tantric practices) and can be channeled in various healing therapies.[24]

The literature of both movements articulates these ideas with a striking language of spiritual forces and empowerments. Take this example from Sun Bear, a Native American and popular New Age teacher: "The invisible powers that are the spirit-keepers come to us, and when we lock ourselves into their energy we conduct it; we are working together, like electricity when it flows through certain kinds of crystals."[25] Or consider this typical example of the language used by Pentecostalists and charismatics to describe this sacred power: "[Pentecostalism] has reminded us that the Holy Spirit makes worship come alive, that the Holy Spirit is not the power stored in unused batteries, but a live current running through our every action."[26] Albanese has posited that an undernoticed feature of America's religious heritage is a metaphysical, mystical strain that knits together self, God, and nature in a way that is directly experienced and provides empowerment in material life.[27] This strain, which has its roots in Native American religions, transcendentalism, early American folk traditions, and the metaphysical healing movements of the nineteenth century, resonates strongly in both the Pentecostal/charismatic and the New Age movements' emphasis on personal encounters with sacred power. The Pentecostal/charismatic emphasis on deeply emotional, ecstatic encounters with the divine also finds paradigmatic antecedents in the recurrent outbreaks of evangelical revivalism that have swept America ever since the First Great Awakening between 1730 and 1760.

Keeping this in mind, one can examine instructively several parallel ways through which the New Age and Pentecostal/charismatic movements believe that they experience sacred power and contact noncorporeal intelligence. One of the most prominent of these ways for many New Agers is through the phenomenon popularly known as "channeling." A channeler is believed to be a human vehicle through whom beings from other dimensions of existence can address persons in this world. To enter the special trance state, the channeler's mind is disengaged from involvement with the sensory space/time world. This state of disengaged attention purportedly allows disembodied entities to use the channel's physical faculties to lecture, counsel, and teach a human audience.[28] The channeling phenomenon has grown more and more popular with New Agers over the past decade. It is estimated that over one thousand active channelers now practice in the Los Angeles area alone.[29]

Many leaders of New Age groups have claimed to be channels of revelatory material from advanced spiritual beings. For example, the popular New Age teacher Ram Dass (Richard Alpert) uses guidance he receives from the entity of the astral plane he calls "Emmanuel," who is channeled through East Coast housewife Pat Rodegast.[30] New Age philosopher and teacher David Spangler claims that he was the channel through which a being identifying itself as "Limitless Love and Truth" dictated the essence of Spangler's New Age bestseller *Revelation: The Birth of a New Age*.

The Pentecostal/charismatic movement's parallels to channeling are the phenomena termed "speaking in tongues" and "prophecy." Charismatic writer Don Basham describes speaking in tongues as "a form of prayer in which the Christian yields himself to the Holy Spirit and receives from the Spirit a supernatural language with which to praise God."[31] The "tongues" phenomenon is usually unintelligible to listeners, and so a second person is often required who, also inspired by the Holy Spirit, is able to "interpret" the tongues message for the community of believers.

Margaret Poloma, who has researched both the charismatic movement in Catholicism and the Assemblies of God, defines prophecy as "a gift of the Holy Spirit through which a person speaks in the name of God by giving an exhortation, reporting a vision, providing a revelation, or interpreting a glossolalic utterance."[32] This can take place in various contexts, including speaking out at meetings in English with a message for the group, interpreting a vision one has received in private prayer, or interpreting a dream.[33] Like the information "channeled" to New Agers, the primary content of this "gift of the spirit" can be described as messages of encouragement, consolation, correction, and future direction.

Some commentators have remarked that these spiritual guidances or ecstatic utterances have similarities to those evidenced by shamans in traditional folk religions.[34] What is clear is that, for both New Agers and Pentecostals/charismatics, these events are experienced as a dramatic breakthrough of sacred power into the ordinary world, as an intensely personal, often ecstatic interaction with this power, and as compelling evidence of the proximity of other realms of being.

Another parallel has to do with each movement's avowed experiential contact with spirit beings, whether they are called angels, demons, spirit guides, spirit helpers, nature spirits, or angelic presences. The reality of demons and angels has long been a fundamental element of Pentecostal cosmology. The activity of the demonic host was believed to be increasing significantly in modern times because of the imminence of the Second Coming. To combat this activity, the authority to exorcise or cast out demons had been given to "spirit-baptized" believers.[35] Pentecostal revivalists such as Oral Roberts and Gordon Lindsay were noted for their power to cast out evil spirits.[36] Sensational stories of exorcism, replete with physical violence, foaming at the mouth, and uncontrolled cursing, abound in Pentecostal groups.[37]

Charismatics, too, believe in a personal devil and discern its influence in the smallest details of their lives. They take regular steps to protect themselves from demonic attacks and perform rituals that use divine power to disperse perceived demonic presences. In numerous books, tapes, and pamphlets, Satan and his minions are portrayed as responsible for all the world's pain, disease, and suffering. Charismatics envision the spiritual realm as inhabited by angels as well as demons, though angels receive far less attention. Some charismatic groups invoke the angels to protect their homes and families from harm.[38] A member of an independent charismatic church I interviewed saw angels as being intimately involved in human lives:

> There are other angels that work in allegiance with God—they're called ministers. . . . There are a lot of instances in the Old and New Testaments where they directly contacted people, spoke to them, came face to face with them or spoke in dreams, visions, things like that. I believe that that's still going on.[39]

Many New Age groups also emphasize the reality of other-than-human persons, though these entities are rarely envisioned within the traditional biblical framework that the Pentecostals and charismatics use. Those groups that have incorporated Native American or shamanic beliefs and practices invoke the aid of spirit helpers and guardians, who help a person cope with and master hidden spiritual forces. These helpers, related to the animal and plant kingdom, are also used in healing practices. Some of these practices closely parallel Pentecostal demon exorcism in that a harmful spirit being is removed from a person whose state of health or state of mind has purportedly been adversely affected by the spirit's presence.[40] The Holy Order of Mysterion, Agape, Nous, and Sophia (MANS), a New Age group founded in the late 1960s in San Francisco, invoked angelic beings in its secret Temple Services and has given each member a special medallion to help ward off negative spirit influences. Findhorn-related groups in America teach "attunements" to nature spirits and *devas*, or spirit beings who rule various plant kingdoms. These attunements, according to Findhorn community members, aid the production of garden vegetables and other crops.[41]

The significant parallel between these beliefs is that each assumes a functional, dynamic relationship between spirit beings (however conceived) and humans. These beings are experienced as *real* and as part of a subtle, sacred dimension that constantly interacts with mundane reality. These beliefs represent, in fact, a cosmological vision similar to that of traditional peoples, who perceive the cosmos as populated with a multitude of malevolent and benevolent noncorporeal entities, who act as causative agents in processes such as disease, plant growth, and human psychological breakdown.

For the traditionalist Pentecostals and charismatics, these spirit beings are conceived as players within a biblically based cosmological battle between the demonic and angelic hosts. Though the exact versions differ from group to group within the Pentecostal/charismatic movement, all contain the belief that Satan is a fallen archangel who, with his armies of demons, conducts spiritual warfare against God and the angelic hosts for the souls of humans. This battle has reached its final stages, and, though God's final victory is assured, the souls of humans are still in the balance. Writers within the Pentecostal/charismatic movement such as Dave Hunt warn that communication with any discarnate entity other than Jesus and the angels is a kind of necromancy that can lead to demonic possession. New Age practices such as channeling and seeking guidance from inner spirit helpers are roundly condemned by these writers.[42]

The cosmological assumptions underpinning the New Age movement's understanding of spirit beings are quite different. As befits its scientific, futuristic character, the New Age movement views the universe as an ever-expanding and evolving reality where persons learn to realize and manifest their innate potentials, however these are conceived. Jesus is one of many discarnate teachers who may be contacted for guidance and healing. Harmful spirit beings do exist, but protective practices, derived from Native American traditions and from the Western occult tradition, are used to combat their influence. New Agers do not believe that spirit beings are arrayed in some vast cosmic struggle for human souls but rather view them as mankind's generally benevolent helpers and guides.

By calling the ecstatic utterances of their adherents "prophecies of the Holy Spirit," Pentecostals and charismatics can enjoy the community-affirming experience of spontaneous guidances and revelations from the realm of the sacred while remaining within their traditional biblical worldview. But however the phenomena are conceptualized by their respective adherents, glossalia, prophesying, and channeling are parallel methods of intense, immediate encounter with sacred power and of the reception of "further light" and revelation on both personal and cosmological issues from sacred beings.

A Parallel Commitment to Sacred Community

Both the New Age movement and the Pentecostal/charismatic movement place a high value on the reintegration of the alienated individual into some form of sacred community. The problem of disintegrating social cohesion and community became particularly acute during the 1960s and 1970s due to such factors as the increased mobility of the work force, the breakup of neighborhoods (through urban decay, riots, and suburbanization), the weakening of the nuclear family, and the increasing depersonalization of life wrought by anonymous bureaucracies and large scale institutions.

In the New Age movement, the attempt to form new structures of social cohesion has taken several forms. The first of these is the creation of intentional communities, where like-minded individuals pool resources and share an urban home or a farm. Richard Fairfield's *Communes, USA* (1972) documents the extensive communal experiments that grew out of the 1960s counterculture. The best known of these, the Lama Foundation in New Mexico, the Farm in Tennessee, the Ananda Cooperative Community in California, and the Chinook Community on Whidby Island, Washington State, were among the first to identify with the New Age vision. A host of New Age groups have sponsored communal living arrangements during their institutional histories. The creation of intentional communities ties in with the desire of many New Agers to build a new planetary society. The communities are believed to provide models for the larger society of how individuals can learn to cooperate, share resources, and discover a deeper sense of human solidarity.

Similarly, both white and black Pentecostals, during their first fifty years of institutionalized existence, tended to be tight-knit religious communities on the fringes of society. Though these groups have advanced in socio-economic terms, they still promote an intense experience of communal identity and belonging.[43] During the charismatic renewal of the 1960s and 1970s, some middle-class converts began establishing communal living arrangements, sharing households and incomes like the early apostolic community described in the Book of Acts.

The New Age movement's one-world vision is paralleled in the Pentecostal/charismatic movement's transcendence of conventional denominational, national, and ethnic boundaries. American Pentecostalism has gone expansionist. Pentecostal-style worshippers are now found within all 150 traditional non-Pentecostal ecclesiastical confessions and families, in 8,000 ethnolinguistic cultures, and in myriads of state-sponsored churches worldwide.[44] Commentators speak of a "grass roots ecumenism" within the Pentecostal and charismatic communities and of the sharing of a common religious language. Though many differences remain between specific groups within the movement as a whole (as is the case in the New Age movement), the emphasis in recent times has been on unity in the Holy Spirit rather than on theological argumentation.

From all this it is clear that both movements seek to create an intense experience of community and to promote actively a worldwide spiritual sister-brotherhood that transcends entrenched racial, national, ethnic, and class boundaries. The worldwide reach and vision of these two movements reflect one of the peculiar traits of the American religious character—its belief that America has been especially chosen by God to lead the rest of the world to some form of spiritual and political enlightenment. This national megalomania is clearly apparent in the highly successful missionizing efforts of the Pentecostal/charismatic movement and in the New Age's planetary vision and alliances with various international religious, environmental, and healing movements.

At the same time, these movements can be seen as reflecting in the sphere of religious communities the realities of late twentieth-century internationalism in the economic and political spheres. With the shrinking of the planet as a result of mass communication, air travel, and unprecedented cultural exchange, these movements can be seen as a part of a larger readjustment of American religion to current geopolitical realities and trends.

Parallels in the Healing and Transformation of Self

Another significant convergence between New Agers and Pentecostal/charismatics is each group's focus on personal healing and transformation. Albanese posits that the healing of self and planet constitutes the central agenda of the New Age movement.[45] Such healing is a form of personal transformation, and for a large segment of New Agers, personal transformation is at the core of a person's spiritual journey. This focus on the self traces its roots back to the humanistic psychology movement, which was launched in 1961 by Maslow. He and those he influenced sought a middle way between the extremes of Freudian psychoanalysis and Skinnerian behaviorism. The movement sought to switch emphasis from the study of pathological behavior to the study of healthy individuals who had learned to "actualize" their full potential. The establishment in 1962 of the Esalen Institute at Big Sur, California, provided a laboratory where human potential theorists could test ideas and techniques on persons seeking to break through what was perceived as modern society's harsh psychological and social conditioning. Theorists found parallels between the emotional opening-up processes of Western cathartic psychotherapies, Maslow's peak experiences, and the altered states of consciousness experienced by practitioners of Eastern techniques of meditation.[46] Thus was born a synthesis of Western psychology (especially the transpersonal variety) and Eastern religion that became normative for the New Age movement.[47] Many New Age groups use techniques derived from humanistic psychology to bring about radical alterations of perspective and personality in their adherents.

The Pentecostal/charismatic movement also focuses a great deal of attention on the personal healing and transformation of its adherents. The "second blessing" or "baptism of the Holy Spirit" is viewed as the major transformative event in a person's life. One of the charismata is the gift of spiritual healing, which is usually administered through a laying on of hands. (This hands motif is paralleled in the numerous therapies of "healing hands" used in the New Age movement.)

Following the "baptism of the Holy Spirit" in the charismatic movement, great emphasis is placed on personal growth and the realization of one's potential. By the late 1970s, New Age group dynamics, popular psychology, New Thought teachings, and meditation techniques had permeated both modernist and traditionalist segments of the charismatic movement. Charismatic leaders like Josephine Ford were recommending the development of democratic, Esalen-type group structures and processes for their prayer groups.[48] Interpersonal honesty and nonverbal forms of communication such as handholding, embracing, and massage were encouraged.[49] Ruth Carter Stapleton, a nationally known charismatic, founded her "Holovita" retreat center outside Dallas in 1978, where she offered an eclectic mix of spiritual therapies including directed visualizations and meditation.[50] (Visualization techniques are, of course, a common staple of New Age self-help therapy.)[51]

Popular New Thought themes such as positive thinking and achieving personal prosperity had gained such adherence in the Pentecostal/charismatic movement by the mid-1980s that conservative Christian leaders were lamenting: "The people are so engaged in making money, subconsciously mammon has become their god until this has clouded, in many places, the real fervor, fire, and New Testament zeal that comes with Pentecostal experience."[52] In 1987, a special six-part series of the John Ankerberg television show highlighted the degree to which such New Age practices as visualization, seeking advice from an inner guide, rebirthing, and listening to relaxation tapes have permeated the Pentecostal/charismatic movement.[53]

Ankerberg and other charismatic leaders often condemn the New Age movement's "anti-Christlike" exaltation and empowerment of the self. But it must be acknowledged that, however much it may be packaged in revivalistic Christian idioms, Pentecostals and charismatics make direct appeals to the suffering individual self and promise *personal* healing, happiness, and prosperity. The fact that this is done within a traditionally salvationist perspective does not change its actual effect on, and appeal to, the personal self of its adherents. As Robert Fuller's *Alternative Medicine and American Religious Life* makes clear, there is a long tradition in America of interest in self-culture and nonmedical healing methods. During the Second Great Awakening of the early nineteenth century, an attempt was made to collapse the distance between the stern Calvinist God and humankind. One manifestation of this attempt was a greatly increased interest in direct encounters with invisible healing power, whether through the instrumentality of revivalist laying on of hands, or through alternative healing systems like homeopathy, mesmerism, and Grahamism. This phenomenon appears to be repeating itself during our current Awakening, whether through the charismatic movement's healing "gifts" or through the New Age's plentiful offerings of alternative healing methods such as crystal healing, polarity therapy, and acupuncture.[54] Clearly, it is in each of these movement's ability to offer an efficacious alternative means to heal and empower body, mind, and soul that we must look for their continued popularity and growth.

Parallel Visions of a New World

Another set of convergences has to do with the elaborate eschatologies that dominate the worldviews of both movements. The scenarios differ in detail but agree on the imminence of a worldwide societal breakdown and the establishment of a spiritually transfigured world community. New Agers generally (Ruth Montgomery and Ramtha are prominent exceptions) envision a "soft" apocalypse wherein much that is of value from our present civilization can be salvaged while the new world community is being built. The Pentecostal/charismatic vision of massive destruction, like the apocalyptic vision in the New Testament that is its prototype, is far less sanguine about the prospects of the modern world. It expects a more radical and sudden breakdown of this civilization and less human agency in bringing the new world about.

Pentecostals have, from their inception as a movement, taught a dispensational premillennialism that entailed the idea of an imminent secret extraction (or "rapture") of the saints to a place of safety, immediately followed by a period of tribulation, the Second Coming of Christ, and a thousand-year messianic reign on earth. Some commentators, following the lead of Robert Mapes Anderson, have argued that this eschatological motif, which permeated the movement's earliest literature and resurfaced in the Latter Rain Revival of the 1940s, is the integrating nucleus of the Pentecostalist message.[55] For these scholars classical Pentecostalism constituted a wholesale rejection and condemnation of the present world order and a longing for its actual destruction so that the millennial reign of the saints could begin.[56] Among modern Pentecostalists and charismatics, these apocalyptic views are quite prominent, and much speculation exists concerning how current events fit into biblical prophecies of the end times. Books like Hal Lindsey's *Late Great Planet Earth* and Doug Clark's *Final Shockwaves to Armageddon* are hugely popular within this movement.[57]

As Robert Bellah has observed about the new religions of the 1960s and early 1970s, many of which were later identified with the New Age movement:

> [they] share a very negative image of established society as sunk in materialism and heading for disaster. Many of them have intense millennial expectations, viewing the present society as in the last stage of degradation before the dawning of a new era. . . . All of these groups . . . have withdrawn fundamentally from contemporary American society, see it as corrupt and illegitimate, and place their hope in a radically different vision.[58]

Mirroring the Second Coming hopes of the Pentecostals, New Agers with theosophical backgrounds speak of the appearance in the last days of a new avatar of the status of Jesus and Buddha. Students of the Arcane School actively advocate this position and have circulated worldwide copies of a prayer invoking the avatar's appearance.[59] A number of "channeled" messages speak of various catastrophic "earth changes" that will accompany the coming period of planetary illumination.

The latest example of New Age millennialism occurred on 16 August 1987, when thousands of New Agers gathered at "power centers" around the world to herald the "harmonic convergence." According to New Age spokesperson Jose Arguelles, this event not only signaled

the return of Quetzalcoatl, but the elimination of Armageddon as well. To some it may even be as another Pentecost and second coming of the Christ. Amidst spectacle, celebration, and urgency, the old mental house will dissolve, activating the return of long-dormant archetypal memories and impressions. Synchronized with the descent of the new mental house, these "return" memories and impressions, corresponding to actual collective archetypal structures, will saturate the field and create the impulse toward the new order and lifestyle.[60]

Donald Dayton has observed that, historically, movements that provide their adherents with an intense experience of divine power also seem to develop a fascination with prophetic and apocalyptic themes and long for a corresponding transformation of the world order.[61] This observation is surely borne out in the two movements we have been studying, who have responded to the societal traumas of the 1960s with varying degrees of world rejection and millennialist visions.

Parallel Anti-Institutionalism and Democratization of Spiritual Authority

The last parallel has to do with each movement's anti-institutional attitudes and tendencies toward democratization. Pentecostals have from their beginnings been criticized for the undignified nature of their worship services, during which the "Holy Spirit" was allowed to move through any believer without institutional control. Early Pentecostal leaders found ready adherence among rural and working-class people who viewed the formal liturgies and extensive bureaucracies of larger denominational churches with a mixture of suspicion and fear.[62]

The charismatic revival of the 1960s and 1970s has adopted a modified version of these attitudes and tends to be decentralized in its authority structures. Leadership is often based on personal charisma rather than formal bureaucratic training within an institutional hierarchy. This movement's most characteristic form is the small prayer group and the "covenant community," which has minimal structure so that it can remain open to the spirit and provide intimate support for its members.[63]

The New Age movement is well known for its anti-institutional and decentralized character. The majority of New Agers embrace a loose form of organization called "networking, " in which informal contacts among New Age groups are maintained by newsletters, shared phone lists, and word of mouth. Decision making in many groups is through consensus, a process wherein a sense of shared responsibility is promoted. The locus of authority for most New Agers tends to reside within the individual. The disciple or seeker decides which teachings or groups meet his needs based upon interior spiritual guidance.

The Pentecostal/charismatic movement's locus of authority also tends to be the individual, who receives the gifts of the Spirit from within and who seeks a "spirit-informed" interpretation of Scripture. These spiritual gifts are not the special province of a priesthood or bureaucratic hierarchy, but are rather seen to be freely distributed by God to all believers. While it is true that some groups have authoritarian *interior* structures, they nevertheless tend to reject the authority claims of normative societal institutions such as the public school and legal systems. Ultimately, as Catherine Albanese argues, the strategy of many New Agers and charismatics toward mainline churches and institutions seems to be to disappear in their midst and to transform them from within. The creation of large separate institutions could only impede this strategy.[64]

The striking underlying similarities between these movements should not make us lose sight of the very real differences between them. The history of the Pentecostalist movement reaches back into the general context of nineteenth-century American Protestantism, with its pre-versus-post-millennialist and fundamentalist-versus-modernist controversies and its questions concerning the proper degree of spontaneity that should be allowed in worship services. The development of twentieth-century Pentecostalism, including the charismatic renewal, has all taken place within the larger socio-historical development of American Protestantism. Its political and moral views, theology, and liturgy thoroughly reflect this fact. Being linked in many ways with the conservative, fundamentalist wing of American Protestantism, Pentecostals and charismatics generally espouse social and political stands that reflect conservative values. These include a pro-life stance on abortion, opposition to homosexuality and the legalization of marijuana, a traditional view of the role of women in society, and support for prayer in public schools.[65]

Though it has important historical roots in the alternative religious movements of the nineteenth century, the contemporary New Age movement is largely a phenomenon of the late twentieth century. The movement's socio-political views and values, including its emphasis on individual freedom and self-empowerment, its willingness to innovate and experiment, and its acceptance of a planetary, as opposed to an ethnocentric or national, perspective, all resonate with identifiable thematic currents in modern society. New Agers' stands on social issues generally fall at the opposite end of the spectrum from those of Pentecostals and charismatics. Despite the elements of the Judeo-Christian tradition in America that can be found within it, the New Age movement is essentially universalist and eclectic (as opposed to exclusivist) in its appropriation of religious traditions and practices.

Summary and Conclusion

It is now possible to posit answers to some of the questions that initiated this inquiry. There do indeed exist significant convergences and parallels between the Pentecostal/charismatic and New Age movements. First, both movements represent attempts to bring an *experience* of sacred power into the daily lives of ordinary people. The actual means of accomplishing this and the theological models for comprehending these experiences may differ, but the underlying theme remains the same. As McLoughlin has observed, in an awakening the divine's manifestations are no longer limited to the institutional churches and their functionaries. Instead, these manifestations occur in intense, personal encounters with all levels of humanity, even the the lowliest. The spiritual and physical worlds intermingle and the boundaries between the two become permeable.[66] The emphasis in both movements on personal experiences with sacred power, whether through channeling, speaking in tongues, prophesying, meditation, laying on of hands, or exorcism, can be understood as aspects of this characteristic manifestation of a great awakening. This democratization of numinous experience can be seen as part of the necessary wresting away from conventional authorities of their hegemony over societal norms, so that the currents of revitalization being pioneered by alternative religious movements can gain some legitimacy in the larger culture.

Second, both movements place a high value on the reintegration of the individual into an intimate, stable, and meaningful sacred community. In each movement this community ultimately extends beyond conventional ethnic, class, national, regional, and denominational boundaries to embrace the human race as a whole. Third, both of these movements place a strong emphasis on the healing and inner transformation of the wounded, fragmented modern individual through various nonmedical means. Finally, each movement sees itself as part of a planetary spiritual transformation that it is helping to bring about, a transformation wherein the locus of authority will be the individual rather than an institution.

Do these convergences tell us something important about the unique religious character of America and its future? That is, are there continuities with the country's religious heritage and yet something that points beyond that heritage to some future synthesis that is as yet in the making?

This essay has demonstrated that each of these movements has its common American features. Each ties into a core part of our long-standing cultural mythos: that we are a chosen people ordained by the divine to embody a glorious new society where peace, community, material prosperity, and equality reign. Though America itself may be the proving ground for this new vision, it is ultimately a vision that Americans feel compelled to share and implement among the rest of humanity. This worldwide vision has a great deal to do with the heterogeneity of the nation's populace. Many of the world's countries have concrete ties of family and tradition to the United States. Each in a sense has a stake in the American experiment. The ability of both the New Age and the Pentecostal/charismatic movements to transcend conventional boundaries and reach out to humanity at large is a reflection of this reality.

The individualistic, egalitarian, and democratizing roots of America's early history are also reflected in both movements' democratization of revelation and mystical experience and in their anti-institutional attitudes. The longstanding revivalistic belief that "God has yet further light to shed upon his revelations" is reflected in each of these movements' privileging of inner voices, visions, and ecstatic utterances over tradition and dogma. Finally, America's pragmatic concern with this-worldly success and material prosperity is strongly reflected in each movement's acceptance of prayer, positive thinking, or visualization as methods for enhancing the individual's spiritual and material conditions.

If indeed a national religious synthesis or consensus is in the making, it will certainly include at least these abovementioned core elements of America's religious heritage. The New Age's attempt to reconcile scientific and religious worldviews in a higher synthesis that enhances the human condition in the here and now is also likely to be part of any emergent religious ethos. Science (and its concrete fruits) has come to dominate modern American society to such an extent that any religious worldview that did not integrate it in some way would be unable to gain a foothold in the majority's thinking. The pragmatic, thisworldly orientation of the American character could never accept a worldview that took people too far afield from the immediate and the concrete. I would also expect that the New Age's individualistic eclecticism and preference for decentralized forms of internal structuring would be characteristic of any emergent religious consensus on American soil.

William McLoughlin's interpretation of the present era as a Fourth Great Awakening has proved useful for identifying the socio-historical factors that may have served as catalysts for the rapid emergence of these movements as well as for understanding them as distinctive yet parallel strategies for dealing with a collective experience of societal crisis. McLoughlin's model of a great awakening, which I discussed briefly at the beginning of this essay, posits a five stage process. In the first stage, growing numbers of individuals within a society begin to lose their bearings and to show signs of psychological or physical illness. This slowly begins to break the institutional bonds of society, especially at the level of families. In the second stage, people begin to shift the blame for their problems away from themselves and onto societal institutions such as churches, schools, courts, and government. Political rebellion, demonstrations, and schisms in churches lead to civil and ecclesiastical disorder. At this stage, there characteristically arise nativist or traditionalist movements that attempt to call people back to traditional beliefs, values, and behavioral norms.[67] In the third stage of an awakening, prophetic movements arise whose adherents articulate a new understanding of the nature and will of God and new social norms for individual and collective behavior. Because of the voluntaristic, pluralistic religious and political structure of our society, these movements have a widely dispersed leadership and outreach in the American context.[68] In the fourth stage, these prophetic movements begin to attract persons willing to experiment with the new "mazeways" or life styles they advocate.[69] In the final phase of an awakening, the prophetic movements win over the undecided majority who, though they themselves have not experienced conversion, are sufficiently impressed by the doctrines and behavior of the prophetic movements that they accept their values and practices. Thus is born the new consensus that remains dominant until the next period of cultural strain and distortion.[70] McLoughlin maintains that the most rigid and reactionary traditionalists are seldom able to make the transition to the new consensus, and soon become a small, dissident minority, clinging to old ways.[71]

Following McLoughlin's schema, I would assert that the Pentecostalist resurgence of the 1960s and 1970s represents one dimension of the traditionalist, revivalist stage of our current Great Awakening. This movement, like the fundamentalist movement of which it is a part,[72] preaches a return to biblical values and a traditional life style. Theologically and morally, it is suspicious of innovation and experimentation. This assertion deviates slightly from McLoughlin's interpretation of Pentecostalism, which sees it as part of the third stage of our current Awakening. McLoughlin bases this judgment on the pietistic, ecstatic dimensions of Pentecostalism, which he views as the Awakening's response to a loss of faith in old religious doctrines and rituals.[73] While I am in agreement with McLoughlin that such a loss of faith in fact occurred during the 1960s and 1970s, I would argue that the Pentecostalist movement is in essence a strategy for dealing with this loss that hearkens backwards to earlier traditions, attitudes, and life styles. It is therefore out of tune with larger societal trends and is not articulating new mazeways that the majority of Americans will adopt over the next generation.

I would also argue that the New Age movement is one of the movements spawned during our present Awakening that is experimental and future-oriented in its effort to create mazeways that are better adapted to current societal conditions. McLoughlin's assertion that the counterculture movement of the 1960s and early 1970s, with its radical politics, communes, interest in Eastern religions, and ecological sensitivity, is a part of the Fourth Great Awakening's third and fourth stages basically concurs with this interpretation. As I have shown, the New Age movement is strongly rooted in the counterculture movement of the 1960s and 1970s.

This leaves the charismatics, who, for the sake of simplicity, I have considered as essentially the same as the Pentecostals throughout the body of this essay. In actuality, charismatics are distinct in several ways. Though they embrace a traditionally Christian theology and worldview, they tend to be far more open to modem social currents and experimentation in matters of life style, spiritual practice, worship, and self-therapy than classical Pentecostals. McLoughlin places the charismatic movement in the third and fourth stages of our current Awakening.[74] This I agree with, for it is clear that the movement has had a powerful effect on the mazeways of the mainstream churches. Ultimately, charismatics may represent a kind of mediating movement, drawing from the strengths of both traditionalists and futurists, formulating their own unique synthesis, and then attempting to revitalize the weakened religious mainstream.

If these observations are accurate, it may be necessary to revise McLoughlin's model somewhat. For, rather than fading into insignificance, as he suggests happens with traditionalist movements after the revivalist phase of an awakening, it is clear from the statistical data quoted earlier that the Pentecostals are still growing rapidly and show no signs of slowing down in the near future. The number of charismatics as well as those with no religious affiliation (who, as Albanese suggests, may be most likely to identify with the New Age movement) is also steadily increasing. As a consequence, it may be more accurate to say that the stages in our present awakening are not occurring within predictable chronological intervals, but in fact are occurring simultaneously.

It is still a matter of debate whether *any* of these three movements has created new social and religious norms that will become the dominant mazeways in twenty-first-century America. However, the growing national concern with environmental issues and the increasing globalization of our culture on the religious, political, and economic fronts would appear to bode well for a larger acceptance of such New Age themes as "the global village," planetary spiritual community, and the healing of self and the planetary ecosystem.

Ultimately, it is too soon to tell whether these movements were indeed part of a larger "Great Awakening" in late twentieth-century American society. Such a judgment can only be made from the perspective of historical hindsight. Nevertheless, each of these movements has clearly had an impact on American society across traditional boundaries of race, creed, class, and nationality and may turn out to have been key harbingers and catalysts of fundamental societal transformation.

PART IV

International Dimensions

The concluding section of this collection, which deals with the international dimensions of the New Age movement, is likely to be the most interesting section, at least in terms of encountering unexpected information. Before compiling the present volume, the editors were aware that the movement was strong in England, Germany, and Australia, but could find no one prepared to write a paper on the New Age in those countries. We were, however, eventually able to contact scholars prepared to contribute chapters on the movement in areas of the world where we did not expect to find significant New Age activity, namely Nigeria, South Africa, Japan, and Italy. Because the topic of the international outreach of new religious movements is as unfamiliar to most Western academics as the international impact of the New Age, contributors in this section were encouraged to discuss the New Age movement in the context of a broader description of alternative spirituality in their respective countries.

Rosalind I. J. Hackett's "New Age Trends in Nigeria" examines the impact of imported new religious movements and ideas in West Africa. Manifesting a pattern which is in some ways comparable to the West's New Age as it existed in the 1970s, the Nigerian New Age is more organizationally focused than the current New Age movement in North America (which, by the 1980s, had become a far more diffuse spiritual subculture). Movements such as the Rosicrucians and the Aetherius Society are, for example, quite strong in Nigeria.

Mark R. Mullins's "Japan's New Age and Neo-New Religions" examines the most recent wave of new religious activity in Japan. After an historical survey of the periods of religious revival that have been experienced by this nation, the bulk of the essay is devoted to a survey of the analyses that have been put forward by Japanese sociologists to explain the current "religion boom." Beyond the usual explanations put forward by social scientists, some of these observers point out that the newer new religions are dominated by emphases that closely resemble the emphases of the folk religion of premodern Japan. Mullins also examines the direct impact of the American New Age movement, and cites some revealing statistics, such as the interesting item of information that Shirley MacLaine's *Out on a Limb*, first translated into Japanese in 1986, is now in its thirty-third printing, having sold some two hundred thousand copies.

Gerhardus C. Oosthuizen's "The 'Newness' of the New Age in South Africa and Reactions to It" presents a very interesting and thorough survey of New Age spirituality in South Africa. The largely hostile reaction of the churches to the New Age movement is examined at some length. Picking up on the discussion in Phillip Lucas's study, Oosthuizen also compares the New Age with South Africa's Black Zionist churches.

Isotta Poggi's "Alternative Spirituality in Italy" examines the Italian New Age in the context of a more general survey of nonmainstream spirituality in Italy. This essay also sets the movement in the historical context of the country's longstanding interest in metaphysical/magical/occult matters. While not as extensive as in northern Europe, the New Age has a definite presence in Italy which is able to boast such Findhorn-like communities as Damanhur and the Green Village. The final section of the chapter examines the Church's response to the utilization of Asian meditation forms by certain segments of the Catholic community.

Chapter 16

New Age Trends in Nigeria: Ancestral and/or Alien Religion?

Rosalind I. J. Hackett

While I was conducting a survey of religious institutions in southeastern Nigeria in the early 1980s, a surprising number of movements came to light whose main focus was the development of spiritual power and esoteric knowledge, and whose associations or origins ranged from places as diverse as India, Indonesia, Britain, and California.[1] These "spiritual science movements," as I termed them, had generally begun to emerge following the end of the Civil War in 1970, although forerunners had been present in Nigeria since the 1930s. To the best of my knowledge, these movements, which did not correspond to recurring types such as neotraditional or independent Christian movements, had received virtually no academic attention. This is still largely the case.

I used the term *spiritual science movement* to describe this very heterogeneous category of movements for a number of reasons: (1) while they displayed little historical, cultural or doctrinal unity, they did share certain definable characteristics, namely a quest for higher states of consciousness, increased spiritual power and knowledge, and a direct religious (sometimes ecstatic) experience, as well as the use of procedures, techniques, and practices which draw on hidden or concealed forces to manipulate the empirical course of existence; (2) it was a term used by Nigerians themselves to describe what they consider to be "higher," more mystical, and "scientific" forms of religion; (3) by using spiritual sciences we avoid confusion with the other major category of new religious movements in Africa—those that are a product of the indigenous culture following the impact of Westernization (in particular the independent African and "spiritual" churches), or with the word *cult*, which has another meaning in the African context; (4) the term is broad enough to cover the occult, mystical, and metaphysical orientations of these movements.[2]

In my first publication on the subject in 1986, I situated these spiritual science movements, whether indigenous or exogenous, as part of a wider phenomenon which I called "spiritual technology": beliefs, attitudes, practices, seeking to manipulate and gain occult knowledge of the divine or sacred as part of a process of spiritual development and empowerment.[3] I argued that magic was but one small part of a resurgence of institutions, specialists, literature, etc. My 1989 publication, *Religion in Calabar*, provided more details on the respective movements and the key figures. While the book was focused on a particular town, my more than eight years of field work in Nigeria from 1975 to 83 and again in 1987 had convinced me of the wider extent of the phenomenon.[4]

My growing awareness of the importance of the New Age movement in the United States, where I have been located since 1984, has led me to identify a number of direct links and parallels between movements and ideas in this country and religious trends in Nigeria. I now believe that many of the movements and techniques I was describing in the Nigerian context bear close resemblance to movements classified elsewhere as "New Age." In this essay, I want to explore whether it is appropriate to talk of a New Age phenomenon existing or developing in the West African context, and to what extent this derives from and reinterprets imported or local sources. I shall be focusing chiefly on the Nigerian context, but this is by no means restrictive, since Nigeria is such a cultural and economic presence in the region (one in five West Africans is a Nigerian). Evidence is gradually coming to light of similar religious trends in Ghana, Liberia, Cote d'Ivoire, Cameroon, and Sierra Leone. Following some discussion of methodological and theoretical considerations, I shall examine those movements where I consider New Age influences to be apparent. I shall be discussing a number of very diverse activities and resources through which personal mystical transformation is believed to occur. I shall then account for the possible appeal of this type of religiosity and the similarities and differences between the African and American versions.

As Melton, one of the major interpreters of the New Age movement in the United States, has argued, the movement is very decentralized and is easier to understand in terms of its ideals and goals rather than the beliefs to which it adheres.[5] It is also very eclectic, drawing on the (often contradictory) ideas and teachings of a host of (alternative) Western traditions ranging from transcendentalism, New Thought, Swedenborgianism, Spiritualism, and Theosophy to Christian Science, as well as of teachers from Eastern religious traditions who flooded the West after 1965.[6] This American social and religious phenomenon which took shape in the early 1970s is generally characterized by the belief in personal, social, and cultural transformation, a desire to achieve a higher synthesis of religious and scientific worldviews in order to enhance the human condition both materially and spiritually, and an "eclectic embrace" of various healing therapies and spiritual beliefs and practices, such as yoga, meditation, crystal healing, macrobiotics, reincarnation, the Western esoteric tradition, tantra, and trance channeling.[7] Lastly, the ethic of self-empowerment focuses on the realization of individual goals and aspirations as a prerequisite for efficacious social transformation. The New Age movement is generally seen as evidence of a religious ferment and revival in a religiously disenchanted West.[8]

I have taken the time to outline briefly the New Age movement as it is perceived in the United States and will compare it with my analysis of the West African situation. We must be careful of not imposing concepts or inventing a tradition, but it is my conviction that there is sufficient evidence, albeit very diverse and fragmented, to support the claim that Nigeria at least is developing her own brand of New Age religion. It may be less formal at this stage and more supplementary than its American counterpart and does not display the same social activism. As a passing observation, it is interesting to note that African spirituality has not been viewed as a source of wisdom, nor commodified or appropriated by the New Age in the same way as Native American and Australian Aboriginal teachings.[9]

"Go Spiritual or Die":[10] The New Momentum

At a very general level, there is plenty of evidence of the West African predilection for things metaphysical, mystical, and occult. Local bookstores are often stocked with occult and metaphysical literature. The West African print media have for at least the last two decades carried advertisements for spiritual healers and Indian experts in palmistry and astrology.[11] Hermetic Science Centres, with branches in western, midwestern, and eastern Nigeria, now advertise several hundreds of occult works on full-page spreads in Nigerian national dailies. Occult and metaphysical literature has circulated for many years in Nigeria, at least. It is mentioned by a government report on the outbreak of a pentecostalist-type Spirit Movement in eastern Nigeria in 1927.[12] Imported religious literature of this nature was banned during the Nigerian Civil War from 1967 to 70. Harold Turner noted the varied inspirational literature of one young West African back in the 1960s. In addition to more conventional Christian texts, he possessed a range of sources on Kabbalism, spiritual and magnetic healing, occultism and Raja Yoga.[13]

It is my contention, for reasons which I will outline later in the paper, that this type of spirituality, which has maintained a low profile for many years, is now gaining momentum. In this section, I propose first to examine the various movements that are actually operating in many parts of West Africa today. Some of them may not be directly classifiable as New Age movements in the American sense, but their leaders, teachings, and practices are fuelling this growing sub-culture of esoteric, mystical, and metaphysical religiosity. It is this subculture, I am arguing, that has direct or indirect links or affinities with the New Age movement elsewhere, or at very least is laying the foundations for its development.[14] These movements have been established by a variety of means: brought back by Africans resident or travelling overseas; direct "missionary" activity;[15] or by Africans acquiring the literature of the organization concerned and then requesting support (although there are some examples of groups having been formed well in advance of official recognition—the Superet Light Mission in southeastern Nigeria, for example).

The Rosicrucians (AMORC) are today the most well known metaphysical movement operating in West Africa, largely owing to their extensive publicity campaign and the fact that they have been active in Nigeria since 1925. In Calabar, in the southeastern corner of Nigeria, where I lived and worked for four years from 1979 to 83, it was hard to ignore the physical presence of the Rosicrucians, since their West African headquarters, in all its Egyptian glory, had been completed there in the early 1980s. I was also very aware of the numbers of male students in our department (Religious Studies and Philosophy) at the University of Calabar who received AMORC mailings. Rosicrucian literature, such as the "Mystic Life of Jesus," was readily available in many bookstores. The appeal of AMORC lies not just in its claimed historical continuity with an ancient Egyptian occult order (several Nigerian historians trace their ancestral roots to Egypt), but also that it claims not to be a religion but a "mystical philosophy" and a "worldwide cultural fraternity" which can help people discover their secret powers of inner vision and cosmic consciousness and attain greater personal success. Nigerians and Ghanaians are reportedly very active in the movement at the international level.

The Aetherius Society was publicized, on the occasion of its introduction to Calabar in 1982, as an "international spiritual brotherhood." It is perhaps more accurately described as a "flying saucer" cult with an explicitly religious structure which incorporates the teachings of occultism and yoga.[16] Founded by a British medium in 1955, the society claims to be able to communicate with extraterrestrial beings for advanced spiritual and material powers through spiritual discipline and "scientific prayer." Groups have reportedly been established in Calabar and Port Harcourt to date. The movement has strong support among politicians and businessmen. Sir S. C. O. Adeyemi, who identifies himself as a "spiritual astrologist" and committed member of the Society, gave an exposition of Aetherius Society teachings in a newspaper interview in one of Nigeria's leading dailies in 1985.[17] He informed readers that the teachings of the cosmic masters have been made available through the founder of the society and must be followed in order to usher in the Aquarian Age, the age of peace and enlightenment. Adeyemi maintains that already the physical and climactic features of the earth have begun to change: "And then, the goddess of the earth will bring forth high vibratory spiritual energies which only spiritually minded people will be able to withstand."

Adeyemi's own spiritual career as "metaphysician" and "spiritualist" is a good example, not just of the type of person who may be associated with this type of movement, but also the eclecticism and experimentation which characterize this growing religiosity. Following a serious illness (occasioned, he claims, by the forces of darkness) and an astral vision, he enrolled in several mystery schools, such as the Ancient Mystical Order of the Sun, the Inner Temple, and the Rosicrucian Fellowship of San Francisco.

Swedenborgian literature has been circulating in Nigeria for over fifty years, and branches of the Church of the New Jerusalem, founded on the teachings of the Swedish mystic, Emmanuel Swedenborg (1668-1772), have existed for almost as long in the eastern and western regions. A group of refugees initiated a small group in the Calabar area during the Civil War (1967-70). In the early 1980s it was being reactivated by a group of students at the University of Calabar. The Institute of Religious Science, which has a very small following in Calabar, stands in the New Thought tradition. In 1982 my research assistant visited the local representative, a car mechanic in Calabar, and came back amazed at his library collection of metaphysical texts. Its metaphysical teachings on healing, as perpetrated through the publication *The Science of Mind*, are the most popular in the Nigerian context. This publication was later observed by one of my students at the Friends of Jesus Church, a Nigerian offshoot of the Church of Christ Unity in Los Angeles, in Calabar. In 1983 there were currently seven branches or study groups of the Institute of Religious Science throughout the country. The Unity Church, which has been an important source of and support for New Age teachings, is now operating in Nigeria.

The Superet Light Mission is primarily concerned with psychic phenomena; it was founded in Los Angeles by Dr. Josephine Trust (Mother

Trust), an aura scientist who claimed to have the mission of bringing into the world Jesus' light teaching. Superet literature found its way to eastern Nigeria in the 1950s, but has only generated two or three groups; the members are barely educated, but claim to be attracted by this "scientific religion." Ministerial training (half the trainees are women) is done by correspondence with the U.S. headquarters. More popular is their "nonsectarian" Peace Movement which holds meetings and rallies for healing and spiritual development and manages to attract a number of nonmembers.

The Eastern-related groups are a far more recent phenomenon. Eckankar or the Secret Science of Soul Travel, based on the teachings of the ECK master, Paul Twitchell, teaches the direct path to God or the path of total awareness. An extensive campaign launched the movement in earnest in the early 1980s, and there are now over 60 branches throughout Nigeria. Eckankar makes frequent use of the broadcasting media to communicate its teachings, and the Area Mahdi, Benjamin Anyaeji, is a popular speaker with accounts of his purported reincarnations, "higher" powers and ability to stop rain.

The Subud Brotherhood is a movement with Indonesian origins which is seeking to gain a foothold on Nigerian soil. The founder, Bapak, taught that through a series of spiritual exercises, known as *latihan*, one can gain access to God's power by complete surrender of the self and the senses. People of all faiths are invited to participate in the direct religious experience of Subud. The National Spiritual Centre is based in Calabar but claims only a few regular members and occasional enquirers. The Grail Movement has been active on university campuses since the 1970s in Nigeria; people are invited to public lectures on spiritual knowledge and "any issue concerning human existence in Creation." The teachings of the founder, Abd-ru-shin ("servant of the light"), are found in his major three-volume work: *In the Light of Truth*.[18] The movement was introduced to Nigeria by a wealthy businessman (Akombi?) and there are reportedly around 1000 members (approximately one seventh of the total membership of the movement). The World Council of Sri Sathya Sai Organization organized an international conference in Ghana in 1986 to "bring to the notice of Africa, teachings of Baba in general and Education in Human Values in particular."[19]

It is worth mentioning a number of other new religious movements which do not necessarily fit into the categories under discussion here, yet their global teachings may be reshaping more locally oriented movements. Baha'ism entered Nigeria from the Cameroons in 1956 via a Ugandan missionary and has since spread to both rural and urban areas of Nigeria. Membership is limited to those with sufficient education to appreciate the egalitarian and global ideals of the organization. Japanese new religions are making inroads into Africa. Tensho-Kotai-Jingu-Kyo toured Nigeria in 1979 advertising itself as "the universal spiritual religion for World Peace and Redemption of evil spirits." It is not known whether this movement with its Buddhist/Shinto elements was able to gain a following. Soka Gakkai has branches in Lagos and Zaria. In a two-part report on Africa, we learn that a young Ghanaian, Joseph Asomani, visiting Japan in the mid-1960s received the Gohonzon and since that time, as general director of Nichiren Shoshu of Ghana, has worked steadily to build the movement in his country.[20] He claims that Africans are very close to nature and for that reason can "fall very easily into the rhythm of Buddhism." Personal revitalization, personal healing, and the realization of world peace also appeal to Nigerians, Liberians, Cameroonians, Zambians, and Kenyans, and there are accounts of growth in those regions.[21] It is also reported that the government of Congo (in Central Africa) recognized the Japanese Tenrikyo movement as one of the six official denominations in the country in 1986.[22]

Hare Krishna devotees have been visiting major Nigerian cities since the 1970s, distributing literature from their "Hare Krishna Bookmobiles." Nigerians are initially drawn to the movement because of the feasts and the festivals, as well as the emphasis on devotionalism. But the comments of a Nigerian devotee of the movement, Omokara Das Oben Nsan, are apposite to our discussion: "[t]here is a difference between the spiritual advancement we make here and the one in the church. . . . But Krishna Consciousness is a practical process you follow and you make advancement till you come into full knowledge of the Supreme Being."[23] He also goes on to show how Krishna Consciousness helps people overcome the three mysteries of material existence that every body suffers.

The Unification Church, with its discourse on a new world order and Unified Family, predicated upon the revelatory teachings of Reverend Sun Myung Moon, has been operating in Nigeria since the 1970s but has not been as successful as in Zaire, for example. They managed to take over two small independent churches in eastern Nigeria to effect government registration, and they have a small staff of foreign missionaries at the headquarters in Lagos. We now turn to the movements of indigenous origin.

Local Initiatives

Indigenous spiritual science movements are still a relatively rare breed. I am here describing those that I researched in more detail in Calabar, but know that similar movements may be found in other locations. The Spiritual Fellowship was founded in Calabar in 1980 by Mr. A. Peter Akpan, a civil servant, in response to a book he wrote entitled: *The Path of Holiness*. The main theme of the book is "spiritual development," which the author understands as a graduated path of knowledge by which the student attains higher levels of consciousness and spirituality and greater power. The author's teachings stem from a variety of religious, mystical and occult sources; a small group of people gather weekly to meditate and discuss these teachings.

The founder of the Esom Fraternity Company (Nigeria), Professor Assassu Inyang-Ibom, is a well-known local "occultist and mystical specialist," who has established a training institution for the "healing arts and sciences" and a "cosmic hospital" (the latter is a joint venture of the Society of Metaphysicians in Britain, an American evangelical church, and some Indian associates). In Calabar in the early 1980s I witnessed the forming of a spiritual science movement known as TUB or The Universal Body. Its founder, Cyril Owan, an ex-policeman and bar owner, had received training from the Psychology School of Thought and the Rosicrucians. He still retained Rosicrucian paraphernalia at his residence, but claimed to have become dissatisfied with "their slow, solid training." He attached great importance to esoteric knowledge and, at times, called this "Christ-consciousness": a state of being Christ-like and having greater illumination and, hence, greater impregnability to dangers and evil forces. His use of symbolism reflected biblical sources as well as a fascination for mystical predictions and calculations.

Two well-known figures in Nigeria who have developed a more autonomous existence after earlier associations with international movements are Benjamin Anyaeji and Guru Maharajji. Both are well-known media personalities. Anyaeji, a member of Eckankar, now reportedly has dozens of people who flock daily to his Eko Boys' High School residence to seek the advice of the "Great Master."[24] His "cosmic consultations" in a weekly Sunday newspaper are extremely popular. Guru Maharajji and his Divine Light Mission have come to prominence over the last few years because of healing claims and prophetic status.

It has become increasingly common for traditional healers to supplement their herbalist and divinatory skills with metaphysical teachings, astrology, astral projection, tarot card readings, etc. In Calabar, I regularly passed a healing home signboard which proclaimed: "Homeopathic and Botanic Medical Clinic: Occultist, Astrologer, Physician." Dr. O. M. J. Obey, a metaphysician with qualifications (obtained by correspondence) from India runs the Obey Super-Science Centre in Ibadan, which I visited in 1987. He claims to offer "alternative medicine" and "metaphysical goods." Perhaps the most well-established of the healing homes in Calabar, by the name of Okopedi Healing Home and Okopedi Enterprises, is a major local supplier of all manner of magical and occult objects and literature. The founder, Okon Okopedi, went to India for a three-month training period in "astro-science." He claims that there is an occult/mystical part to traditional healing; in fact, he refers to "occultists" (such as himself) as the modern versions of "witch-doctors."[25] I intend to investigate more closely the Indian connections of some of these traditional healers in the course of my next research trip to Africa in 1991.

Influence of the Spiritual Sciences on Other Religious Institutions

In this section we examine the ways in which some religious institutions have incorporated and adapted spiritual science teachings into their own beliefs and practices.

The Brotherhood of the Cross and Star, which has established itself as one of the largest spiritual or independent churches in eastern Nigeria, is drawing increasingly on the support of occultists and metaphysicians. This is done primarily to enhance the image and status of the Sole Spiritual Head and founder, Leader Olumba Olumba Obu. For instance, the front page of one of the Brotherhood newspapers—the *Herald of the New Kingdom* (18-24 May 1984)—reveals how three of the "world's great occultists" have acknowledged Obu to be the source of Ultimate Power. Professor Assassu Inyang-Ibom describes how he travelled to various planes and into the astral world to test the power of Obu—"Every result was that the leader of the Brotherhood of the Cross and Star was a Super-Human being." Dr. J. S. Bazie (alias Dr. Aggarwal), an occult and mystical specialist based in Delhi, wrote in 1972 (in reference to Obu) to say: "I am convinced that God has his representative here on earth who comes into the world as God in disguise." Dr. Bazie's letter, as well as a later declaration that he had been visited by Obu in spirit in India, have been much publicized by the Brotherhood as testimonies to the power of their leader. Dr. Bazie and a small entourage from India visited Calabar in the late 1970s.

The Brotherhood also publishes numerous testimonies by its members (both in Nigeria and overseas) regarding their visions and auditions of Obu and their miraculous cures performed by him. He is generally believed to be omnipresent and omniscient. Obu claims that the power of Brotherhood is above that of any church or secret society or cult. Of particular interest here is the fact that a Brotherhood delegation visited the Rosicrucian (AMORC) headquarters in San Jose, California in 1981. There have also been negotiations with the Unification Church concerning a joint fishing industry on the Cross River.

The Crystal Cathedral Church began in 1964 as a small healing home in Lagos. The founder, Leader Brother A.E. Inyang, who is from Oku-Iboku in the Cross River State, is a fairly well educated man, with a Presbyterian background. He has read a number of spiritual science works, and this is partly reflected in some of his teachings on spiritual power and communication which are set down in a booklet on the history of the church. For instance, there is reference to the leader's "premier psychic initiation" in a dream and to the later development of his "clairvoyance, clairaudience and strong inspiration of the body."[26] Inyang is described as a "great mystic"; in a Revival address he stated the following: "I invoke the Light of the Ancient Power to encircle you all and may the vibration of the creation demonstrate its power today."[27]

There are examples of other independent church leaders being influenced in similar ways by their readings of occult and mystical literature. Bishop Dr. V.A. Oluwo, the founder of the Cross of Christ World Ministry in Ibadan, confesses to being an avid reader of comparative religious texts, as well as theosophical, magical, and mystical materials. While he sees this in terms of his own personal edification and not as a determinant of church ideology and activities, it nonetheless influences his teachings on spiritual power and discipline. The Cherubim and Seraphim Church (an Aladura or spiritual church) regularly places the following advertisement regarding its London branch in the news magazine, *West Africa*:

PRAYER AND SCIENCE
Prayer books, candle burning Psalms,
and Seraphic Sciences.
For your difficulties, knowledge, success
and easy life Contact:
Mother Prophetess Janet Awojobi

CHERUBIM AND SERAPHIM
7 Ranelagh Road, Tottenham

The introduction of the concept of "science" has occurred over the last few years.

We may also include here the influence of the spiritual sciences on the media. For example, a popular evening television program in Calabar is "Contemplation," billed as "our spiritual and metaphysical programme for mature minds." It features local leaders or representatives of spiritual science movements or any prominent "thinker" who is able to express himself (they are nearly always men, although the presenter is sometimes a woman) on "philosophical" (i.e. nonchurch) issues. The local Sunday newspaper in Calabar, the *Sunday Chronicle*, carries a lively column entitled the "Philosophy of Life. " The writer, Mr. B. I. Otu-Odofa, a lecturer in General Studies at the University of Calabar, is described by his readers as a "Christian mystic." He admits to having had early training in lodges and philosophical schools before recognizing the "power of Jesus." In his articles he addresses himself to moral and religious issues of the day, with a language heavily infused with concepts such as 'karma,' 'power,' and 'reincarnation.' The beginning of each calendar year is also an important time for Nigeria's parapsychologists whose front-page predictions proclaim Nigeria's fate for the coming twelve months. The increasing influence of these metaphysicians and parapsychologists is the object of a satirical play—*Requiem for a Futurologist*—by the Nigerian playwright and Nobel laureate, Wole Soyinka.[28] The fact that this type of religious figure is singled out for satire by one of Nigeria's leading social critics is a testimony to the growing significance of the phenomenon.

Ancestral Links?

In this section let us consider those areas of possible affinity between some traditional African and New Age beliefs and practices. In many cases, these are undeveloped and exploratory reflections. Wande Abimbola, a leading diviner or *babalawo* in the Ifa divination system of the Yoruba of Nigeria, claims that the training received by the Ifa priest aims to tap and unleash unlimited human and spiritual potential.[29] This notion of spiritual development, often associated with esoteric knowledge and initiation within the context of cults and secret societies, is common to many parts of West Africa. Sir Adeyemi, the Aetherius Society spiritualist, draws an interesting parallel between Ifa and Kabbalism: "Ifa is the Kabala of the Yorubas. Both are used for divination, healing, etc."[30] There are obvious links between traditional forms of divination and the strong interest in astrology that is observable among West Africans.

Healing has always been central to African concepts of the human and the divine and their interrelationship. Healing rituals reflect a holistic view of sickness; the individual as a composite configuration of natural, divine and human forces is healed from and by society, as well as the divine and natural worlds. Such a holistic paradigm characterizes the New Age attitude to healing, according to Catherine Albanese.[32] As the result of his work on the Yoruba of southwestern Nigeria, Peel was able to state that "[t]he wonderful power of healing might be explained by such scientistic doctrines as Rosicrucianism, Pelmanism or hydropathy, which have a surprisingly wide currency among literate Yorubas."[32] In similar vein, Robin Horton argues that the independent Aladura (or "prayer-healing") churches among the Yoruba have adopted innovative strategies of interpretation which allow them to reconcile custom with Christianity by focusing on those aspects of Western religion which are most consistent with their own beliefs, such as faith healing, spiritualism, and occultism.[33]

The idea of reincarnation is a feature of a number of African societies. This is linked to the belief in the ancestors, who may return partially or wholly in the form of a newborn child. Hence, the Yoruba practice of naming a child, for example, as Babatunde or Yetunde (father or mother has returned). The Institute of Parapsychology at the University of Virginia has shown much interest in this phenomenon among the Yoruba and Igbo. Igbo students of mine were commissioned by the Institute to report on signs and incidents of reincarnation among their people. While in some ways the African belief in partial or total reincarnation is a far cry from Shirley MacLaine's belief in former lives, it is possible that some may make the connections in their "welded cosmologies."[34] Benjamin Anyaeji, the "teleguru" as I have heard him termed, is fond of recounting his past lives on the air.

Spirit possession is a major form of communication between the human and divine worlds in many African societies. Such possession may be temporary or long-term. A human being may be a conduit for a deity, which may lead to a "marriage" with the deity, in terms of a full-time priestly commitment. There are obvious parallels here with the phenomenon of channeling among New Agers. We might also point to the shared belief in the importance of dreams as a medium of communication with the spirit world.

One of the aspects of New Age religion in America that has been particularly subject to attack by some Christian groups is the notion that one may become divine. Apotheosis is an integral feature of Yoruba religion, for example. But the process occurs in the next life. Individuals are commonly believed to have special powers or at least access to the (pantheistic) power source, ase. These are often the elders in the society. There may also be perceived links between the pantheistic aspects of some African worldviews and the New Age movement. At the very least, the monistic tendencies of New Age religion are consonant with the lack of differentiation between "religion" and other aspects of traditional African society. This idea of God within, or God and humans as one is highlighted as the primordial African state by the (Sri Lankan?) writer of a Nigerian-produced publication, entitled *Universal Brotherhood and Practical Meditation.*[35]

In the only article that I have encountered on this subject by a West African scholar, Onunwa argues that the emphasis upon self-realization in the new movements that he has studied is un-African, given that a basic concept of life is commensality, in which a person is part of a redeemed society.[36] He claims that the "cold contemplation of mysticism" is elitist and only appeals to those with an intellectual bent or who may already be involved in secret societies that emphasize mental discipline.[37] He also maintains that the "new guru movements" are often too mystical to appeal to ordinary Africans who are looking for practical solutions to problems. Here he is not taking account of the many movements which emphasize "empowerment" or "cosmic power" and which are very much world-affirming and pragmatic. According to Onunwa, the new movements do not offer the type of social solidarity found in kin-based religions. That may be the case, but many Africans are experimenting with the newer movements as a result of having found Christianity wanting.

Music is an important part of many traditional African rituals, not just as entertainment, but in terms of its transformative effects regarding spirit possession, for example. Within the African independent churches, music which is composed "in spirit" (through prophetic revelation) is believed to heighten the spiritual power of the church and its members. (Several of these African-instituted churches have shunned Western music for its lack of cultural relevancy and spiritual appeal.) I have encountered a number of Nigerians and Ghanaians (especially male university professors) who are avid listeners of New Age music because of its capacity to induce a state of peace or higher consciousness. I am not sure at this point in my research whether it is possible to purchase New Age-style music in West Africa. The individuals I am referring to were either expatriates or visitors who purchased or recorded the music in this country for use here or back in Africa. Some of them have been influenced directly or indirectly by the Rosicrucian use of classical music to generate spiritual states.

Evidence is fragmentary, but, as suggested above, these newer movements seem to appeal predominantly to Western-educated males who are disillusioned churchgoers.[38] They are attracted to the freedom from orthodoxy and orthopraxis and the absence of the religious label and its denominational divisiveness.[39] They are also drawn to the possibility of constructing their own religious destiny, through eclectic, quasi-scientific experimentation. The whole notion of empowerment is central to the appeal of these movements. It is a power that is mediated and acquired esoterically and often externally (cosmically, geographically) and therefore perceived as greater. In the words of R. M. Umukoro, the director of the "Kabbalistic Order: Home of Mysticism" in Ijesha-Tedo, Nigeria, " [U]nlike African voodooism, mysticism is a foreign culture which makes use of external forces that are beyond human understanding."[40] In an article on Christianity and magic in a Nigerian newspaper, C. Offiong claimed that "magic is an advanced form of Christianity" and tried to argue that Jesus belonged to a mystical society.[41]

In the course of his field work on the Aladura churches, Peel notes that Rosicrucianism was considered more socially acceptable than the Aladura or indigenous churches. He maintains that these beliefs and interest in such books as *Sixth and Seventh Books, The Kabbalah Revealed* . . . seemed especially prominent among solid bourgeois families, often with Lagos Saro links or connected with the African (separatist) churches. He believes that the phenomenon goes back to the 1920s and would have been diffused from such centers as Lagos and Calabar, which possessed their own bourgeoisie. He also maintains that the strand of "ancient Egyptianism" which appeared in such books as Olumide Lucas' *Religion of the Yorubas* was another important belief, circulating among the coastal peoples from Freetown (Sierra Leone) to Calabar.[42]

Jean Comaroff, commenting on Horton's observation that dissenting African movements have often lighted upon the "side-alleys" of Western culture such as faith healing and occultism, notes that European counterorthodoxies (among which she lists Spiritualism, Rosicrucianism and Theosophy) have been an important source of symbols and practices for dissidents in Africa, Latin America, and the Caribbean.[43] People find in them, she maintains, "a rejection of the logic of rational materialism and its reified religion." She goes on:

> Despite their diverse origins, these symbolic orders share an opposition to the categories of bourgeois liberal secularism; and all promise to subvert the divisive structures of colonial society, returning to the displaced a tangible identity and the power to impose coherence upon a disarticulated world.[44]

While Peel and Comaroff disagree on the social class this type of religion appeals to, they share the conviction that its discourse on power and order resonates with those whose life-experiences have been disrupted in some way and who feel compelled to regain control through a process of cultural reinterpretation, negotiation, and experimentation.

There are additional factors which have promoted the growth of these new movements. First, the process of internationalization, whereby individuals or groups seek to (re)establish links with international or overseas religious or spiritual organizations. As we have already noted, India and America seem to have a special draw in terms of perceived power sources. One booklet that I acquired in Ibadan, entitled *Universal Brotherhood and Practical Meditation*, is written by a Sri Lankan for a northern Nigerian audience, based on the teachings of the Sri Lankan Theosophical Society. Such a trend does not run counter to that of greater religious self-determination, which has characterized the postcolonial period. It reflects a desire on the part of individuals and groups to branch out and be part of international religious networks and control their own religious destiny.[45]

There is also the moral question, which we shall only briefly allude to in the present essay, but suffice it to say that, in a situation of moral dislocation, rather than advocating a stronger morality (as is characteristic of many churches), the problem may be transposed by identifying the problem as metaphysical rather than moral. This is identified as one of the reasons for the appeal of "guruism" by Onunwa—"We are not sinners: we are simply ignorant of our true nature and self."[46]

Religious pluralization has become the order of the day in a number of African societies since independence. Nigeria, in particular, has become a veritable marketplace of religions. Religious and spiritual groups compete for clients, in a way that departs from traditional patterns of cultic coexistence. It has been argued that the treatment of religion as a consumer item is characteristic of the New Age movement. Religious affiliation is now more closely linked to individual choice among Nigerians, rather than family, ethnic or marital determination.[47] This is in turn linked with an increasing privatization of religion. This is epitomized by the Rosicrucian claim so frequently seen in their advertisements in Nigerian newspapers that "Your Home is Your Temple" (which is in many respects a recreation of the domestic shrine so common to traditional ways of worship) and the abundance of "mail-order religion" and supplemental literature.

From Community to Cosmos?

In many respects, the patterns of belief and practice described above and identified as belonging to a subculture referred to as "spiritual science" are lacking some vital ingredients of the New Age movement in the United States. There is no social activism, no networking, no health and fitness and dietary concerns, and limited earth awareness.[48] Specialized New Age newspapers and magazines do not circulate. Further research is needed to see whether these categories are emerging. The vision of the New Age is not prominent in the Nigerian context and is generally expressed in terms of an imminent Aquarian Age, or some future ideal time where peace and harmony will reign.[49] Yet one cannot fail to be struck by the historical similarities, i.e., the New Thought, Spiritualist, metaphysical and occult foundations, and the common denominators of "radical mystical transformation,"[50] self-knowledge, convergence of religions, and empowerment. It may be that Nigerian New Age religion bears a closer resemblance to the American movement as it was in the 1970s rather than in its later phase.[51] It has also been my observation in this country that many people are New Agers by default rather than conscious commitment. In other words, they only gradually become aware of the wider extensions and implications of their tastes, life style and commercial choices. Yet they are sustaining as consumers the various facets of the New Age movement. Furthermore, we should not expect Africa to mirror religious developments in other parts of the world. Africa has never failed to provide a creative and selective filter for exogenous beliefs and practices. The Salvation Army or the Methodist Church in Nigeria, for example, differ from their parent bodies on a number of counts.

Melton has suggested that in the American context, "[t]he concern with the planet and the development of networks to engage in social change has become a significant factor separating New Age people from more traditional occultists who tended to avoid social activism as irrelevant to spiritual development."[52] On the basis of my limited research to date, I do not believe that occultism is the end of the line, so to speak, in the Nigerian context. As New Age literature circulates more freely (economic restrictions notwithstanding), and because of more general trends, namely religious pluralization and globalization (of which Roland Robertson speaks), growing consumer culture, increased communications and environmental awareness, we are likely to witness New Age-style religious developments in Nigeria and other West African countries. The *bricolage* offered by such a multimedia religious perspective provides an important material and symbolic interface between the local and the global.[53] Its international appeal, together with its roots in and affinities with traditional beliefs, suggest a firm basis for continued growth. We should not forget that the New Age movement only really began in the early 1970s in the United States. There is every evidence that these beliefs and practices, while remaining, for logistical reasons, more privatized, fragmented, and supplemental in Africa than in the American context, will continue to permeate and influence other religious institutions and affiliations. They will probably develop a wider base of support than their currently ostensible connection with a wealthy, male, educated élite. There will likely be an attendant increase in attacks by the mainline and evangelical churches on the larger, more visible, and esoteric movements such as AMORC (which is already much maligned as a "secret society" by many churches). Perhaps we may even witness the emergence of African New Age culturebrokers who will ensure the inclusion of African ideas and practices at a more international level (in the same way as African evangelists have now broken into the international evangelical and Pentecostalist scene).

Much more research remains to be done, not just along the lines suggested above, but also focusing on such areas as the relative absence of women in these movements in the Nigerian context, despite the key founding roles of American women. While my data selections, juxtapositions, and interpretations positing the emergence of a New Age movement in the Nigerian context may be subject to debate, what remains unquestionable is the rich and varied religious spectrum of modern-day Nigeria, whose complexities and implications we have only partially explored and sought to understand in the present essay.

Chapter 17

Japan's New Age and Neo-New Religions: Sociological Interpretations

—————————————— *Mark R. Mullins*

Introduction

Over the past several years journalists and scholars have been giving considerable attention to what has been variously referred to as a "religious awakening," a "revival of magic and occultism," and a "religion boom" in contemporary Japanese society. Journals and magazines have devoted entire issues to exploring the nature and significance of this renewed interest in spiritual, religious, and supernatural matters. Even the journal *Shiso to gendai* [Thought and Modernity], sponsored by the Materialism Research Association, published a special issue on "The Religious Awakening" in 1988.

Until the 1970s, the most widely accepted viewpoint on religion in modern Japanese society was that it would continue to decline in significance. The recent resurgence of religiosity, however, has forced scholars to rethink this interpretation. Sociologists of religion have long been preoccupied with the Weberian question of the role of religion in the process of modernization and rationalization. Recently, Japanese scholars have begun to address a post-Weberian concern by considering new religions as reactions or responses to modernization.[1] Past research has indicated that new religions flourish in periods of anomie and deprivation. What are we to make of the recent "religion-magic-occult boom" in light of Japan's present economic prosperity and abundance?[2] In order to understand the New Age phenomena and new religions presently flourishing in Japan, it is important to remember that interest in magic and the occult and the emergence of numerous new religions have occurred several times over the past century. While there are many similarities to religious trends in other societies characterized by advanced modernization, the present revival of religious and quasi-religious concerns must be understood in light of this earlier history.

The New Age and New Religions in Socio-historical Perspective

Omura suggests that there have been four such periods during which new religions have flourished in Japan.[3] Over the course of a century Japan has been transformed from a traditional feudal society into a modern technological society. Accompanying or following close behind the major stages of this modernization process have been periods during which new religions have arisen and grown rapidly. We will briefly review the first three periods and then consider in more detail the nature and significance of new religions and New Age phenomena in the midst of the present so-called "boom" of religion, magic, and mysticism.[4]

Period I

The first growth period for new religions began in the latter part of the nineteenth century, shortly after the *Meiji* Restoration (1868). The Restoration marked the beginning of a modernization process (and to a certain extent, a Westernization process) that was to transform Japanese society. As Nagai has observed, "nineteenth-century Japan was the epitome of confusion and chaos."[5] The feudal order was disintegrating rapidly by the end of the *Tokugawa* period (1603-1868) and the new Meiji government was only in the "process" of building a new order. During the transition period, Japanese society experienced a phase of acute anomie.[6]

There were two social groups that suffered most directly from the new policies of the Meiji government. The first was the samurai (warrior) class. When the government promulgated the conscription law in 1873, it "eliminated the last of the privileges of the samurai class.[7] The special status enjoyed by the members of the samurai class seemed to vanish almost overnight, particularly for those belonging to clans that had supported the Tokugawa government. Dispossessed samurai from these clans found that they were subsequently excluded from positions in the new Meiji government. Small land owners and farmers represent a second and much larger group that felt the negative consequences of new government policies most keenly. In 1873 the government began carrying out its land tax reform. Taxes were no longer to be based on crops but on the assessed value of the land. Consequently, farm families began living with new insecurities—whether they would be able to pay their taxes or be forced to sell to a wealthy landlord, and whether they would become tenant farmers or move to the cities as laborers. The deterioration of the situation of farmers during this period is well-documented: "It is estimated that as of 1873 over a quarter of the land was already tenant farmed; by the 1890s this figure had increased to 40 percent" (p. 279). The farmers faced an additional problem was well; that is, whether they would lose their sons to military service (traditionally the responsibility only of the samurai class) through the new conscription law.[8]

It was from among these two groups that new religions found a receptive audience during this first period. *Tenrikyo, Konkokyo,* and *Kurozumikyo,* though they began in the late Tokugawa period, were three new religions that experienced their most significant growth after the Meiji Restoration. These groups were particularly popular among farmers who were oppressed by the government's new land tax policies and grew most rapidly between 1873 and 1881, the years during which the land tax reform was being carried out.[9] Christianity, as a new religion to Japan, had its initial and primary appeal among the dispossessed samurai class. The samurai class, the most literate and intellectual class of Japanese society, was overrepresented in Christian churches. While the samurai class comprised only about 5 percent of the Japanese population at this time, approximately 30 percent of Protestant church membership came from this class.

Period II

According to Omura, a second religious boom occurred from the late Meiji, lasting through the *Taisho* period (1912-1926), and on into the early part of the *Showa* period.[10] By this time Japan was well into its industrial revolution and experiencing the many problems associated with a rapidly changing economy. While in 1889 the urban population was only 9 percent, by 1920 it had climbed to 18 percent as laborers streamed in from rural areas to meet the demands of the developing industries.[11] Poor working conditions and recurring unemployment problems characterized the lives of laborers in urban areas. Not long after the Great Kanto earthquake of 1923, there was a serious depression and growing insecurity, particularly among industrial workers.[12] The situation in rural areas also continued to deteriorate during this period. By 1920 land under tenancy had grown to almost 50 percent as many middle- to lower-class farmers were unable to meet the demands of the Meiji land tax system.

New religions, political ideologies, and social movements flourished in this fluid social climate. The 1920s were especially pluralistic as socialist, communist, and democratic movements attempted to address the many pressing social and economic problems. Many individuals seeking some kind of security and salvation found solace in *Omotokyo, Reiyukai, Hito no Michi Kyodan* (after World War II renamed *PL Kyodan*) and *Seicho-no-Ie*, new religions formed during this period. These groups, with the exception of Seicho-no-Ie (whose primary appeal was among intellectuals), grew particularly in urban centers among the laborers who had been uprooted from rural areas. They also had some success among farmers whose conditions progressively worsened. The growth of these new religions subsided from around 1941 when Japan entered the Pacific War. All citizens were expected to give their full support to the religion of the emperor system and the war effort.[13]

Period III

The third growth period of new religions began shortly after the end of World War II. This again was a period of acute anomie. The ideology which had united and propelled Japan as a nation since the 1930s disintegrated within moments of the war's end. Under General Douglas MacArthur, the Supreme Commander of the Allied Powers (SCAP) during the Occupation, the new "Bill of Rights" issued in October 1945 effectively dismantled the old social order. State *Shinto* was disestablished and reduced to a voluntary organization, and the Religious Bodies Control Law, which had both suppressed and used religious minorities for State purposes, was abolished. During the war, the government had forced various religious groups to unite and had reduced the number of religious bodies to forty-one. Under the Occupation's freedom of religion guarantee, many of these groups separated and resumed their former independent status. In this new environment, scores of new religions were also organized, so that by 1951 there were over seven hundred religious bodies.[14] In an attempt to gain some control over this situation, the Diet passed the Religious Juridical Persons Law in 1951. In order to qualify as a tax-exempt organization, religious groups were forced to properly register and comply with laws for property holding. When this law went into effect, the number of recognized religious bodies was reduced by several hundred.

Wartime devastation and the shock of defeat created a large-scale crisis of meaning. The new religions which emerged from the war's aftermath provided one means of coping with this crisis. Some of these new religions were simply reorganized groups that had been suppressed during the war, while others were appearing for the first time. The five groups experiencing the most phenomenal growth during this postwar period were *Sokagakkai, Risshokoseikai*, Reiyukai, Seicho-no-Ie, and PL Kyodan. Sokagakkai membership, for example, grew from thirty-five thousand households to a membership of more than one million households in just over a decade.

The growth of these new religions should be understood in light of the rapidly occurring processes of industrialization and urbanization. By 1950, Japan's economic recovery was underway, and due to the boost provided by the Korean War, "industrial production had risen to 134.5 percent of the prewar level" by 1953.[15] The progress of industrialization required, of course, another major population shift from rural areas to the cities. Laborers poured into urban areas to meet the demands of the recovering industrial economy. Earhart explains that: "In postwar times, the population shifted from 70 percent rural, 30 percent urban, to 70 percent urban, 30 percent rural."[16] It was from among these laborers and factory workers that the new religions gained most of their adherents. Lacking the support of their families and rural communities, individuals found these new religions able to meet fundamental human needs.[17] Caldarola notes that theses new religions also had considerable appeal to "economically and psychologically insecure persons employed in small enterprises which in the Japanese productive system is the sector most exposed to business uncertainties."[18] From the 1960s, these new religions became more sophisticated and began to attract members from the increasing numbers of white-collar workers and the new middle class.[19]

By the 1960s the Japanese were enjoying new levels of prosperity. The 1964 Tokyo Olympics clearly signaled that Japan was a significant economic power recognized by the international community. This new prosperity, however, was accompanied by a leveling off of religious interest, and organizational growth subsided. Not until the oil shock and crisis of 1973 did the rate of economic growth slow down.

Period IV

Omura suggests that a fourth religious boom began around 1978 as the period of unlimited economic growth came to an end.[20] Since the mid-1970s there has been a growing recognition of the problems of modern industrial society and the limits of science and technology. This has been accompanied by a revival of traditional Japanese religiosity as well as the emergence of another wave of new religious movements and New Age phenomena. The findings of the NHK Survey on Japanese religious consciousness provides important background for understanding the current social climate.[21]

The NHK study discovered that the percentage of the Japanese population claiming to have a personal faith increased from 25 percent in 1973 to 33 percent in 1981. It also found that the observance of traditional Japanese religious practices was relatively high. As many as 53 percent of the sample worshiped before a Shinto god-shelf and 57 percent before a Buddhist Altar in the home. The percentage of Japanese participating in *Hatsumode*, the first visit to a Shinto shrine during the New Year holidays, was 81 percent. Of the sample, 77 percent received protective amulets or talismans from shrines and temples, and 89 percent indicated that they participated in *Obon* or *Ohigan*, Buddhist festivals which usually involve visiting ancestral graves (pp. 4-9).

Other findings of this study are also important for interpreting the recent revival of religion, magic, and mysticism. Regarding attitudes toward science, "about 73 percent of the NHK survey respondents answered that 'science is not almighty,' while 76 percent stated that 'even as science develops further, it will not necessarily bring more happiness to people'; and 55 percent agreed that 'the more science develops, the more people will have a longing for the mysterious.'"[22] Commenting on these findings, Swyngedouw suggests that these expressions of disbelief in science indicate a certain openness to religion, magic, and the occult.

Nishiyama's 1985 survey of religious consciousness among first- and second-year university students supports Swyngedouw's interpretation. This study discovered that while students have a negative image of organized religion they nevertheless express a strong interest in mysterious or supernatural phenomena. Some of the findings of this survey are as follows: 56.5 percent expressed an interest in transcendental (supernatural) power, while 40.8 percent actually believed in the existence of such power; 62.4 percent expressed an interest in UFO phenomena, while 53.4 percent indicated a belief in the existence of this phenomena; 52.6 percent expressed an interest in ghosts, while 46.8 percent indicated believe in their existence; and 60.2 percent expressed an interest in miracles, with 49.1 percent expressing belief in their occurrence.[23]

A look back over the past decade reveals a growing interest in the occult, mysticism, and New Age phenomena. This is particularly evident in bookstores across Japan. One could say that over the past decade a new spiritualistic counterculture or subculture has emerged and become a visible feature of contemporary Japanese society.[24] If one strolls through almost any bookstore in Japan (it is unnecessary to go to a special "New Age" bookstore) one will come across a section of books under the label "the spiritual world." This is usually a rather large collection of books found next to a smaller counter of books on traditional religion.[25] Here one will find books, magazines, cassettes and videos on a wide range of topics, including astrology, divination, UFO phenomena, psychic science, techniques of magical healing, communication with spirits of the dead, the occult, and training methods for controlling the spiritual world.

While there are numerous indigenous contributions to this relatively new spiritualism, the influence of imported New Age phenomena is not without significance. Modern forms of communication and travel have made it possible for ideas, beliefs, and movements to spread across national, cultural and linguistic boundaries at dizzying speeds. It is probably not uncommon for a New Age trend of religious movement to make it to the streets of Tokyo before ever penetrating communities in the southeastern United States.[26] Book after book by Edgar Cayce, Rudolf Steiner, Krishnamurti, Gurdjieff, and various Eastern gurus line the shelves in Japanese translation.[27] While most of these volumes never become best sellers, publishers have indicated that they usually sell between five- and ten-thousand copies. More recently books by Carlos Castaneda, Shirley MacLaine, and Osho Rajneesh have appeared in Japanese. Shirley MacLaine's *Out on a Limb*, for example, was first translated into Japanese in 1986. It is now in its thirty-third printing and has sold some two hundred thousand copies. Four other of her books have also been translated, bringing her book sales to over five hundred thousand. Some twenty-five books by Rajneesh have appeared in Japanese, with one selling as many as forty-three thousand copies. Numerous videos, and cassettes of music from the "world of Osho" also line the shelves with Rajneesh books. The Japanese version of the *Osho Times International* magazine is also distributed in Japan. While the Rajneesh movement is quite visible in print, it has not met with spectacular success as an organized religious movement. It has some eleven centers scattered across Japan and a membership of approximately three thousand.[28]

There are also many indigenous expressions of the New Age movement in Japan. A recent edition of *Tama Mind Network*, a monthly New Age magazine, contained articles on paranormal healing, principles of UFO, the establishment of the new science paradigm, and on how to obtain unlimited spiritual energy. This journal also advertises the latest books in New Age spiritualism and news of various group activities. There are currently several hundred loosely organized spiritualistic groups, some with memberships ranging from only one or two hundred to over a thousand. While some of these groups have been formed in the past ten to twenty years and are heavily influenced by the New Age movement in North America, the Association for Spiritual Science traces its history back to 1929, when it was first organized in Tokyo under the influence of the Western Theosophical movement. A number of these spiritualistic groups are a part of the network "International Spiritual Science Forum" and together sponsor lectures, hold an annual conference, and publish a journal.[29]

The Rise of "Magical" Religions

While "organized religion" has on the whole a very poor image and little appeal, there are some new religious movements meeting with success. In the present environment, however, the religions that grew so rapidly during the postwar period are not experiencing significant growth. While Sokagakkai, Reiyukai, Risshokoseikai, Seicho-no-Ie, and PL Kyodan still remain the largest of the new religions, they are now regarded as "established" new religions and are apparently not benefitting from the recent surge in Japanese religiosity. A new set of religious groups is meeting the needs of the present wave of "seekers," many of whom are under thirty years of age.

In order to understand the nature and significance of recent religious trends and movements, Nishiyama classifies new religions into two types: "belief" religions *(shin no shukyo)* and "magical" religions *(jutsu no shukyo).*[30] The former are movements which tend to be exclusivistic and emphasize doctrine, and the latter emphasize mystical experience and magical rituals. According to Nishiyama, the "neo-new religions" that emphasize magic are meeting with the most success in the present situation.[31] The most representative groups of the current religious boom are Agon Shu, Mahikari Kyodan, GLA (God-Light Association) and Shin'nyoen. The combined membership of these so-called "neo-new religions" is approximately 2,700,000.[32] Religious experience, performance of esoteric rituals, and techniques for controlling the spiritual world, are the most important aspects of these groups. Exclusivistic beliefs or doctrines tend to have little importance.[33]

Recently some new personalities and cult movements have begun attracting considerable media attention.[34] One prominent new age figure is Ryuho Okawa, the founder of the Science of Happiness Association *(Kofuku no Kagaku).* While this Association began as an "audience cult" in 1986, it has rapidly evolved into a new religious movement. Thirty-three year old Okawa, a graduate of Tokyo University and former salary man (company employee), began to attract a following through the publication of his "spirit world" books. In a period of four years, Okawa has written almost 150 books, which together have sold around 4 million copies. A casual perusal of almost any bookstore will likely uncover twenty to thirty Okawa titles. One can legitimately ask how a single person can produce two or three books per month. The answer is that Okawa does not write alone: over half of the books published by Okawa are "spirit messages." In trance Okawa communicates with spirits from the "other world" and writes down the messages he receives. These have been published as collections of spirit revelations *(reijishu)* and consist of messages from such luminaries as Buddha, Jesus Christ, Edgar Cayce, Swedenborg, Newton, and Picasso.[35] From all of these "guiding spirits" Okawa has synthesized an eclectic vision for building a New Age civilization which integrates personal and public happiness.

In addition to books and tapes, Okawa communicates his messages from the spirit world in lectures throughout Japan. In spite of the fact that tickets cost 2,000 yen (approximately U.S. $13.00), in the spring of 1990 Okawa's lectures drew crowds of 7,000 in Kobe, 4,000 in Hiroshima, 12,000 in Chiba, and 5,000 in Nagoya. In only four years, Okawa's Science of Happiness Association has grown to include 100 employees in the Tokyo headquarters and 15,000 members associated with 9 centers across Japan.[36] According to a recent report, Okawa is presently seeking to register the Science of Happiness Association with the government as an official religious body.[37]

Folk Religion and the New Shamanism

The many features and characteristics of the New Age and religious revival in North America—shamanistic practices, non-medical healing, and communication with the spirits of the dead, for example—may appear cultic and bizarre in a highly rationalized Judeo-Christian context. Apart from spiritualism and Native American Indian traditions, such phenomena have been rather unusual and outside of mainline religion. In Japan, however, these elements have long been basic ingredients of folk religion. As Miyake has pointed out, "it is within the frame of reference provided by folk religion that the organized religions have made their way into Japanese society."[38] Recent new religions and imported New Age phenomena must also be seen in relation to folk religion. While there are clearly novel elements in the New Age and new religions, their popularity and relative success in contemporary Japan is clearly due in part to their effectiveness in relating to the "old" concerns for ancestors, spirits, and magical healing which have dominated folk religion for centuries.

Folk religion, with its animism, syncretistic beliefs and practices, has been referred to as the comparatively stable "substructure" of Japanese religion.[39] Central to the cosmology of folk religion is the interdependence between two spheres: the world of the living and the spirit world of the dead. The world of the dead, traditionally associated with mountains, is populated by various *kami* (gods), animal spirits, spirits of dead ancestors, and protective spirits.[40] In traditional Japanese society, the shaman served as an intermediary between this world and the spirit world. Through trance the shaman was able to make direct contact with supernatural beings and various ancestral spirits. In addition to transmitting messages from the spirit world, the shaman was usually empowered by a protective spirit and able to prophesy and heal.

It has long been recognized that the ancestral cult is a central feature of Japanese folk religion. In its classical or traditional form, the ancestral cult refers to the "belief in the superhuman power of the dead who are recognized as ancestors, and the rituals based on this belief."[41] Ancestors were originally understood as the founder of a household and successive household head. Thus, ancestor veneration was essentially a patrilineal phenomenon. Studies have indicated that modernization and urbanization have modified both the family structure and conception of ancestors in significant ways. Nevertheless, the concern with ancestors and appropriate care for the deceased is still a dominant feature of contemporary Japanese religion and culture.

According to the worldview of Japanese folk religion, one's situation in this life in causally influenced by the spirit world. Health problems, business failures, and personal problems are frequently attributed to the failure of descendants to properly care for their ancestors. If appropriate rituals are not performed, the ancestor suffers and cannot achieve "buddhahood" *(jobutsu)* or lasting peace.[42] Often wandering spirits "are said to be suffering from the emotional state of *urami*-bitterness, ill will, enmity, spite or malice."[43] Individuals suffering misfortune in this life often see the cause in the "urami" of some unpacified spirit.

In order to pacify such spirits, individuals follow the instructions of shamans to perform memorial services or make special food offerings. Until the needs of the ancestors are met through rituals and offerings, the ancestor will more than likely function as a malevolent spirit and bring a curse *(tatari)* and problems upon the descendants. If descendants perform the proper rituals, then the ancestor becomes a protective spirit and brings blessings upon the household. The land of the living and the dead is in this way interdependent and linked symbolically through ritual behavior.

This animistic worldview dominated by the shaman has faced a number of challenges over the past century. Since the Meiji Restoration, the Japanese government actively suppressed the activities of shamans and proscribed magical healing and exorcism.[44] Clearly indebted to Weber and his view that modernization (rationalization) involves the elimination of magic under the influence of ascetic Protestantism, Shimazono argues that westernization, nationalism, and state control of religion have functioned similarly to eliminate animistic (i.e. magical) beliefs and practices, although the rationalization process has not reached the level found in the Western world.[45]

In spite of the rationalization process and government control of religion over the past century, shamanistic folk religion has been revived again and again by new religions. The founders of many Japanese new religions have functioned essentially as traditional shamans and articulated the basic worldview of traditional folk religion.[46] While founders of new religions have introduced "new" revelations, gods, and rituals, these movements are most accurately understood as a new expression of folk religion and a revival of animism.[47] The "new" syntheses of both indigenous and foreign beliefs and practices in various movements over the past century have not fundamentally altered the cosmology and framework of traditional folk religion.

While the message is essentially the same, it is transmitted with the power of modern technology: books, cassettes and videos are widely marketed and sold. Unhappiness, illness, and problems in this life are still, for the most part, related either to the bad karma accumulated in one's previous existence or to the spirits of the dead. An examination of almost any of the "older" new religions as well as the neo-new religions will reveal an emphasis upon magical rituals that enable their members to cope appropriately with the dead and transform malevolent spirits into protective spirits.

The central place of ancestors and spirits in new religions has been noted in numerous studies.[48] Hardacre's research indicates that both Reiyukai and Kurozumikyo stress the importance of ancestor worship in one form or another.[49] Earhart's study of *Gedatsu-Kai* revealed that the founder of this movement had provided innovative means of more effectively dealing with spirits and ancestors.[50] The *amacha* memorial ritual and the mediumistic technique of *goho shugyo* are two new methods of restoring harmonious relations with the dead. Davis' study of Mahikari discovered a similar preoccupation with the dead: "Knowing how to feed and worship the spirits of one's ancestors has been the key to health and happiness for many Mahikari followers."[51] Likewise, Reader (1988:240) notes that the *taizo* fire, one of the two *gomagi* fire rituals performed at Agonshu's popular *hoshi matsuri* (Star Festival) is for the veneration of ancestors and salvation of suffering souls who in their unfulfilled state simply cause physical and spiritual trouble for the living.[52] It is significant to note here that in recent years both traditional religious institutions as well as new religions have given considerable attention to the spirits of *mizuko* (literally "water-child") or aborted and stillborn children. Many Buddhist temples as well as new religions provide memorial services for mizuko in response to the felt needs of Japanese women who are struggling with the sense of guilt and curse associated with their spirits.[53] In fact, it is difficult to find a new religion that does not provide special memorial services for mizuko.

Sociological Interpretations

Japanese scholars suggest that the growth of these neo-new religions reflects a larger shift in Japanese culture.[54] In the postmodern situation, consciousness and life style have shifted from an emphasis upon instrumentalism to expressivism. There has been a movement away from "instrumental" concerns (production and labor), and "expressive" behavior related to consumption, play, and leisure has begun to be valued more highly. While the economic prosperity of contemporary Japan has increased leisure and cultivated the "spirit of play" *(asobi no seishin)*, the current involvement of youth in new religions has deeper significance than simply "play" or "experimentation." Unlike previous periods, the present surge in religiosity is occurring in a society characterized by affluence and material security. For the most part it seems to be boredom with the routine and restrictions of the educational system and the business world that is giving birth to the new wave of seekers. Nishiyama suggests that many individuals see themselves as stuck on the escalator of modern bureaucratic society with little control or freedom to direct their own lives.[55] For this reason, perhaps, magical religions which emphasize "sacred techniques for gaining power and well-being" are increasingly attractive.[56] While physical conditions have certainly improved since the war, a "new kind of poverty" has appeared and exists alongside material abundance. By-products of the modernization (rationalization) process have been boredom, fatigue, and the loss of meaning. Youth in particular, Nishiyama argues, have felt this new form of poverty most keenly as they are enclosed in a competitive and bureaucratic educational system from kindergarten to university.

The work of Sakurai, a Japanese folklore scholar, provides the basis for Nishiyama's analysis of the social function of neo-new religions.[57] The role of these new religions is explained with reference to the Japanese term *ke* which means "life force" or "spiritual energy." The loss of this life force is called *kegare* and the recovery of this principle of vitality is called *ketsuke*. Using this framework, Nishiyama suggests that the new religions successfully perform the function of ketsuke or revitalization. It is in the sacred space and through the ketsuke rituals and festivals provided by the neo-new religions that individuals are able to experience the spontaneity and freedom so lacking in their daily existence. The emergence of this new form of expressive individualism, particularly in the youth culture, is often referred to with the catchphrase *shinjinrui* or "new human kind." It is among the "new human kind" that these new religions seem to have their greatest appeal. They offer exciting religious experience without the excessive pressures of conformity demanded by the larger social system and without the requirement of adherence to a rigorously defined belief system.

The classic Weberian perspective on the process of modernization emphasizes the role of rationalization in the elimination of magic or the "disenchantment of the world."[58] Nishiyama points out, on the other hand, that the modernization process in fact gives birth to nonrational phenomena.[59] In other words, revivals of mysticism and magic are inevitable reactions to the rationality and predictability of contemporary society. Nishiyama observes that the problem of kegare (loss of vitality) is not limited to contemporary Japanese society. It can be seen in other countries characterized by advanced modernization. The ketsuke or revitalization function is performed in North America, for example, by the charismatic movement and various new religious movements emphasizing meditation.

According to Shimazono, other factors are also important for understanding the current revitalization of animistic beliefs and practices in the new religions.[60] First, Shimazono points out that the "democratization of religious culture" has accompanied the process of modernization. For many years, intellectual elites (representing education) and the government had the power to suppress or exclude folk religion. In recent times, however, the general population has experienced economic mobility and an increase in political power. This in turn has increased the ability or power of the masses to articulate their own beliefs and practices. The number of intellectuals interested in and identifying with folk culture and religion has also increased; consequently, through journalism and mass media the influence of popular religion upon middle class culture has been steadily growing since the 1970s.

Secondly, Shimazono suggests that the pragmatic (utilitarian) orientation of modern technological society and its fragmentary/specialized approach to knowledge is well-suited to the animistic beliefs of popular religion (p. 6). For the most part, understanding of modern technology is limited to specialists. Individuals simply use various forms of technology to meet specific needs. A pragmatic or utilitarian type of orientation to the world is becoming dominant. Shimazono maintains that this type of orientation fits the approach to life found in popular religion. It is also based upon a fragmentary or isolated use of spirits and magical powers to deal with particular problems and situations. The systematic worldviews of the historical religions, based upon scriptures, myths, and tradition, have attempted to provide a comprehensive guide for all of an individual's decisions. It is becoming increasingly difficult, Shimazono explains, to maintain such a worldview in the present pluralistic and fragmented situation. In sum, there is a kind of compatibility between a utilitarian-fragmentary approach to the spiritual world and our modern technological culture.[61] Shimazono concludes that the present religious revival and growth of neo-new religions have brought the revival of animism to Japan's middle class.[62]

Conclusion

Almost two decades ago Blacker's study of Japanese shamanism concluded with the suggestion that the spiritualistic worldview of the ancient shamans, a separate world of spirits and supernatural beings able to causally effect our world, is a thing of the past:

> The vision of another plane utterly different from our own, ambivalent, perilous and beyond our control, has faded. Instead the universe has become one-dimensional; there is no barrier to be crossed, no mysteriously other kind of being to be met and placated. The storms, droughts, sicknesses, fires which used to be laid at the door of kami, ancestors, foxes and ghosts, are now believed to lie within the competence and control of man. . . . When the view of the other world fades, and its inhabitants dwindle to the predictable regularities called the laws of nature, the shaman and his powers are no longer needed.[63]

It is apparent that since Blacker wrote these words, there has been a significant resurgence in belief in this "other world." Furthermore, a number of modern shamans have appeared and are advocating new and old ways of controlling this "other world" of spirits and powers for personal protection, happiness, and success in this world.

Religious trends in contemporary Japanese society reveal many striking similarities to forms of religious belief and behavior in other societies characterized by advanced modernization. Bird and Reimer, commenting on the new religions and para-religious movements in North America, suggest that the phrase "religion and the rise of magic" captured the character of recent religious concerns and involvements.[64] In the context of Japanese religious history it is probably more appropriate to speak of recent trends here in terms of the "revival of magic." While many elements have been imported from Western New Age movements, most new religions currently prospering in Japan are dominated by concerns and a religious world view which closely resembles that of premodern Japan.

Chapter 18

The "Newness" of the New Age in South Africa and Reactions to It

——————— *Gehardus C. Oosthuizen*

The New Age movement was forcibly brought to the attention of South Africans when two aluminum poles were planted in Capetown on 11 November 1989 (Armistice Day) and on Table Mountain, Capetown on 12 November 1989 (Remembrance Day) by the "Movement for Peace through Prayer" (an organization which originated in Japan after World War II). Some were shocked that such "foreign" religious activities were carried out in Capetown on the country's most prominent mountain. Has the Cape of Good Hope become a symbol of foreign religious invasion? Has the Mayor of Capetown, with sympathies for Sufism and the New Age movement, become a traitor of all that is dear to so many conservative Christians? The Mayor of Capetown, Gordon Oliver, made no excuses for his participation in the planting and consecration of the Peace Poles. On the contrary, he emphasized, "There are many paths to the same source. My role as mayor is one of bridge-building with love."[1] He himself goes to Jewish synagogues and takes part in Buddhist meditation sessions.

The Mayor further stated: "I am a Christian but not an orthodox one." And added, "I feel at home in any form of religion and support the idea of one world religion and one God."[2] He criticized Christians for being intolerant and stated that it should not be necessary to accept the religious views of others to be able to pray for peace with them. This was said at a time when the country was in deep turmoil, especially within the Black townships. He stated that it was the New Age movement which organized the activation of the "Energy Centre," but he did not wish to be described as a member of the movement. He emphasized that, as a result of a decision of the Municipal Council of Capetown, the Peace Poles would not be removed. Ms. Susan Kaschula, coordinator of the World Peace Movement, stated that there is nothing "demonic or evil" on the Peace Poles. If they were demonic, the Pope would not have one on St. Peter's Square, nor would Mother Theresa have one at her hospital in India. Before the abovementioned event took place, the Shekum Foundation stated, "Table Mountain is a major planetary focal point in beaming energies of Aquarius and New World consciousness."[3]

Table Mountain had special significance for General J. C. Smuts. His book, *Holism and Evolution* (first published in 1926), has received special attention from New Agers in South Africa. The man who received inspiration from his regular walks and climbs in and on this mountain has become one of the central figures to be adopted as a predecessor by the New Age movement. His approach tried to overcome the Newtonian, mechanistic concept of nature (i.e., that all events in nature are merely physically-chemically directed). Smuts emphasized that an "inner energy," a *vis vitalis*, exists in matter; there is a teleological factor which governs the material processes. Smuts also had difficulties with the Judeo-Christian concept of God, and the position he eventually adopted—the Divine as the dynamic energy active in matter—has marked affinities with certain New Age concepts.

The planting of the two aluminum poles, carrying the words "May Peace Prevail on Earth," in Capetown and on Table Mountain was an independent act of the "Movement for World Peace through Prayer." At the same time, New Agers decided to "positively activate the negative energy" in Table Mountain through meditation and prayer, carried out at propitious moments determined by consulting the astrological calendar. It was anticipated that these activities would bring a spirit of peace, love, friendship, and harmony to Capetown. An ecological act was also performed in clearing away litter. Songs were sung, such as "*Nkosisikelela*" (God Bless Africa—a kind of national anthem [for Blacks] which originated in South Africa, and which was translated and sung in many other African countries). It is a prayer directed to God, asking that Africa and its people be blessed. Whites often interpreted this beautiful song as a kind of war cry. The songs on Table Mountain at the abovementioned ceremony were sung to the accompaniment of Buddhist gongs.

Very few people had been conscious of the fact that the New Age movement was active in South Africa. Some Christians who have been in contact with it condemn it; others have been more careful. Several incidences of strong reactions by fundamentalist Christians have been reported, such as chopping down the poles and accusing New Agers of being inspired by the spirit of Satan.

New Age Activities in South Africa

It is difficult to describe here more than the main tenets of this movement in South Africa. Beyond the inherent complexity of the New Age worldview, there are differences between the various "Communities" and between individuals, although there are broad areas of general agreement. Many aspects of what is designated as "New Age" hail from ancient philosophies and religions, so that this movement appeals to people who are dissatisfied with the secular and religious status quo. The movement's agenda includes holistic health and healing, education, relationships on all levels (family, marriage, social, and business), various dimensions of ethics, alternate technology, conflict management, nonadversarial politics, nonadversarial law, new ways to care for the dying, the environment, green issues, and peace issues. Not only is the intensity of New Age activities increasing, but their scope has widened as more people are convinced that the new vision gives them hope and satisfaction. Many New Agers have a history of discontent with the churches, and experienced rejection and accusations of being "unorthodox" and "heretical." The first "Link-Up" in South Africa came into existence in order to help such persons connect with each other (an activity that is referred to as "networking"). Each region has its own "Link-Up." It provides a communication service and gives free information on forthcoming events, workshops and talks, on the ongoing groups that are spread throughout the country, and on other activities available in and around the various cities.

The Wellstead of Wynberg, Capetown became the first resource center in South Africa. New Age information is now available through *Odyssey*, Link-Up, and the vast array of books to be found at the Wellstead (which is a meeting place, information center, bookroom, and lending library). The Wellstead is responsible for the publication of *Odyssey* and *Link-Up Western Cape*, and assistance is given in organizing and running seminars and workshops. Other New Age bookshops flourish in Capetown (such as East-West Bookshop, The ID Booksellers, and The International Bookshop); in Johannesburg (such as Aquarian Book Centre and Isis); and in Durban (Adams Bookshop and others, especially those that concentrate on Eastern religions—Durban has about half-a-million Indians of whom the largest section are Hindus). New Age material is proliferating at great speed in all South African cities. Articles associated with the New Age movement appear in South Africa in magazines such as *Femina, Fair Lady, Cosmopolitan, Personality,* and in Afrikaans magazines such as *Die Huisqenoot, Sarie, Rooi Rose, Insiq, Basuin,* etc. One popular anti-New Age book in Afrikaans is a translation of Walter Martin's, *The New Age Cult*.

The various and differentiated activities of the New Age movement started to surface during the latter part of the seventies, and their impact has rapidly expanded. The bookshops mentioned above sell a great variety of books, videos, and cassettes on subjects related to the movement's agenda. Books that are in demand at the various shops (as reported to the author by the Wellstead bookroom in Capetown, Aquarius Book Centre and House of Isis in Johannesburg and Adams in Durban) are *inter alia*: Shirley MacLaine's *Out on a Limb* (as well as her other books); Lazaris' writings; The Scott Peck Books; Dr. Deepak Chopra's *Creating Health, Perfect Health, Quantum Health and Return of the Rishi*; B. Segall, *Love, Medicine and Miracles*; Juriannes's *Bridges*; J. C. Smuts, *Holism and Evolution*; Crawford's *The Guide to Mysteries*; Lobsang Rampa's *The Third Eye*; Elizabeth Haich's *Initiation*; O'Phiel's *Kabbalah Magic*; H. K. Challoner, *The Man Triumphant*; P. B. Bowen, *The Sayings of the Ancients*; *The Occult Way*; Alice Bailey, *The Works of Alice Bailey*; A. A. Bailey, *Ponder on This*; *Prophecies*; *Serving Humanity*; Aldous Huxley, *The Perennial Philosophy*; Lesley Weatherhead, *The Christian Agnostic*; F. C. Happold, *The Journey Inward*; William Kingsland Christos, *The Religion of the Future*; Sri Krishna Prem, *The Yoga of Bhagavadgita*; *The Yoga of the Upanishads*; *Man the Measure of All Things*; Dion Fortune, *Esoteric Philosophy of Love and Marriage*; Joseph Head and S. L. Cranston, *Reincarnation*; and Helen Greaves, *Testimony of Light*. Tarot cards are also in regular demand at New Age bookstores.

Emphasis on Healing

The emphasis on alternative healing is one of the outstanding features of the New Age movement in South Africa. Alternative healing also has a special place in the African Independent/Indigenous Churches, as will be discussed later (the [African] Traditional Healers Council's Secretary estimates that, in South Africa, eighteen million blacks, out of the greater than twenty-four million black population, visit traditional healers—e.g., diviners and herbalists).

New Age healing methods come from various parts of the world, such as Asia. The impact of East Asia is evident in such organizations as the British Tai Chi Chuan and Shaoli Kung Fu Association in Capetown. This is an ancient system of martial arts that has only recently been introduced in the West. It is considered to be a holistic means of attaining and maintaining optimum health. For the body it is a form of exercise and relaxation; for the mind a study in concentration, will-power and visualization; and for the soul a system of meditation and spiritual development. *Shin Sen Do* is practiced *inter alia* in Johannesburg.

This Taoist energy practice, which includes healing, diet, meditation, acupuncture, herbology, and macrobiotics, is quite popular.

The Holistic Health Centre in Constanttia, Capetown, sponsors courses and seminars on medicinal herbs, message, aromatherapy, energy balancing, crystals, candida, and building the immune system. Other centers offer homeopathic remedies and psychotherapeutic medicines. Various healing centers are highlighted in *Odyssey* and in Link-Up circulars, such as Dr. John Bell's (a medical practitioner in Johannesburg) center. His practice utilizes holistic message therapy, and he maintains that real health is a synthesis of all aspects of life—physical, emotional, intellectual, and spiritual—as well as relationships with others. His work represents a synthesis of Western and Eastern approaches.

Health for Africa is a forum for holistic health care in South Africa and operates on a compassionate, united, and multiracial basis. The Festival of Mind, Body and Spirit was presented in Durban on 27 and 28 January 1991 and included exhibitions and lectures on reflexology, crystals and their healing powers, circle dancing, astrology, the future of the planet, meditation, and quantum healing. Dr. Deepak Chopra's book and Maharishi Ayur-Veda products are in demand at all centers in the country, especially after his recent visit.

"The Leeward," referred to as the realization and healing center of the Healing Association of South Africa, operates in Johannesburg. Services available through The Leeward include clairvoyant counseling, aura readings, regressions, spiritual healing, metamorphic techniques, acupressure, Swedish massage, and *Jin Shin Do*. Regular events are evening meditation classes, afternoon Tai Chi classes, hatha Yoga classes, and spiritual healing courses.

One of the active centers in Johannesburg is the Font, which was started on 29 May 1990, and is directed by Christopher Nevill (whose reflections on the New Age in South Africa are contained in the Appendix). This is one of the mushrooming centers for learning, holistic healing, and metaphysical research—a retreat which "recognizes the divine uniqueness of man and his ability to control his own destiny." In 1991 courses were offered on herbs, meditation, hypnotism, "memory," relationships, rebirthing-breathing, Tai Chi, Buddhism, reflexology, etc.

Much attention is given by various New Age centers and groups to human relationships, such as the Insight Training Centres in various cities in the country (said to "enhance the quality of your personal and professional life"). The Yoga-Kabbalah Meditation Society teaches Burmese Zen and Kabbalah Tantra Meditation. Burmese Zen concentrates on the release of tension, stress, and anxiety; Kabbalah-Tantra

Meditation focuses on yoga meditation technology and improved relationships through centering on the Universal Love Energy. There are various yoga centers in the country, especially in the greater Durban area where there are more than half-a-million Indians. Esoteric healing practices are practiced *inter alia* at the Raja Yoga Meditation Centre, the Ananda Kutir Yoga Centre, Yoga Today Ministry Centre, Sahaja Yoga, and other centers. The main emphasis is on self-realization. The Reflexology Academy of South Africa in Johannesburg offers various courses emphasizing the experience of "genuine togetherness."

Wholistic World Vision (WWV) emphasizes togetherness on a global scale moving beyond the "disturbing religious, cultural, ethnic and political" barriers because "we ALL share the same planet and have the same conscious responsibility." Planetary networking and healing in its holistic context is a major emphasis of WWV.

Ongoing groups and their activities are mentioned in the Link-Up newsletter of each region. Groups mentioned in such regional Link-Ups include Circle/Sacred dance; Meditation; the Homeopathic Society of South Africa; Theosophical Society, ECKANKAR; First Church of United Religious Science in South Africa Abundant Living Centre; International School of Reflexology and Meridian therapy; and the Liberal Catholic Church, which has various churches in the country. As reflected in these newsletters, the New Age movement also encompasses the Road Less Travelled discussion groups (based on Scott Peck's book, which emphasizes a new psychology of love, traditional values, and spiritual growth); the Order of Truth (an esoteric school specializing in the mystic teachings of the Masters); the Sandton Church of Religious Science (which advertises services on Sunday mornings that feature "inspirational lectures on positive thinking"); the Three in One Spiritual Centre; the Spiritualist Church; the South Africa Study group of the Summit Lighthouse ("study the teachings of ascended Masters"); the Aetherius Society (lectures available on "The Cosmic Plan," New Age Holy Mountains, Karma and Reincarnation, Flying Saucers and their Message to Earth); the School of Metaphysics ("classes in every aspect of positive living"); Astrology ("Astrological natal chart analysis; astrological consultations; computer assisted astrological reports, astro-intelligence; an in-depth psychological horoscope analysis"). Workshops are announced which will "include exercises in breathing and relaxation, healing of self and others, guided imagery and meditation. It will explore the use of color and sound, dreams, symbols, mandalas, the use of crystals and past life therapy as keys to awakening and releasing our inner wisdom and power. It will look at nature and how to live in harmony with all life." Crystals—rainbow crystals, cosmic crystals, healing crystals—play a significant role ("the crystal is capable of receiving, sending and holding energy. It is uniquely a tool of communication and as our age is an age of communication, it might be in fact called the 'Age of the Crystal'"). Another advertisement emphasizes that "crystals from deeper than anywhere in the World—from 4000 feet below the ground—are now brought into light." Tarot cards, tarot numerology and palmistry are also significant.

Much attention is given to ecology by New Agers. Earthlife Africa admits that there are many environmental conservation organizations and groups doing important work in achieving a common goal. A gap, however, has to be filled to complement the work done by these organizations and groups. Earthlife Africa is the South African equivalent of Greenpeace, and tries to serve as a watchdog, especially in such areas as industrial pollution. Scientists, doctors, lawyers, and other professional people serve as advisers. They assist in investigating and exposing particular pollution problems. Earthlife Africa stimulates environmental awareness and research and upholds six principles: 1) ecological wisdom; 2) reverence towards the earth; 3) grassroots democracy; 4) rejection of all forms of discrimination; 5) nonviolence; and 6) ending of exploitation.

A Proto "New Ager": A DRC Minister's Wife

Johanna van Warmelo (1875-1964), who married a Dutch Reformed Church (DRC) Minister, the Rev. L. E. Brandt, came to the fore with a number of ideas which are now central concepts in the New Age movement (NAM). After assisting Boer spies against the British, she worked in a concentration camp near Pretoria among the Boer inmates. She later contracted cancer, but cured herself with a grape diet and through "sunbaths."

She had a vision at the death bed of her mother in which the Messenger anointed her with the gift of prophecy. After the decease of her mother, she had four visions concerning events in the future and had them published in a book entitled *Millennium*. In this book she maintains that after a time of judgment the millennium will commence in South Africa. Harmony will be the key of the future. She founded the Order of Harmony which was a mystic covenant—a secret covenant of men, women, and children who pledged before God to do everything in their power to prepare South Africa, and through South Africa the world, for the coming of the Redeemer. The aim of the Order was the promotion of harmony on earth—between races, genders, religion and politics, spirit and reason, nature and science—harmony between God and the human being.

The primary aim of members of the Order was to reform themselves and experience the harmony of bodily health. Physical health was a precondition for a pure spirit. The grape cure, which the founder experienced as being so efficacious, became an indispensable part of physical purification. Healing was viewed as taking place through all seven of nature's healers, through the agency of water therapy, pure air, sunbath, spinal adjustments, fruit diet, and the Spirit. Genuine healing was based on living according to the laws of nature.

She also taught that, to understand the present age, the "scientific truths which influence this period should be understood," namely, that every two thousand years the earth enters a new cycle and that a new tempo of vibration is established. The unrest in every corner of the world in 1916 was taken to be evidence of such a change of cycle. She maintained that the earth was in a transitional stage between the era of the Fish and the age of Aquaria (she used the feminine form of Aquarius). She maintained that Aquaria is also the giver of life, who is the Mother. The era of Aquaria is that of the woman which, according to her, will be the worldwide era of the emancipation of women. The Order also taught that matter is spirit, but in a lower state of vibration.

In 1927, she went to New York for two years to make known her ideas and healing procedures through the grape cure. While in North America, she received an honorary degree from the American School of Naturopathy. After returning from the United States she published *The Paraclete—or Coming World Mother*, a book which announced the coming of God-the-Mother in the New Era. The outpouring of the Spirit will first be on women and later on the other generations and genders so that the finer qualities of intuition, imagination, and mysticism will be able to develop. She believed in the Fatherhood of God, the Motherhood of the Holy Spirit, and Jesus Christ as the Elder Brother, the representative of the heavenly home. The Mother will teach humanity to do the will of the Father, and this will transform conditions on earth. Humanity will then have the right to claim its status of being sons and daughters of the most High.

She believed in the universality of what is good. In the "New Era" this universality will be evident irrespective of color, faith, age, or gender. Peace, tranquility, redemption from poverty and sickness will characterize the New Era. Johanna Brandt could have been the first person to describe the New Era of Aquarius in a manner foreshadowing the ideals of the present New Age movement. The emphasis on the new spiritual era, on healing, on the closeness and compassion of the human being towards nature, on a fruit and vegetable diet, on self-development—all are prominent in the New Age movement.[4] It would be

unthinkable today to find the wife of a moderator of the DRC pro-
pounding these ideas. The substance of her books on the abovementioned issues is far removed from the Calvinist doctrines of the DRC.
Irving Hexham maintains she was the first person to give a systematic
exposition of the "New Era." She died at the age of eighty-seven in
1964.

Reaction of the Churches to the New Age Movement

A variety of reactions are to be discerned among the various churches.
Desmond Tutu, Archbishop of the Church of the Province of South
Africa, criticized the attitude of "fundamentalist Christians" who tried
to disrupt the New Age prayer and meditation meetings. The Rev. John
Hawkridge, moderator of the Presbytery of Capetown (Presbyterian
Church), while disagreeing with the New Age philosophy as being
against "orthodox Christianity," stated, "I do not think we should run
the New Age down." The reaction of Bishop James Gribble of the
Methodist Church, District Bishop for the Cape of Good Hope was that
"there is a deep longing for peace all over the world, and 'Blessed are
the Peacemakers,' says the Bible. I cannot support the kind of antago-
nism being displayed against them." A Dutch Reformed Church Minister in Capetown at the time, Professor B. Loubser (now Professor of
New Testament studies at the University of Zululand) assessed the new
development as follows: "Within my experience there is room for plurality of religion, but the confusion between science and the mystical is
too real. Is it not merely an updated revival of the Millennialistic and
mystical tendencies of the past? Is a religion based on the planet and the
future really necessary? Many New Age terms are woolly, New Agers'
thoughts naive, and certain practices sinful. Penetrating and critical
questions are necessary."

Self-searching is discernable in the reaction of a distinguished member of the Baptist Church, Rev. John Herbert: "I am totally opposed to it.
It carries the seed of complete anarchy. The message is very subtle and
plausible. I feel for the New Agers very deeply because they are
deceived; it is wrong to become a law unto your own self. But this puts
the question to us as a Church: 'Why are we not attractive enough?'"

Pastor Don White of the Apostolic Faith Mission of South Africa
(in Capetown) stated "I am totally against it. It's a false doctrine and a
false cult. Their principles are not based on the Word of God." Pastor
Paul Daniel of the Lighthouse (associated with the International Fellowship of Christian Churches) described the Movement as preparing
"the platform for the coming of the anti-Christ," while a spokesman

for another group, called "an open ministry for the Body of Christ in Capetown," stated: "We reject the New Age Movement totally and utterly. It is an evil and satanic embodiment of the Anti-Christ."[5]

The Dutch Reformed Church (DRC)
and the New Age Movement (NAM)

The strongest DRC reaction to the New Age movement thus far has come from Dr. J. Malan, who ministers to an "Upper Income" congregation at Aasvoelkop, Johannesburg, and who was at the time Moderator of the Southern Transvaal (Regional) Synod of the DRC. He gave a lengthy analysis of the NAM in an article published in the mouthpiece of the DRC, *Die Kerkbode*, on 7 July 1989. The article had a photo of the wife of a leading industrialist with children's articles in her hands—a "horror pencil box" in the form of a coffin with R.I.P. on it; another, a "horror bag" with a skeleton on it and a "horror eraser" with a few skulls painted on it. The article is entitled "Misleading New Age Movement Also in South Africa." It commences with Luke 12:56: "You hypocrites! You know how to interpret the present time?" The article asserts that Christianity faces "one of the greatest threats in its history" (i.e. the subtle ways of distorting the Bible). "Falsehoods" are not directly launched but come under "the cloak of so-called scientific techniques" which are presented as improving one's religious experience, and which "could transform one into a better Christian."

Malan provided his readers with a background to the New Age movement, with its emphasis on the eradication of the evils of the Age of Pisces and the promises of the Age of Aquarius. He described the movement as stressing the significance of what is useful and advantageous to each individual; that distinctions between races and gender, between "heathen" and Christian as "sinner and Redeemed," should disappear as well as the distinction between Satan and God. One world religion, one world government, and one world economy are the aim. It was pictured as presenting a false concept of peace; the World Council of Churches is accused of advocating such a type of peace; that peace has become the greatest clarion call of our time without circumscribing this "peace." All people are described as brothers whether they have the same father or not; all people are "anonymous" Christians who belong to the so-called "latent Church" which strives for the "Perfect Society" on earth. The article responded to this picture of the New Age with the biblical reference from Luke 12:51—"Do you think that I have come to give peace on earth? No I tell you, but rather division."

Dr. Malan ascribes these developments to the longing for inner peace which the explosion of knowledge, technology, and science could not bring. The potential of human thought has been tapped to explore the world of outer space, and now the sensory world of the human soul should be expanded. The new emphasis should be on the "inner space" of man. The "occultic religions of the East," such as the Shamanism from Korea, are presented as especially dangerous. Much emphasis is placed on the changing world view of Newton in response to developments in modern physics. The psychological sphere also receives attention from the NAM. From the beginning of the second half of this Century, the "Human Potential Movement," with its emphasis on the latent powers of the human spirit and the rise of group dynamics and sensitivity training, opened up new avenues to develop the dormant potential of the human being. Modern psychology thus prepared people to be influenced by Eastern thought, according to Dr. Malan.

The movement aims to create a new unity within the context of the political and economic world order, when humanity will be in harmony with the cosmos. The ultimate ideal of the New Age vision is for the human being to be completely in unison with the cosmos, and through reincarnation, to develop his soul to perfect divinity. Ontologically, no distinction exists between God and the human being. Dr. Malan views the NAM as a human-centered program to establish a total unity without God—the old heresy of the tower of Babel. Its methods and techniques are seen as a combination of Western science and Eastern idolatry whereby human beings are taught how to meditate and, through visualization, extend their consciousness in order to make the transformation from the old to the new era.

Dr. Malan warns that the powers of evil are prepared to enter open doors—opened by this humanistic, pantheistic worldview and practice. All these efforts prepare the way for the Antichrist. The warnings are also extended to the sphere of children, especially the small children, who will be the main generation after 2000—in the Age of Aquarius. He warns that the schools have already been infiltrated with New Age ideas. Children are taught to get in contact with "guides," "wise persons," demons, and demonic powers. Toys, plays, cartoons, symbols, and all kinds of methods are used, including music that employs such hideous methods as "back masking." Dr. Malan described the NAM as an "unstoppable movement in the last decade of this Century in order to introduce the non-Christian era."[6]

Dr. Malan was threatened with legal action by a music company for a statement that a specific record gave evidence of "back masking." He maintained that another specific record "addresses the subconscious mind," distorting the Christian message and attacking basic Christian values. The production manager of the record firm rejected the allegations and stated that "musicians react on the basis of moral obligations, over against a Society, and part of these moral obligations is to indicate injustices in the society. Dr. Malan's attitude is typical of that type of distorted conservatism against which young South Africans react."

This extensive reference to the reaction of a prominent Minister in the DRC in South Africa—he was the second oldest Minister at the recent General Synod—indicates that the sources relied upon for his reaction against the movement originate from outside of South Africa, principally from the United States. Very little empirical research has been done by the DRC in this country. The General Synod of the DRC, which had its quadrennial Synod in October 1990, decided to refer the whole New Age issue to one of its committees for further investigation. The concern with regard to the movement remains, but there is little clarity on the precise approach that should be taken concerning the NAM. The Methodist Church of Southern Africa has also appointed a commission to investigate NAM.

The NAM attracts the younger people who see in this movement an answer to their longing for a more dynamic and meaningful expression of their convictions. This is also evident in the Pentecostal/Charismatic Churches which, however, are not expanding at the rate they did from the 1960s to the early 1980s. None of the denominations have done an in-depth analysis of the influence of the NAM on their churches, although concern is expressed about its activities. More attention has been given to Satanism.

The NAM, being an inclusive movement, is appealing because of its emphasis on a global stance over against the parochialism that has prevailed in South Africa. The New Agers seek wider contact in a country which is a religious microcosmos, with its nine world religions, many new religious movements, and Independent Charismatic and Pentecostal Churches. A section of the youth find the NAM attractive because of its open, universalistic stance in an environment where the Apartheid syndrome has destroyed real contact among people. It is usually the more intellectualized middle- to higher-income group who experiment with new possibilities. This leads some to occultic practices which emphasize self-realization and the rediscovery of the Divine in oneself. The hidden knowledge, wisdom, and power which are found outside the bounds of ordinary sensory and experiential reality have to be sought in extraordinary ways. What many South African youths have experienced of this country's traditions have been unappealing. The NAM is nothing else than a longing from the heart of modern man for a more hopeful world than the one in which s/he was reared. This challenge of the NAM to the Churches in South Africa will become more severe in the future. Many of the white youth are filled with genuine guilt. The NAM is especially attractive for a section among them, as it gives them the opportunity to contact congenial spirits. Many New Agers in South Africa are sincere people, believing firmly that they serve God in what they are doing. They attract other people who want to do good, and the NAM satisfies genuine human needs.

The movement has something for everybody, whatever kind of people they are. Many New Agers are sad that people don't understand their intentions and accuse them of being unchristian. Many of them could have been candidates for membership in the charismatic Churches because of their deep longing for meaning, but they found the New Age first.

The Hindus in South Africa and the New Age Movement

There are, among the one million Indian South Africans, over six hundred thousand Hindus, whose ancestors were brought to this country from 1860 onwards. About 12.5 percent of the Indian population are Christians, whose proportions have increased very rapidly since 1970. Lately, there have been complaints among some Christian Missionaries that the NAM has made their missionizing activities difficult among the Hindus. The missionary message of redemption is challenged by the Hindus as never before, because they maintain that there is nothing they need to be redeemed from. A Reformed Church missionary maintains that the New Age movement in the Capetown area is responsible for the emphasis of Hindus on the ongoing significance of the Hindu religion. The Hindus react against the proclamation that Christ came to save people—Christianity is not the future of the people, but rather, as is evident in the New Age movement, Hinduism is the bearer of the future of mankind.[7]

Divali or *Deepavali*, the Festival of the Lights, was again celebrated on 17 and 18 October 1990 in South Africa. One day is for the Hindi and Gujarati-speaking Hindus (whose ancestors came from North India), the other for the Tamil and Telugu-speaking Hindus (whose ancestors came from South India). Divali is described as a record of the two ages of the cycle—the dark age and the golden (or new) age. The lighting of millions of tiny lamps throughout the world signifies the enlightenment of souls through the spiritual knowledge that God gives through the *Gita* in the midst of the age of darkness and unrighteousness that prevails at the end of each cosmic cycle. This spiritual awakening results in great joy and happiness, which is a foreshadowing of what is to be experienced in the golden age of the cycle.

The above description was given by a spokeswoman of the Brahama Kumaris Yoga Organization, highlighting the spiritual significance of Divali/Deepavali. There were also statements concerning the time cycles which are determined by the movement of the sun through the constellations of the stars (the sun takes approximately two thousand years to pass through one of these constellations, and this period of time constitutes an "age"). Before the close of the last century, Hindu astrologers and Gurus started speaking about an age that is soon to dawn, an age which would be known as the Age of Kali (a feminine deity). They predicted that the characteristics of Kali would surface and mold the face of society. This is said to explain the rise of feminism and the social revolution followed in the wake of it. Helena Blavatsky, of the Theosophical Society, at the last quarter of the last century, picked up on these Hindu notions and began preparing for the New Age. (Statement by Rev. G. H. Denyschen, Reformed Church of Africa, Missionary in Indian Community).

Over the last two decades the sun has been moving out of the sign of the fish (Christian era) and into the sign of Aquarius. Those involved in the esoteric sciences speak of the "dawning of the New Age." For Hindus the evidence of change in the world and society is a confirmation of their belief in astrological determination and the "truth" of the teachings of Hinduism. This New Age is being eagerly awaited by informed Hindus as the new age of peace and prosperity.

Many Hindus in South Africa adhere to what has been termed "Village Hinduism," and are not well informed regarding the basic teachings of Hinduism (i.e., the theological framework within which the ceremonies are performed). There is, however, a new breed of academics and professionals who began delving seriously into their Hindu roots as a result of the favorable attention their religion has been receiving in the West, particularly in the new movements such as the New Age movement. There was a time when academics and professionals who were Hindus kept their religion in the background. Efforts to have Hinduism taught in the Indian schools were not only thwarted as a result of counteractivities from biased white Christian educational authorities, but also from teachers who were Hindus. The situation has now drastically changed. South Africa is experiencing a resurgence of Hinduism.

Western input and guidance is steering the academics and professionals who are Hindus toward the vocabulary utilized by New Agers. Words like *karma, avatar, reincarnation,* and *meditation* originate from Hindu Scriptures. But words such as *altered states of consciousness, holism, paradigm shift, Quantum Leap,* even *New Age* are Western contributions. There is, however, a rapid awakening of awareness, especially among the intelligentsia in need of a defense against the moral argument of Christianity, of the powerful and relevant role that Hinduism will play in the modern world. A revival in philosophical Hinduism in South Africa is also taking place as a reaction to the penetration and proliferation of the Pentecostal and Charismatic Churches in their midst. Posters are going up regularly advertising visits of Gurus and Swamis from India; more and more are drawn to meditation and yoga; and the Brahma Kumaris, an organization run by women, offers meditation and yoga. There are many yoga schools in the greater Durban area among the white and Indian communities, but not among the blacks.

Hindus have many of the basics of the New Age in their cultural tradition and are mostly not aware that they are involved with the NAM, but, in point of fact, they are involved in a closely related thought world. The average Westerner who converts to the New Age experiences a radical change of worldview when he or she accepts a worldview with close affinities to Hinduism. For the Hindu, much in the NAM is not "new," but is rather a continuation of his or her basic beliefs concerning religious practices, traditional healing methods, occultic practices, visiting astrologers, following the calendar, etc. Westerners are already responsible for an increase in the awareness of the NAM among the Indian people, which has led to a reaction against the missionizing attempts of the protagonists of Christianity. This reaction has become understandably strong among all sections of Hindus. Many Hindus believe that time is on their side and not on the side of the type of Christianity practiced in many churches.

Movements of Spiritual Freedom in South Africa— NAM and Black Zionism (BZ)

The New Age movement and Black Zionism have, in spite of specific differences, many similarities. If so, in what sense is the NAM "new"? Black Zionism is, in the Southern African context, a vast indigenous Pentecostal/charismatic movement. Three movements—Ethiopian, Zionist, and Apostolic—constitute the African Independent Church (AIC) movement which reacted against the ecclesiastical establishment because of its association with missionary control. The largest section is the Zionists, established as a result of influences from the Christian Catholic Church in Zion (Illinois, USA). Eighty percent of the eight million strong AIC movement (i.e., 28 percent or 6.5 million Africans) belongs to the Zionists.[8]

Reaction Against Staleness in Empirical Christianity

BZ, like the Ethiopians and Apostolics, reacted against missionary control, but more against the Westernized expressions of Christianity. BZ is by and large an expression of ecclesiastical democracy—an expression of ecclesiastical freedom in a situation of political oppression. This movement's Church structures are largely decentralized, with numerous house congregations, many of which are full-fledged denominations. These face-to-face church groups strengthen the traditional sense of community. They reintegrate, as does the NAM, individuals who have lost their relationships with the extended family and who have become alienated from traditional bonds in the new social situation. Many blacks migrated to the cities in a short space of time with the result that BZ became a major factor in reintegrating religiously and culturally rudderless people. The sense of community is as strong in the NAM as it is in Zionism. The relatively small NAM groups transcend the barriers of race—of narrow, closed, suffocating, isolated communities. The NAM cherishes wider contacts, as does Black Zionism. The NAM has grown at a great pace during the last few years. New Agers themselves find it surprising that there is such a genuine and deep interest in the various aspects of what has become known as the NAM. In the faceless cities and in the context of faceless churches, many find the NAM activities "refreshing and inspiring."

New Agers and Black Zionists both feel free to choose their own religious expressions. The former do so by borrowing from East and West as well as from the ancient Middle East and also Africa, and the latter combine religious expressions from African traditional religion with Christianity. Both broke through conventional boundaries to reach the people. Black Zionists express their liturgy through singing, dancing, handclapping—in a spontaneous manner which is not evident in most mainline Churches. Such spontaneity is also evident in many of the New Age groups.

In both, symbols play an important role. Sacred power is relayed by way of symbols—in BZ through crosses, staves, holy water, color symbolism, candles, stars, and certain acts, and in the NAM through such universalistic symbols as the rainbow and through symbols associated with ancient mythologies. In BZ the spirit (Holy Spirit) as a powerful force is greatly emphasized.[9] This is at least partially attributable to their experience of powerlessness in the face of powerful negative forces in South Africa. "The Spirit" as a powerful macrocosmic counterforce to the realities of their situation acts within the microcosmic context (i.e., within the group). These small communities or denominations isolate themselves from the wider context of human existence with the idea of retaining their spiritual power in order to be, in a centripetal manner, the salt of the earth. "The Spirit," with its sacred power, identifies itself with their group—it is for them a vivid experience. The NAM also has its numerous small groups, most of which strongly believe in the omnipotent mystical power which transforms them through various spiritual acts, such as meditation.

BZ and NAM React Against Structural Institutionalism

Black Zionism's reaction against structural institutionalism resulted in no less than five thousand denominations in South Africa. Relatively few groups have authoritarian structures. Their finances are not spent on keeping the organization, as an institution, going, but on the needs of their flock and others who need their help. Ministers or leaders are often not paid for their services—BZ is largely a "tent making" ministry. Personal charisma is the major "gift" expected for ministry, without undue emphasis on theological training. Thousands upon thousands of small groups gather in houses (only about 5 percent of Black Zionists gather in Church buildings) or open spaces in nature for services. Many of these groups become closely knit entities with very little formal structure. Various persons assist with different tasks, such as the leader, the evangelist who is a probationer, the lay preacher, the prayer healer, the prophet, and the woman's leader (the latter three offices can all be held by women). The role of women here is as prominent as it is within the New Age movement.

The antiestablishment and anti-institutional character of the New Age movement is a remarkable parallel to BZ. Many New Agers, however, remain in mainline Churches, especially the more "liberal" churches. A tremendous variety of activities go under the designation New Age, and the term "networking" aptly describes the loose contact between many of them (as is, *inter alia*, evident in the "Link-Ups" and *Odyssey*, the bi-monthly magazine). Many of the groups know about each other through personal contacts, newsletters, Link-Up and sharing of information. Every New Ager decides for him or herself what direction is most advantageous to his or her spiritual taste and longings. There are elements of Eastern universalist spirituality which are attractive for a section of the New Agers. The BZ emphasis on traditional African worldviews, and the particular healing procedures practiced, make them attractive to black Africans, while the New Age movement attracts mainly urban whites and a small number of Indians—Hindus rather than Indian Christians.

The Role of Universal Energy in ZB and NAM

Most NAM adherents and all Black Zionists accept the existence of a universal energy. There is a life force or energy for the African in everything, though some objects and persons have more of this mysterious energy than others. This is referred to in Black Zionism as "power": an energy, a force that effects healing, that gives a person the power to heal, to prophesy, to exorcise. Like the NAM, BZ thus believes in the universal power which permeates all existence. Some places have special power, so that dancing and praying on a specific mountain, for example, is more effective than other places. The sea, with its white, blue, and green "colored" water and salt, is effective in transforming this power and in making contact with the "living dead" ancestors in the beyond. The sea serves as a contact medium with the forces in the metaphysical world.

Although New Agers see this power as a natural energy that permeates everything in the cosmos, certain persons with supernatural qualities convey it more effectively than others. They contact a higher form of energy through specific methods which enable a person to tune in and relay it to others.

Channeling and Prophecy in NAM and ZB

In traditional African society the diviner plays a prominent role. This important office has been replaced in BZ by the faith healer *(Umthandazi)* and the prophet *(Umprofeti)*. These prophets work through visions, and transfer the healing powers which they receive from the "Holy Spirit" and the ancestors onto the sick; they exorcise, counsel, and transfer healing energies and powers to patients and also serve as seers. They have the gift of "prophecy," and speak in tongues while other members interpret the content during the prophet(ess)'s state of trance. New Agers concern themselves with "channeling," just as the prophet in BZ is a medium or channel through whom specific ancestors operate. Such contact from the ancestors is important for the diviner in traditional African religion and so is also important for the prophet, who is the substitute for the diviner in most of BZ. For both New Agers and BZ, contact with these powers occurs in a dramatic manner, not because they are remote, but because of the significance of such contact.

Negative Evil Forces: The BZ and NAM

While in the traditional Pentecostal/charismatic Churches much emphasis is placed on Satan and demonic powers, in BZ Satan is in the background, and demonic evil spirits are more threatening to the group (they are used by sorcerers to harm people). The reaction against these forces by Black Zionists holds them together. One of the most important activities in Black Zionism is the removal of various kinds of demons from the flock, and this is usually done at dams, rivers, and the sea. BZ is second century Christianity, and the Christianity of the first few centuries after the ascension of Jesus Christ had much to do with exorcism, especially after his religion became the religion of the Roman Empire in the fourth century A.D. For these Christians, as for BZ, evil and well-meaning spirits were a reality. They affected, as in the case of BZ, their health, well-being, relationships, and the future.

New Agers are, on the whole, not evading the issue of negative spirit influences but do not give much attention to any evil disposition in the unseen world as being an evil threat to mankind. The spirit world is rather benevolent and helpful to human existence. For both Black Zionists and New Agers the metaphysical world is a world of sacred power, and from this world enlightenment and revelations are received for the personal life and human existence.

Healing in ZB and NAM

Healing in the holistic sense is a central issue in BZ. This is one of the main reasons for the rapid growth of the movement.[10] They understand the psyche of their people, speaking the "language" of people at the grassroots, and address the problems these people encounter with cultural diseases, such as the effects of evil spirit possession, witchcraft, sorcery, and the usual diseases. The world of spirits is still very real for most of the adherents of BZ (as for first and second century Christians). Much of their concentration on evil spirits is due to the fact that socio-economic and political issues are viewed as resulting from the activity of evil forces. Bewitchment and sorcery are frequently directed at depriving one of life, often through mysterious events and diseases. BZ concentrates on purification rites as a fortification against misfortune and the forces of evil.[11] Because there are typical African diseases which are ignored by the mainline church leadership, people are not able to fortify themselves against their onslaughts. They then go to herbalists, diviners, or to the prayer healers and prophets of the African Independent Churches. These Churches are spiritual "freedom fighters" — they free their flock from the vicissitudes of evil forces projected into evil spirits. They have their own approach to group dynamics based on the sensitive, in-depth understanding of the African psyche.

Summary

Many of the activities of the NAM are associated with healing, as is evident from our earlier discussion of NAM healing. Many kinds of healing techniques are utilized in the movement, and encompass such practices as spiritual therapies, meditation techniques, mind healing procedures, New Thought teachings, visualization, yoga, and various other physical techniques.

In both Black Zionism and NAM, the healing and empowerment of the body, the soul, and the mind (the latter perhaps indirectly in Black Zionism) accounts for the rapid growth of these movements. Both Black Zionism and the New Age emphasize the role of holy power personally experienced in the lives of individuals. The duality between this world and the world beyond has been broken down—there is a deep, sensitive relationship between the physical and the spiritual world. In both movements personal experiences with the numinous power are emphasized. In Black Zionism this experience is manifested through speaking in tongues, prophesying, praying, intercessing, laying on of hands, singing, shouting, and exorcism, while in the NAM personal experience with sacred powers comes through channeling, prophesying, and meditation. Experiences of the sacred are thus not the prerogative of the mainline, institutional Churches, but are accessible to every individual.

The stability and human caring that individuals experience in these movements make them places where they can feel at home. They have been seeking this familial atmosphere in the hustle and bustle of urban life, and the traditional Churches could not provide it. In these meaningful house congregations and sacred communities they found what they were seeking.

The healing of people through nonmedical means by giving wholeness to their lives is a great attraction in both movements: Here they receive a freedom to interact with the metaphysical forces that support them, a freedom they did not experience in the mainline Churches. Mystical experience and revelation are not limited to a few, but are the birthright which every human being can claim without reference to any institution or hierarchy.

While the NAM ventures to synthesize scientific, metaphysical, and religious worldviews, Black Zionism concentrates on the metaphysical and the religious without regard for the scientific worldview. Black Zionists take their traditional roots seriously without losing touch with developments around them. Not less than five million traditionalist blacks joined Black Zionism during the last quarter of a century. For them a new future opened up. They are much more open to the needs of their people than "classical" Westernized Pentecostals.

Black Zionism has proved itself as the church of the future for the black community in South Africa. The NAM has, in spite of its "newness" on the South African scene, the momentum among those who wish to experience more dynamic responses to their quest for meaning than what the mainline churches offer. A section, however, combine their churches and the NAM. The NAM is for the largest majority still new, but challenging. The indications are clear that this movement will become a force to be reckoned with in the South African context. The mainline churches have lost the dynamic stance which attracts the youth, and with them lies the future.

Conclusion

The NAM has only recently come to the attention of South Africans. It appears that this movement is extending its influence among middle income whites, especially those in the age group twenty to forty-five. The average New Ager is a seeker who could have been a candidate for the charismatic movement. They come from that segment of the population which has become marginal to the mainline churches, including the Afrikaans language churches and those who have already left these churches. People who wish to overcome what they consider to be the narrow and biased outlook of white South Africa feel attracted to such movements as the NAM. On the basis of current trends, we can predict that the NAM will continue to gain momentum, and that fundamentalist Christianity, feeling itself threatened by the New Age, will continue to react strongly. THe Hindu section of the population will discover more and more the central role that aspects of their religion plays in the NAM.

Whether the Pentecostal/charismatic movement will be able to expand its influence in this context remains to be seen. The black community, deeply religious and not easily moved by other than Christian-oriented movements, will not produce many New Agers. For this community, Black Zionism, and the African Independent Church movement more generally, will be the main force in the lives of those who look for a dynamic expression of religiosity. It could be that the NAM will attract more and more blacks from the intelligentsia. A small number of them increasingly visit the NAM bookshops, but few are yet actively involved.

The development of the NAM in South Africa is an interesting phenomenon which, in retrospect, makes Johanna Brandt, who highlighted the contours of the NAM during the first quarter of this century, appear to be somewhat of a prophet. That she and Jan Christiaan Smuts, both products of a Calvinist upbringing, should become forerunners of the NAM is indeed remarkable. Thus, in spite of the apparent "newness" of the New Age in South Africa, it is, from a historical perspective, merely the latest incarnation of a form of spirituality that has been present since at least the early part of the twentieth century.

Appendix

The New Age—South African Version
Christopher Nevill

Up until the middle of 1980 South Africa boasted only one of what are today becoming known as Centers of Light. This was The Wellstead in Cape Town. In the rest of the world many of these centers had sprung up since the Second World War. Some of these like Findhorn, the Paul Solomon Center in America, and Esalen Institute in California have become almost household names even amongst those who view the whole idea of a New Age with more than a healthy dose of skepticism. There are today possibly thousands of centers worldwide, all offering an alternative viewpoint on the rather prickly subject of life. Some of these viewpoints were and still are somewhat unusual, and their activities have cast a pall over the activities of the New Age movement. None of this seems to have really mattered, as the prognostications of various seers about this movement from the Piscean to the Aquarian Age seem—in broad terms at least—to have materialized as facts. It is extremely difficult not to be impressed.

South Africa has seemed to lag behind. Books like the *Aquarian Conspiracy*, by Marilyn Ferguson, *Supernature*, by Lyall Watson, the wealth of material put out by people like Colin Wilson, Alan Watts, Fritjof Capra and the plethora of books on Eastern mysticism, yoga, Buddhism—all these have been as eagerly devoured by South Africans as they were by the Americans and Europeans. It is in the formalization of structures that we have lagged behind.

A myriad of sitting rooms in private homes have been the meeting places for groups of varying sizes, who, rather like the early Christians, have met almost in secret to pursue their interests. As elsewhere, these have ranged from pure discussion groups to other groups who meet with more specific purposes—such as healing, meditation, astrology, and so on—in mind. Some of these activities have excited the attention of the authorities, and more than one police file contains the terse notation "Harmless loonies," or words to that effect.

Despite the occasionally hysterical opposition by the charismatic movement and the more measured tones of the conventional Churches, the New Age movement is now quite firmly a part of the South African scene. As is so often the case when genuinely concerned people start to worry about what is going on, the cause of the particular concern is producing some old bedfellows. If one can keep a sense of proportion, the results are really very funny. It is difficult for a charismatic church to rail (which seems to be their first instinct) against alternative healers when both come out as anti-CFCs. Again, it is not easy to put down a meditation movement that expresses concern about racial injustice or the polluted state of the planet. Nonetheless, the legacy of the spiritually barren Piscean Age continues to hold and will continue to hold sway for some time yet. This is characteristic of any time of change when the influences of both the old and the new continue to have effect until the new slowly displaces the old.

In the world of medicine, for example, Americans and Europeans are, albeit slowly, beginning to recognize the value and efficiency of alternative methods of healing. There is a recognition that both allopathic and alternative methods have validity and complement, rather than contradict, one another. Sadly, this is far from being the case in this country.

Some small cracks in the monolithic edifice of the S.A. Mental and Dental Council have materialized with the recognition of homeopaths and chiropractors as legitimate practitioners. Other healers must exist on the edges of respectability and, on occasion, suffer persistent harassment from the authorities. This is a pity, for they have much to offer.

There is, however, some hope. Organizations such as Health for Africa have come into being. Membership is drawn from both the conventional and alternative fields, and the organization conducts a reasonably vigorous program of education. Regular seminars are held. Other organizations batter away at the recognized authorities. The battering is also beginning to come from within as more and more general practitioners begin to explore the possibilities of hypnotism and even refer some patients to the like of spiritual healers, aromatherapists, reflexologists and acupuncturists.

So far, and there is only anecdotal evidence for this, the New Age consciousness in South Africa seems to have been limited to the white segment of the population, and the upper income groups at that. One can speculate about the reasons for this, but it is really beyond the scope of this monograph. For the meantime it seems safe to say, and again the evidence is anecdotal, that, as people become more and more disillusioned with the answers trotted out glibly by the conventional sources of wisdom, they will turn more and more to alternative sources for possible answers to their problems. Bookshops are still nervous about their displays of esoteric books, and these are usually pushed to the back of the shop—but they keep stocks all the same, which can only mean that they sell. Even such bastions of the cliché and the mundane as the CNA devote considerable shelf space to their (carefully?) unlabeled sections of esoteric books.

The movement is, of course, unstoppable and will, in time, lose the label of *New Age movement* as it becomes the standard by which society operates. New so-called "Centers of Light" are appearing all over the country. Three have been established in Johannesburg alone and all appear to be going from strength to strength. The Leeward Concentrates on healing, and the Nest seems to direct its activities more to meditation and related activities, while the Font takes a broad holistic view and provides both venue and facilitation of all manner of disciplines, as well as its own courses, which are based firmly in the Western esoteric tradition.

Chapter 19

Alternative Spirituality in Italy

——————————— *Isotta Poggi*

An appreciation of the New Age in Italy cannot be separated from a prior examination of certain historical and cultural factors which have influenced the country's reception of the New Age movement. These factors include, especially, the past and more recent history of alternative spirituality in the country as well as the influence of foreign religious movements which began immigrating to Italy during the 1970s. As the Italian scholar Giovanni Filoramo[1] has noted, most academic studies—as well as mass media coverage—of new religious movements in Italy are undeveloped and uneven and tend to take an adversarial stance towards new religions or, at least, to denounce their more sensational aspects. According to Filoramo, this is partially due to the fact that in Italy this phenomenon is in its beginning stages. The principal reason for this lack of development can be explained in terms of the cultural background of Italy, which has not been historically sensitive to contact with religious minorities, and not very informed or educated "in general on the religious world, particularly the non-Christian ones."[2] My initial investigation of the New Age phenomenon in Italy widened when I discovered the broad range of new groups, not exclusively New Age but intertwined with it, which have taken hold in this country. The present paper aims to describe the current situation in a way that will give the reader some sense of the breadth of this phenomenon.

The New Age developed out of various religious, philosophical, and psychological traditions which originated in the nineteenth century and earlier. These traditions, the best known of which are probably the Spiritualist, New Thought, and Theosophic traditions, constituted a kind of spiritual subculture out of which the New Age emerged. As a modern social movement, the New Age was born during the 1960s in Great Britain, from whence it spread in the 1970s to North America and

271

continental Europe in coincidence with large numbers of former counterculturists who began to explore alternative spirituality.[3]

The New Age can be characterized as a new approach to spirituality, focused on the experience of individual transformation as well as
participation in the universal power, or the energy "which supports
and permeates all of existence."[4] This participation in Universal Energy
involves the individual as a whole—body, mind, and spirit. "Evil" is the
lack of union, whereas "good" is the harmony and balance between
the two. The principal tool for this inner growth is the practice of meditation, adopted in its Oriental mode, which has become very popular in
the Western world. Meditation enlarges the consciousness and develops
awareness of the here and now. The renewal of the body is realized by
the use of a correct diet, often strictly vegetarian. The body's healing is
assisted by the practice of alternative medicine, which draws upon the
natural products of the earth, and the practice of such alternative treatments as relaxation techniques and yoga asanas.

The New Age also accepts the idea of universal religion, and such a
belief often implies a form of syncretism. For example, the ideas of 'reincarnation' and 'karma', adopted to explain certain aspects of personal
development and spiritual growth, has become a common notion in
the Western world. Theosophical and anthroposophical traditions,
astrology, channeling, UFO revelations, polytheism, and paganism are
often combined with elements from Christianity, Hinduism, Buddhism,
Islam, and Zoroastrism. This open syncretist tendency is an important
aspect of the New Age, especially when contrasted with the beliefs of
the Christian religion, in general, and of the Roman Catholic Church, in
particular.

Italy, where the Roman Catholic Church is the official religion, is
mostly a Catholic country, with 92 percent of its population being bap-
tized into the faith. Nevertheless, since the 1960s, historical, political,
and social changes have occurred which have resulted in greater freedom of religious choice.[5] As part of those changes the New Age also
arrived in Italy and settled, though rather underground. It is not, however, an isolated phenomenon; it has arisen along with the "boom" of
new religious movements, which are catching on in many countries of
the world where a fragmented society is looking for new spiritual
answers: "the sacred, kicked out of the front door, manifests an irre-
pressible desire to get back in through the back door" ("il sacro, cacciato
dalla porta, manifesta un desiderio insopprimibile a rientrare dalla
finestra") says Massimo Introvigne, a well-known Italian phenomenol-
ogist on new religions in Italy and abroad.[6]

Within Europe, the New Age has been most influential across the central part of the continent—from the United Kingdom to Holland, and Germany to Switzerland, where many new religious organizations were established during the last few decades. In their larger cities New Age books, magazines, and brochures advertising yoga classes and meditation courses are easily available in New Age bookstores, health food shops, or simply in the newsstands along the streets. These countries are swarming with new churches, magical movements, and secret societies which claim to continue the traditions of their pre-christian culture, or try to combine new ideas and practices with orthodox beliefs. Their land is fertile and open for the growth and development of new movements and new thinkers.

Italy is also involved in this phenomenon, but a smaller number of publications, reviews, and magazines advertising new religious activities, meditation courses, or New Age seminars indicates that the New Age is a less substantial movement in this country, or at least is not as manifest as in other European countries. It may thus appear that Italy is not sensitive to new spiritual developments and renewals. As a matter of fact, Introvigne explains how many people eligible for new religious movements in Italy tend to become involved in Catholic organizations and activities.[7]

The Alternative Tradition in Italy

Alongside its Catholic heritage, Italians have shown a deep interest and passion for both syncretism and alternative spirituality, and though in the minority, a lineage of thinkers has kept the tradition alive. Italy transmitted to us the heritage of great philosophers and other thinkers who promoted a universal religion and influenced contemporary European thought with their metaphysical speculations. An example of this strand can be found in the prophecies and visions of Joachim de Flores (1145-1202), a Cistercian monk who had his own interpretation of Scriptures. He viewed the history of the world as divided into three stages, from the Age of the Father, through the Age of the Son, to the Age of the Holy Spirit. The first Age was identified chronologically with the period of the Old Testament, which was expressed by the Jewish religion. The second stage, the Age of the Son, was represented by Christianity. The next stage will be the Age of the Holy Spirit, which will signal the beginning of a new religion. Since first articulated by Joachim, his millennial schema has reappeared under various guises as an expression of the longing for individual and cultural transformation. It attained a significant restatement in contemporary astrology, in which the Age of the Father reappears as the Age of Aries, the Age of the Son as the Age of

Pisces, and the Age of the Holy Spirit as the Age of Aquarius. This astrological myth of the Age of Aquarius is integral to the New Age milieu, where it is conceived as the age of wisdom and renewal. In Italy this view has been developed by the New Age thinker Bernardino del Boca.

Another example of the Italian contribution to the Western tradition of alternative spirituality can be found in the Italian Renaissance with the intense intellectual activity at the Medici court in Florence. The Byzantine philosopher Georgius Gemistus Plethon (1355-1450) learned pre-Christian philosophy and religion from a Jew. In Florence, in the 1430s, he suggested to Cosimo de Medici to open the Platonic Academy, wherein the philosopher Marsilio Ficino (1433-1499) translated Plato's and Plotinus's works and disseminated astrological and hermetic thought. For a generation Platonism, Neoplatonism, and Neopythagoreanism flourished. His most noteworthy disciple, G. Pico della Mirandola (1463-1494), studied in Padua Averroé, and was one of the first Christian scholars to study the Kabbala. He was interested in the study of the occult and astrology, and, like his master Ficino, he promoted the study of philosophy in the search for religious truth. The academy promoted a syncretism in which Christianity, Islam, and Judaism mingled with magic, with orphism, and with astrology. However, the flowering of Florentine Neoplatonism was cut short by such historical circumstances as the intervention of the Church through the agency of the Inquisition. In 1493 Pico della Mirandola found it convenient to move to France, where he spent some years before being absolved by Pope Alexander VI. The Inquisition was less clement with another relevant figure in the astrological and occultist tradition, Giordano Bruno, who died at the stake in 1600. A former Dominican, Bruno traveled throughout Europe teaching Copernicus's astronomical system, integrating it into his own combination of magic, astrology, and Pythagorism. Tommaso Campanella, author of the famous *Città del Sole (City of the Sun)* and a student of magic, Kabbala and alchemy, was also indicted by the Inquisition in 1591 for his doctrines and a few years later moved to Paris.

During the following centuries the Roman Inquisition played a predominant role in the control of the official religion, and no relevant thinkers in Italy contributed to a development of alternative forms of spirituality. More popular approaches to magic, practiced in the peasants' villages, were also persecuted by the Church. An example, among many throughout Europe, is attested to in Ginzburg's work, *Witchcraft and Agrarian Cults in the Sixteenth and Seventeenth Century*, wherein the author describes the proceedings of the Venetian Inquisition against the *Benandanti* (good walkers), men and women who, in a trance, would go in the form of spirits during the night to "fight for the faith of God" against witches and warlocks,[8] as one of the women arrested testified. The trials went on and on until the beginning of the eighteenth century, when all this tradition no longer interested anybody.

Modern Italy

While the Inquisition operated in the Italian peninsula to cope with witchcraft and popular superstition, in Northern Europe Rosicrucianism and Masonic Lodges were developing into organized movements. At the end of the eighteenth century a great change occurred in Europe. The Age of the Enlightenment and the Revolutionary worldview of the French salons set in motion a cultural and spiritual renewal in the Western world that included in its agenda the goal of creating an alternative spirituality which would replace, or at least drastically alter, the official Christian religion.[9] This renewal drew primary inspiration from three different traditions. The first was the *pre-Christian traditions*—Celtic, Egyptian, Roman, and Greek—which became manifest in the introduction of Greek, Roman, and Druidic cults in seventeenth-century Paris. A second tradition was the *illuministic cult of Reason*, which developed, on one hand, into the study of inner human potential and aimed at the discovery of mankind's powers, and on the other hand, formulated an atheist worldview which would provide roots both to psychoanalysis and to Marxism. Finally, a third position was represented by *magic, occultism*, and *spiritism*, which spread out of private small elite circles and reached the more general audience, now interested in the Mesmer's discoveries on animal magnetism. During the nineteenth century, these trends assumed shapes that foreshadowed those of recent decades.

In the eighteenth century ancient Egyptian esoterism was developed in the work of mysterious Alessandro Cagliostro (1743-1795). Cagliostro's life is surrounded by questions as to his birth and identity. According to the main tradition, he is to be identified with the Sicilian Giuseppe Balsamo, who was born in 1743 and disappeared in 1775. The following year Cagliostro, who was initiated into the secrets of alchemy and the hermetic sciences by a certain Althotas, was seen in Malta, where he obtained the title of Count. From Malta he traveled throughout Europe. In London he was initiated into the free masonry, in Germany met the Count of St. Germain, and afterwards established his own lodges based upon the Egyptian Masonic rite. He became a mythic ancestor for the magical tradition in Italy and also reappeared as the reincarnated founder of an Italian UFO contactee group called "We are not alone." The Egyptian tradition introduced by Cagliostro was also developed within the Masonic lodges of Misraim (Misr is the Egyptian name for Egypt) and Memphis, which developed in France in the same period. Another Italian contributor to the West's alternative spiritual tradition was the Neapolitan healer Ciro Formisano (1861-1930), better known as Giulian Kremmerz, who in the 1890s founded a magical brotherhood (Magic Therapeutical Brotherhood of Myriam) inspired by the model of ancient Egyptian cult of Isis.[10]

Other strands feeding into the tradition of alternative spirituality originated in organizations based on the ancient Italian heritage. The ancient Roman pagan religion and Neopythagoreanism were reconsidered in the new atmosphere of the *Risorgimento*, the renewal movement which aimed at the unification of Italy. Relevant leaders of the unification, Mazzini and Garibaldi, were free masons. The latter was Great Master in the rite of the Brotherhood of Misraim and Memphis, Masonic Egyptian orders which originated in Cagliostro's work. At the beginning of the twentieth century, Fascism was seen by some people as providing the opportune conditions for developing an official new neopagan religion, based on the occult tradition which went back to the ancient Roman Age. Arturo Reghini (1878-1946), who was a free mason and a member of the *Ordo Templi Orientis*, established the Theosophical Society in Italy. He founded the "Pythagorean Association," based on a tradition which counted various historical learned persons of the Italian world as continuing the ancient Pythagorean thought, from Dante Alighieri to Napoleone Bonaparte (as an Italian), and from Giordano Bruno to Cagliostro. Ancient Roman paganism was promoted by Julius Evola through his movement the *Gruppo di Ur*, which issued the magazine called *Ur* when he was collaborating with Reghini, and *Krur* afterwards. This neopaganism was intended to be adopted as the new state religion, to give a "soul" to the Fascism which was taking shape in those years.[11] The pact between church and state disappointed these ideologists, and their activity officially disappeared, to reemerge in different forms with different names during the 1970s in some southern cities.

Also in Italy along with this return to the ancient pagan religion, a Theosophical tradition was developed by Roberto Assagioli (1888-1975), a friend of Alice Bailey and a psychologist, who created psychosynthesis, a method to integrate our perception of our inner self and the transpersonal dimensions which go beyond it with spiritual development. His thought, along with the traditional Theosophical variations, such as Agni Yoga, and the channeled messages of Benjamin Creme, would inspire the *Ordine Esoterico del Loto Bianco* (Esoteric Order of the White Lotus), an order founded in 1980 by Giuseppe Filipponio, as a "'magic' version of the Theosophic tradition," aiming to reach a larger general audience, beyond the few exclusive circles of initiated.[12]

Over the course of the last several centuries, as well as up through the middle of the twentieth century, this alternative spirituality was rather bound to a cultural and political elite. Members of Societies and Lodges were limited in number. The predominant religion was still represented by the Catholic Church. However, these restricted neopagan groups began to reemerge from underground, while a wave of new traditions, cults, and religions began to enter and spread in Italy. These new importations further stimulated the development of the country's subculture of alternative spirituality.

Imported Movements

The recent wave of religious movements and alternative traditions originated in countries other than Italy. The New Age is part of this new wave. Italy, although seemingly disinterested on the surface, has actually been quite receptive. Almost all of the principal new religious movements are represented. It is well known that the Jehovah's Witnesses are very numerous in Italy. The Mormons are also very active. The Children of God, with their new name "Family of Love," are present as well, although they are declining.[13]

The beginnings in Italy of the Holy Spirit Association for the Unification of World Christianity, commonly known as Unification Church, can be traced to 1965. It spread mostly in the Northern part of the country, and since the mid-1970s has issued a monthly magazine called *La Nuova Era* (The New Age) besides two other reviews bound to their communities. Active members of the Church are now around three hundred, but part-time followers are reported to be four thousand five hundred. One of the most popular of the imported new religious movements is the Church of Scientology, which was established in Italy in 1974. Like the Unification Church, its strength is more in the Northern part of the country, with centers located in Lombardia and Veneto. Scientology has attracted some of its Italian followers through the development of Narconon, an institution which addresses the issue of heavy drug use, a major problem in this country. Active members of the Church of Scientology number around six hundred. Organizations in competition with it are Advanced Ability Center, a group established in Milan, and Silva Mind Control, present in Turin, Rome, and Milan.

Within the New Thought tradition, the Church of Christ, Scientist established three churches in Italy (in Milan, Rome, and Florence), and two societies (in Turin and Aosta). The Unity School of Christianity also has a few followers. The largest prophetic movement in the country, with between 500 and 800 members, is Universal Life-The Inner Religion, founded in Germany in 1984 by prophetess, channel, and healer Gabriele Wittek.[14] A small group that is attempting to grow is the Grail Movement, founded in Austria in 1928 by the German Oskar Ernest Bernhardt (Abd-ru-shin) (1875-1941).

The Theosophical Society was established in 1902 and now has centers spread throughout the country. The United Lodge of Theosophists is also present. The Lucis Trust, founded by Alice Bailey, established the *Associazione Culturale dei Triangoli e della Buona Volontà Mondiale* in Rome and broadcasts the news of its organization in Italian. The Universal White Brotherhood of Peter Deunov, established in France in 1937, and Rudolf Steiner's Anthroposophical Society have some hundreds of followers in Italy. The *Associazione Igenista Italiana*, headquartered in Genua, is the Italian representative of the International Biogenic Society, founded in France in 1928 by Hungarian Edmond Bordeaux Szekely. The Great Universal Brotherhood of Serge Raynaud de la Ferriere (1916-1962) has some centers in Italy, with headquarters in Rome. The Great Universal Brotherhood-Sun Line *(Linea Solare)*, founded by his disciple Manuel Estrada, has a good number of centers with related activities established in the northeastern part of Italy (in Venice, Padua, and Mestre, for example).

From Argentina the International Organization New Acrople, founded in Buenos Aires by Jorge Angel Livraga and Ada Albrecht, arrived during the 1970s, with centers located throughout the country. Reiki, a Japanese healing group, is also active in the country. Among the channeling movements, the most organized is the *Scuola Scientifica Basilio*, founded in Argentina in 1917 by Blanca Aubreton and Aires Eugenio Portal. The School established its headquarters in Florence, and now has about 300 members. The work of Italian channel Pietro Ubaldi, author of *The Great Synthesis*, was brought to Italy from Brazil through the Ubaldian Nucleus of Methaphysics. A movement imported from the United States that is still not too well known is neopagan Wicca, which is present only in some feminist circles and organizes courses in Milan on magic. The Raelian movement, founded in France by contactee Claude Vilhord, has attracted some Italian followers. Much smaller but still present is the postspiritist movement called Antoinism, founded in Belgium in 1910 by Lois Antoine (1846-1912).[15] A movement inspired by Gandhian thought was established in the South of Italy; it is called the "Ark Community" *(Comunità dell'Arca)* and was founded in France in 1948 by philosopher Giuseppe Lanza Del Vasto (1901-1981), after his experience as one of Gandhi's disciples in 1937. All of these groups, as well as movements of Hindu and Buddhist origin, contributed to the development of new religious and philosophical traditions in Italy. Among the Hindu groups, the "Hare Krishna," also known as ISKCON, first came to Italy in 1973 and now reports a membership of 300 totally involved believers and 50,000 followers. They are the most significant in terms of number of members. They established their headquarters in Tuscany and then spread throughout the country. World Plan Executive Council (originally called Transcendental Meditation) was established in Italy in 1972 and has since organized twenty-five centers, mostly in the northern part of the country. There are in Italy around thirty-five thousand followers of this movement. Again during the 1970s, Bhagwan Shree Rajneesh's movement (now Osho Meditation Center) established centers in the country. Before Rajneesh's expulsion from the United States, the active members in Italy, who used to be called the *Arancioni* ("The Orange People") because of the colour of the robe of *Neo-Sannyasin*, numbered in the hundreds. Sai Baba's movement has also established many centers in Italy, issues a monthly magazine called *Sai Sangita-Il Canto del Signore* (Sai-Sangita-The Lord's Song), and now reports a membership of around 1,000 Italian followers. Ananda Marga was brought to Italy in 1974, organizing centers mostly in the northeastern part of the country. It also issues two magazines (*Yoga per una Rinascita Universale*, and *Dharma*). *Il Centro Bhole Baba* is the Italian representative of Haidhakan Samaj. The movement organized two centers in the north and in the south of Italy.

There are also in Italy relevant Buddhist groups which are recognized at an international level. During the 1970s the Mahayana Institute, properly called the "Institute Lama Tzong Khapa," was established. It is located at Pomaia (Pisa), and represents the international headquarters of the Foundation for the Preservation of the Mahayana Tradition. It has also organized a branch in Milan, called "*Centro GHE-PEL-LING*." The International Institute for Tibetan Studies Shang Shung, connected with the Merigar community, and related in the United States with the Dzoch-chen Community, was inaugurated in 1990 by the Dalai Lama. The Japanese Buddhist Sokagakkai, the lay organization of the Nichiren Shoshu Temple, has between 3,000 and 5,000 followers. Sukyo Mahikari, another Japanese Buddhist group, has 3,000 followers, with centers spread mostly in the North. Reiyukai has a center in Milan. Sant Mat was also introduced in Italy during the 1970s, with the establishment of Elan Vital, here represented by the *Missione della Luce Divina*, which organized an ashram in Milan and coordinates work in other Italian towns. ECKANKAR is also present in Italy.

This overview has been intended to show the extensive interest in, and the success of, new religious traditions in the country. This interest is even more evident when we consider the movements which have been founded in Italy.

"Made in Italy" New Movements

An eminent Italian scholar, Massimo Introvigne, to whom we have already referred, has been very helpful as a source of information for the present work. The following survey draws heavily on his analysis of these movements. In his main works in this field, *Le Nuove Religioni*[16] and *Il Cappello del Mago*,[17] he analyzes several of the new and not so new religious movements which developed during recent decades, mostly in Europe, but also with many references to the North American situation. Introvigne's volume *Il Cappello del Mago* provided much information for the present work, mostly for the present section (the following references refer to this book).

Within the magic tradition, two Italians claim to be avatars. In 1988 Francesco Isa Atmananda, also known as Babaji and author of *The Seventh Gospel*, announced that he was an avatar of universal consciousness itself. He has since attracted a hundred followers in Milan and Rome (319). Sicilian Guglielmo Marino, founder of the Association Avatar-Cultura e Umanità, also declared himself to be an avatar. He published *La Via dell'Amore* (The Way of Love), a gospel which preaches the return to a true original Christianity, excluding the Old Testament from the Holy Scriptures (319).

Graal, Rivista di Scienza dello Spirito is the name of a monthly magazine which has been issued since 1982 in Rome by an intellectual spiritual circle. It is centered upon the thought of Giovanni Colazza (1877-1953), who formerly participated in the publication of the magazine *Ur*, and the thought of Massimo Scaligero (1906-1980) (originally called Antonio Scabelloni). The periodical draws heavily upon Rudolf Steiner's thought, the "perfect synthesis between East and West" (320). In Turin during the 1970s, esoterist Giancarlo Barbadoro and Rosalba Nattero organized the Jules Laforgue Foundation, Grail Center for Study and Research, which issues the magazine *Meditazione Oggi* (Meditation Today). Spiritism, ufology, meditation, and neoshamanism are some of the traditions drawn upon by the center. Barbadoro is also the founder of the Order of the Shan Masters, an initiatic school where the "oldest esoteric doctrine is taught," as transmitted through an ancient language called "Shannar" (320-1).

UFO contactee revelations and Marian apparitions mingle in the spirituality of the group *Nonsiamosoli* ("We are not alone"), centered upon the apocalyptic visions and teachings of Sicilian contactee Eugenio Siragusa (b. 1919), who claimed to be, among many others, the reincarnation of Cagliostro, the mythic ancestor. The movement was founded in 1962 under the name of *Centro Studi Fratellanza Cosmica* (Cosmic Brotherhood Study Center), and now has one thousand followers (130-133). Channeling activity is at the base of *Cerchio Firenze 77* (65), a circle of people who participated in the work of Roberto Setti (1930-1984), channel for the messages and teachings of spiritual guides called the "Masters."

Ancient polytheism continues in contemporary Italy in the "Neo-Hellenic Centers of Polytheistic Religiousness," organized by Milanese Antonino de Bono and his followers, who claim to be the only heirs of ancient Neoplatonic philosophers (347-8). In Naples a group generally called *Unione Trifoglio* (Clover Union), also the name of its magazine, was founded in 1975 by Giorgio Punzo. The organization's official name is "*Sodalitas Aedis Nemorumque Custodum,*" the Union of the Guardians of the Temple and the Woods. Besides an ecological message, it also preaches a cult of Nature worship to people who are "committed to harmonize the individual life and the human individual within Nature" (362-3).

"Made in Italy" New Age

Beyond all the groups mentioned above are two movements which are particularly interesting in their effort to spread in the country and beyond the borders of Italy. They base their activities on a community life style, sharing property and working for the collectivity on a spiritual basis. These movements are reminiscent of the well-known Findhorn community. Because these groups are still in their developmental stages, it has not been easy to find information on them.

In 1975, anthropologist and esoterist Bernardino del Boca (b. 1919) published the *International Guide to the Aquarian Age,*[18] a wide-ranging and accurate directory and collection of information on the Aquarian Age movements around the world. This was one of the first efforts to give a comprehensive overview of the new awareness. That work was only the beginning. Bresci Editore, is the publishing house which issued that volume. Since 1970, the date of its founding, this publishing house has been working to promote the development of a *Nuovo Piano di Coscienza* ("New Level of Consciousness") and to indicate the forces at work in the world for the promotion of New Age values. The year 1975 is conceived of as being the end of the Age of Pisces, a 2,155-year cycle, and the beginning of the Aquarian Age, which will also last 2,155 years. "The Reign of the Son is over. The dawn of the Reign of Holy Spirit is arising."[9] Middle Age prophecies are quoted to testify to the arrival of a New Age. Mankind is starting to experience a new level of consciousness, based no longer on the search for knowledge, but rather on the search for wisdom. The Pagans before, and now the Neopagans, are tolerant toward "every religion and every human behavior."[20] The Age of Pisces is characterized by the notion of education as something imposed on a society that is unaware, and "perpetuates the system of power." Only the "forces of spiritual wisdom" can "limit the ignorance of such an intellectual and childish conformism."[21] (ibidem). During the Age of Pisces exploitation of nature and pollution has resulted in the chaos of contemporary society.[22] Fearfulness, indifference, egoism, and ignorance are the evils of this age. Only the person who achieves the "Level of Consciousness" will be able to change this reality.

Del Boca developed what he termed the "psychothematic" *(psicotematica)*, the ability to perceive reality with the soul more than with the mind, the "only tool to reach intuition."[23] By the "psychothematic" mankind will be able to perceive "in one hundred, one thousand years, the mysterious reality of the Continuum-infinite-present."[24] The goal of the Aquarian Age individual is to perceive the "Parallel Reality," that can be understood only by intuition, not verbally. "Man is living to carry on a message from Nature. If he does not sense his relation with the universe, he will never understand this message."[25] Del Boca's books are written, and are to be read, through the psychothematic: he writes "to testify to the complexity of life which is nothing but a painted veil. Beyond the veil you can see, getting closer, the parallel reality, and perhaps to leave a guide to those people who wish to be contacted by 'Those who walk on the High Roads of the World.'"[26] He wrote a diary in which two different realities, in terms of both space and time, alternate. He worked during the late 1940s in Singapore and described his "initiation to the High Roads" page by page, following the diary he was writing at that time. In these recent works, he associates his Singapore human and spiritual experience with the events of his 1980s life, in Italy, and his activity as a Theosophist.

In agreement with del Boca's thought and teachings in Milan, the first Center of the Aquarian Age was established in 1971, where seminars and courses are held for the psychological and spiritual development of participants. "Green Villages" are also another initiative which grew out of del Boca's teachings. They are "Theosophical-aquarian" villages based on an alternative economic and political system, "for people who want to develop self-consciousness."

In 1975, another Italian initiative based on the principle, typical of the New Age, of working to create a new world, was started through the work of healer Oberto Airaudi (b. 1950). He founded in Turin the Center for Research and Parapsychologist Information, HORUS. The following year he organized the "Airaudi Hands On Healing School," which gives lectures and teaches classes in several Italian cities. The school deals mostly with the "hands on" ability and therapy, such as bioenergy, selfica (see below), hypnosis, and others. In 1979 a proper community started taking shape under his leadership and now reports a membership of over two hundred citizens. This initiative has developed many activities through the work of its members, operating together for the improvement of society, against "ignorance, . . . ideas growing out of Egoism, . . . consumerism."[27] It is called "Damanhur"[28] (name of an ancient Egyptian site with an esoteric school) and is located in the countryside near Turin (in Baldissero Canavese) as a city-community whose purpose is to achieve total self-sufficiency: they run a publishing house (called "Edizioni Horus"), a travel agency, and various agricultural, educational, medical activities. They also have their own code language, and even use their own coin, called "credito."

Airaudi was the author, at the age of seventeen, of the *Cronaca del Mio Suicidio*[29] (Chronicle of My Suicide), and later he became a *pranoterapeuta* (spiritual healer). Part of the founder's thought is published in his *Pietre dell'Età dell'Acquario* (Stones of the Aquarian Age),[30] where he states that the group is not a religion. (He prefers to be considered a philosopher.) The community reflects ideas typical of the New Age in the teachings that are illustrated in *La Via Horusiana*.[31] There is only one God, a "*Motore immobile*," which can be contacted only through intermediate divinities. Among these divinities, some are autogenerated *Divinità Primeve* (the primeval divinities), whereas others are created by *Uomo* (Mankind). Mankind is a *Divinità Primeva* which for some reason descended into matter and shattered. Man can still return to the original "splendor" by going through a conscious evolutionary process, aided by such tools as magic, alchemy, and the *selfica*. The selfica is centered upon the image of the spiral, and is manifested in the paintings of Airaudi, in the jewelry designed in the community and used by the members, and in the meditation path, which follows a spiral line. Airaudi's notion of universe is that it is made up of three *Mondi Madre* (Mother Worlds), *Mondo dell'Uomo* (the Human World), the Vegetal Realm (Mondo Vegetale), and the *Mondo degli Spiriti della Natura* (Spirits of the Nature World). These worlds cannot communicate except through the *Mondi Eco* (Echo Worlds), formed by the resonance originating in the Mother Worlds. Through the practice of specific techniques, every living race can draw upon its astral *"serbatoio"* (container, tank),[32] as an archive. Mankind can also draw upon the astral memory of animals (this is the reason why every member of the community adopts the name of an animal). It is also possible to foresee and plan reincarnation, through the *linee sincroniche* (synchronic lines) which frame the earth. The school teaches how to die, in order to be ready for the next incarnation, and to overcome its cycle. The dead, soon after their deaths, spend about seventy days (depending on their preparation) tied to their physical body. Either liberation or reincarnation will occur after that. Spiritism is practiced in Damanhur not only to communicate and to "receive much information," from the dead. They believe that *entità appena nate* (just born entities) originate from these spiritist meetings, drawing energy from the members of the meeting, and still autonomous and often able to give useful information.[33]

According to the school, the inner faculty is developed and amplified by the use of magical techniques and tools, such as the *pentacolo* (pentacle), which is supposed to be made with red clay during a night of full moon. It will enlarge the individual's personal energy. Airaudi's spiritism is conceived as an inner subconscious paranormal ability: it is a "Magic Syncretism," as Introvigne defines it, which draws upon the most typical elements of the new magical movements (such as mesmerism, spiritism, and ritual magic). The pentacle, meditation, and other "spiritual" practices help mankind to achieve in the former "splendor." This is at the antipode of Christian belief as it is expressed in the Catholic tradition.

"Against a Pernicious Syncretism"

Although I have found no Catholic statements regarding the New Age specifically, Church publications considering the development and success of the new religious movements exist, and some of the positions taken in these documents are applicable to the New Age movement.[34] It will thus be relevant to consider what the Church has to say regarding this subject. In the Italian world these new religious initiatives provoked a reaction from the Catholic Church, which perceives its spiritual leadership as being undermined by this wave of alternative approaches to spirituality. The Church considers this problem, the propagation of new religious movements, as a challenge, a "Pastoral Challenge." In 1985 a "temporary statement" was issued by the Church on the phenomenon of the "Sects" or "New Religious Movements."[35] The purpose of this statement was to show the results of research organized through the work of a number of Episcopal Conferences in different parts of the world. The project aimed to understand this new phenomenon, its definition (what is a sect or a new religious movement?), its reasons, and its effects (which were often, according to the document, negative) (Part 4).

Four years later, in 1989, from the Sacred Congregation for the Doctrine of the Faith, a document was published by Cardinal Ratzinger in the form of a letter bound to the Bishops of the Catholic Faith on "some aspects of the Christian meditation."[36] This document aimed to explain and define prayer within the Christian Catholic faith, mostly in its "theological and spiritual implications" (4). It grew out of an awareness of the popularity and diffusion of spiritual practices, which mainly originate from the Buddhist and Hindu traditions (such as zen, transcendental meditation, and yoga), that have been adopted by some Christians. In the third part of the document the author delineated two "wrong ways to pray" that came into being during the first centuries of the Church, Pseudognosis and Messalianism. The former was based upon the belief that prayer would free the soul from the ignorance which is caused by impure matter, the latter on the identification of the grace of the Holy Spirit with the psychological experience of him in the soul. Pseudognosis and Messalianism eliminate the distance between God the creator and Man, which is mediated by Jesus Christ (10). The practice of Oriental meditation can be of "psychophysical support" (12) but the human "I" can not be absorbed in the divine "I"; an absorption of the human "I" in the divine "I" (*"un assorbimento dell'io umano nell'io divino"*) will never occur, not even in the highest stages of grace (13). A "life of perfection" can be achieved through the three stages originally defined during the first centuries by the non-Christian classics: purification, enlightenment, and union (15). Purification is conceived as liberation from egoistic attachment to passions (16). Enlightenment is achieved by the grace of the Baptism. "A special experience of union, if God wants it" (18) can be achieved, however, the "authentic Christian mystic" does not depend on any "technique" (19). In fact techniques (e.g., the attention to the position of the body), "if not adequately perceived," can even prevent one from achieving the "elevation of the spirit to God" (22). If the moral behavior does not correspond to the experienced "gratifying feelings," such as "light or heat phenomena," a "kind of mental schizophrenia" can occur (22).

This is what a "pernicious syncretism" (12) could cause if non-Christian religious practices were to be adopted by Catholics for the purpose of achieving union with God. The Catholic critique of Oriental spiritual practices is not confined to specific techniques, but also to the ideology from which they originate, e.g., Hindu pantheism, the belief in reincarnation, or the "irrationalist Zen doctrine."[37] For the Catholic Faith, Christian contemplation is a "supernatural reality" (24) achieved by the creature through the mediation of Jesus Christ and by the grace of God. Manuel Guerra, scholar of history of religions, hopes for a return of Christians who forgot the "treasures of Christianity," "perhaps because fascinated by mythic scientific technological progress, and by the despotism of images and sensoriality" (26).[38]

The position of the Church is largely incompatible with the new religious traditions mentioned above. As in past centuries, the Church cannot accept the introduction of syncretism. The Concordat which declared the Catholic Church no longer the sole official religion, will "offer greater possibilities to the new emerging cults."[39] It will be interesting to observe the future development of the Italian religious scene, which among the new religious movements will be lasting, and which solutions and alternatives will be offered by the Catholic Church. Although the Italian and the more general European academic milieu still tends to adhere to the belief that secularization is continuing to spread in Europe, closer field research shows that alternative forms (as well as certain more traditional forms) of spirituality are widespread and expanding. New religious variety can perhaps be related to the increase of social pluralism, which is already well developed in North American society, and which in Italy has started taking hold only in very recent years.

CONTRIBUTORS

Catherine L. Albanese is professor of religious studies at the University of California, Santa Barbara. She holds a Ph.D. in American religious history from the University of Chicago (1972) and is the author of numerous books and articles, including, recently, *Nature Religion in America: From the Algonkian Indians to the New Age.*

Kay Alexander received her Ph.D. from the Department of Religious Studies of the University of California at Santa Barbara in 1988. She has a particular interest in developments of new spiritual directions resulting from encounters between religions and psychologies in California since the Second World War.

Mary Farrell Bednarowski is Professor of Religious Studies at United Theological Seminary of the Twin Cities. Her publications include *American Religion: A Cultural Perspective* and *New Religions and the Theological Imagination in America* as well as essays on religion in nineteenth and twentieth century America.

Susan Love Brown is Candidate in Philosophy in the Department of Anthropology, University of California, San Diego. She is currently completing fieldwork in the Bahamas on national identity and socio-cultural integration.

Stephen M. Clark is currently a graduate student in Anthropology at the University of California, San Diego.

Andrea Grace Diem received her M.A. degree in comparative religion from UC Santa Barbara. She is currently an instructor in the Philosophy Department of Mt. San Antonio College. Her publications include *The Gnostic Mystery: A Connection between Ancient and Modern Mysticism.*

Robert Ellwood is Professor of Religion at the University of Southern California. He received his Ph.D. In History of Religion from the University of Chicago, and is the author of books on Japanese religion, the history of religion, and new religious movements in Japan, New Zealand, and the United States.

Shoshanah Feher is currently a graduate student in the Sociology Department at the University of California, Santa Barbara. Her areas of study are the sociology of religion, sociology of culture, and social psychology. Currently, she is interested in New Religious Movements and in American Judaism, especially where the two areas overlap.

Rosalind I. J. Hackett is Associate Professor in the Department of Religious Studies at the University of Tennessee, Knoxville. She has conducted many years of fieldwork on new religious movements in Africa. She is the editor of *New Religious Movements in Nigeria* and author of *Religion in Calabar: The Religious Life and History of a Nigerian Town*.

Irving Hexham, Associate Professor in the Department of Religious Studies at the University of Calgary, is the author of *The Irony of Apartheid*, co-author with Karla Poewe of *Understanding Cults and New Religions*, and editor of several books on African Religion. Hexham is an Evangelical Christian and member of the Anglican Church who taught at Regent College, Vancouver, from 1977 to 1980 and is a contributor to such magazines as *Christianity Today* and *Charisma*.

Aidan A. Kelly has worked in publishing as an editor for 27 years, and is currently senior editor for Jeremy P. Tarcher, Inc. After receiving his Ph.D. in Religious Studies from the Graduate Theological Union in 1980, he taught at the University of San Francisco, Holy Family college and the World University of America. Among many other publications, he is the author of *Crafting the Art of Magic*.

James R. Lewis is Senior Editor for the Center for Academic Publication and Senior Research Fellow for the Institute for the Study of American Religion. He received his Ph.D. in Religious Studies from the University of North Carolina, Chapel Hill (1989). He has published extensively in the fields of New Religious Movements, Sikh Studies, and Native American Religions.

Phillip C. Lucas is a doctoral candidate in the Department of Religious Studies at the University of California, Santa Barbara. His research focuses on religious movements in American history and the internal changes they undergo in response to such factors as societal change, leadership succession, doctrinal elaboration and shifting value orientations. Lucas also has interests in the history of the early Christian period, especially as it relates to the disputes between heretical and orthodox groups.

J. Gordon Melton is Director of the Institute for the Study of American Religion and a Research Specialist with the Department of Religious Studies at the University of California, Santa Barbara. He received his Ph.D. in American Religious History from Garrett Theological Seminary (1975) and is the author of such standard reference works as the *Encyclopedia of American Religion* and the *Encyclopedic Handbook of Cults in America,* and of such recent works as *Religious Leaders of America* and the *New Age Encyclopedia.*

Mark R. Mullins is an Associate Professor at Meiji Gakuin University, Tokyo/Yokohama,Japan. His Ph.D. is in the Sociology of Religion from McMaster University, Hamilton, Ontario. He has published widely in the area of the indigenization of religions and is author of *Religious Minorities in Canada: A Sociological Study of the Japanese Experience.* Currently he is serving as an associate editor for the *Japan Christian Quarterly* and as guest co-editor for the *Japanese Journal of Religious Studies* for a special double issue on "Japanese New Religions Abroad."

G. C. Oosthuizen is Professor and Head of the Department of Theology at the University of Fort Hare and Head of the Department of Science of Religion at the University of Durban, Westville. He is presently Director of a Research Unit for Indigenous Churches and New Religions in Southern Africa. He has published extensively on black African religion and Indian religion in Southern Africa.

Isotta Poggi received her Laurea degree from the University Ca'Foscari, Venice, Italy, Facolta di Lettere e Filosofia, in 1988. From 1989 to 1990 she was a Fulbright scholar in the Department of Religious Studies at the University of California, Santa Barbara. At present she is a Research Associate with the Institute for the Study of American Religion.

Suzanne Riordan is a graduate student at the University of California in Santa Barbara. Her publications include articles on alternative education, the Green movement, and various facets of the New Age movement. She is currently doing research for a book on faith healing.

Glenn Rupert is a graduate student in the Department of History at Texas A & M University. He is currently finishing his Master's Thesis on the emergence of infant baptism in the early church.

NOTES

Introduction

1. In a recent paper on the religious makeup of the baby boom generation, Wade Clark Roof pointed out that New Age spirituality has touched too large a number of people to be regarded as a marginal religious phenomenon. He further anticipated that in the future we would see an expansion, rather than a diminishment, of this form of spiritual expression. Wade Clark Roof, "Narratives and Numbers," J. F. Rowny Inaugural Lecture, UCSB (May 30, 1990).

2. On this point refer to the introductory essay in J. Gordon Melton, Jerome Clark, and Aidan A. Kelly, *New Age Encyclopedia* (Detroit: Gale Research, 1990).

3. As a significant social movement, the New Age began in the early seventies. Gordon Melton has suggested the publication of Baba Ram Dass's *Be Here Now* (dominated by the metaphor of transformation that Melton views as the distinguishing characteristic of the New Age) in 1972 as a useful event from which to date the movement. The first New Age directories, the *Spiritual Community Guide* and *The Year One Catalog*, were published in the same year. Other significant events in the emergence of the New Age were the appearance of the first New Age magazine, *East West Journal*, in 1968, the World Symposium on Humanity in 1976 (the first large-scale New Age gathering), and the publication of Marilyn Ferguson's *Aquarian Conspiracy* in 1980 (a survey that, more than any other book before or since, made participants in the New Age subculture aware that the New Age had become a mass movement).

Chapter 1. Approaches to the Study of the New Age Movement

1. Paul Zuromski, "Is 'New Age' Dead?" *Body Mind Spirit* 10 (March/April 1991): 4.

2. Shoshanah Feher, "Who Holds the Cards? Women and New Age Astrology," elsewhere in this volume.

3. See, for example, J. Gordon Melton, "New Thought and the New Age," elsewhere in this volume.

4. See, for example, his introductory essay to J. Gordon Melton, Jerome Clark, and Aidan A. Kelly, *New Age Encyclopedia* (Detroit: Gale Research, 1990).

5. The metaphysical message conveyed by New Age channels is treated in Suzanne Riordan, "Channeling—A New Age Revelation?" elsewhere in this volume.

6. The New Age entry into the business world is amply documented in Glenn A. Rupert's "Employing the New Age," elsewhere in this volume.

7. Excerpted from a flyer, *A Powerful New Dimension in Business Consulting*. For researchers interested in further investigating this phenomenon, Evelyn Oliver can be contacted at: Box 5097, Stanford, CA 94309, (408) 236-3387.

8. This appears to be the opinion of Wade Clark Roof, a prominent scholar of mainstream religion; see, for example, his "Numbers and Narratives," J. F. Rowny Inaugural Lecture, May 30, 1990.

9. Don Lattin, "'New Age' Mysticism Strong in Bay Area," *The San Francisco Chronicle* 24-25 April 1990, discussed in *Sequoia* 10 (July/August 1990): 1.

10. G. C. Oosthuizen notes a similar pattern in South Africa; see his "The 'Newness' of the New Age in South Africa and Reactions to It" elsewhere in the present volume. The adoption of Asian meditation forms is so widespread within Catholicism that the Church has issued an official pronouncement against such practices. In this regard, refer to the discussion in the last section of Isotta Poggi's "Alternative Spirituality in Italy," elsewhere in this volume.

11. Using the expression "Paradigm Shift" (taken from Thomas Kuhn, *The Structure of Scientific Revolutions* 1962), the notion of cultural and individual change as a sudden change in perspective was popularized by Marilyn Ferguson in *The Aquarian Conspiracy* (Los Angeles: J. P. Tarcher, 1980).

12. Eileen Barker, *New Religious Movements* (London: Her Majesty's Stationery Office 1989), 189.

13. Robert S. Ellwood and Harry B. Partin, *Religious and Spiritual Groups in Modern America*, 2d ed. (Englewood Cliffs, NJ: Prentice-Hall, 1988), 14-15.

14. Roy Wallis, "Reflections on When Prophecy Fails," Zetetic Scholar 4 (1979). Colin B. Campbell's influential article is "The Cult, the Cultic Milieu and Secularization," *A Sociological Yearbook of Religion in Britain*, Vol. 5 (London: SMC Press, 1972), 119-136.

15. Melton *et al.*, *New Age Encyclopedia*, xiii.

16. Mary Farrell Bednarowski, *New Religions and the Theological Imagination in America* (Bloomington: Indiana University Press, 1989).

17. Catherine L. Albanese, "Religion and the American Experience: A Century After," *Church History* 57 (1988): 337-351. Albanese's suggestive comparison of seemingly opposed movements formed the starting point for Phillip Lucas's paper, "The New Age Movement and the Pentecostal/Charismatic Revival," which in turn shaped parts of G. C. Oosthuizen's "The 'Newness' of the New Age in South Africa and Reactions to It." Both of these latter two papers can be found elsewhere in this volume.

18. Hans Sebald, "New-Age Romanticism: The Quest for an Alternative Lifestyle as a Force of Social Change," *Humboldt Journal of Social Relations* 11 (Spring/Summer 1984): 106-127.

19. The movement's attitude toward science can best be described as ambivalent, in that the New Age integrates those facets of science that appear to support its view of things into its mythology while denying the applicability of those aspects of mainstream science that appear to contradict its viewpoint. This attitude is discussed in Maureen O'Hara's critical article on the 100th Monkey concept, "Of Myths and Monkeys: A Critical Look at a Theory of Critical Mass," *Journal of Humanistic Psychology* 25 (Winter 1985): 61-78.

20. As indicated in the introduction to the present volume, prior to the channeling and crystals fad the New Age subculture was dominated, particularly in the 1970s, by the newly imported Asian groups.

21. The perception of the New Age as "irrationalist" has made it a favorite target of rationalist skeptics, who repeat ad nauseam the accusation that the movement is "escapist." In this regard refer to the New Age issue of the *Skeptical Inquirer* 13, no. 4 (Summer 1989). The heavy-handed polemic undertaken in most rationalist discourse tends to make such literature barren of genuine insight.

22. See Irving Hexham's "The Evangelical Response to the New Age" elsewhere in this volume. To be fair to conservative Christians, it should be noted that most mainstream Christian responses to the New Age have been similarly empty of insight; see, e.g., Ted Peters, "Discerning the Spirits of the New Age," *The Christian Century* 31 August-7 September 1988, 25.

23. As Jeremy Tarcher, a prominent Los Angeles publisher has remarked, the serious core of the New Age movement doesn't "make the 'good copy' that weird ideas do and so are neglected" by the mainstream media. Jeremy P. Tarcher, "The New Age as Perennial Philosophy," *Science of Mind* 61 (June 1988): 37. [Reprinted from the *LA Times*] A good example of a study that undercuts potential insights with overheated polemics is Steven J. Hendlin, "Pernicious Oneness," *Journal of Humanistic Psychology* 23 (Summer 1983): 61-81. On the other side of the coin, it should be noted that the reflections of academics who "go native" are usually as empty of insight as the scholars who take up a harsh critical stance; an example of a paper in this category is Earl Babbie's "Channels to Elsewhere," in Thomas Robbins and Dick Anthony, eds., *In Gods*

We Trust: New Patterns of Religious Pluralism in America, 2d. ed. (New Brunswick: Transaction, 1990), 255-268.

24. In the effort to distance themselves from the "New Age" label, even otherwise thoughtful figures in the metaphysical subculture have picked up such media stereotypes as narcissism and hurled them back at the movement; see, e.g., Ken Wilber, "Baby-Boomers, Narcissism, and the New Age," *Vajradhatu Sun* (October/November 1987).

25. Readers who have accepted uncritically the media stereotype of the New Age as apolitical should refer to Mark Satin's *New Age Politics* (New York: Dell, 1979).

26. E.g., Refer to Susan Love Brown's "Babyboomers, American Character, and the New Age," elsewhere in this volume.

27. The dominant role that millenarianism has played in American religion is one of the uniting themes of Catherine L. Albanese's *America: Religions and Religion* (Belmont, California: Wadsworth, 1981). A useful overview of millenarianism can be found in Vittorio Lanternari, "Messianism: Its Historical Origin and Morphology," *History of Religions* 2 (Summer 1962): 52-72. A more recent historian of religion to give serious attention to such movements is Charles H. Long; see, e.g., his entry on "Popular Religion" in Mircea Eliade, ed., *The Encyclopedia of Religion*, Vol. 11 (New York: Macmillan, 1987), 442-452.

28. See, for example, Sherry Hansen Steiger and Brad Steiger, "The Star People and the Pleiades Connection," *Connecting Link* 1 (November/December 1989): 16-18. Certain spokespeople are even willing to assert that "The New Age is essentially a millennialist movement." Cited in Margaret Jones, "New Age on the Brink," *Publishers Weekly* 3 November 1989, 15.

29. For recent work on the Ghost Dance, see Alice Beck Kehoe, *The Ghost Dance: Ethnohistory and Revitalization* (New York: Holt, Rinehart and Winston, 1989). While not the focus of his analysis, David J. Hess suggestively discusses the millenarian dimension of the New Age Movement in an as yet unpublished manuscript, "Science in the New Age: A Cultural Interpretation of Skepticism, Parapsychology, and the New Spiritualism in the United States" (1989). It should be noted that, because of the diversity within the New Age subculture, many prominent figures within the movement are highly critical of its millenarian aspect, e.g., see David Spangler, "Defining the New Age," *New Realities* (May/June 1988).

Chapter 2. New Thought and the New Age

1. This paper has grown out of the convergence of two projects being pursued by the Institute for the Study of American Religion. Several years ago a concerted effort to assemble and organize the materials on the first generations

of New Thought led to the formation of the Society for the Study of Metaphysical Religion (organized by a group of interested scholars at the 1987 meeting of the American Academy of Religion). About the time of the organization of the society, ISAR began to compile a *New Age Encyclopedia*, a 400,000 word reference work that appeared in the spring of 1990.

2. Typical of the secondary material on New Thought can be seen in the chapter on the Unity School of Christianity in the frequently republished anticult classic, *The Chaos of Cults* by Jan Karel Van Baalen (Grand Rapids, MI: Wm. B. Eerdmans Publishing Company, 3d ed., 1960), or the more recent volume, *Rest from the Quest* by Elissa Lindsey MacClain (Shreveport, LA: Huntington House, 1984). The number of secondary sources on the New Age Movement is staggering. A colleague has recently prepared an annotated bibliography as a guide through the extensive literature: James R. Lewis, *A Bibliography of Conservative Christian Literature on the New Age Movement* (Santa Barbara, CA: Santa Barbara Centre for Humanistic Studies, 1989).

3. See, for example, Frederick R. Harm, *How to Respond to the Science Religions* (St. Louis: Concordia Publishing House, 1981).

4. New Thought has fared much better than the New Age since Charles Braden did the pioneering work on New Thought in his *Spirits in Rebellion* (Dallas: Southern Methodist University, 1963). His work was followed by equally excellent volumes such as J. Stillson Judah, *The History and Philosophy of the Metaphysical Movements in America* (Philadelphia: Westminster Press, 1967) and Gail Thain Parker, *Mind Cure in New England* (Hanover, NH: University Press of New England, 1973). However, one can not help but suspect that the attitude of Donald Meyer's *The Positive Thinkers* (Garden City, NY: Doubleday, 1965), which attacks the spiritual worth of New Thought, expresses a more common attitude.

The Scholarly treatment of the New Age has begun in such important works as Mary Bednarowski's *New Religions and the Theological Imagination in America* (Bloomington: Indiana University Press, 1989). The more typical attitudes of elitist disdain, however, are expressed in, for example, Martin Gardner, *The New Age, Notes of a Fringe Watcher* (Buffalo, NY: Prometheus Books, 1988) and Henry Gordon, *Channeling in the New Age* (Buffalo, NY: Prometheus Books, 1988). As will probably be recognized, both of these volumes emanate from the humanist press, which has dedicated itself to attacking any form of what it considers supernatural or esoteric religion.

5. On Hopkins and the beginnings of New Thought, see J. Gordon Melton, "Emma Curtis Hopkins: The Forgotten Founder of New Thought." *META* 1, 1 (1989).

6. (London: George Redway, 1888).

7. For the complete texts of both Declarations see J. Gordon Melton, *The Encyclopedia of American Religion: Religious Creeds* (Detroit: Gale Research Company, 1988).

8. The understanding of the major thrust of the New Age and its boundaries as presented in this paper has been significantly informed, first, by the perusal of the many New Age periodicals of which over a hundred are currently being published. The Institute for the Study of American Religion regularly receives around 50 such periodicals. Second, the programs of major New Thought gatherings have been examined to determine the most popular themes repeated in lectures, workshops and booths.

9. The many groups which flow from the lineage of the Theosophical Society are detailed in the chapter on the "Ancient Wisdom Family" in J. Gordon Melton, *The Encyclopedia of American Religions*, 3d ed. (Detroit: Gale Research Company, 1988).

10. (New York: Lucis Publishing Company, 1948).

11. The most important of Spangler's books are *Revelation, The Birth of a New Age* (San Francisco: Rainbow Bridge, 1976) and *Emergence, The Rebirth of the Sacred* (New York: Dell, 1984).

12. (Garden City, NY: Doubleday, 1980).

13. (New York: E. P. Dutton, 1976).

14. (New York, 1882. Rept.: Montrose, CO: Essenes of Kosmon, 1950).

15. (Los Angeles: The Author, 1907).

16. (Englewood Cliff, NJ: Prentice-Hall, 1970).

17. Jane Roberts, *Seth Speaks* (Englewood Cliffs, NJ: Prentice-Hall, 1972).

18. (New York: Foundation for Inner Peace, 1975).

19. *Scientific Properties and Occult Aspects of Twenty-two Gems, Stones, and Metals* (Virginia Beach, VA: A.R.E. Press, 1960).

20. *Exploring Atlantis* (Thousand Oaks, CA: Quantum Productions, 1982).

21. I want to acknowledge the assistance for this section of the paper I have drawn from conversations with and the writings of Dell deChant, a Unity minister who had taken a lead in exploring the relationship of New Thought and the New Age from a very critical stance.

Chapter 3. Roots of the New Age

1. New Thought can be understood as composed of groups and individuals who agree with the basic declarations of the International New Thought Alliance. New Thought movements differentiate themselves from Christian Science, and the Unity School of Christianity is not formally part of the group. The Declaration of Principles adopted at the Congress of the International

New Thought Alliance held in St. Louis in 1917 included the following affirmations:

> ... the freedom of each soul as to choice and as to belief ... the essence of New Thought is Truth ... health is man's divine inheritance ... every cell of (man's body) is intelligent ... spiritual healing has existed among all races in all times (and) has now become part of the higher science ... within us are unused resources of energy and power ... the teachings of Christ ... God (is) Love, Life, Truth and Joy ... His mind is our mind ... Heaven (is) here and now ... the universe is spiritual and we are spiritual beings. Quoted in J. Gordon Melton, *New Thought—A Reader* (Santa Barbara, CA: The Institute for the Study of American Religion, 1987), 3.

2. J. Gordon Melton, "The Forerunners of New Thought," Ibid., 17.

3. *Isis Unveiled* (NY: J. W. Bouton, 1877) and *The Secret Doctrine* (London: Theosophical Publishing Co., 1889).

4. A prominent Theosophical periodical.

5. Arthur H. Nethercot, see *The First Five Lives of Annie Besant* (Chicago: University of Chicago Press, 1960).

6. Walter Truett Anderson, *The Upstart Spring: Esalen and the American Awakening*, (Menlo Park, California: Addison-Wesley Publishing Co., 1983), 54.

7. The term 'Gnosticism', as I am using it, refers to the syncretistic first- and second-century Hellenistic movements broadly present in the Roman Empire and emanating originally probably from Alexandria in Egypt, which variously taught a salvation religion based on having knowledge or *gnosis*. Knowledge given by a revealer saves the Gnostic from the evil, material world and permits, at death, his divine spark within to rejoin the light in the heavenly pleroma. The central idea or myth of Gnosticism concerns the presence in man of the divine "spark" ... which has proceeded from the divine world and has fallen into this world of destiny, birth and death and which must be reawakened through its own divine counterpart in order to be finally restored. This idea ... is ontologically based on the conception of a downward development of the divine whose periphery (often called Sophia or Ennoia) has fatally fallen victim to a crisis and must—even if only indirectly—produce this world, in which it then cannot be disinterested, in that it must once again recover the divine "spark" (often designated as *pneuma*, "spirit").

This was identified as the central myth of Gnosticism at the Messina Conference on the Origins of Gnosticism in 1966. Quoted in Kurt Rudolph, *Gnosis*, ed. and trans. by Robert McLachlan Wilson (San Francisco: Harper and Row, 1983), 57.

8. The first source Mead lists, published in 1569 in Latin as were all of the

following, is *Lives, Secrets and Dogmas of all the Heretics* published in 1669 by Marcossius. He was followed by Macarius who wrote on the Basilidians (1659); Siricius on Simon Magus (1664); a dissertation he attributes to Michaelis on Indian Gnostic philosophy at the time of the Septuagint (1667); Ittig on heresies of the apostolic period (1709); Strunz on Bardesanes (1710); Massnet on heresies of the second century in his prolegomena to Irenaeus (1710); Beausobre on Basilides, Marcion, Bardesanes and Manicheism (1734); Mosheim on the Dositheans (1739); and Schumacher on the Ophites (1756) to list just works that were written before the death of Swedenborg. In George R. S. Mead, *Fragments of a Faith Forgotten* (NY: New Hyde Park, 1960).

9. See Marguerite Beck Block, *The New Church in the New World* (New York: Octagon Books, 1968).

10. Ibid., 63.

11. Ibid., 93.

12. Ibid., 130.

13. Ibid., 132. Block notes:

In 1851 the *Medium* makes the statement that the great majority of the New Church fully acknowledge their belief in spiritualistic manifestations. But though this was probably true, it does not mean that they were actively engaged in spiritualistic practices—in fact, quite the contrary—the majority of New Churchmen have always heeded Swedenborg's warning concerning the dangers of intercourse with spirits, and the Church has officially kept coldly aloof from Spiritualism. . . . But the Spiritualists' side of the story is a very different one. They claim Swedenborg as the first Spiritualist, that is, the first to have communications with departed souls, and much of their belief concerning the kind of future life to look forward to after death comes directly from *Heaven and Hell*. 133

14. Block quotes Podmore: "Animal magnetism became the fertile matrix from which sprung all the shadowy brood of latter-day mysticisms—Spiritualism, Theosophy, the New Thought, culminating in the Christian Science of Mrs. Mary Baker Eddy." Ibid., 131.

15. Ibid.

16. Horatio Dresser, "The Spirit of New Thought," in Melton, *New Thought*, 6.

17. Ibid.

18. Ibid.

19. Charles Brodie Patterson, "What New Thought Stands For," in *The Will to be Well* (New York: Alliance Publishing Company, 1901). Quoted in Melton, Ibid., 12.

20. J. Gordon Melton, "Prosperity, the Psychic and Reincarnation," in Melton, Ibid., 179.

21. Charles S. Braden, Spirits in Rebellion: The Rise and Development of New Thought (Dallas, Texas: Southern Methodist University Press, 1963).

22. Ibid., 255.

23. Anderson reports Brady's description as follows:

"She told about the shacks they lived in, their beards and sandals and tattered clothes, the abstract painting on their walls, their parties and poetry-reading sessions. Their philosophy, she wrote, was based on opposition to the traditional institutions of Western civilization—church, state and family—and it expressed itself in an erotic, sentimental mysticism. The new Bohemia, she reported with surprise, was religious. Its religion, however, was nothing like the standard American fare. It was a belief in something that went by such names as 'the life force' or the 'great oneness.'" Walter Truett Anderson, *The Upstart Spring*, 20.

24. Anderson describes California in the sixties as follows:

"The Sufis say that ordinary life is a kind of slumber from which only a few extraordinary human beings have ever truly awakened. They also say that there are occasions in the lives of the rest of us when we awaken for a moment and catch a fuller glimpse of the true vastness of our being before we fall asleep again. I find that a cogent and unusually scrutable piece of Oriental wisdom, and I think a good case could be made that that is true for societies as well as for individuals—that there are periods in the history of any civilization when its rest is disturbed, and that in such periods the inner life runs near the surface, ordinary people crave mystical experience, there is much odd behavior, and many things seem possible." Ibid., 8.

25. Rexroth describes Santa Barbara as follows:

"There still exists tucked away in the interstices of a most conventional population a survival of that almost forgotten community—bohemia. A stranger attending a mid-summer part or a wine pressing on Mountain Drive would think he had landed by time machine back in the days of Jack London's and George Sterling's Carmel, the days before intellectual was wolf to intellectual. There is nothing to fight about. Even sex, food, clothing, and shelter and mild intoxicants are abundant and can be obtained practically for the asking. Then too, not least, the extremely conventional citizenry have passionately defended the beauty of their city so that it is today the least fouled up of any place with a mediterranean climate." Kenneth Rexroth, "Introduction" in Lee Mallory, *20 Times in the Same Place*, (Santa Barbara: Painted Cave Books, 1973).

26. Anderson quotes Huxley as follows:

"Let us begin[would say Huxley, in his kindly Oxonian accents] by asking a question: What would have happened to a child of 170 I.Q. born into a Paleolithic family at the time of, say the cave paintings of Lascaux? Well, quite obviously, he could have been nothing except a hunter and a food gatherer. There was no opportunity for him to be anything else. The biologists have shown us that, physiologically and anatomically, we are pretty much the same as we were twenty thousand years ago and that we are using fundamentally the same equipment as the Aurignacian man to produce incredibly different results. We have in the course of these twenty thousand years actualized an immense number of things which at that time and for many, many centuries thereafter were wholly potential and latent in man. This, I think, gives us reason for tempered optimism that there are still a great many potentialities—for rationality, for affection and kindliness, for creativity—still lying latent in man; and, since everything has speeded up so enormously in recent years, that we shall find methods for going almost as far beyond the point we have reached now within a few hundred years as we have succeeded in going beyond our Aurignacian ancestors in twenty thousand years. I think this is not an entirely fantastic belief. The neurologists have shown us that no human being has ever made use of as much as ten percent of all the neurons in his brain. And perhaps, if we set about it in the right way, we might be able to produce extraordinary things out of this strange piece of work that a man is." Walter Truett Anderson, *The Upstart Spring*, 11.

27. Ibid.

28. See Anthony Sutich, "Introduction," *Journal of Humanistic Psychology*, Vol. I, No. 1. (1969), viii.

29. James S. Simkin, "Gestalt Therapy," in Corsini, Ibid., 277-278.

30. Ibid., 273. Raymond J. Corsini, *Current Psychotherapies* (Itasca, IL: F. E. Peacock, 1979, 2d ed.).

31. Donald Stone, "The Human Potential Movement," in Charles Y. Glock and Robert N. Bellah, *The New Religious Consciousness* (Berkeley: University of California Press, 1976), 102-104.

32. Eugene Gendlin, "Experiential Psychotherapy," Corsini, *Current Psychotherapies*, 340.

33. Ibid.

34. Ibid., 344. Gendlin notes:

Yoga and Wilhelm Reich's systems work directly with the body, with muscles, movements and postures. Such work does lead to improvements in psyche and ways of living. Both Yoga and Reich stress that while working with the body, certain psychological processes are necessary. Yoga stresses meditation. Reich urges one to 'work through' the psychological and interpersonal feelings that arise when one releases certain muscles and works with one's body. Systems that work with the body directly want to consider body and psyche as one and want to work not only with muscles but also with feelings.

35. Ibid., 347.

36. Ibid., 354.

37. Patterson, "What New Thought Stands For," 10.

38. Leon J. Fine, "Psychodrama," in Corsini, *Current Psychotherapies*, 435.

39. Sutich, "Introduction."

40. Abraham Maslow, "Health as Transcendence of Environment." *Journal of Humanistic Psychology*, Vol. I, No. 1, 3.

41. Ibid.

42. Ibid.

43. John H. Mann, "Human Potential," in Corsini, *Current Psychotherapies*, 511.

44. Ibid.

45. Abraham Maslow, quoted in Mann, Ibid.

46. Ibid.

47. Ibid.

48. Ibid.

49. Ibid.

50. Ibid., 512.

51. Ibid., 516.

52. Roberto Assagioli. Quoted in Donald Stone, "The Human Potential Movement," 101.

53. Mueller notes that

this nonformalized, independent 'emerging force' had already been seeded in many different ways. A short sample of a long list might include the many inroads of particularly Tibetan and Zen Buddhism; Hindu derived yoga schools, ashrams, fellowships, and even Transcendental Meditation; Sufism and the Arica Institute; the vast psychedelic drug experiment of the youth culture; advances in parapsychology related especially to human energies such as kundalini, auras, Kirlian photography, and life fields; the many converging interests in consciousness, notably through the development and application of techniques of mind control, psycholytic drugs (as LSD), hypnosis, meditation, biofeedback and autogenic training; and so on. Donald J. Mueller, "Transpersonal Psychology: Religion or Science," (A paper presented to a colloquium of The Comparative Study of Religion Program at the University of Wisconsin-Milwaukee on April 19, 1978) (Milwaukee, Wisconsin: School of Social Welfare, The University of Wisconsin-Milwaukee), 2..

54. Ibid.

55. Ibid., 3. Mueller quotes Sutich's definition of Transpersonal psychology:

Transpersonal (or "Fourth Force") Psychology is the title given to an emerging force in the psychology field by a group of psychologists and professional men and women from other fields who are interested in those *ultimate* human capacities and potentialities that have no systematic place in positivistic or behavioristic theory ("second force"), or humanistic psychology ("third force"). The emerging Transpersonal Psychology ("fourth force") is concerned specifically with the *empirical*, scientific study of, and responsible implementation of the findings relevant to, becoming, individual and species-wise meta-needs, ultimate values, unitive consciousness, self-actualization, essence, bliss, wonder, ultimate meaning, transcendence of the self, spirit, oneness, cosmic awareness, individual and species-wide synergy, maximal interpersonal encounter, sacralization of everyday life, transcendental phenomena, cosmic self-humor and playfulness; maximal sensory awareness, responsiveness and expression; and related concepts, experiences and activities.

56. Ibid.

57. Ibid., 4.

58. Ibid., 23.

59. Ibid.

60. Ibid.

61. See *The Journal of Transpersonal Psychology.*

62. Mueller, "Transpersonal Psychology."

Chapter 4. Imagining India: The Influence of Hinduism on the New Age Movement

1. See the discussion of New Age beliefs in the introductory essay in J. Gordon Melton, Jerome Clark, and Aiden A. Kelly, *New Age Encyclopedia* (Detroit: Gale Research, 1990).

2. For the impact of Indian philosophy on the transcendentalists, see J. Stillson Judah, *The History of the Metaphysical Movements in America* (Philadelphia: Westminster, 1967), 31-32. Judah also mentions the impact of Indian philosophy on New Thought on pp. 146, 160, 198, and 249. Much of the Hindu influence on New Thought was mediated through transcendentalism.

3. While Theosophy is probably the most important single influence in the constellation of ideas that make up the New Age worldview, Theosophy's heavy borrowing from Hindu thought, in combination with the more direct contribution of later Hindu spiritual teachers, would allow one to argue that Hinduism constitutes the most significant component of the contemporary New Age movement.

4. J. Gordon Melton, "The Attitude of Americans toward Hinduism from 1883 to 1983 with Special Reference to the International Society for Krishna Consciousness," in David G. Bromley and Larry D. Shinn, *Krishna Consciousness in the West* (Lewisburg: Bucknell University Press, 1989), 79.

5. Mozoomdar's presence in the West was one of the results of a very interesting connection between Anglo-American Unitarians and the Indian reformer Ram Mohan Roy. This connection is the subject of Spencer Lavan, *Unitarians and India* (Boston: Beacon, 1977).

6. We might also note in passing that Swami Kriyananda, one of Yogananda's more important American disciples, has been an active participant in many New Age gatherings. In this regard, see Susan Love Brown's paper in the present volume.

7. Fritjob Capra, *The Tao of Physics* (Boulder: Shamballa, 1965), 90.

8. E.g., to pull out a few relevant statements from the *Crest Jewel of Discrimination*: "If you really desire liberation, hold the objects of sense enjoyment at a distance, like poison." Shankara, *Crest Jewel of Discrimination*, trans. Swami Prabhavananda and Christopher Isherwood (Hollywood: Vedanta Press, 1947), p. 53; "The body can never be the same as the self-existent Atman, the knower. The nature of the Atman is quite different from that of the body." Ibid., 68.

9. Capra, *The Tao of Physics*, 25.

10. Harvey Cox, *Turning East* (New York: Simon & Shuster, 1977), 149.

11. Many parallel phenomena, such as the early Jesuit scholarship about

PERSPECTIVES ON THE NEW AGE

China and D. T. Suzuki-Alan Watts Zen, will not be considered, both for lack of space and for lack of expertise in these areas.

12. India had already found a place in the European imagination prior to his time, but the influence of this image increased markedly in the wake of the large number of texts translated by Sir William Jones and company. In this regard see Raymond Schwab, *The Oriental Renaissance*, trans., Gene Patterson-Black and Vitor Reinking (New York: Columbia, 1984).

13. David Kopf, *British Orientalism and the Bengal Renaissance* (Berkeley: University of California, 1969), 22.

14. Ibid., 24.

15. E.g., to cite a relevant passage from Jones: "[H]ow degenerate and abased so ever the Hindus may now appear, . . . in some early age they were splendid in arts and arms, happy in government; wise in legislation, and eminent in various knowledge." Sir William Jones, "The Third Anniversary Discourse" in *The Works of Sir William Jones* (London: John Stockdale and John Walker, 1807), 32. The link between the Indian and the Mediterranean classical civilizations is made in a number of places in this same discourse.

16. C. L. Becker, *The Heavenly City of the Eighteenth Century Philosophers* (New Haven: Yale University, 1964), 107-108.

17. Voltaire, *The Philosophy of History*, trans. Thomas Kiernan (New York: Philosophical Library, 1965), 76.

18. Cited in Rick Fields, *How the Swans Came to the Lake* (Boulder: Shamballa, 1981), 42.

19. Edward W. Said, *Orientalism* (New York: Vintage, 1979), 93, 52.

20. Ibid., 99.

21. Ibid., 92.

22. Ibid., 86.

23. E.g., William Jones asserted that contemporaneous Indians "were so wedded to inveterate prejudices and habits, if liberty could be forced upon them by Britain, it would make them miserable as the cruelest despot." Cited in Fields, *How the Swans Came to the Lake*, 40.

24. Kopf, *British Orientalism and the Bengal Renaissance*, 40-41.

25. P. C. Majumdar, *British Paramountcy and Indian Renaissance* (London: G. Allen & Unwin, 1965), 114.

26. Jawaharlal Nehru, *The Discovery of India* (New York: John Day, 1946), 37.

27. "It was from Jones's books, especially his translation of the *Laws of Manu*, and the essays in *Asiatic Researches*, that literate Americans . . . drew their knowledge of Indian literature and comparative religion." Fields, *How the Swans Came to the Lake*, 55.

28. On this point see Schwab, *The Oriental Renaissance*, 200-201.

29. Fields, *How the Swans Came to the Lake*, 64.

30. In this regard, see the discussion in Said, *Orientalism*, 137 and elsewhere. This notion was also picked up and utilized by Indian reformers and nationalists; for this latter point, see Bernard S. Cohn, *India: The Social Anthropology of a Civilization* (Englewood Cliffs: Prentice-Hall, 1971), 57.

31. Henry David Thoreau, *Walden*, in *The Writings of Henry David Thoreau* (Boston: Haughton Mifflin, 1906), 328. For a more general discussion of this theme see Said, *Orientalism*, 51 and elsewhere.

32. E.g., "Helping the lama or brahman as he trims the lamps of idols, Dancing through the streets in a phallic procession . . . Drinking mead from the skull-cup, to Shastas and Vedas . . . " In Walt Whitman, *The Portable Walt Whitman* (New York, Viking, 1963), 85. For a general discussion of this theme see Said, *Orientalism*, 187-188 and elsewhere.

33. See his poem "Passage to India," in *The Portable Walt Whitman*, 275-284.

34. Also present was Soyen Shaku, the teacher of D. T. Suzuki. Although less influential than Vivekananda at the time, this Zen lineage would—through Suzuki and his emulator, Alan Watts—shape American perceptions of Asian religion as significantly as the Hindu missionaries.

35. Vivekananda, *The Complete Works of Swami Vivekananda* (Calcutta: Advaita Ashram, 1972), 23.

36. Ibid., 350.

37. Ibid., 347-348.

38. Ibid., 7.

39. Ibid., 15.

40. Cited in Majumdar, *British Paramountcy and Indian Renaissance*, 127.

41. Kopf, *British Orientalism and the Bengal Renaissance*, 41.

42. Gary Snyder, "Buddhism and the Coming Revolution," in *Earth House Hold* (New York: New Directions, 1969), p. 91. Snyder was an important Beat literary figure.

43. Snyder, "Why Tribe," in Ibid., 114-115.

Chapter 5. How New is the New Age?

1. The ephemerality of early Spiritualism should not be overemphasized. Although the "craze" of the 1850s did not last, the movement certainly continued, showing periodic upsurges, as in the 1870s and 1920s, and graduating from platform demonstrations and home "circles" to regular churches and denominations around the turn of the century. More importantly, Spiritualism paved the way for such subsequent movements as Theosophy, New Thought, and psychical research. For many Spiritualism was, to be sure, an ephemeral episode in their lives. But not a few sometime Spiritualists found that, subsequently, there was no turning back to previous dogmatic slumbers: They were open to other fresh and modern infusions of the spirit, such as those cited.

2. See R. Laurence Moore, *In Search of White Crows: Spiritualism, Parapsychology, and American Culture* (New York: Oxford University Press, 1977), Ch. 4, and Ann Braude, *Radical Spirits: Spiritualism and Women's Rights in Nineteenth-Century America* (Boston: Beacon Press, 1989).

3. For a study of Spiritualism and proletarian radicalism in England, see Logie Barrow, *Independent Spirits: Spiritualism and English Plebeians, 1850-1910* (London and New York: Routledge and Kegan Paul, 1986). Unfortunately, a full scholarly history of modern Spiritualism in the land of its birth and its interaction with other social movements has yet to be written.

4. Michael Grosso, *The Final Choice: Playing the Survival Game* (Walpole, NH: Stillpoint Publishing, 1985); Kenneth Ring, *Heading Toward Omega* (New York: William Morrow, 1984, 1985).

5. Raymond Moody, *Life After Life* (Atlanta: Mockingbird Press, 1975). This is a composite scenario; most experiencers report only certain of these features.

6. Letter from John F. Grey, *The Shekinah* 3, (1853), 190. Cited in Moore, *In Search of White Crows*, 77-78.

7. "A Doctor of Hermetic Science," ed., *The Harmonial Philosophy: A Compendium and Digest of the Works of Andrew Jackson Davis* (Chicago: Advanced Thought Pub. Co., 1917), from *Arabula*.

8. Ibid., 290. From *The Principles of Nature*.

9. Rutland Free Convention, *Proceedings*, 1858. Cited in Braude, *Radical Spirits*, 70.

10. *The Liberator*, 17 Dec. 1852. Cited in Moore, *In Search of White Crows*, 78-79.

11. A. B. Child, *Whatever Is, Is Right* (Boston: Berry, Colby, 1861), p. 144. Cited in Moore, *In Search of White Crows*, 79.

Chapter 6. The Magical Staff:
Quantum Healing in the New Age

1. This account is based on Andrew Jackson Davis, *The Magic Staff: An Autobiography of Andrew Jackson Davis*, 5th ed. (1859; reprint, Mokelumne Hill, Calif.: Health Research, 1972), 227-39. *The Magic Staff* is Davis's first autobiography, covering almost the first thirty years of his life.

2. Ibid., 240-45, 262-63. Emphasis in Davis.

3. Davis's New York series of trance lectures were published as Andrew Jackson Davis, *The Principles of Nature, Her Divine Revelations, and a Voice to Mankind* (New York: S. S. Lyon and W. Fishbough, 1847). My own copy of the thirty-fourth edition (reprint, Mokelumne Hill, Calif.: Health Research, 1984) bears the imprint 1881. For the quotation, see Andrew Jackson Davis, *Beyond the Valley: A Sequel to "The Magic Staff: An Autobiography of Andrew Jackson Davis,"* (Boston: Colby & Rich, 1885), 360 (emphasis in Davis). My summary here is based on a fuller discussion of Davis in Catherine L. Albanese, "On the Matter of Spirit: Andrew Jackson Davis and the Marriage of God and Nature," *Journal of the American Academy of Religion*, forthcoming.

4. For a discussion of Poyen's tour and the introduction of mesmerism to the United States, see Robert C. Fuller, *Mesmerism and the American Cure of Souls* (Philadelphia: University of Pennsylvania Press, 1982), esp. 17-22.

5. Franz Anton Mesmer, "Dissertation by F. A. Mesmer, Doctor of Medicine, on His Discoveries" (1799), in Franz Anton Mesmer, *Mesmerism: A Translation of the Original Medical and Scientific Writings of F. A. Mesmer*, trans. and comp. George Bloch (Los Altos, Calif.: William Kaufmann, 1980), 119-21.

6. For a recent and insightful discussion of the materiality of Swedenborg's heaven, see Colleen McDannell and Bernhard Lang, *Heaven: A History* (New Haven: Yale University Press, 1988), 181-226, esp. 191-99. The best single-volume account by Swedenborg of his thought on matters of correspondence, influx, the Divine Human, and heaven is Emanuel Swedenborg, *Heaven and Its Wonders and Hell, from Things Heard and Seen*, trans. J. C. Ager (1852; reprint, New York: Swedenborg Foundation, 1964). And for "conjugial love," see Emanuel Swedenborg, *The Delights of Wisdom pertaining to Conjugial Love after which follow The Pleasures of Insanity pertaining to Scortatory Love*, trans. Samuel M. Warren, and rev. trans. Louis H. Tafel (1856; reprint, New York: Swedenborg Foundation, 1980).

7. On the *North American Review* and the *Western Repository*, see D. Michael Quinn, *Early Mormonism and the Magic World View* (Salt Lake City: Signature Books, 1987), 129, 174.

8. For a more extensive discussion of the mental world of early osteopathy and chiropractic, see Catherine L. Albanese, *Nature Religion in America: From*

the Algonkian Indians to the New Age, Chicago History of American Religion (Chicago: University of Chicago Press, 1990), 142-49.

9. See Victor Guillemin, *The Story of Quantum Mechanics* (New York: Charles Scribner's Sons, 1968), 42, 174.

10. My discussion in this and the next several paragraphs is based mostly on Albanese, *Nature Religion in America,* 150-52. Accounts of quantum physics especially germane for students of religion include Fritjof Capra, *The Tao of Physics: An Exploration of the Parallels between Modern Physics and Eastern Mysticism,* 2d ed. (Boston: Shambhala, New Science Library, 1985); and Gary Zukav, *The Dancing Wu Li Masters: An Overview of the New Physics* (New York: Bantam Books, 1980).

11. For Heisenberg and the "unsharpness principle" or principle of uncertainty, see Guillemin, *Story of Quantum Mechanics,* 91-101. Heisenberg's own statements may be found in Werner Heisenberg, *The Physical Principles of the Quantum Theory,* trans. Carl Eckart and Frank C. Hoyt ([New York]: Dover, 1930), 3, 20; and Werner Heisenberg, *Physics and Philosophy: The Revolution in Modern Science,* World Perspectives, vol. 19 (New York: Harper, 1958), 55-58.

12. Werner Heisenberg, *Natural Law and the Structure of Matter* (London: Rebel Press, 1970), 32; Heisenberg, *Physics and Philosophy,* 81, 205.

13. J. Gordon Melton, *Encyclopedic Handbook of Cults in America* (New York: Garland Publishing, 1986), 108; and J. Gordon Melton, "New Thought and the New Age" (Paper delivered at the American Society of Church History Meeting, San Francisco, Calif., 29 December 1989), 4. See, in this volume,
Sociological information on the composition and size of the New Age movement is exceedingly hard to come by. Melton has suggested that its "largest constituency" is "from single young upwardly mobile urban adults" (*Encyclopedic Handbook,* 116). Meredith McGuire's study of alternative healing among suburban New Jerseyites—not specifically identified as New Agers but in many cases conforming to a New Age profile—emphasizes the middle-class status of her subjects (Meredith G. McGuire with the assistance of Debra Kantor, *Ritual Healing in Suburban America* [New Brunswick: Rutgers University Press, 1988], esp. 3-17). Meanwhile, David J. Hufford's study of contemporary folk medicine—dealing in many cases with advocates of the kinds of holistic therapies that New Agers favor—points to higher levels of education than in the general population for those who follow the folk therapies (David J. Hufford, "Contemporary Folk Medicine," in Norman Gevitz, ed., *Other Healers: Unorthodox Medicine in America* [Baltimore: Johns Hopkins University Press, 1988] 228-64, esp. 245-46). On the other hand, my own acquaintance with the New Age community in southwestern Ohio has suggested to me a strong component of working-class people with only average levels of education, and in the Santa Barbara, California, area, I have also encountered not a few New Agers from the working class. As for numbers of adherents to New Age beliefs and practices,

see my discussion in Catherine L. Albanese, "Religion and the American Experience: A Century After," *Church History* 57, 3 (September 1988): 337-51, esp. 241, 245-46.

14. Melton, "New Thought and the New Age," 3, 9-10. See, in this volume,

15. Robert Ellwood, "How New Is the New Age?" (Paper delivered at the American Society of Church History Meeting, San Francisco, Calif., 29 December 1989), 1-3. See, in this volume,

16. Melton, *Encyclopedic Handbook*, 113; Mary Farrell Bednarowski, *New Religions and the Theological Imagination in America*, Religion in North America (Bloomington: Indiana University Press, 1989), 15 (brackets Bednarowski's). The Spangler quotation is from David Spangler, *Emergence: The Rebirth of the Sacred* (New York: Dell, 1984), 167.

17. This is my own paraphrase of linked questions initially suggested to me by Meredith McGuire, *Ritual Healing*, 247.

18. For an assessment, see Melton, *Encyclopedic Handbook*, 112; and for a sample New Age publication, see any issue of the *Whole Life Times*, available in cities like Los Angeles and Cincinnati.

19. Richard Gerber, *Vibrational Medicine: New Choices for Healing Ourselves* (Santa Fe: Bear, 1988), 58-59, 67, 59-60, 69. Emphasis in Gerber.

20. Deepak Chopra, *Quantum Healing: Exploring the Frontiers of Mind/Body Medicine* (New York: Bantam Books, 1989), 17-18, 71, 40, 95, 105, 112, 129. I am indebted to Chopra for the "quantum healing" portion of this essay's title, although I use the term with a more extended designation than he does.

21. Hufford, "Contemporary Folk Medicine," 236; and on the difference between healing and curing, see McGuire, *Ritual Healing*, 233-34.

22. Marilyn Ferguson, *The Aquarian Conspiracy: Personal and Social Transformation in the 1980s*, 2d ed. (Los Angeles: J. P. Tarcher, 1987), 241-42, 246-47, 256, 248, 257. Emphasis in Ferguson.

23. Larry Arnold and Sandy Nevius, *The Reiki Handbook* (Harrisburg, Pa.: PSI Press, ParaScience International, 1982), 13; Barbara Weber Ray, *The Reiki Factor: A Guide to Natural Healing, Helping, and Wholeness* (Smithtown, N.Y.: Exposition Press, 1983), 35-36, 39, 30-31, 50 (emphasis in Ray). For further discussion of Reiki, see Albanese, *Nature Religion in America*, 186-90.

24. Robert C. Fuller, *Alternative Medicine and American Religious Life* (New York: Oxford University Press, 1989), 112-13.

25. Gurudas [Kevin Ryerson], *Flower Essences and Vibrational Healing* (Albuquerque: Brotherhood of Life, 1983), 29, 31.

26. Ibid., 35-36.

27. Shakti Gawain, *Creative Visualization* (San Rafael, Calif.: New World Library, 1978), 17-19. Emphasis in Gawain.

28. Ibid., 19, 44, 55.

29. Ibid., 76.

30. Jeanne Achterberg, *Imagery in Healing: Shananism and Modern Medicine* (Boston: Shambhala, New Science Library, 1985), 6, 8, 13, 17.

31. Ibid., 50, 144, 50.

32. Michael Harner, *The Way of the Shaman: A Guide to Power and Healing* (New York: Bantam Books, 1982).

33. Ibid., 55-56, 175-76. Emphasis in Harner.

34. Ibid., 179. Emphasis in Harner.

35. McGuire, *Ritual Healing*, 240-44.

Chapter 7. Baby Boomers, American Culture, and the New Age: A Synthesis

Acknowledgments. This paper was presented in briefer form at the 1989 annual meeting of the American Anthropological Association in Washington, D.C. As always, I am grateful to Sri Kriyananda and the members of the Ananda community for sharing their lives so generously. I owe a special debt of gratitude to Vivian Rohrl, who encouraged and supervised the original Ananda research. My special thanks to Roy D'Andrade, whose course in national character served as an impetus for the baby boomer research, and to Ted Schwartz for the opportunity to present these ideas publicly.

1. My research was conducted in the summer of 1986 when I lived at Ananda for six weeks. I later participated in weekly meditations with Ananda members in San Diego from 1986-87, visited the community again in 1987 for a week, and attended Ananda church services in San Diego from 1987-88.

2. For a detailed study of the New Age interest in witchcraft in Great Britain, for example, see T. M. Luhrmann's *Persuasions of the Witch's Craft* (Cambridge, Massachusetts: Harvard University Press, 1989).

3. Alexis de Tocqueville, *Democracy in America* (New York: Vintage, 1945), 2:142.

4. Benjamin Zablocki, *Alienation and Charisma* (New York: The Free Press, 1980), 40.

5. D. Michael Quinn, *Early Mormonism and the Magic World View* (Salt Lake City: Signature Books, 1987).

6. For example, see Daniel Weizmann, "Getting Clear as Crystals," *California*, July 1989, for a popular, if scathing, assessment of New Age variety.

7. Carl T. Jackson, *The Oriental Religions in American Thought: Nineteenth Century Explorations* (Westport, Connecticut: Greenwood Press, 1981),14, 30-31.

8. Robert S. Ellwood, *Eastern Spirituality in America: Selected Writings* (New York: Paulist Press, 1987), 21.

9. Paramahansa Yogananda, *Autobiography of a Yogi* (Los Angeles: Self-Realization Fellowship, 1985), 404-410.

10. Ananda has had many names. In the beginning it was called Ananda Cooperative Village. When I was there in 1986, it was Ananda Village. But that summer, Kriyananda changed the name to Ananda World Brotherhood Village, because world brotherhood villages were something Yogananda had talked about but never achieved in his lifetime.

11. Paramahansa Yogananda, *The Science of Religion* (Los Angeles: Self-Realization Fellowship, 1982), 14.

12. Paramahansa Yogananda, *Man's Eternal Quest* (Los Angeles: Self-Realization Fellowship, 1982), 283.

13. This phrase is from Anthony F. C. Wallace, "Revitalization Movements: Some Theoretical Considerations for Their Comparative Study," *American Anthropologist* 1956, 58(2):264-281.

14. Ananda celebrated its twentieth anniversary from 1987 to 1989 to avoid confusion over which was actually the beginning date.

15. Sri Kriyananda, *Cooperative Communities: How to Start Them and Why.* (Nevada City, California: Ananda Publications, 1979), 92-93.

16. Baba Ram Dass, *Be Here Now* (San Cristobal, New Mexico: Lama Foundation, 1971).

17. Susan Love Brown, *Ananda Revisited: Values and Change in a Cooperative, Religious Community.* M. A. Thesis. (Unpublished. San Diego: San Diego State University, 1987), 132.

18. Ibid, 120.

19. For example see Wade Clark Roof, "Narratives and Numbers." J. F. Rowny Inaugural Lecture. University of California, Santa Barbara. 30 May 1990.

20. Cheryl Russell, *Predictions for the Baby Boom* (New York: Plenum Press, 1987), 27-28.

21. Ibid., 27.

22. Ibid., 29.

23. Ibid., 10.

24. Ibid., 30.

25. Charles E. Strickland and Andrew M. Ambrose, "The Baby Boom, Prosperity, and the Changing Worlds of Children, 1945-1963" in Joseph M. Hawkes and N. Ray Hiner, eds., *American Childhood, a Research Guide and Historical Handbook*, 533-585 (Westport, Connecticut: Greenwood Press, 1985), 533.

26. Ibid., 546.

27. Cheryl Russell, *Predictions for the Baby Boom*, 39.

28. Strickland and Ambrose, "The Baby Boom," 544-45.

29. Ibid., 565.

30. Susan Love Brown, *Ananda Revisited*, 128-29.

31 .Daniel Yankelovich, *New Rules: Searching for Self-Fulfillment in a World Turned Upside Down* (New York: Random House, 1981).

32. Ibid., 4.

33. Ibid., 5.

34. Ibid., 9.

35. Ibid., 10.

36. Peter Clecak, *America's Quest for the Ideal Self: Dissent and Fulfillment in the 60s and 70s* (New York: Oxford University Press, 1983), 9.

37. Ibid., 10.

38. For a description of the original orientation interviews, see Florence Kluckhohn and Fred Strodtbeck, *Variations in Value Orientations* (Evanston, Illinois: Row, Peterson, 1961). For a look at the raw data and results of the interview at Ananda, see Susan Love Brown, *Ananda Revisited*, 101-115, 176-192.

39. Kluckhohn and Strodtbeck, *Variations in Value Orientations*, 258.

40. Susan Love Brown, *Ananda Revisited*, 112.

41. Anthony F. C. Wallace, "Revitalization Movements," 264.

42. Kriya yoga is a form of raja yoga and a particular form of meditation. It is taught only to those who have been initiated into it.

43. Ted A. Nordquist, *Ananda Cooperative Village: A Study in the Beliefs, Values and Attitudes of a New Age Religious Community* (Uppsala, Sweden: Religionhistorika Institutionen, 1978), 83-84.

44. Benjamin Zablocki, *Alienation and Charisma*, 118.

45. Joseph Veroff, Elizabeth Douvan, and Richard A. Kulka, *The Inner American: A Self Portrait 1957-1976* (New York: Basic Books, 1981).

46. Ted A. Nordquist, *Ananda Cooperative Village*, 86.

47. See, for example, Thomas Robbins, "Eastern Mysticism and the Resocialization of Drug Users: The Meher Baba Cult," *Journal for the Scientific Study of Religion* 8 (1969):308-317.

48. Susan Love Brown, *Ananda Revisited*, 137.

49. George Gallup, Jr. and Jim Castelli, *The People's Religion: American Faith in the 90s* (New York: Macmillan, 1990).

Chapter 8. Myth, Metaphor, and Manifestation: The Negotiation of Belief in a New Age Community

1. Hans Toch, *The Social Psychology of Social Movements* (Indianapolis: Bobbs-Merril, 1965).

2. L. Festinger, *A Theory of Cognitive Dissonance* (Stanford: Stanford University Press, 1957).

Chapter 9. Channeling: A New Revelation?

1. James Hillman, *Re-Visioning Psychology* (New York: Harper & Row, 1975), 3.

2. Robin Western, *Channelers, A New Age Directory* (New York: Putnam, 1988).

3. Ceanne DeRohan, *Right Use of Will: Healing and Evolving the Emotional Body* (Santa Fe: Four Winds Publications, 1986), viii.

4. Jon Klimo, *Channeling: Investigations on Receiving Information from Paranormal Sources* (Los Angeles: Jeremy Tarcher, 1987), 86.

5. Ibid., 100.

6. Samuel M. Warren, *A Compendium of the Theological Writings of Emmanuel Swedenborg* (New York: Swedenborg Foundation, 1977), 618.

7. Gary North, *Unholy Spirits* (Ft. Worth: Dominion Press, 1986), 74.

8. Dick Anthony, Bruce Ecker, and Ken WIlber, eds., *Spiritual Choices* (New York: Paragon House, 1987).

9. Ibid., 284.

10. Allan Kardec, *The Gospel According to Spiritism* (London: The Headquarters Publishing Co., 1987), 7. Originally published in 1864 as *L'Evangile Selon le Spiritisme*.

11. Jane Roberts, *The Afterdeath Journal of an American Philosopher* (New Jersey: Prentice-Hall, 1978), 14.

12. Pat Rodegast and Judith Stanton, comp., *Emmanuel's Book* (Weston, CT: Friend's Press, 1985), 38.

13. "Introduction," in Lazaris, *The Sacred Journey: You and Your Higher Self* (Palm Beach, FL: NPN Publishing, 1987).

14. Westen, *Channelers, A New Age Directory*, 105.

15. Ramon Stevens, *Whatever Happened to Divine Grace?* (Walpole, NH: Stillpoint, 1988), 377.

16. Ibid.

17. Mission Control & Dianna Luppi, *E.T. 101: THe Cosmic Instruction Manual, An Emergency Remedial Edition* (Santa Fe: Intergalactic Council Publications, 1990), 1.

18. Robert Skutch, *Journey Without Distance* (Berkeley: Celestial Arts, 1984), 54.

19. Ann Braude, *Radical Spirits, Spiritualism and Women's Rights in Nineteenth-Century America* (Boston: Beacon Press, 1989), 56.

20. Willis Harman, *Global Mind Change, The Promise of the Last Years of the Twentieth Century* (Indianapolis: Knowledge Systems, Inc., 1988), 35.

21. Ken Carey, *Starseed, The Third Millennium, Living in the Posthistoric World* (San Francisco: Harper, 1991), 196.

22. Ibid., 197.

23. Ibid., 200.

24. Ken Carey, *Return of the Bird Tribes* (Kansas City: Uni*Sun, 1988), 51.

25. Stevens, *Whatever Happened to Divine Grace?*, 166.

26. Mission Control & Dianna Luppi, *E.T. 101*, 7.

27. Ibid., 18.

28. Ibid., 35.

29. Stevens, *Whatever Happened to Divine Grace*, 87.

30. Ibid., 109.

31. Jane Roberts, *Seth Speaks* (New Jersey: Prentice Hall, 1972), 401.

32. Ibid., 403.

33. Jane Roberts, *The Nature of the Psyche, Its Human Expression* (New Jersey: Prentice Hall, 1979), 80.

34. Ibid., 81.

35. Jane Roberts, *The Afterdeath Journal of an American Philosopher*, 217.

36. Raphael, *The Starseed Transmission, An Extraterrestrial Report*, Kansas City: Uni*Sun, 1982), 12.

37. Ibid., 15.

38. Ibid., 10.

39. Ibid., 44.

40. Ibid.

41. Statement made by Emmanuel in public appearance in Santa Barbara in 1988.

42. Rodegast and Stanton, *Emmanuel's Book*, 80.

43. Ibid., 247.

44. Ibid., 249.

45. Pat Rodegast and Judith Stanton, comp., *Emmanuel's Book II, The Choice for Love* (New York: Bantam Books, 1989), 168.

46. Ibid., 138.

47. Rodegast, *Emmanuel's Book*, 39.

48. Rodegast, *Emmanuel's Book II*, 117.

49. Rodegast, *Emmanuel's Book*, 111.

50. Rodegast, *Emmanuel's Book II*, 10.

51. Ibid., 5.

52. *A Course in Miracles* (Tiburon, CA: Foundation for Inner Peace, 1975), I:14.

53. Ibid.

54. Ibid., I:53.

55. Ibid., I:77.

56. Ibid.

57. Ibid., I:229.

58. Ibid.

59. Bartholomew, *From the Heart of a Gentle Brother* (Taos, NM: High Mesa Press, 1987).

60. *A Course in Miracles*, I:18.

61. Ibid., I:32.

62. Ibid., I:21.

63. Ibid., I:420.

64. Ibid., I:118.

65. Ibid., I:121.

66. Ibid., I:15.

67. Ibid., I:464.

68. Ibid., I:27.

69. Ibid.

70. Rodegast, *Emmanuel's Book II*, 4.

71. Ibid., 10.

72. Bartholomew, *From the Heart of a Gentle Brother*, 51.

73. Stevens, *Whatever Happened to Divine Grace?*, 120.

74. *A Course in Miracles*, I:74.

75. Bartholomew, *Reflections of an Elder Brother, Awakening from the Dream* (Taos, NM: High Mesa Press, 1989), 6.

76. Raphael, *Starseed Transmissions*, 42.

77. Westen, *Channelers, A New Age Directory*, 107.

78. Rodegast, *Emmanuel's Book*, 110-111.

79. Quote taken from a videotaped presentation by Emmanuel entitled *A*

Meeting with Emmanuel (Westport, CT: Friend's Production, 1989).

80. Rodegast, *Emmanuel's Book*, 133.

81. Stevens, *Whatever Happened to Divine Grace?*, 61 and 62.

82. Lazaris, *The Sacred Journey: You and Your Higher Self* (Beverly Hills, CA: Synergy Publishing), 20; Carey, *Return of the Bird Tribes*, 51-52.

83. Bartholomew, *From the Heart of a Gentle Brother*, 150.

84. Roberts, *The Nature of the Psyche*, 15. On dreams see: Jane Roberts, *Seth: Dreams and Projection of Consciousness* (Walpole, NH: Stillpoint Publishing, 1987); Jane Roberts, *Dreams, "Evolution," and Value Fulfillment, Volume II*, (New York: Prentice Hall Press, 1986).

85. Roberts, *The Nature of Personal Reality*, 509.

86. Stevens, *Whatever Happened to Divine Grace?*, 76.

87. Ibid., 74.

88. Roberts, *The Afterdeath Journal of an American Philosopher*, 196.

89. Ibid.

90. Ibid., 211.

91. Ibid., 197.

92. Bartholomew, *From the Heart of a Gentle Brother*, 24.

93. Stevens, *Whatever Happened to Divine Gracer?*, 61.

94. Ibid., 62.

95. Raphael, *Starseed Transmission*, 48.

96. Rodegast, *Emmanuel's Book*, 24.

97. Carey, *Return of the Bird Tribes*, 184 and 29.

98. Carey, *Starseed: The Third Millennium*, 167.

99. Rodegast *Emmanuel's Book II*, 184. See also Rodegast, *Emmanuel's Book*, 243; Ken Carey, *Vision* (Kansas City: Uni*Sun, 1985), 68.

100. See articles by these authors in this Volume.

101. Carey, *Starseed: The Third Millenium*, 195.

102. Rodegast, *Emmanuel's Book*, 38.

103. Carey, *Starseed: The Third Millenium*, 48.

104. As in *A Course in Miracles* and portions of *Starseed Transmissions*.

105. Carey, *Starseed: The Third Millenium*, 195.

106. Raphael, *Starseed Transmissions*, 67; *A Course in Miracles*, II:84.

107. Joseph Campbell, *The Power of Myth* (New York: Doubleday, 1988).

108. Lazaris, *The Sacred Journey*, 15.

109. Douglas Groothuis, *Unmasking the New Age* (Downer's Grove, IL: Intervarsity Press, 1986), 152.

110. Carey, *Starseed: The Third Millenium*, 154.

111. *A Course in Miracles*, 4.

Chapter 10. Employing the New Age: Training Seminars

1. Michael Ray and Rochelle Myers, *Creativity in Business* (New York: Doubleday and Co. 1986), 9.

2. Ibid., 36-38.

3. Robert Lindsey, "Spiritual Concepts Drawing a Different Breed of Adherent," *The New York Times*, 29 September 1986, A1.

4. Ibid., B12.

5. *Enhancing Human Performance* (Washington D.C.: National Academy Press, 1988). Quoted in John Alexander, "Enhancing Human Performance: A Challenge to the Report," *New Realities*, 9, no. 4 (March/April 1989): 53.

6. See Alexander, "Enhancing Human Performance."

7. Annetta Miller and Pamela Abramson, "Corporate Mind Control," *Newsweek* 4 May 1987, 38.

8. Lindsey, "Spiritual Concepts," B12. This quote was taken from Dr. Edwin Morse, a specialist on religious groups and counselor to ex-members of controversial sects.

9. Leonard L. Glass and Michael A. Kirsch, "Psychiatric Disturbances Associated with Erhard Seminars Training: I. A Report of Cases," *The American Journal of Psychiatry* 134 (March 1977): 245.

10. For a thorough discussion of est training methods and the psychology behind them, see Sheridan Fenwick, *Getting It: the Psychology of est* (Philadelphia: J. B. Lippincott Co., 1976).

11. Paul Keegan, "Into the Void," *Boston Business*, 1 February 1990.

12. Ibid.

13. Janice Haaken and Richard Adams, "Pathology as 'Personal Growth': A Participant-Observation Study of Lifespring Training," *Psychiatry*, 46 (August, 1983): 270.

14. Jeremy Main, "Trying to Bend Managers' Minds," *Fortune*, 23 November 1987, 105.

15. Miller and Abramson, "Corporate Mind Control," 39.

16. Perry Pascarella, "Create a Breakthrough in Performance by Changing the 'Conversation,'" *Industry Week*, 15 June 1987, 52.

17. Main, "Trying to Bend Managers' Minds," 104.

18. Pascarella, "Create a Breakthrough," 55.

19. "From Rosemead Teacher to Spiritual Leader of a New Age Empire," *Los Angeles Times*, 14 August 1988.

20. Ibid.

21. Ibid.

22. Main, "Trying to Bend Managers' Minds," 104.

23. Ibid., 103-104.

24. For exact case histories, see Glass and Kirsch, "Psychiatric Disturbances I," and their other article "Psychiatric Disturbances Associated with Erhard Seminars Training: II. Additional Cases and Theoretical Considerations," *The American Journal of Psychiatry*, 134 (November 1977).

25. Keegan, "Into the Void."

26. Miller and Abramson, "Corporate Mind Control," 39.

27. Main, "Trying to Bend Managers' Minds," 100.

28. Miller and Abramson, "Corporate Mind Control," 39.

29. Main, "Trying to Bend Managers' Minds," 100.

Chapter 11. An Update on Neopagan Witchcraft in America

1. An earlier version of this paper was delivered to a session of the Group on New Religious Movements of the American Academy of Religion at the annual meeting in Boston, December 1987.

2. Although the general public would actually be welcome, the policy of "by invitation only" is intended to keep out the Christian fundamentalists, who, like fundamentalists in general, seem unable to believe that the "sacred spaces" of other religions are in fact sacred. Neopagans have experienced everything from rudeness in, to wanton destruction of, their places of worship.

3. Most of the local councils of COG carry out this function. As other examples of such local associations, I can mention: the covens of the NROOGD tradition in the San Francisco area; South Bay Circles, San Jose area; the New Wiccan Church, Sacramento; the Midwest Pagan Council, Illinois; Circle, Wisconsin; Council of the Isis Community, Salem, Massachusetts; the Earth Song Community and the Free Spirit Alliance, Baltimore; the Earth Spirit Community, Medford, Massachusetts; the Eleusis Foundation, Brooklyn; the Heartland Pagan Association, Kansas City; the Southwest Earth Festival Association, Albuquerque; and there are yet others in Atlanta, Houston, and many other cities.

4. I have listings in my database for more than a hundred such periodicals. The *Green Egg* mailing list includes more than five hundred at last count. The Neopagan movement must surely hold a world record for number of small periodicals produced.

5. Adler's resource list on organizations, pp. 510-535, listed six organizations that call themselves Temples; there are at least twice as many now. My description of them is based on what I know of the Aquarian Tabernacle Church in Seattle, and the Temple of the Wiccan Church of Canada in Toronto; I am not familiar with the actual operations of any others.

6. Melton, "Modern Alternative Religions," p. 467; Melton, cited by Adler, p. 444.

7. There are, of course, some orthodox Gardnerians who refuse to admit that this coven is really Gardnerian, even though Michael always invites a Third-Degree Gardnerian High Priestess (usually Judith Harrow) to cast the circle for the initiations, as Gardnerian tradition in America requires. I am reminded of a joke whose punchline is, "But then, by Orthodox Rabbis, who is?"

8. E.g., the recent works by Joan Engelsman, Donald Gelpi, and Elisabeth Schüssler Fiorenza. There is also a great deal of embarrassingly bad work being done by women who are regarded by other women as scholars.

9. I am citing information he mentions in his autobiography, pp. 387-91; he is citing results published in his *Sociology of the Paranormal*, co-authored with Nancy McCready in 1984.

Chapter 12. The Evangelical Response to the New Age

1. Francis A. Schaeffer, *The Complete Works of Francis A. Schaeffer*, 2d ed. (Westchester: Crossway Books, 1985), 69.

2. Irving Hexham, "Some Aspects of the Contemporary Search for an ALternative Society," (M.A. dissertation, Department of Theology and Religious Studies, University of Bristol, January, 1972).

3. Only the relatively obscure Toronto magazine *Vanguard* accepted my work, but even then I had to focus on Glastonbury rather than the New Age as such. *Vanguard*, Toronto, (May/June, 1972): 18-22. In 1973 I managed to publish *The New Paganism: Yoga and UFOs*, (Potchefstroom: Potchefstroom University, 1973), which was the edited text of a lecture I gave to the student society *Korps Veritas Vincet* at Potchefstroom University where I was using the archives for my Ph.D.

4. J. Gordon Melton, *New Age Encyclopedia* (New York: Gale Research Inc., 1990), 135-137.

5. Based on the book by Shirley MacLaine, *Out on a Limb* (New York: Bantam Books, 1983).

6. This was Oakhill Theological College, which is an Evangelical Anglican graduate school.

7. As far as I am aware the first popular British Evangelical article on the New Age Movement was John Allen's "Peace and Harmony," *Cubit*, (Spring, 1988).

8. The American influence on British Evangelical views of the New Age can be seen from Michael Cole, Jim Graham, Tony Higton and David Lewis' *What Is the New Age? A Detailed Candid Look at This Fast Growing Movement*, (London: Hodder and Stoughton, 1990), 198-208. This is curious given the general cultural superiority of British clergy and academics who usually disdain all things American.

9. This observation was vividly illustrated recently when a colleague submitted a highly creative article to *The Christian Scholar's Review*. They rejected it because they were "unsure" about its scholarly merit. The article was then sent to a prestigious secular journal where it became a lead article.

10. Francis A. Schaeffer, *The Complete Works* 1: 57-90; 5: 9-19, and 229-244.

11. The root cause of his rejection by Evangelical academics is probably his strong condemnation of Communism which must be understood against the European background of his work but which was inevitably interpreted in terms of McCarthyism in America. Since his death a number of biting critiques of his work have been published by Evangelical academics. Cf. Ronald W. Ruegsegger, ed., *Reflections on Francis Schaeffer* (Grand Rapids: Zondervan, 1986).

12. The effects of upward mobility on Evangelicals is discussed by Richard Quebedeaux in *The Worldly Evangelicals* (San Francisco: Harper & Row, 1987); Cf. Robert Wuthnow, *The Restructuring of American Religion* (Princeton: Princeton University Press, 1988), 187-194.

13. Secular scholars have been much kinder to Schaeffer than Evangelicals. Cf. Harold Coward, *Pluralism: The Challenge to World Religions* (Maryknoll: Orbis, 1986) 36-37.

14. Critics of Schaeffer insist on judging him by the standards of academic scholarship and not popular writing. As a result it is easy to pick holes in his arguments. Many criticisms are, however, unfair, as can be seen from Ronald A. Wells's criticism of his views on the Reformation in *History: Through the Eyes of Faith* (San Francisco: Harper & Row, 1989), 89 ff; and G. Thomas Stadler's, "Renaissance Humanism: Francis Schaeffer Versus Some Contemporary Scholars," *Fides et Historia*, 2 (June, 1989): 4-20. In both cases the authors criticize Schaeffer's scholarship but fail to tell the reader that their own views are one possible interpretation among many, including Schaeffer's. For a generalist to overlook the fine points of academic debate is permissible. For academics to criticize the generalist and then make the same mistake is not. On intellectuals generally, see F. A. Hayek, *Studies in Philosophy, Politics and Economics* (Chicago: University of Chicago Press, 1967), 179-182.

15. The best introductory books on this scholarly tradition are: Herman Dooyeweerd, *Roots of Western Culture: Pagan, Secular and Christian Options* (Toronto: Wedge, 1979); and L. Kalsbeek, *Contours of a Christian Philosophy* (Toronto: Wedge, 1975).

16. Contrary to what Ronald Wells says in "Schaeffer on America" in Ronald W. Ruegsegger, ed, *Reflections on Francis Schaeffer*, 234-235, Rousas J. Rushdooney and Christian Reconstructionism were *not* the source of Schaeffer's views. True, Schaeffer used one of Rushdooney's books as the basis for a lecture series in the mid-1960s. But, his essential philosophy came from Dooyeweerd through the person of Professor Hans Rookmaaker as both Schaeffer and Rookmaaker freely admitted. Another source for Schaeffer's ideas was the evangelical philosopher E. J. Carnell, although Schaeffer was reluctant to admit this unless directly asked.

17. Francis A. Schaeffer, *The Complete Works* 5: 229-244.

18. Ibid., 1: 57-90.

19. Ibid., 5: 9-19.

20. Gary North, *None Dare Call It Witchcraft*, (Los Angeles: Arlington House, 1976).

21. Gary North, *Unholy Spirits: Occultism and New Age Humanism* (Fort Worth: Dominion Press, 1988). Several other evangelical writings have been updated by adding "New Age" to their titles, apparently to cash in on the evangelical New Age market. One example is Paul C. Reisser, Terri K. Reisser and John Weldon's, *New Age Medicine: A Christian Perspective on Holistic Health* (Downers Grove: Inter-Varsity Press, 1987), which was originally published in

1983 as *The Holistic Healers*. While in some cases the addition of "New Age" to a title can be justified because of the contents, Jay Howard's *Confronting the Cultist in the New Age* (Old Tappan, New Jersey: Fleming H. Revell Col, 1990) appears to be an example of a book the title of which was almost entirely determined by marketing considerations. In fact the book has very little to say about the New Age movement.

22. Constance Cumbey, *The Hidden Dangers of the Rainbow: The New Age Movement and the Coming Age of Barbarism* (Shreveport: Huntington House, 1983).

23. Ibid., 13-25, and 99-120. In fact there may well be a link between certain aspects of New Age thought and Fascism. But, none of the Evangelicals I have read make a convincing case. Forging such a link has been begun by Jane Bramwell in her excellent book *Ecology in the Twentieth Century*, (New Haven: Yale University Press, 1989).

24. Dave Hunt, *Prosperity and the Coming Holocaust: The New Age Movement in Prophecy* (Eugene: Harvest House, 1983).

25. Douglas Groothuis, *Unmasking the New Age: Is There a New Religious Movement Trying to Transform Society?* (Downers Grove: Inter-Varsity, 1986).

26. Douglas Groothuis, *Confronting the New Age: How to Resist a Growing Religious Movement* (Downers Grove: Inter-Varsity Press, 1988).

27. Douglas Groothuis, *Revealing the New Age Jesus* (Downers Grove: Inter-Varsity, 1990).

28. Space does not allow for a discussion of all Evangelical works on the New Age. The ones chosen here have been selected because they are representative of the better critiques.

29. To discuss such works in detail would probably result in libel suits. Suffice to say that in one case, where I know the writer, the author gives a highly romanticized version of his life, omitting such significant details as his divorce, to make it acceptable to an Evangelical readership.

30. Karen Hoyt, ed., *The New Age Rage: A Probing Analysis of the Newest Religious Craze* (Old Tappan: Fleming H. Revell, 1987).

31. Russell Chandler, *Understanding the New Age* (Waco: Word, 1988).

32. Elliot Miller, *A Crash Course on the New Age Movement* (Grand Rapids: Baker, 1989).

33. Walter Martin, *The New Age Cult* (Minneapolis: Bethany House, 1989).

34. Norman L. Geisler & J. Yutaka Amano, *The Reincarnations Senation* (Wheaton: Tyndale House, 1986).

35. Mark Albrecht, *Reincarnation: A Christian Appraisal* (Downers Grove: Inter-Varsity, 1982).

36. Arthur L. Johnson, *Faith Misguided: Exposing the Dangers of Mysticism* (Chicago: Moody Press, 1988).

37. Paul C. Reisser, Teri K. Reisser and John Weldon, *The Holistic Healers: A Christian Perspective on New-Age Health Care* (Downers Grove: Inter-Varsity, 1983).

38. Frank E. Peretti, *This Present Darkness* (Westchester: Crossway Books, 1986).

39. It is important to recognize that, while the novel is popular among Evangelicals, its ethos is fundamentalist. For a discussion of the differences between Evangelicals and Fundamentalism see: E. J. Carnell, *The Case for Orthodox Theology* (London: Marshall, Morgan and Scott, 1961), 113-126; and Robert Campbell, ed., *Spectrum of Protestant Beliefs* (Milwaukee: Bruce Publishing, 1968).

40. Cf. Richard Quebedeaux, *The Worldly Evangelicals* (New York: Harper & Row, 1978).

41. While the better evangelical writers would avoid such crude labeling, many ordinary church members eagerly accept and use it in their daily life.

42. It should be noted that some evangelicals, such as Ken Blue of the Vineyard Movement, are aware of the dangers of a "new fundamentalism" even though they do not see the role played by books like that of Peretti. Lecture series given at St. James Anglican Church, Ranchlands, Calgary, Alberta, Canada, 22-24 February 1990.

43. A very mild form of such criticism is to be found in Shirley MacLaine's best-selling, *Out on a Limb*, 50-51.

44. For example he has appeared on James Dobson's radio program as an authority on "Satanism."

45. This misuse of footnotes is common among students and many popular New Age writers as well as Evangelicals.

46. Michael Cole, Jim Graham, Tony Higton and David Lewis' *What Is the New Age?*, 29, cf. note 1, pg. 199.

47. As a result Tony Higton cites Abraham Maslow, Carl Jung and others as "quoted in" Marilyn Ferguson's *The New Age Conspiracy* (London: Paladin Grafton, 1988). Ibid., 44, cf. note 4 and p. 200; 45, cf. note 10, p. 200.

48. Dave Hunt and T. A. McMahon, *The Seduction of Christianity: Spiritual Discernment in the Last Days* (Eugene: Harvest House, 1985).

49. These are essentially charismatic and social action ministries.

50. Dave Hunt and T. A. McMahon, *The Seduction of Christianity*, 101-114.

51. Ibid., 101.

52. Paul Yonggi Cho, *The Fourth Dimension: The Key to Putting Your Faith to Work for a Successful Life* (Plainefield: Logos International, 1979), 36-37.

53. Ibid., 40.

54. Gary North, *Unholy Spirits*, 98-101.

55. Ibid., 52-56.

56. Kirlian Photography is discussed and shown to be a natural and nonoccult phenomenon in Arleen J. Watkins and William S. Bickel's article "A Study of the Kirlian Effect," *The Skeptical Inquirer* (1986); a number of cases of so called "human combustion" are examined and shown to be a myth by Joe Nickell and John F. Fischer in "Incredible Cremations: Investigating Spontaneous Combustion Deaths," *The Skeptical Inquirer* (1987).

57. Dave Hunt and T. A. McMahon, *America: The Sorcerer's New Apprentice—The Rise of New Age Shamanism* (Eugene: Harvest House, 1988), 213.

58. Douglas Groothuis' best-selling *Unmasking the New Age*, 18-31.

59. Cf. Karen Hoyt, ed., *The New Age Rage*, 248-255; and Elliot Miller, *A Crash Course on the New Age Movement*, 17.

60. Even such an orthodox Calvinist as Gordon H. Clark could write "actually Christianity is more successfully monistic than Neoplatonism was. God alone is the eternal substance, the independent principle; apart from the creation of the world nothing exists besides him. . . ." *Thales to Dewey: A History of Philosophy* (Boston: Houghton Mifflin, 1957), 231.

61. Bertrand Russell, *The Scientific Outlook* (New York: Norton, 1931), 98.

62. David K. Clark and Norman L. Geisler, *Apologetics in the New Age: A Christian Critique of Pantheism* (Grand Rapids: Baker, 1990).

63. Ibid., 14.

64. Ibid., 13.

65. Ibid., 8.

66. Ibid., 9.

67. It needs to be recognized that Clark and Geisler are correct when they see pantheism as a central tenet of popular New Age thinking. Where they go wrong is in projecting an essentially modern view onto writers in the past and in identifying pantheism with religious traditions which contain pantheistic elements but are not necessarily pantheistic.

68. David K. Clark and Norman L. Geisler, *Apologetics in the New Age*, 24.

69. Cf. S. Radhakrishna, *Indian Religions* (New Delhi: Vision Books, 1979), 130-131. Radhakrishna denied that he was a pantheist in many other places.

70. Ninian Smart, *Doctrine and Argument in Indian Philosophy* (London: George Allan and Unwin, 1964), 97-105; cf. *Reasons and Faiths* (London: Routledge & Kegan Paul, 1958), 35-41.

71. A good discussion of the complexities of interpreting Plotinus is to be found in Phillip Merlan's article "Plotinus" in *The Encyclopedia of Philosophy*, ed. Paul Edwards (New York: Collier Macmillan), 6: 351-359.

72. Robert Basil, *Not Necessarily the New Age: Critical Essays* (Buffalo: Prometheus Books, 1988).

73. Significantly, one never sees references to books like Eric J. Sharpe's *Faith Meets Faith: Some Christian Attitudes to Hinduism in the Nineteenth & Twentieth Centuries* (London: SCM, 1977) even though Sharpe is essentially an Evangelical writer. I suspect the problem is that he raises too many difficult questions.

74. RightWriter Version 3.1. Sarasota, Florida: RightSoft.

75. Cf. Peter F. Drucker, *The New Realities* (New York: Harper & Row, 1989).

76. Cf. Harold Coward, *Pluralism: The Challenge to World Religions* (Maryknoll: Orbis, 1986).

77. For example David K. Clark and Norman L. Geisler, in *Apologetics in the New Age*, speak about the Hare Krishna Movement in terms of the New Age, 63, 163, while Tony Higton, in Michael Cole, Jim Graham, Tony Higton and David Lewis' *What Is the New Age?*, includes Buddhism, Hinduism, and Islam under the general rubric of the New Age, as does at least one other writer in the same book, 10 and 52-57.

78. To the extent that courses on world religions are taught at theological colleges, they are usually a secondary interest of someone trained in another theological discipline. As a result the course books, at least those I have examined, are unbelievably bad.

79. This is an excellent introductory book on world religions in Western society written by the former editor of *Christianity Today*, who holds a doctorate in Buddhism. Although very simply written, it is ideal for the average Evangelical minister and his congregation.

80. It also provides Evangelical writers and speakers with an additional source of income.

Chapter 13. The New Age Movement and Feminist Spirituality: Overlapping Conversations at the End of the Century

1. David Spangler, *Emergence: The Rebirth of the Sacred* (New York: Dell, 1984), 79-81.

2. Marilyn Ferguson, *The Aquarian Conspiracy: Personal and Social Transformation in the 1980s* (Los Angeles: J. P. Tarcher, 1980).

3. David Spangler, *Emergence: The Rebirth of the Sacred*, 80-8 1.

4. This critique is so widespread in New Age and feminist writing that it almost doesn't need documentation. A recent publication that catalogues the critique in a series of essays from the feminist perspective is *Weaving the Visions: New Patterns in Feminist Spirituality*, ed. Judith Plaskow and Carol P. Christ (San Francisco: Harper & Row, 1989).

5. David Ray Griffin, ed., *The Reenchantment of Science: Postmodern Proposals* (Albany: State University Press, 1988), 2. Griffin does not identify himself as a New Age thinker, but his opening essay in this volume, 'Introduction: The Reenchantment of Science," presents much of the New Age case against Newtonian science. There are other essays in the volume which offer insights that coincide with a New Age worldview, particularly those by David Bohm, Willis W. Harman, and Stanley Krippner.

6. David Toolan, *Facing West from California's Shores: A Jesuit's Journey into New Age Consciousness* (New York: Crossroad, 1987), 180.

7. David Bohm, "Postmodern Science and a Postmodern World," in David Ray Griffin, ed., *The Reenchantment of Science*, 66.

8. See Ken Wilber, "Physics, Mysticism and the New Holographic Paradigm: A Critical Appraisal," in *The Holographic Paradigm and Other Paradoxes: Exploring the Leading Edge of Science*, ed. Ken Wilber (Boston & London: Shambhala, 1985), 157-86.

9. David Toolan, *Facing West from California's Shores*, 217.

10. Much of the work that has been compelling to feminists on the goddesses of ancient matriarchies has been done by Merlin Stone and Maria Gimbutas. See, particularly, Stone, *When God Was a Woman* (New York: Dial Press, 1978); and Gimbutas, *The Gods and Goddesses of Old Europe, 6500-3500 B.C.: Myths and Cult Images* (Berkeley: University of California Press, 1974, 1982), and *The Language of the Goddess: Unearthing the Hidden Symbols of Western Civilization* (San Francisco: Harper & Row, 1989). However, the topic of the historical reality of goddess-ruled matriarchies has not been without controversy in feminist writings. See, for example, the exchange in *The Politics of*

Women's Spirituality: Essays on the Rise of Spiritual Power Within the Feminist Movement, ed. Charlene Spretnak (New York: Doubleday, 1982) in the section titled "Are Goddesses and Matriarchies Merely Figments of Feminist Imagination?"

11. Whether Goddess spirituality is by nature polytheistic or monotheistic is a subject of controversy in some circles of Women's Spirituality.

12. Linda Ann Hoag, "Isis at the Supermarket," in *Heresies: A Feminist Publication on Art and Politics*," (Spring, 1978): 39.

13. Merlin Stone, "Introduction," *The Goddess Reawakening: The Feminine Principle Today*, comp. Shirley Nicholson (Wheaton, Illinois: The Theosophical Publishing House, 1989), 19.

14. Nelle Morton, "The Goddess as Metaphoric Image." in *Weaving the Visions*, ed. Judith Plaskow and Carol P. Christ, 111.

15. Shakti Gawain, *Living in the Light: A Guide to Personal and Planetary Transformation* (Mill Valley, CA: Whatever Publishing, 1986), 10.

16. Corinne McLaughlin, "The Mystery of the Veiled Mother of the World," *The Quest*, 3 (Summer, 1990): 56.

17. David Bohm, "Postmodern Science and a Postmodern World," 67.

18. Thomas Berry, *The Dream of the Earth* (San Francisco: Sierra Club Books, 1988), 123.

19. Ibid., 120.

20. Brian Swimme, *The Universe Is a Green Dragon: A Cosmic Creation Story* (Santa Fe: Bear & Company, 1984), 38.

21. Ibid., 39.

22. David Spangler, *Emergence: The Rebirth of the Sacred*, 38.

23. Some of the emphasis on unity and planetary culture in the New Age movement comes from the influence of Pierre Teilhard de Chardin, whom Marilyn Ferguson identifies in *The Aquarian Conspiracy* (420) as the most frequently cited influence on the thinking of the "aquarian conspirators" she surveyed. For a further discussion of the influence of Teilhard's thinking on this subject, see *Teilhard and the Unity of Knowledge*, ed. Thomas M King, S.J. and James F. Salmon, S.J. (New York: Paulist Press, 1983).

24. Alla Bozarth, Julia Barkley, Terri Hawthorne, *Stars in Your Bones: Emerging Signposts on Our Spiritual Journeys* (St. Cloud, MN: North Star Press of St. Cloud, 1990), 1. The book is dedicated to "the explorers and storytellers of the future, who will continue to tell the cosmic stories in healing and creative ways." It includes the poetry of Alla Bozarth, an Episcopalian priest, the paint-

ings of Julia Barkley, an artist, and the commentary of Terri Hawthorne, a feminist educator, writer, and counselor, and offers an instructive blend of the New Age and Women's Spirituality perspectives.

25. Corinne McLaughlin, "The Mystery of the Veiled Mother of the World," 58.

26. Alla Bozarth, Julia Barkley, Terri Hawthorne, *Stars in Your Bones: Emerging Signposts on Our Spiritual Journeys*, 49.

27. Starhawk, *Truth or Dare: Encounters with Power, Authority, and Mystery* (San Francisco: Harper & Row, 1987), 32-33.

28. Judith Plant, "Remembering Who We Are: The Meaning of Ecofeminism," in *Healing the Wounds: The Promise of Ecofeminism*, ed. Judith Plant (Philadelphia and Santa Cruz: New Society Publishers, 1989), 5.

29. Starhawk, "Feminist, Earth-based Spirituality and Ecofeminism," in *Healing the Wounds*, ed. Judith Plant, 174-75.

30. Charlene Spretnak, "Toward an Ecofeminist Spirituality," in *Healing the Wounds*, ed. Judith Plant, 127.

31. David Spangler, *Emergence; The Rebirth of the Sacred*, 66-68.

32. Ibid., 68.

33. Carol W. Parrish-Harra, *Messengers of Hope* (Black Mountain, NC: New Age Press, 1983). See Chapters 4 and 20.

34. Corinne McLaughlin, "The Mystery of the Veiled Mother of the World," 63.

35. Many scholars have noted the interest of women in nineteenth century occult and metaphysical spiritualities. See, for example, Mary Farrell Bednarowski, "Women in Occult America," in *The Occult in America: New Historical Perspectives*, ed. Howard Kerr and Charles L. Crow (Urbana and Chicago: University of Illinois Press, 1983); Ann Braude, *Radical Spirits: Spiritualism and Women's Rights in Nineteenth-Century America* (Boston: Beacon Press, 1989); and Robert Ellwood, *Alternative Altars: Unconventional and Eastern Spirituality in America* (Chicago: University of Chicago Press, 1979). See also J. Gordon Melton's essay in this volume.

36. Rodney Stark and William Sims Bainbridge in *The Future of Religion: Secularization, Revival, and Cult Formation* (Berkeley: University of California Press, 1985), suggest a thesis of this sort when they claim that there is nothing new in contemporary culture about secularization, revival, or innovation; all three activities are always going on in any culture in regard to religion.

Chapter 14. Who Holds the Cards?
Women and New Age Astrology

I would like to thank the Institute for the Study of American Religion for their help in funding this project. I also wish to warmly thank the people who helped at various stages of the endeavor: Naomi Abrahams, Michael Delucchi, Elsa Feher, Valerie Jenness, Phillip Hammond, Gordon Melton, Martha McCaughey and Mark Shibley. This paper was presented at the regional American Academy of Religion meetings in Oakland, California, March 1990.

1. The New Age is a movement that emphasizes that a spiritual transformation will occur after which people will be better aware that they are one with the natural world. This transformation can be achieved through various healing therapies as well as spiritual beliefs and practices (P. Lucas, "The New Age Movement and the Pentecostal/Charismatic Revival." Paper presented at the annual meeting of the American Academy of Religion, Anaheim, Ca., 1989).

2. J. Davis and J. Weaver, "Dimensions of Spirituality" and R. Rennie and K. Grimstad, "Spiritual Explorations Cross Country." Both in *Quest* (Spring, 1975).

3. G. Haddon, *Body Metaphors* (New York: Crossroad Publishing Co., 1988); D. Riddle, "New Visions of Spiritual Power" in 1 *Quest* (Spring 1975); J. Davis and J. Weaver, "Dimensions of Spirituality"; M. Daly, "The Quantitative Leap Beyond Patriarchal Religion," 1 *Quest* (Spring 1975).

4. For ease of comprehension, I will refer to all of the people at the conference interested in astrology as "astrologers." Where it is necessary to distinguish between practicing astrologers and people vaguely interested in astrology, I will refer to the former as "practicing astrologers" or "professional astrologers."

5. Robert Bellah et al, *Habits of the Heart* (California: University of California Press, 1985), 75.

6. R. Stark and W. Bainbridge, *The Future of Religion* (California: University of California Press, 1985).

7. B. Zikmund, "The Feminist Thrust of Sectarian Christianity," in *Women of Spirit*, ed. Ruether and McLaughlin (New York: Simon and Schuster, 1979); M. Bednarowski, "Women in Occult America," in *The Occult in America: New Historical Perspectives* (Illinois: University of Illinois Press, 1983).

8. A. Braude, "Spirits Defend the Rights of Women: Spiritualism and Changing Sex Roles in Nineteenth-Century America," in *Women, Religion and Social Change*, ed. Haddad and Findly (New York: State University of New York Press, 1985); J. Davis and J. Weaver, "Dimensions of Spirituality"; G. Ward, *The Feminist Theme of Early New Thought* (Santa Barbara, California: Institute for the Study of American Religion, 1989).

9. C. Fischler, "Astrology and French Society," in *On the Margin of the Visible*, ed. Tiryakian (New York: John Wiley and Sons, 1984).

10. New Thought has been considered the predecessor to the New Age.

11. As cited in Ward, G., "The Feminist Theme of Early New Thought," 9.

12. B. Zikmund, "The Feminist Thrust of Sectarian Christianity"; M. Bednarowski, "Women in Occult America."

13. A. Braude. "Spirits Defend the Rights of Women,"; J. Davis and J. Weaver, "Dimensions of Spirituality."

14. B. Zikmund. "The Feminist Thrust of Sectarian Christianity."

15. B. Zikmund, "The Feminist Thrust of Sectarian Christianity"; G. Ward, "The Feminist Theme of Early New Thought."

16. S. Bordo, "The Cartesian Masculinization of Thought," in *Sex and Scientific Inquiry*, ed. Harding and O'Barr (Illinois: University of Chicago Press, 1987).

17. D. Riddle, "New Visions of Spiritual Power"; G. Haddon, *Body Metaphors*.

18. M. Bednarowski, "Women in Occult America."

19. C. Gilligan, *In a Different Voice* (Massachusetts: Harvard University Press, 1982).

20. N. Chodorow, *The Reproduction of Mothering: Psychoanalysis and the Sociology of Gender* (California: University of California Press, 1978).

21. J. Davis and J. Weaver, "Dimensions of Spirituality," 6.

22. S. Rennie and K. Grimstad, "Spiritual Explorations Cross Country," 50.

23. Minerva, "Chart Yourself" in 4 *Quest* (Spring 1975): 71.

24. Ibid., 70.

25. Daly, M., "The Quantitative Leap Beyond Patriarchal Religion," 50.

26. Ibid.

27. S. Rennie and K. Grimstad, "Spiritual Explorations Cross Country."

28. Minerva, "Chart Yourself," 70.

29. R. Stark and W. Bainbridge, *The Future of Religion*.

30. Whether the question was answered.

31. Chi-square showed significance at the .01 level.

Chapter 15. The New Age Movement and the Pentecostal/Charismatic Revival: Distinct Yet Parallel Phases of a Fourth Great Awakening?

1. Catherine L. Albanese, "Religion and the American Experience: A Century After," *Church History* 57:337-51.

2. Ninian Smart, *Religion and the Western Mind* (London: Macmillan Press Ltd, 1987), 14.

3. William G. McLoughlin, *Revivals, Awakenings, and Reform: An Essay on Religion and Social Change in America, 1607-1977* (Chicago: University of Chicago Press, 1978), 10.

4. Ibid., 14.

5. Ibid., 22.

6. Ibid., 214-15.

7. Ibid., 18.

8. Ibid., xiv.

9. Ibid., 19-20.

10. Ibid.

11. Ibid., 21.

12. For an excellent analysis of the theological fundamentals of New Age religion, see Mary Farrell Bednarowski's *New Religions and the Theological Imagination in America* (Bloomington: Indiana University Press, 1989).

13. J. Gordon Melton, *Encyclopedic Handbook of Cults in America* (New York: Garland Publishing, 1986), 108-9.

14. Ibid., 116.

15. Sociological survey entitled *Values and Belief Study*, conducted September, 1988. Project headed by Wade Clark Roof and Phillip Hammond.

16. Grant Wacker, "America's Pentecostals: Who They Are," *Christianity Today*, 16 Oct. 1987, 20.

17. Terry Muck, "Spiritual Lifts," *Christianity Today*, 16 Oct. 1987, 14-15.

18. Wacker, "America's Pentecostals," 20.

19. Ibid., 16.

20. David B. Barrett, "The 20th Century Pentecostal/Charismatic Renewal in the Holy Spirit, With Its Goal of World Evangelization," in Stanley Burgess and Gary McGee, eds., *Dictionary of Pentecostals and Charismatic Movements* (Grand Rapids: Zondervan Publishing House, 1988), 1-19.

21. Abraham H. Maslow, *Religions, Values, and Peak-Experiences* (New York: Viking Press, 1970), viii.

22. For instance: Seraphim Rose, *Orthodoxy and the Religion of the Future* (Platina: Saint Herman of Alaska Brotherhood, 1983), 149; Richard Quebedeaux, *The New Charismatics II* (San Francisco: Harper and Row, 1983), 217-18; Carol Flake, *Redemptorama: Culture, Politics, and the New Evangelicalism* (Garden City: Anchor Press, 1984), 221-22.

23. Melton, *Handbook of Cults*, 113-14.

24. Catherine L. Albanese, *Nature Religion in America: From the Algonkian Indians to the New Age* (Chicago: University of Chicago Press, 1990), 281-82.

25. Sun Bear, *The Path of Power, as told to Wabun and to Barry Weinstock* (Spokane: Bear Tribe Publishing, 1983), 245-46.

26. Muck, "Spiritual Lifts," 15.

27. Albanese, "Religion and American Experience," 339, 345.

28. Brooks Alexander, "Theology from the Twilight Zone," *Christianity Today*, 18 Sept. 1987, 22.

29. Alexander, "Theology from the Twilight Zone," 23.

30. Ibid., 24.

31. Don Basham, *A Handbook On Holy Spirit Baptism* (Monroeville: Whitaker Books, 1973), 80.

32. Margaret M. Poloma, *The Charismatic Movement: Is There a New Pentecost?* (Boston: Twayne Publishers, 1982), 246.

33. Mary Jo Neitz, *Charisma and Community: A Study of Religious Commitment within the Charismatic Renewal* (New Brunswick: Transaction Books, 1987), 42.

34. Rose, *Orthodoxy*, 170.

35. Robert Mapes Anderson, *Vision of the Disinherited: The Making of American Pentecostalism* (New York: Oxford University Press, 1979), 199-202.

36. For an expanded treatment of Pentecostalist spirit exorcism, see David E. Harrell, *All Things are Possible* (Bloomington: Indiana University Press, 1975).

37. Neitz, *Charisma and Community*, 32.

38. Ibid.

39. Donna Bilow, interview with author, Goleta, California, 9 August 1989.

40. Michael Harner, *The Way of the Shaman* (New York: Bantam Books, 1982), 145-61.

41. See Paul Hawkin, *The Magic of Findhorn* (New York: Harper and Row, 1975).

42. Dave Hunt, *The Seduction of Christianity: Spiritual Discernment in the Last Days* (Eugene: Harvest House Publishers, 1985), 172-88. See also Constance E. Cumbey, *The Hidden Dangers of the Rainbow* (Shreveport: Huntington House, 1983).

43. Flake, *Redemptorama*, 221.

44. Barrett, *Pentecostal/Charismatic Renewal*, 1.

45. Albanese, "Religion and American Experience," 348.

46. As Gordon Melton has shown, the Theosophical movement has been instrumental in introducing Eastern mysticism and meditation to the American public since the late nineteenth century. See *The Encyclopedia of American Religions*, 3d ed. (Detroit: Gale Research Inc, 1989), 129-32.

47. Win McCormack, "The Rajneesh Files: 1981-86," *Oregon Magazine, Collector's Edition* (Portland: New Oregon Publishers, Inc., 1985), 85-86.

48. Quebedeaux, *The New Charismatics II*, 229.

49. Neitz, *Charisma and Community*, 238.

50. Poloma, *The Charismatic Movement*, 95; Quebedeaux, *The New Charismatics II*, 230.

51. See, for instance, Hunt, *Seduction of Christianity*, 137-48; Shakti Gawain, *Creative Visualization* (New York: Bantam New Age Books, 1978); "Under Fire: Two Christian Leaders Respond to Accusations of New Age Mysticism," *Christianity Today*, 18 Sept. 1987, 17-21.

52. Wacker, "America's Pentecostals," 21.

53. Transcript of the John Ankerberg Show, "The New Age and the Church," undated.

54. Robert C. Fuller, *Alternative Medicine and American Religious Life* (New York: Oxford University Press, 1989).

55. Donald W. Dayton, *Theological Roots of Pentecostalism* (Metuchen: The Scarecrow Press, Inc., 1987), 143.

56. Anderson, *Vision of the Disinherited*, 201-2.

57. Hal Lindsey, *The Late Great Planet Earth* (Grand Rapid, Michigan: Zondervan, 1970) and Doug Clark, *Final Shockwaves to Armageddon* (Vail: Doug Clark Ministries, 1982).

58. Robert Bellah, "New Religious Consciousness and the Crisis in Modernity," in Charles Glock and Robert Bellah, eds., *The New Religious Consciousness* (Berkeley: University of California Press, 1976), 343-44.

59. Melton, *Handbook of Cults*, 115.

60. Jose Arguelles, *The Mayan Factor: Path Beyond Technology* (Sante Fe: Bear and Company, 1987), 169-70.

61. Dayton, *Theological Roots*, 144.

62. Erling Jorstad, *The Holy Spirit in Today's Church: A Handbook of the New Pentecostalism* (Nashville: Abingdon Press, 1973), 13.

63. Kilian McDonnell, "Catholic Charismatics: A Critique," *Commonweal*, 5 May 1972, 210-11.

64. Albanese, "Religion and American Experience," 348.

65. For statistical support of these statements, see Chapter 6 of Wade Clark Roof's and William McKinney's *American Mainline Religion* (New Brunswick: Rutgers University Press, 1987), 186-228.

66. McLoughlin, *Revivals, Awakenings, and Reform*, 20.

67. Ibid., 12-14.

68. Ibid., 16-17.

69. Ibid., 19-20.

70. Ibid., 22.

71. Ibid., 16.

72. As mentioned in my introduction, I view the Pentecostalist movement as a subset of the fundamentalist revival of the 1960s, 1970s, and 1980s. In terms of theology, biblicism, moral and political attitudes, use of telecommunications, and regional strength, enough similarities exist to justify this view.

73. McLoughlin, *Revivals, Awakenings, and Reform*, 191-92.

74. Ibid., 192-93.

Chapter 16. New Age Trends in Nigeria: Ancestral and/or Alien Religion?

1. Approximately fourteen or 12 percent of all distinct religious bodies in the town of Calabar were identified. See Rosalind I. J. Hackett, *Religion in Cal-*

abar: the Religious Life and History of a Nigerian Town (Berlin: Mouton de Gruyter, 1989), chap. 6.

2. I am grateful to Andrew F. Walls for helpful suggestions regarding the issue of terminology. Ndiva Kofele-Kale and Charles H. Reynolds, together with other colleagues in my department, also provided important critical observations. Katherine Finch provided invaluable help in assembling and interpreting the data on the New Age movement in this country.

3. See Rosalind I. J. Hackett, "Religious Encounters of the Third Kind: Spiritual Technology in Modern Nigeria," in *Identity Issues and World Religions*, ed. V. C. Hayes (Bedford Park, S.A.: Australian Association for the Study of Religion, 1986), 155-166.

4. In their interim, I received personal communications from Elisabeth Isichei, John Peel and Bennetta Jules-Rosette, in response to my earlier 1986 paper, confirming the important, yet underresearched nature of this topic.

5. J. Gordon Melton, "The New Age Movement," in *Encyclopedia Handbook of Cults in America*, ed. J. Gordon Melton (New York: Garland Publishing, 1986), 113.

6. Ibid., 108.

7. These characteristics are taken from Philip Lucas's excellent synthesis of the New Age movement, "The New Age Movement and the Pentecostal/Charismatic Revival: Distinct Yet Parallel Phases of a Fourth Great Awakening?" elsewhere in this volume.

8. Melton, "The New Age Movement," 107f.

9. I am basing my observations on a survey of primary sources and the radio program "New Dimensions," for example. One exception that I have noticed, however, would be music. "Hearts of Space," the popular New Age music program, has broadcast programs with African themes. See my discussion below of the African interest in New Age music.

10. From the interview with Sir Adeyemi, the Aetherius Society spiritualist. See interview below.

11. This is especially the case for the London-based *West Africa* news magazine, which is widely read by West Africans both overseas and in Africa.

12. See H. W. Turner, "Pentecostal Movements in Nigeria," in *Religious Innovation in Africa: Collected Essays on New Religious Movements* (Boston: G. K. Hall, 1979), 123-124.

13. H. W. Turner, "Searching and Syncretism: a West African Documentation," in *Religious Innovation in Africa: Collected Essays on New Religious Movements* (Boston: G. K. Hall, 1979), 159-164.

14. I am influenced here by Melton's paper elsewhere in this volume, "New Thought and the New Age," which examines the historical roots of the New Age movement and how certain philosophical orientations and syntheses facilitated the emergence of New Age spirituality.

15. Udobata Onunwa claims that the phenomenon dates back to the late 1960s and early 1970s when Asian gurus began penetrating West African campuses and cities. See "African Response to Guruism," *Areopagus*, 1 (Spring/Summer 1988): 24-28.

16. See R. S. Ellwood, *Religious and Spiritual Groups in Modern America* (Englewood Cliffs, NJ: Prentice-Hall, 1973), 150.

17. *Sunday Times* (Lagos), 8 January 1984.

18. The movement was founded by a German prisoner of war, Oscar Ernst Bernhard, as the result of his experiences during the First World War. He moved to Vomperberg, Austria, where the headquarters are now located under the direction of a woman, Irmingard Bernhardt. Personal communication from a member of the movement for twenty years, C. J. Lammers, Lienden, the Netherlands, 23 September 1985.

19. Advertisement in *West Africa*, 28 July 1986.

20. *Soka Gakkai International*, 2 February 1985.

21. *Soka Gakkai International*, 3 March 1985.

22. *West Africa*, 7 July 1986, 1446.

23. *The African Guardian*, 11 December 1989, 16.

24. Ibid.

25. See Hannelore Vögele and Daniel Fraiberg, "Heilung, Heil and das Okkulte: Gespräche mit einem traditionale Heiler in Nigeria," *Curare* 5 (1986): 179 [an interview with Okopedi regarding his traditional healing practices and knowledge].

26. See *Short History of the Crystal Cathedral Church* (Lagos: the Church, 1976), 6f.

27. Ibid., 13.

28. London: Rex Collings, 1985.

29. Wande Abimbola, personal communication, 19 April 1990.

30. Interview, *Sunday Times*, 8 January 1984.

31. Catherine L. Albanese, "The Magical Staff: Quantum Healing in the New Age," elsewhere in this volume.

32. J. D. Y. Peel, "Understanding Alien Belief-Systems," *British Journal of Sociology* 20 (1969): 78.

33. Robin Horton, "African Conversion," *Africa* 41 (1971): 106-107.

34. Yet see "We are Born Seven Times," *Sunday Times* (Lagos), 25 May 1980—an interview with Dr. John Nkameyin Ibok, a Lagos-based "parapsychologist, metaphysicist, research psychic and an accomplished traditional healer."

35. K. Mailva Ganam, *Universal Brotherhood and Meditation* ([Jos, Nigeria], n.d.), 3.

36. Onunwa, "African Response to Guruism," 27.

37. Ibid.

38. This evidence is based on discussions with interested individuals and attendance at public meetings of many of the organizations in question.

39. See Mailva Ganam, *Universal Brotherhood and Practical Meditation*, 1, 3.

40. In an article entitled, "Of Mysticism, Occultism and all that," *Daily Times* (Lagos), 22 August 1986.

41. *Sunday Chronicle*, 1 May 1983.

42. Professor John D. Y. Peel, personal communication, 4 February 1986.

43. Jean Comaroff, *Body of Power, Spirit of Resistance* (Chicago: University of Chicago Press, 1985), 254.

44. Ibid.

45. See Hackett, *Religion in Calabar*, 342-43.

46. Onunwa, "African Response to Guruism," 25.

47. Cf. C. Albanese, "Religion and the American Experience," *Church History* 57 (September 1988): 337-51, where she speaks of the "new pluralism" and "new voluntarism" being linked to an "ethos that possesses a flexibility in institutional commitments" (343).

48. Although it might be argued that the latter is a spurious point in the African context, where people have traditionally lived in close contact, even communion, with the natural world. My choice of categories here is influenced by those suggested by the New Age Publishing and Retailing Alliance (NAPRA) for booksellers and publishers classifying New Age materials. See the *Library Journal* (August 1989).

49. Back in 1982 in Calabar, I remember being handed an invitation by a university colleague to a celebration of traditional religious festivals in the

neighboring small town of Oron, which would herald the Aquarian Age. I was struck then by the creative blend of traditional and metaphysical ideas. But, lacking vision, I unhappily failed to preserve the documentary information.

50. See J. Gordon Melton, "A History of the New Age Movement," in *Not Necessarily the New Age*, ed. Robert Basil (Buffalo, NY: Prometheus Books, 1988), 35-53.

51. See the comment by James Lewis in his introduction to this volume.

52. Melton, 1986, 115.

53. See Comaroff, *Body of Power*, 252f.

Chapter 17. Japan's New Age and Neo-New Religions: Sociological Interpretations

1. Just this year, for example, a series of lectures largely concerned with this issue were published in a book entitled *Kindaika to shukyo bu-mu* [Modernization and the Religion Boom] by Nobutaka Inoue et al. (Tokyo: Kokugakuin University Institute for the Study of Japanese Culture, 1990). This volume indicates that there is a serious need to reconsider the relationship between religion and modernity in light of the emergence and growth of new religions from the mid-1970s and the recent interest in magic and the occult.

2. The current discussion clearly resembles the debate regarding secularization in the West, which began as sociologists struggled to make sense of the counterculture movement and new religious movements from the late 1960s.

3. Eisho Omura, "Gendaijin no shukyo." [The Religion of People Today] in Eisho Omura and Shigeru Nishiyama, eds. *Gendaijin no shukyo* [The Religion of People Today] (Tokyo: Yuhikaku, 1988), pp. 12-16.

4. This sections draws upon an earlier essay in which I examined the growth of Christianity in the context of these four periods, "The Situation of Christianity in Contemporary Japanese Society," *Japan Christian Quarterly* 55:2 (1989).

5. Michio Nagai, "Tradition and Modernization of Japan." In Robert I Rothberg, ed. *The Mixing of Peoples: Problems of Identity and Ethnicity* (Stamford, Conn.: Greylock, 1978), p. 107.

6. Jun Miyake, "Nihon no shakaigaku shukyo gaisetsu." [Japanese Sociology: An Introduction to Religion] in Jun Miyake, Mitsugu Komoto, and Shigeru Nishiyama, eds. *Nihon no shakaigaku: shukyo* Japanese Sociology: Religion] Readings, Vol. 19 (Tokyo: Tokyo University Press, 1986), p. 34.

7. John Whitney Hall, *Japan: From Prehistory to Modern Times* (Tokyo: Charles E. Tuttle Edition, 1971), p.

8. Mikiso Hane, *Peasants, Rebels. and Outcasts: The Underside of Modern Japan* (New York: Pantheon Books, 1982), pp. 21-23.

9. Hiro Takagi, *Nihon no shinko shukyo* [Japan's New Religions] (Tokyo: Iwanami Shinsho, 1959), pp. 87-

10. Omura, *Op. Cit.*, p. 13.

11. William A. Caudill, "Social Change and Cultural Continuity in Japan." In George A. DeVos, ed., *Response to Change: Society, Culture and Personality* (NY: D. Van Nostrand, 1976), p. 32.

12. Miyake, *Op. Cit.*, p. 34.

13. Takagi, *Op. Cit.*, p. 61.

14. Mika Tokuchika, "Reminiscences of Religion in Postwar Japan," *Contemporary Religions in Japan* 6:2 (1965), p. 171.

15. Hane, *Op. Cit.*, p. 247.

16. Byron H. Earhart, *Japanese Religion: Unity and Diversity* (Belmont, CA: Dickenson Publishing Co., 1974), p. 123.

17. Miyake, *Op. Cit.*, p. 36.

18. Carlo Caldarola, "Japan: Religious Syncretism in a Secular Society." In Caldarola, ed., *Religions and Societies: Asia and the Middle East* (The Hague: Mouton Publishers, 1982), p. 647.

19. Shigeru Nishiyarna, "Shin shin shukyo no shutsugen," [The Appearance of the New New Religions] in Jun Miyake, Mitsugu Komoto, and Shigeru Nishiyama, eds., *Nihon no shakaigaku: shukyo* [Japanese Sociology: Religion] Readings, Vol. 19 (Tokyo: Tokyo University Press, 1986), pp. 199-202.

20. Omura, *Op. Cit.*, p. 13.

21. The NHK Survey was conducted in November, 1981. It was based upon 3,600 interviews with individuals age 16 or older at 300 different locations throughout Japan. Of that number 2,692 (74.8 percent) were usable.

22. Jan Swyngedouw, "The Quiet Reversal: A Few Notes on the NHK Survey of Japanese Religiosity," *The Japan Missionary Bulletin* 31:1(1985), p. 11.

23. The Results of the "Survey of the Religious Consciousness of University Students" conducted by Professor Nishiyama and his seminar students cautions us in our interpretation of recent trends in religious practice as evidence for "religious revival." This was a study of first- and second-year university students, and the results are based upon an analysis of 363 usable questionnaires. In their study they also found that participation in these traditional religious activities was high among university students. However, in each case,

only a small percentage indicated that these actions were performed with religious motivation. While 75.8 percent of the sample participated in hatsumode, 71.7 percent indicated that they observed it simply as a "custom" and without religious motivation. Similarly, of the 76.3 percent observing Obon only 8.5 percent did so out of religious motivation. Nevertheless, it is clear that the religious consciousness of many university students predisposes them to experiment and participate in the new religions.

24. Since in many ways it represents a revival of folk religiosity, to refer to this phenomenon as a "counterculture" might be misleading. In any case, it represents a movement or development outside of established religious institutions.

25. In a personal conversation, Professor Shimazono of Tokyo University informed me that bookstores began this special section of "spiritual world" books in 1978, having found that books under the usual label of "religion" did not sell too well.

26. It is worth noting here that there is considerable movement of ideas and groups in both directions. The transplantation of "Japanese new religions abroad" will be analyzed in an upcoming double issue of the *Japanese Journal of Religious Studies* (1991).

27. The presence of these older traditions of spiritualism are not limited to the printed medium; in fact, this past year Gurdjieff-Ouspensky centers were opened in Tokyo.

28. Throughout this paper I have relied heavily upon Nobutaka Inoue et al.'s recently published *Shin shukyo jiten* [Dictionary of New Religions] (Tokyo: Kobundo, 1990) for current information on a variety of Movements and organizations.

29. This information is based upon the article by Umehara on "Seishin sekai no undo" [Spirit world movements] in *Ibid.*, pp. 155-158.

30. Nishiyama's broad distinction between the established new religions (such as Sokagakkai) as "belief religions" and the neo-new religions as "magical religions" has not escaped criticism. Shimazono, for example, maintains that the continuity and similarity of new religions is much more significant than the differences suggested by Nishiyama. For example, belief in various types of spirits and communication with the spirit world has a long history in new religions (going all the way back to the Edo period). This phenomenon was central to Omotokyo, Reiyukai, Seicho no Ie, as well as more recent movements. While some of the older movements have become institutionalized and rationalized to a considerable degree, direct religious experience of the spirit world and emphasis upon magic are still maintained at the level of the individual believer. For this reason, Shimazono argues that it is not helpful to designate the neo-new religions as "magical religions" and the established new religions as "belief

religions." While there may have been some shift in emphasis and more individualistic expression in the current period, the neo-new religions are basically
revivals of animism—something they have in common with new religions
which began over a century ago. Susumu Shimazono, "Spirit-Belief in New
Religions Movements and Popular Culture: The Case of Japan's New Religions," *The Journal of Oriental Philosophy* 26:1 (1987), p. 4.

31. Nishiyama began calling this new wave of new religions *"shin shin
shukyo"* [new new religions] over a decade ago. The inadequacy of *"shin shin
shukyo"* as a sub category of classification has been argued by Inoue in his
review of Nishiyama's work. Nobutaka Inoue, "Book Review: *Gendaijin no
shukyo* [The Religion of People Today] in *Journal of Religious Studies* 63:282,
pp. 106-110. In any case, the so-called "neo new religions" refers to the various
groups which began or experienced significant growth from the mid-70s.

32. It is important to recognize that membership statistics for the new religions are somewhat inflated. In his study of Mahikari, Davis estimated that
the actual membership was 10 to 20 percent of the number reported by the
movement and represented the number of amulets distributed. Winston Davis,
Dojo: Magic and Exorcism in Contemporary Japan (Stanford: Stanford U. Pr., 1980),
p. 7. Furthermore, there is considerable movement from group to group as individuals experiment with various "products." Davis writes: "In Mahikara, for
example, almost a third of the present members once belonged to other New
Religions. Judging from my interviews and survey, these people often join a religious group in search of a miraculous cure or some other concrete benefit. If the
sect proves ineffective, they drop out until they are introduced to an alternative
'thaumaturgical product' by another 'ad,' friend or relative. Thus they go from
product to product (or rather, from religion to religion), comparing the cost-
benefit only in retrospect." (p. 101)

33. For helpful English introductions to some of these neo-new religions,
see Davis, *Op Cit.*; Fredrik Spier, "Introducing Agon-Shu," *Japanese Religions*
14 (1986); Shinji Kanai, "The New Religions in Japan," in Allan R. Brockway and
J. Paul Rajashekar, eds., *New Religious Movements and the Churches* (Geneva:
WCC Publications, 1987); and Ian Reader, "The Rise of a Japanese 'New New
Religion'—Themes in the Development of Agonshu," *Japanese Journal of Religious
Studies* 15:4 (1988).

34. A helpful review of the most recent New Age phenomena appeared in
a volume entitled *Imadoki no Kamisama* [The Gods of the Present Age] (1990).
This was published as number 114 in the Bessatsu Takarajima Series (JICC Publishing). All kinds of New Age phenomena are reviewed in this journal, including: occult bookstores, the mail-order occult business, and various forms of religious experimentation.

35. Less familiar to westerners, but vitally important to Okawa's Japanese
audience, are his books of spirit messages from important Japanese religious

teachers and leaders, such as Dogen (Zen), Taniguchi (Seicho-no-Ie), Takahashi (GLA), and Uchimura (Japanese Christianity). Okawa's father, who experimented with Christianity, Seicho-no-Ie, and GLA, undoubtedly had a significant influence upon him. It is important to point out here that members of other religious bodies do not look too favorably upon the "new revelations" Okawa is receiving from "their" founders.

36. There are two types of membership in the Association. Full membership requires that one read over ten of Okawa's books, submit a written application and essay, and pass an examination. One receives notification within two weeks if membership has been granted. One can become an associate member and receive the monthly magazine for a modest monthly fee. This also qualifies one to attend study sessions and retreats sponsored by the Association. It is unclear whether the 15,000 membership figure noted above refers to full or associate members.

37. Okawa's group is not the only "audience cult" which has developed into a new religious movement. Minoru Kuroda, a former member of Mahikari and veteran comic *(manga)* artist, began a religious movement called "Subikar-iha Sekai Shindan" in 1980. Kuroda gathered a following (a large percentage of whom are junior high and high school girls) when he began publishing a series of "spirit world comics." A recent book contains cartoons which deal with the tormenting spirits of *mizuko* (aborted or stillborn fetuses) and the reality of the spirit world. At the present time, this new religion has a membership of 4,500 and 75 trained teachers.

38. Jon Miyake, "Folk Religion," in Ichiro Hori, gen. ed., *Japanese Religion*, trans. Abe Yoshiya and David Reid (Tokyo: Charles E. Tuttle, 1972), p. 122.

39. Ichiro Hori, *Folk Religion in Japan: Continuity and Change*, Joseph Kitagawa and Alan Miller, eds. (Chicago: Univ. of Chicago Pr., 1968), p. 18.

40. Carmen Blacker explains that this simple cosmology became rather complex with "the superimposition onto these ancient holy mountains of the Buddhist cosmos of heavens, hells and other realms to which sentient beings may be prescribed by their past karma to transmigrate." *The Catalpa Bow: A Study of Shamanistic Practices in Japan* (London: George Allen and Unwin, Ltd., 1975), p. 81.

41. Kiyomi Morioka, "Ancestor Worship in Contemporary Japan: Continuity and Change," in George A DeVos and Takao Sofue, eds., *Religion and Family in East Asia* (LA: Univ. of Calif. Pr., 1984), p. 201.

42. This conception of "buddhahood" or the idea that one can become a "buddha" *(hotokesama)* is a popular understanding of death which developed over many years in Japanese folk religion. See Nagayki Koike, *Nihon no shukyo shi* [Japan's Religious History] (Tokyo: Gakugei Tosho, 1963), pp. 166-168; Eiki Hoshino and Dosho Takeda, "Indebtedness and Comfort: The Undercurrents of

Mizuko kuyo in Contemporary Japan," *Japanese Journal of Religious Studies* 14:4 (1987), pp. 306-308. Hoshino and Takeda point out that, Buddhologically speaking, it is not appropriate to identify "buddha nature" with spirits of the dead who are pacified by various rituals. Nevertheless, this view is prominent in many of the new religions.

43. Robert J. Smith, *Ancestor Worship in Contemporary Japan* (Stanford, CA: Stanford U. Pr., 1974), p. 44.

44. Shigeyoshi Murakami, *Japanese Religion in the Modern Century*, trans. by H. Byron Earhart (Tokyo: Tokyo U. Pr., 1980), p. 50; Blacker, *Op. Cit.*, p. 127.

45. Susumu Shimazono, "Gendai shukyo to animizumu—minshu shukyo no fukko o megutte." [Modern Religion and Animism—With Reference to the Revival of Popular Religion] (a revised version of a paper first presented to the Annual Meeting of the Kanto Sociological Association, 1986).

46. Hori, *Op. Cit.*, p. 181; Blacker, *Op. Cit.*, p. 130; Kenya Numata, *Gendai nihon no shin shukyo* [the New Religions of Modern Japan] (Osaka: Sogansha, 1988), pp. 4148.

47. Shimazono, *Op. Cit.*; Michio Araki, "Minzoku shukyotoshite no shin shukyo" [New Religions as Folk Religion], in Inoue, Nobutaka et al., *Kindaika to Shukyo bu-mu* [Modernization and the Religion] (Tokyo: Kokugakuin University, 1990), pp. 30-44.

48. Mitsugu Komoto, "The Place of Ancestors in the New Religions," trans, Norman Havens. *Transactions of the Institute for Japanese Culture and Classics* (Kokugakuin Univ.), No. 62 (1988).

49. Helen Hardacre, *Lay Buddhism in Contemporary Japan: Reiyukai Kyodan* (Princeton, NJ: Princeton U. Pr., 1984); Helen Hardacre, *Kurozumikyo and the New Religion of Japan* (Princeton, NJ: Princeton U. Pr., 1986).

50. Earhart, *Op. Cit.*

51. Davis, *Op. Cit.*, p. 41.

52. This section draws upon my paper, "Japanese Pentecostalism and the World of the Dead: A Study of Cultural Adaptation in Iesu no Mitama Kyokai," *Japanese Journal of Religious Studies*, 17, No. 4 (1990).

53. See Hoshino and Takeda, *Op. Cit.*, for helpful background and discussion of this growing trend in contemporary Japanese religion.

54. Shigeru Nishiyama, "Kegare shakai no reijutsu shukyo" [The Magical Religions of 'Devitalized' Society] *Shiso to gendai* [Thought and Modernity], No. 13 (1988); Shimazono, *Op. Cit.*

55. Shigeru Nishiyama, "Gendai no shukyo undo" [Modern Religious

Movements], in Eisho Omura and Shigeru Nishiyama, eds., *Gendaijin no shukyo* [The Religion of People Today] (Tokyo: Yuhikaku Press, 1988), p. 26.

56. Frederick Bird and Bill Reimer, "Participation Rates in New Religions and Para-Religious Movements," *Journal for the Scientific Study of Religion* 20:1 (1982), p. 13. A particular emphasis of most recent movements is that shamanistic powers are not restricted to the founder. With proper training all members can achieve similar power over the spirit world. Mahikari, for example, assures its followers that after three days of training in the class for beginners they too will be able to exercise "hand power" and have the spirit light from the palm of their hands heal and purify. Each member receives a pendant *(omitama)* following this first session of training which assures them that the life-energy of the True Light (Mahikari) resides within them. Commenting upon this aspect of Mahikari, Davis *(Op. Cit.,* p. 302) writes: "Thanks to the democratization of magic, modern believers can face the challenges of life with the courage of the primitive shaman and wizard." This "empowering" of members is not restricted to Mahikari. Shin'nyoen, GLA, and Agonshu also have various levels of training for their members so that they can also communicate with different dimensions of the spirit world and exercise powers of healing, clairvoyance and exorcism. Shin'nyoen and Agonshu, in particular, claim to make available to members the secrets and powers of esoteric *(mikkyo)* Buddhism which priests have monopolized in the past. One can become a spiritual "superman" with only a modest amount of effort and training. While not all members take advantage of these opportunities for cultivating such spiritual powers, most new religions have trained a number of mediums and spiritual guides.

57. Tokutaro Sakurai, *Kesshu no genten* [The Origin of Regimentation] (Osaka: Kobundo, 1985).

58. Max Weber, *The Protestant Ethic and the Spirit of Capitalism* (New York: Charles Scribner's Sons, 1958), p. 125; H. H. Gerth and C. Wright Mills, eds., *From Max Weber: Essays in Sociology* (NY: Oxford U. Pr., 1946), p. 51.

59. Nishiyama, "The Magical Religions . . . ," p. 23. This perspective strikingly resembles the view advanced by Stark and Bainbridge regarding secularization: that it "is a self-limiting process prompting religious revival and innovation." Rodney Stark and William Sims Bainbridge, "Secularization and Cult Formation in the Jazz Age," *Journal for the Scientific Study of Religion* 20:4 (1981), p. 362.

60. Shimazono, *Op. Cit.,* 1987.

61. A similar observation has been made with reference to the religiously unaffiliated in North America. Reviewing research on cult consumption in Canada, Thomas Robbins writes that: "Rather than embracing organized 'new religions,' today's religiously detached persons are more likely to opt for fragmentary a-scientific beliefs (e.g. astrology, ESP, or magic). " And that: "A-ratio-

nal fragments are chosen over integrated systems because the former 'are more conducive to life in our present age,' as well as the ('secular') context of life in a highly differentiated and pluralistic society." *Cults, Converts & Charisma* (London: Sage Publications, 1988), p. 59. Robbins's citation [are . . . age] from: Reginald W. Bibby and Harold J. Weaver, "Cult Consumption in Canada," *Sociological Analysis* 46:4 (1982), p. 458.

62. Shimazono, *Op. Cit.*, 1987, p. 3. Shimazono suggests that similar revivals of animism occurred over a century ago in the Spiritualism movement in the United States (1848) and later in the Pentecostal movement which began in 1906. Since the late 1960s, through the new religions and the charismatic movement, this revival of animism finally made it to the middle class in North America.

63. Blacker, *Op. Cit.*, p. 315.

64. Bird and Reimer, *Op. Cit.*, p. 13.

Chapter 18. The "Newness" of the New Age in South Africa and Reactions to It

1. *Cross Times*, January 1990.

2. *Die Burger*, 15 November 1989.

3. Unpublished, p. 1.

4. Cf., C. Steyn, "Dominee se vrou formuleer 'New Age'," *Insiq*, (November 1989) 20-23: Also Irving Hexham on Johanna Brandt. Unpublished.

5. James Giles; see *Cross Times* January, 1990, 13.

6. *Die Kerkbode*, 7 July 1989, 6-7.

7. Cf. D. Pypers, *Die Kerkbode*, 27 July 1990, 1.

8. Cf. G. C. Oosthuizen, *The Birth of Christian Zionism in South Africa* (Durban, South Africa: University of Zululand, 1987).

9. Cf. B. G. M. Sundkler, *Bantu Prophets in South Africa* (London: Oxford U. Pr., 1961).

10. Cf. G. C. Oosthuizen, S. D. Edwards, J. Hexham, and W. H. Wessels, *Afro-Christian Religion and Healing in Southern Africa* (Lewiston: Edwin Mellen Press, 1988).

11. Cf. G. C. Oosthuizen *Baptism in the Context of the African Indigenous/Independent Churches* (Durban, South Africa: University of Zululand, 1985).

Chapter 19. Alternative Spirituality in Italy

1. Giovanni Filoramo, *I Nuovi Movimenti Religiosi. Metamorfosi del Sacro* (Bari, Italy: Laterza, 1986).

2. Ibid., 147.

3. *The Tao of Physics*, written by Fritjof Capra in 1975, was one of the precursor works of the New Age, and *The Aquarian Conspiracy*, by Marylin Ferguson, published in 1980, one of the most important propagators.

4. J. Gordon Melton, *New Age Encyclopedia* (Detroit: Gale, 1990).

5. Gustavo Guizzardi, "New Religious Phenomena in Italy. Towards a Post-Catholic Era?" in *Archives de Sciences Sociales des Religions*, 42 (1976): 97-116.

6. Massimo Introvigne, *Il Cappello del Mago* (Turin, Italy: Sugarco, 1990), 41.

7. Massimo Introvigne, *New Religious Movements in Italy* (Conference of Lugano, Switzerland, 1990), 9.

8. Carlo Ginzburg, *I Benandanti: Stregoneria e Culti Agrari tra Cinquecento e Seicento* (Einaudi, 1966). English Edition: *Witchcraft and Agrarian Cults in the Sixteenth and Seventeenth Century* (New York: Penguin, 1985), 209. Ibid., 103.

9. Massimo Introvigne, *I Nuovi Culti* (Milano, Italy: Mondadori, 1990).

10. Massimo Introvigne, *Il Cappello del Mago*, 301.

11. Julius Evola, *Imperialismo Pagano* (Padova, Italy: Edizioni di Ar, 1978). See in Massimo Introvigne, *Il Cappello del Mago*, 346.

12. Massimo Introvigne, *Il Cappello del Mago*, 318.

13. Maria Macioti, "New Religious Movements in Italy," in *Update: A Quarterly Journal of New Religious Movements*, 8 (1984): 54-58.

14. Massimo Introvigne, *Le Nuove Religioni* (Torino, Italy: Sugarco, 1989), 163-165.

15. Massimo Introvigne, *Il Cappello del Mago*, 74-79.

16. Massimo Introvigne, *Le Nuove Religioni*, 429.

17. Massimo Introvigne, *Il Cappello del Mago*, 487.

18. Bernardino del Boca, *Guida Internazionale dell'Età dell'Acquario* (Torino, Italy: Bresci, 1975), 318.

19. Bernardino del Boca, *Il Segreto* (Torino, Italy: Bresci, 1986), 210.

20. Bernardino del Boca, *Guida Internazionale dell'Età dell'Acquario*, 171.

21. Ibid.

22. Ibid., 205.

23. Ibid., 316.

24. Bernardino del Boca, *Iniziazione alle Strade Alte* (Torino, Italy: Bresci, 1985).

25. Bernardino del Boca, *Guida Internazionale dell'Età dell'Acquario*, 217.

26. Bernardino del Boca, *Iniziazione alle Strade Alte*, 48.

27. Oberto Airaudi, *Pietre dell'Età dell'Acquario. Editoriali 1975-1988* (Torino, Italy: Horus, 1988), 183.

28. Massimo Introvigne, *Il Cappello del Mago*, 87-90.

29. Oberto Airaudi, *Cronaca del Mio Suicidio* (Torino, Italy: CEI, 1978).

30. Oberto Airaudi, *Pietre dell'Età dell'Acquario. Editoriali 1975-1988*.

31. Mauro Gagliardi, *La Via Horusiana. Il Libro. Principi e Concetti Fondamentali della Scuola di Pensiero di Damanhur* (Turin, Italy: Horus, 1988).

32. Introvigne associates this astral "serbatoio" to the Akhashik Memory, present in other postspiritist movements such as the "Association des Chercheur en Science Cosmique," a movement born in Québec, and centered upon the thought of Adéla Tremblay de Montréal (d. 1980). Massimo Introvigne, *Il Cappello del Mago*, 85-87.

33. Massimo Introvigne, *Il Cappello del Mago*, 89.

34. "La Sfida dei 'Movimenti Religiosi Alternativi,'" in *Civiltà Cattolica* 3337, vol. III, 1989, 3-15. "Una Valutazione Cattolica dei 'Movimenti Religiosi Alternativi,'" in *Civiltà Cattolica* 3338, vol. III, 1989, 105-117. "La Chiesa Cattolica e i 'Movimenti Religiosi Alternativi,'" in *Civiltà Cattolica* 3342, vol. III, 1989, 449-461.

35. *Rapporto Provvisorio delle Sette o Nuovo Movimenti Religiosi. Sfida Pastorale* (Bologna, Italy: Ed. Dehoniane, 1986), 30. (Temporary Statement on Sects or New Religious Movements. Pastoral Challenge). This document was issued by the Secretariat for Union of Christians, the Secretariat for non-Christians, the Secretariat for non-Believers, and by the Papal Council for Culture.

36. Joseph Cardinal Ratzinger, *Alcuni Aspetti della Meditazione Cristiana* (Milano, Italy: Ed. Paoline, 1990), 29.

37. Manuel Guerra, "Yoga, Zen, Meditazione Trascendentale: Moda o Eclettismo Mascherato?" in *Informatore di Urio* (Gennaio-Febbraio 1990): 17-27.

38. Within the Church in Italy there are some "experimental" religious communities led by Catholic clergy that are open to nontraditional forms of prayer, such as meditation. But they are very clear about not wanting to be associated with such movements as the New Age.

39. Macioti, Maria. "New Religious Movements in Italy," 58.

REFERENCES

Chapter 7. Baby Boomers, American Culture, and the New Age: A Synthesis

Brown, Susan Love. *Ananda Revisited: Values and Change in a Cooperative. Religious Community.* M.A.Thesis. San Diego: San Diego State University, 1987.

Clecak, Peter. *America's Quest for the Ideal Self: Dissent and Fulfillment in the 60s and 70s.* New York and London: Oxford University Press, 1983.

Dass, Baba Ram. *Be Here Now.* San Cristobal, New Mexico: Lama Foundation, 1971.

Ellwood, Robert S. *Eastern Spirituality in America: Selected Writings.* New York: PaulistPress, 1987.

Gallup, George, Jr., and Jim Castelli. *The People's Religion: American Faith in the 90s.* New York and London: Macmillan Publishing Company and Collier Macmillan Publishers, 1990.

Jackson, Carl T. *The Oriental Religions in American Thought: Nineteenth Century Explorations.* Westport, Connecticut: Greenwood Press, 1981.

Kluckhohn, Florence, and Fred Strodtbeck. *Variations in Value Orientations.* Evanston, Illinois: Row, Peterson & Company, 1961.

Kriyananda, Sri. *Cooperative Communities: How to Start Them and Why.* Nevada City, California: Ananda Publications, 1979.

Luhrmann, T. M. *Persuasions of the Witch's Craft.* Cambridge: Harvard University Press, 1990.

Nordquist, Ted A. *Ananda Cooperative Village: A Study in the Beliefs, Values, and Attitudes of a New Age Religious Community.* Uppsala, Sweden: Religionhistorika Institutionen, 1978.

Quinn, D. Michael. *Early Mormonism and the Magic World View.* Salt Lake City: Signature Books, 1987.

Robbins, Thomas. "Eastern Mysticism and the Resocialization of Drug Users: The Meher Baba Cult." *Journal for the Scientific Study of Religion* 8 (1969):308-317.

Roof, Wade Clark. "Narratives and Numbers." J. F. Rowny Inaugural Lecture. University of California, Santa Barbara. 30 May 1990.

Russell, Cheryl. *Predictions for the Baby Boom.* New York and London: Plenum Press, 1987.

Strickland, Charles E., and Andrew M. Ambrose. "The Baby Boom, Prosperity, and the Changing Worlds of Children, 1945-1963." In *American Childhood, a Research Guide and Historical Handbook*, Edited by Joseph M. Hawkes and N. Ray Hiner, 533-585. Westport, Connecticut: Greenwood Press, 1985.

Tipton, Steven M. *Getting Saved from the Sixties.* Berkeley: University of California Press, 1982.

Tocqueville, Alexis de. *Democracy in America.* 2 vol. New York: Vintage, 1945.

Veroff, Joseph, Elizabeth Douvan, and Richard A. Kulka. *The Inner American: A Self Portrait 1957-1976.* New York: Basic Books, 1981.

Wallace, Anthony F. C. "Revitalization Movements: Some Theoretical Considerations for Their Comparative Study." *American Anthropologist.* 58 (1956):264-281.

Weizmann, Daniel. "Getting Clear on Crystals." *California* (July 1989).

Yankelovich, Daniel. *New Rules: Searching for Self-Fulfillment in a World Turned Upside Down.* New York: Random House, 1981.

Yogananda. *The Science of Religion.* Los Angeles: Self-Realization Fellowship, 1982.

————. *Man's Eternal Quest.* Los Angeles: Self-Realization Fellowship, 1982.

————. *Autobiography of a Yogi.* Los Angeles: Self-Realization Fellowship, 1985.

Zablocki, Benjamin. *Alienation and Charisma.* New York: The Free Press, 1980.

Chapter 8. Myth, Metaphor, and Manifestation: The Negotiation of Belief in a New Age Community

Caddy, Eileen. *The Dawn of Change: Selections from Daily Guidance on Human Problems.* Findhorn, Scotland: The Findhorn Foundation, 1979.

Elixir [Caddy, Eileen]. *God's Word Through Elixir.* Findhorn, Scotland: The Findhorn Trust, 1971.

Festinger, L. *A Theory of Cognitive Dissonance.* Stanford: Stanford University Press, 1957.

Findhorn Community. *Faces of Findhorn: Images of a Planetary Family.* New York: Harper & Row, 1980.

——— . *The Findhorn Garden: Pioneering a New Vision of Man and Nature in Cooperation.* New York: Harper & Row, 1975.

Spangler, David. *Explorations: Emerging Aspects of the New Culture.* Findhorn, Scotland: Findhorn Publications, 1980.

——— . *The New Laws of Manifestation.* Findhorn, Scotland: The Findhorn Press, 1978.

——— . *Revelation: The Birth of a New Age.* Findhorn, Scotland: The Findhorn Foundation, 1977.

Toch, Hans. *The Social Psychology of Social Movements.* Indianapolis: Bobbs-Merrill, 1965.

Chapter 10. Employing the New Age: Training Seminars

Alexander, John, "*Enhancing Human Performance:* A Challenge to the Report." *New Realities,* 9 (March/April 1989): 10-15, 52-53.

Fenwick, Sheridan. *Getting It: the Psychology of est.* Philadelphia: J. B. Lippincott Co., 1976.

"From Rosemead Teacher to Spiritual Leader of a New Age Empire." *Los Angeles Times,* 14 August 1988.

Haaken, Janice, and Richard Adams. "Pathology as 'Personal Growth': a Participant-Observation Study of Lifespring Training." *Psychiatry* 46 (August 1983): 270-280.

Keegan, Paul. "Into the Void." *Boston Business,* 1 February 1990.

Kirsch, M., and L. Glass. "Psychiatric Disturbances Associated with Erhard Seminars Training: I. A Report of Cases." *American Journal of Psychiatry* 134 (1977): 245-247.

——— . "Psychiatric Disturbances Associated with Erhard Seminars Training: II. Additional Cases and Theoretical Considerations." *American Journal of Psychiatry* 134 (1977): 1254-1258.

Main, Jeremy. "Trying to Bend Managers' Minds." *Fortune,* 23 November 1987, 95-106.

Miller, Annetta, and Pamela Abramson. "Corporate Mind Control." *Newsweek,* 4 May 1987, 38-39.

Pascarella, Perry. "Create a Breakthrough in Performance by Changing the 'Conversation.'" *Industry Week*, 15 June 1987, 51-57.

Ray, Michael and Rachelle Myers. *Creativity in Business*. New York: Doubleday and Co., 1986.

Chapter 11. An Update on Neopagan Witchcraft in America

Adler, Margot. *Drawing Down the Moon*. NY: Viking, 1979. Boston: Beacon Press paperback, 2d ed., 1987.

Bonewits, P. E. I. *Real Magic*. NY: 3d ed. Weiser, 1988.

Buckland, Raymond. *Witchcraft from the Inside*. St. Paul, MN: Llewellyn, 1971.

Budapest, Zsuzsana E. *The Feminist Book of Lights and Shadows*. Venice, CA: Luna Publications, 1976. Created by rewriting the Gardnerian Book of Shadows to leave out all references to males.

――――. *The Holy Book of Women's Mysteries*. Los Angeles, CA: Susan B. Anthony Coven, part I, 1979; part II, 1980. An expanded edition of the preceding.

Burland, C. A. *Echoes of Magic: A Study of Seasonal Festival Through the Ages*. London: Peter Davies, 1972. Burland was a member of the Gardnerian inner circle in the late 1950s.

Crowley, Aleister. *Magick in Theory and Practice*. NY: Castle, n.d. [ca. 1930]

Downing, Christine. *The Goddess: Mythological Images of the Feminine*. NY: Crossroads, 1981.

Eliade, Mircea. *Shamanism: Archaic Techniques of Ecstasy*. Translated by W. Trask. Princeton, NJ: Princeton University Press, 1964.

――――. "Some Observations on European Witchcraft." *History of Religions* 14 (Feb. 1975): 149-172.

Ellwood, Robert S., Jr. *Alternative Altars: Unconventional and Eastern Spirituality in America*. Chicago: University of Chicago Press, 1979.

――――. *Religious and Spiritual Groups in Modern America*. Englewood Cliffs, NJ: Prentice-Hall, 1973.

Engelsman, Joan Chamberlain. *The Feminine Dimension of the Divine*. Wilmette, IL: Chiron, 1987.

Farrar, Stewart. *What Witches Do: The Modern Coven Revealed*. NY: Coward, McCann, 1971.

———, and Janet Farrar. *Eight Sabbats for Witches.* London: Robert Hale, 1981.

———. *The Witches' Way: Principles, Rituals, and Beliefs of Modern Witchcraft.* London: Robert Hale, 1985. (These two volumes are available in the U.S. in paperback, under the title *A Witches Bible*, from Magickal Child.)

Fiorenza, Elisabeth Schüssler. *In Memory of Her: A Feminist Theological Recon-struction of Christian Origins.* New York: Crossroads, 1983.

Galbreath, Robert. "The History of Modern Occultism: A Bibliographical Sur-vey." *Journal of Popular Culture* 5 (Winter 1971): 98-126.

Gardner, Gerald B. "Ye Book of ye Art Magical." Unpublished MS., written between about 1945 (or earlier) and 1953, formerly owned by Ripley's Inter-national, Ltd., now owned by Richard and Tamara James of the Wiccan Church of Canada, Toronto.

———. *High Magic's Aid.* London: Michael Houghton, 1949.

———. *The Meaning of Witchcraft.* London: Aquarian Press, 1959.

———. *Witchcraft Today.* London: Jarrolds, 1954.

Gelpi, Donald L. *The Divine Mother: A Trinitarian Theology of the Holy Spirit.* Lan-haun, MD: University Press of America, 1984.

Glanvil, Joseph, and Henry More. *Saducismus Triumphatus: or, Full and Plain Evidence Concerning Witches and Apparitions.* 3d ed. London: Lowndes, 1689. Scholar's Facsimiles, 1966. One of Murray's major sources of information.

Glass, Justine. *Witchcraft, the Sixth Sense—and Us.* London: Spearman, 1965.

Glock, Charles Y., and Robert N. Bellah, eds. *The New Religious Consciousness.* Berkeley: University of California Press, 1976.

Graves, Robert. *The Greek Myths.* Baltimore: 2 vols. Pelican, 1955.

———. *The White Goddess: A Historical Grammar of Poetic Myth.* 1948. NY: 3d, rev. ed. Noonday, 1966.

Greeley, Andrew. *Confessions of a Parish Priest.* NY: Pocket Books, 1987.

———. "Implications for the Sociology of Religions of Occult Behavior in the Youth Culture." In Tiryakian, 295-302.

The Green Egg. Journal of the Church of All Worlds. Otter G'Zell, ed.

[Hill, Gregory.] *The Principia Discordia of Malaclypes the Younger; or, How I found Goddess and What I Did to Her When I Found Her.* 4th ed. San Francisco, 1970; Loompanics reprint, 1985.

Iron Mountain: A Journal of Magical Religion. Edited by Charles Clifton and Mary Currier-Clifton. Artemisia Press.

Kelly, Aidan A. *Crafting the Art of Magick, Book I: A History of Gardnerian Witchcraft, 1939-1964.* St. Paul, MN: Llewellyn, 1991.

————. *Crafting the Art of Magick, Book II: Neopagan Witchcraft in America, 1964-1990.* St. Paul, MN: Llewellyn, forthcoming.

————, ed., with Introduction. *Neo-Pagan Witchcraft.* 2 vols. (Volumes 22 & 23 of the series *Cults and New Religions: Sources for Study of Nonconventional Religious Groups in Nineteenth- and Twentieth-Century America,* edited by J. Gordon Melton.) New York: Garland, 1990.

————. "An Evolutionary Model for New Religious Movements." Paper presented to a session on New Religions and Political Movements at the Western Regional meeting of the AAR, Santa Clara Univ., March 1986.

————. "In the Season of Scarlet Herrings: Some Rather Personal Observations on Methodology in Religious Studies." In *Devils, Witches, Pagans, and Vampires: Studies in the Magical World View* (Fort Hayes Studies, Third Series, Humanities, No. 5., 1985). [Subsumes a paper given to the Women and Religion Section of the AAR/West in Pasadena, March 1981, entitled "Observations on Some Systemic Methodological Problems with Theories of Ancient Female Monotheism."]

————. "The Invention of Witchcraft: Uses of Documentary and Oral-Historical Materials in reconstructing the History of the Gardnerian Movement." *Zetetic Scholar* no. 10 (Fall 1982). Originally given to the Religion and Social Science Section of the AAR, in San Francisco, December 1981. Reprinted as "Inventing Witchcraft" in *Iron Mountain* No. 1 (Summer 1984).

————. "Looking Reasonably at Outrageous Religions: Satanism as a Normal Phase of Religious Maturation." Paper delivered to a session of Philosophers for Social Responsibility at the Pacific Division meeting, American Philosophical Association, Los Angeles, March 1986.

————. "Questions About the Evolution of New Religious Movements." Paper given to the Group on New Religious Movements of the AAR, Atlanta, GA., Nov. 1986.

————. "Witchcraft and the Techniques of Disinformation." Paper given to the Group on New Religious Movements of the AAR, Anaheim, Calif., Nov. 1985.

King, Francis. *Ritual Magic In England, 1887 to the Present.* London: Spearman, 1970.

Leland, Charles Godfrey. *Aradia: The Gospel of the Witches of Tuscany.* NY: Scribner's, 1897. Buckland Museum reprint, 1964.

Lethbridge, T. C. *Witches: Investigating an Ancient Religion.* London: Routledge & Paul, 1962.

Mathers, S. L. MacGregor, ed. and trans. *The Greater Key of Solomon.* Chicago: De Laurence, Scott, 1914.

Melton, J. Gordon. *The Cult Experience: Responding to the New Religious Pluralism.* NY: Pilgrim Press, 1982.

——— . *Magic, Witchcraft, and Paganism in America: A Bibliography.* NY: Garland, 1982.

——— . "Modern Alternative Religions in the West." In J. R. Hinnells, ed., *A Handbook of Living Religions* (Baltimore: Penguin, 1984), 455-474.

——— . "Origins of Modern Sex Magick." Paper delivered to the Soc. for the Scientific Study of Sex, Midcontinent Region, Chicago, June 1985.

Miller, David L. *The New Polytheism: Rebirth of the Gods and Goddesses.* NY: Harper and Row, 1974.

Murray, Margaret A. *The God of the Witches.* Oxford: Oxford University Press, 1934. NY: Doubleday Anchor, 1960.

——— . *The Witch-Cult in Western Europe.* Oxford: Oxford University Press, 1921. Oxford paperback, 1962.

Needleman, Jacob, and George Baker, eds. *Understanding the New Religions.* NY: Seabury, 1978.

Nugent, Donald, "Witchcraft Studies, 1959-1971: A Bibliographic Survey." *Journal of Popular Culture* 5 (Winter 1971): 82-97.

Regardie, Israel. *The Golden Dawn: An Account of the Teachings, Rites, and Ceremonies of the Order of the Golden Dawn.* 1937-1940. 4th ed. St. Paul, Minn: Hazel Llewellyn, 1971.

Roberts, Susan. *Witches USA.* Dell, 1971; Surrey, B.C.: 2d ed. Phoenix House, 1974.

Rose, Elliott. *A Razor for a Goat: A Discussion of Certain Problems in the History of Witchcraft and Diabolism.* Toronto: Univ. of Toronto Press, 1962.

Russell, Jeffrey B. *A History of Witchcraft: Sorcerers, Heretics, and Pagans.* London: Thames and Hudson, 1980.

Starhawk [Miriam Simos]. *Dreaming the Dark: Magic, Sex, and Politics.* Boston: Beacon Press, 1982.

——— . *The Spiral Dance: A Rebirth of the Ancient Religion of the Great Goddess.* NY: Harper & Row, 1979.

——— . *Truth or Dare: Encounters with Power, Authority, and Mystery.* NY: Harper & Row, 1987.

Tiryakian, Edward A., ed. *On the Margin of the Visible: Sociology, the Esoteric, and the Occult.* NY: Wiley, 1974.

Truzzi, Marcello. "The Occult Revival as Popular Culture: Some Random Observations on the Old and the Nouveau Witch." Paper presented to the Ohio Valley Sociol. Society, Akron, May 1970. *Sociol. Quarterly,* 13 (Winter 1972): 16-36. Excerpted in Tiryakian, 215-222.

———. "Towards a Sociology of the Occult: Notes on Modern Witchcraft," in Zaretsky and Leone.

Valiente, Doreen. *An ABC of Witchcraft Past and Present.* NY: St. Martin's, 1973.

———. *Where Witchcraft Lives.* London: Aquarian Press, 1962.

———. *Witchcraft for Tomorrow.* NY: St. Martin's, 1978.

———. Letter to the Editors, *Iron Mountain* No. 3 (Fall 1985): 3-6.

———. *The Rebirth of Witchcraft.* London: Robert Hale, 1989.

Zaretsky, I. J., and M. P. Leone, eds. *Religious Movements in Contemporary America.* Princeton, NJ: Princeton University Press, 1974.

INDEX